The Autobiography of Benvenuto Cellini

One Volume Edition

Translated by

J. Addington Symonds

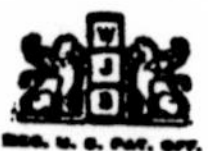

WALTER J. BLACK INC.
NEW YORK, N. Y.

Printed in the United States of America

THE AUTOBIOGRAPHY
OF
BENVENUTO CELLINI

INTRODUCTORY NOTE

"All men of whatsoever quality they be, who have done anything of excellence, or which may properly resemble excellence, ought, if they are persons of truth and honesty, to describe their life with their own hands." With these words Benvenuto Cellini begins his autobiography, which to-day holds a unique place among the autobiographies of the world.

Born in 1500, he hewed his way through the years that mark the peak of the Italian Renaissance in art, "taking much more pride," to use his own words, "in having been born humble and having laid some honourable foundation for my family, than if I had been born of great lineage and had stained or overclouded that by my base qualities."

Benvenuto, meaning "Welcome," proved an appropriate name for Cellini so far as his accomplishments are concerned; as artist, metal worker, and sculptor his services were demanded by pope, prince, and king. With the greatest of difficulty did he gain release from one patron to serve another, finding it necessary at times to flee in secret. Everywhere commissions poured in upon him, at which he laboured assiduously often "day and night together, for the sake alike of honour and of gain."

Mingled with and greatly hindering his pursuit of art, however, went a course of tempestuous living that gave promise of early terminating his career. In spite of all of which he lived to the good age of seventy-one years. Perhaps it was that he merited much; it is his own philosophy expressed with considerable complacence when a rival of his broke a leg and died, that "even may it be seen that God keeps account of the good and bad, and gives to each one what he merits."

He was something of a psychologist, reading aright his turbulent disposition. "I was perhaps more inclined by nature to the profession of arms than to the one I had adopted, and I took such pleasures in its duties that I discharged them better than those of my own art." He admits too to being "also by nature somewhat choleric." A delightful touch of naîveté, that "somewhat," as a reading of the book will disclose.

A workman runs away owing him money. Out rushes Benvenuto resolved to seek redress. "At first I thought of lopping off an arm of his; and assuredly I should have done so, if my friends had not told me that it was a mistake, seeing I should lose my money and perhaps Rome too a second time, forasmuch as blows cannot be measured." So he contents himself with suing the man and having him thrown into prison. In his words, "I should have liked to conduct the affair more freely," one recognizes, however, a sigh for an opportunity lost.

Then he punishes a friend for refusing to furnish bail for him. With his dagger he rushes to the house, where he finds the family at table and, as he tells the story, "Gherardo, who had been the cause of the quarrel, flung himself upon me. I stabbed him in the breast, piercing doublet and jerkin through and through to the shirt, without however grazing his flesh or doing him the least harm in the world. When I felt my hand go in, and heard the clothes tear, I thought that I had killed him, and seeing him fall terror-struck to earth, I cried, 'Traitors, this day is the day on which I mean to murder you all.' " He spares father, mother, and sisters, nevertheless, who, screaming for mercy, offer no resistance. But, storming down the stairs he charges the rest of the household, "more than twelve persons," armed with iron shovel, iron pipe, hammers, anvil, and cudgels. "Raging like a mad bull, I flung four or five to earth and fell down with them myself, continually aiming my dagger now at one and now at another . . . but inasmuch as God does sometimes mercifully intervene, He so ordered that neither they nor I did any harm to one another."

The victims of his wrath did not always come off so happily, however. As for himself—twice his life was attempted by poison, and several times by foul conditions in prison where it is generally conceded he was unjustly held. But he miraculously escaped—his escape from the castle, from which he is found "crawling on all fours and streaming with blood," is as vividly told as any tale of fiction—and he lived to carry on the art he so passionately loved.

Friend to Leonardo da Vinci, Titan, and the "divine" Michelangelo, whom he describes as "the most amusing comrade and heartiest good fellow in the universe, that prince of sculptors and of painters," and in whose praise he could not say enough, he was also a thorough scorner of such as aroused his indignation. For Bandinelli, the ruling motive of whose life, so unprejudiced authorities tell us, seems to have been jealousy both of Cellini and Michelangelo, his contempt was colossal; he pitied the very blocks of marble that came into the hands of such a bungler. Yet in the opinion of some, Bandinelli as a sculptor stands second only to Michelangelo himself.

The autobiography carries the story of Cellini up to 1562. Regarding his movements thereafter, there is some disagreement. The introductory note in the edition to be found in the Harvard Classics states that the remainder of his life "seems to have been more peaceful. In 1565 he married Piera de Salvadore Parigi, a servant who had nursed him when he was sick; and in the care of his children, as earlier of his sisters and nieces, he showed more tenderness than might have been expected from a man of his boisterous nature." According to the Encyclopedia Britannica, he remained unmarried and left no posterity.

Cellini died in Florence in 1571 and was buried in the church of the Annunziata. To this church some years before he had presented a crucifix, a "Christ of the whitest marble set upon a cross of the blackest, exactly the same size as a tall man." Beneath this the "virtuous friars" had permitted him to make his grave according to his "will and pleasure"—as he pictured it in the Autobiography, "a little sarcophagus upon the ground beneath the feet of Christ, into which I might creep when I was dead."

Of the objects of art in existence to-day executed by Cellini, most of which are medallions and coins, the outstanding piece is the bronze statue of Perseus holding the head of Medusa, a work now in the Loggia dei Lanzi at Florence, described by one commentator as "full of the fire of genius and the grandeur of a terrible beauty, one of the most typical and unforgettable monuments of the Italian Renaissance."

The uncompleted chalice intended for Clement VII, the gold cover for a prayer book, the silver statues of Jupiter, Vulcan, and Mars wrought for Francis I, the bust of Julius Cæsar, the silver cup for the Cardinal of Ferrara have all perished. The magnificent gold "button" so graphically described, made for the cope of Clement VII, "appears to have been sacrificed by Pius VI with many other priceless specimens of the goldsmith's art, in furnishing the indemnity of 30,000,000 francs demanded by Napoleon at the conclusion of the campaign against the States of the Church in 1797."

To such readers as may be within reach of the Metropolitan Museum of Art in New York City it may prove of interest to see the cup attributed to Cellini in the Altman collection. It is a gold shell ribbed like that of a scallop, perhaps eight or ten inches across. The ridges on the under part are decorated with designs worked out in bright colors with enamel. The shell is supported by a winged dragon which in turn stands upon a turtle. On the curve of the bowl, at the hinge of the shell, rests a fish-like body with two tails and the head of a woman. One wonders whether the face may be that of the fair Caterina, the model in whose beauty the artist took such joy, but whom, on occasion, in blind rage, yet apparently to her own satisfaction, he seized by the hair and dragged up and down the room. Whatever of emotional abandon may lie buried in the cup, the whole betokens an exquisite workmanship.

The Autobiography is vividly written, and all the more extraordinary in that by far the major portion of it was casually dictated to a boy of fourteen while the author was busy about his work. That it is extravagant at times one must admit; but it is never insincere. Although it is valuable as a document of the age it depicts, its chief interest lies in the record it gives of one of the most remarkable careers in the history of fine art.

INA WEYRAUCH

BENVENUTO CELLINI'S AUTOBIOGRAPHY

BOOK FIRST

I

ALL men of whatsoever quality they be, who have done anything of excellence, or which may properly resemble excellence, ought, if they are persons of truth and honesty, to describe their life with their own hand; but they ought not to attempt so fine an enterprise till they have passed the age of forty. This duty occurs to my own mind now that I am travelling beyond the term of fifty-eight years, and am in Florence, the city of my birth. Many untoward things can I remember, such as happen to all who live upon our earth; and from those adversities I am now more free than at any previous period of my career—nay, it seems to me that I enjoy greater content of soul and health of body than ever I did in bygone years. I can also bring to mind some pleasant goods and some inestimable evils, which, when I turn my thoughts backward, strike terror in me, and astonishment that I should have reached this age of fifty-eight, wherein, thanks be to God, I am still travelling prosperously forward.

II

It is true that men who have laboured with some show of excellence, have already given knowledge of themselves to the world; and this alone ought to suffice them; I mean the fact that they have proved their manhood and achieved renown. Yet one must needs live like others; and so in a work like this there will always be found occasion for natural bragging, which is of divers kinds, and the first is that a man should let others know he draws his lineage from persons of worth and most ancient origin.

I am called Benvenuto Cellini, son of Maestro Giovanni, son of Andrea, son of Cristofano Cellini; my mother was Madonna Elisabetta, daughter to Stefano Granacci; both parents citizens of Florence. It is found written in chronicles made by our ancestors of Florence, men of old time and of credibility, even as Giovanni Villani writes, that the city of Florence was evidently built in imitation of the fair city of Rome; and certain remnants of the Colosseum and the Baths can yet be traced. These things are near Santa Croce. The Capitol was where is now the Old Market. The Rotonda is entire, which was made for the temple of Mars, and is now dedicated to our Saint John. That thus it was, can very well be seen, and cannot be denied, but the said buildings are much smaller than those of Rome. He who caused them to be built, they say, was Julius Cæsar, in concert with some noble Romans, who, when Fiesole had been stormed and taken, raised a city in this place, and each of them took in hand to erect one of these notable edifices.

Julius Cæsar had among his captains a man of highest rank and valour, who was called Fiorino of Cellino, which is a village about two miles distant from Monte Fiascone. Now this Fiorino took up his quarters under the hill of Fiesole, on the ground where Florence now stands, in order to be near the river Arno, and for the convenience of the troops. All those soldiers and others who had to do with the said captain, used then to say: "Let us go to Fiorenze;" as well because the said captain was called Fiorino, as also because the place he had chosen for his quarters was by nature very rich in flowers. Upon the foundation of the city, therefore, since this name struck Julius Cæsar as being fair and apt, and given by circumstance, and seeing furthermore that flowers themselves bring good augury, he appointed the name of Florence for the town. He wished besides to pay his valiant captain this compliment; and he loved him all the more for having drawn him from a very humble place, and for the reason that so excellent a man was a creature of his own. The name that learned inventors and investigators of such etymologies adduce, as that Florence is flowing at the Arno, cannot hold; seeing that Rome is flowing at the Tiber, Ferrara is flowing at the Po, Lyons is flowing at the Saone, Paris is flowing at the Seine, and yet the names of all these towns are different, and have come to them by other ways.[1]

[1] He is alluding to the name *Fluenzia*, which some antiquaries of his day thought to have been the earliest name of the city, derived from its being near *Arno fluente*. I have translated the word *fluente* in the text literally, though of course it signifies "situated on a flowing river." I need not call attention to the apocryphal nature of Cellini's own derivation from the name of his supposed ancestor.

Thus then we find; and thus we believe that we are descended from a man of worth, Furthermore, we find that there are Cellinis of our stock in Ravenna, that most ancient town of Italy, where too are plenty of gentle folk. In Pisa also there are some, and I have discovered them in many parts of Christendom; and in this state also the breed exists, men devoted to the profession of arms; for not many years ago a young man, called Luca Cellini, a beardless youth, fought with a soldier of experience and a most valorous man, named Francesco da Vicorati, who had frequently fought before in single combat. This Luca, by his own valour, with sword in hand, overcame and slew him, with such bravery and stoutness that he moved the folk to wonder, who were expecting quite the contrary issue; so that I glory in tracing my descent from men of valour.

As for the trifling honours which I have gained for my house, under the well-known conditions of our present ways of living, and by means of my art, albeit the same are matters of no great moment, I will relate these in their proper time and place, taking much more pride in having been born humble and having laid some honourable foundation for my family, than if I had been born of great lineage and had stained or overclouded that by my base qualities. So then I will make a beginning by saying how it pleased God I should be born.

III

My ancestors dwelt in Val d' Ambra, where they owned large estates, and lived like little lords, in retirement, however, on account of the then contending factions. They were all men devoted to arms and of notable bravery. In that time one of their sons, the younger, who was called Cristofano, roused a great feud with certain of their friends and neighbours. Now the heads of the families on both sides took part in it, and the fire kindled seemed to them so threatening that their houses were like to perish utterly; the elders upon this consideration, in concert with my own ancestors, removed Cristofano; and the other youth with whom the quarrel began was also sent away. They sent their young man to Siena. Our folk sent Cristofano to Florence; and there they bought for him a little house in Via Chiara, close to the convent of S. Orsola, and they also purchased for him some very good property near the Ponte a Rifredi. The said Cristofano took wife in Florence, and had sons and daughters; and when all the daughters had been portioned off, the sons, after their father's death, divided what remained. The house in Via Chiara with some other trifles fell to the share of one of the said sons, who had the name of Andrea. He also took wife, and had four male children. The first was called Girolamo, the second Bartolommeo, the third Giovanni, who was afterwards my father, and the fourth Francesco. This Andrea Cellini was very well versed in architecture, as it was then practised, and lived by it as his trade. Giovanni, who was my father, paid more attention to it than any of the other brothers. And since Vitruvius says, amongst other things, that one who wishes to practise that art well must have something of music and good drawing, Giovanni, when he had mastered drawing, began to turn his mind to music, and together with the theory learned to play most excellently on the viol and the flute; and being a person of studious habits, he left his home but seldom.

They had for neighbour in the next house a man called Stefano Granacci, who had several daughters, all of them of remarkable beauty. As it pleased God, Giovanni noticed one of these girls who was named Elisabetta; and she found such favour with him that he asked her in marriage. The fathers of both of them being well acquainted through their close neighbourhood, it was easy to make this match up; and each thought that he had very well arranged his affairs. First of all the two good old men agreed upon the marriage; then they began to discuss the dowry, which led to a certain amount of friendly difference; for Andrea said to Stefano: "My son Giovanni is the stoutest youth of Florence, and of all Italy to boot, and if I had wanted earlier to have him married, I could have procured one of the largest dowries which folk of our rank get in Florence;" whereupon Stefano answered: "You have a thousand reasons on your side; but here am I with five daughters and as many sons, and when my reckoning is made, this is as much as I can possibly afford." Giovanni, who had been listening awhile unseen by them, suddenly broke in and said: "O my father, I have sought and loved that girl and not their money. Ill luck to those who seek to fill their pockets by the dowry of their wife! As you have boasted that I am a fellow of such parts, do you not think that I shall be able to provide for my wife and satisfy her needs, even if I receive something short of the portion you would like to get? Now I must make you understand that the woman is mine, and you may take the dowry for yourself." At this Andrea Cellini, who was a man of rather awkward temper, grew a trifle angry; but after a few days Giovanni took his wife, and never asked for other portion with her.

They enjoyed their youth and wedded love through eighteen years, always greatly desiring to be blessed with children. At the end of this time Giovanni's wife miscarried of two boys through the unskilfulness of the doctors. Later on she was again with child, and gave birth to a girl, whom they called Cosa, after the mother of my father.[1] At the end of two years she was once more with child; and inasmuch as those longings to which pregnant women are subject, and to which they pay much attention, were now exactly the same as those of her former pregnancy, they made their minds up that she would give birth to a female as before, and agreed to call the child Reparata, after the mother of my mother. It happened that she was delivered on a night of All Saints, following the feast-day, at half-past four precisely, in the year 1500.[2] The midwife, who knew that they were expecting a girl, after she had washed the baby and wrapped it in the fairest white linen, came softly to my father Giovanni and said: "I am bringing you a fine present, such as you did not anticipate." My father, who was a true philosopher, was walking up and down, and answered: "What God gives me is always dear to me;" and when he opened the swaddling clothes, he saw with his own eyes the unexpected male child. Joining together the palms of his old hands, he raised them with his eyes to God, and said "Lord, I thank Thee with my whole heart; this gift is very dear to me; let him be Welcome." All the persons who were there asked him joyfully what name the child should bear. Giovanni would make no other answer than "Let him be Welcome—Benvenuto;"[3] and so they resolved, and this name was given me at Holy Baptism, and by it I still am living with the grace of God.

IV

Andrea Cellini was yet alive when I was about three years old, and he had passed his hundredth. One day they had been altering a certain conduit pertaining to a cistern, and there issued from it a great scorpion unperceived by them, which crept down from the cistern to the ground, and slank away beneath a bench. I saw it,

1 Cosa is Florentine for Niccolosa.

2 The hour is reckoned, according to the old Italian fashion, from sunset of one day to sunset of the next—twenty-four hours.

3 Benvenuto means Welcome.

and ran up to it, and laid my hands upon it. It was so big that when I had it in my little hands, it put out its tail on one side, and on the other thrust forth its mouths.[1] They relate that I ran in high joy to my grandfather, crying out: "Look, grandpapa, at my pretty little crab." When he recognised that the creature was a scorpion, he was on the point of falling dead for the great fear he had and anxiety about me. He coaxed and entreated me to give it him; but the more he begged, the tighter I clasped it, crying and saying I would not give it to any one. My father, who was also in the house, ran up when he heard my screams, and in his stupefaction could not think how to prevent the venomous animal from killing me. Just then his eyes chanced to fall upon a pair of scissors; and so, while soothing and caressing me, he cut its tail and mouths off. Afterwards, when the great peril had been thus averted, he took the occurrence for a good augury.

When I was about five years old my father happened to be in a basement-chamber of our house, where they had been washing, and where a good fire of oak-logs was still burning; he had a viol in his hand, and was playing and singing alone beside the fire. The weather was very cold. Happening to look into the fire, he spied in the middle of those most burning flames a little creature like a lizard, which was sporting in the intensest coals. Becoming instantly aware of what the thing was, he had my sister and me called, and pointing it out to us children, gave me a great box on the ears, which caused me to howl and weep with all my might. Then he pacified me good-humouredly, and spoke as follows: "My dear little boy, I am not striking you for any wrong that you have done, but only to make you remember that that lizard which you see in the fire is a salamander, a creature which has never been seen before by any one of whom we have credible information." So saying, he kissed me and gave me some pieces of money.

V

My father began teaching me to play upon the flute and sing by note; but notwithstanding I was of that tender age when little children are wont to take pastime in whistles and such toys, I had an inexpressible dislike for it, and played and sang only to obey him. My father in those times fashioned wonderful organs with pipes of

1 The word is *bocche*, so I have translated it by *mouths*. But Cellini clearly meant the gaping claws of the scorpion.

wood, spinets the fairest and most excellent which then could be seen, viols and lutes and harps of the most beautiful and perfect construction. He was an engineer, and had marvellous skill in making instruments for lowering bridges and for working mills, and other machines of that sort. In ivory he was the first who wrought really well. But after he had fallen in love with the woman who was destined to become my mother—perhaps what brought them together was that little flute, to which indeed he paid more attention than was proper—he was entreated by the fifers of the Signory to play in their company. Accordingly he did so for some time to amuse himself, until by constant importunity they induced him to become a member of their band. Lorenzo de' Medici and Piero his son, who had a great liking for him, perceived later on that he was devoting himself wholly to the fife, and was neglecting his fine engineering talent and his beautiful art.[1] So they had him removed from that post. My father took this very ill, and it seemed to him that they had done him a great despite. Yet he immediately resumed his art, and fashioned a mirror, about a cubit in diameter, out of bone and ivory, with figures and foliage of great finish and grand design. The mirror was in the form of a wheel. In the middle was the looking-glass; around it were seven circular pieces, on which were the Seven Virtues, carved and joined of ivory and black bone. The whole mirror, together with the Virtues, was placed in equilibrium, so that when the wheel turned, all the Virtues moved, and they had weights at their feet which kept them upright. Possessing some acquaintance with the Latin tongue, he put a legend in Latin round his looking-glass, to this effect—"Whithersoever the wheel of Fortune turns, Virtue stands firm upon her feet:"

Rota sum: semper, quoquo me verto, stat Virtus.

A little while after this he obtained his place again among the fifers. Although some of these things happened before I was born, my familiarity with them has moved me to set them down here. In those days the musicians of the Signory were all of them members of the most honourable trades, and some of them belonged to the greater guilds of silk and wool;[2] and that was the reason why my father

[1] The Medici here mentioned were Lorenzo the Magnificent, and his son Pietro, who was expelled from Florence in the year 1494. He never returned, but died in the river Garigliano in 1504.

[2] In the Middle Ages the burghers of Florence were divided into industrial guilds called the Greater and the Lesser Arts. The former took precedence of the latter, both in political importance and in social esteem.

did not disdain to follow this profession, and his chief desire with regard to me was always that I should become a great performer on the flute. I for my part felt never more discontented than when he chose to talk to me about this scheme, and to tell me that, if I liked, he discerned in me such aptitudes that I might become the best man in the world.

VI

As I have said, my father was the devoted servant and attached friend of the house of Medici; and when Piero was banished, he entrusted him with many affairs of the greatest possible importance. Afterwards, when the magnificent Piero Soderini was elected, and my father continued in his office of musician, Soderini, perceiving his wonderful talent, began to employ him in many matters of great importance as an engineer.[1] So long as Soderini remained in Florence, he showed the utmost good-will to my father; and in those days, I being still of tender age, my father had me carried, and made me perform upon the flute; I used to play treble in concert with the musicians of the palace before the Signory, following my notes: and a beadle used to carry me upon his shoulders. The Gonfalonier, that is, Soderini, whom I have already mentioned, took much pleasure in making me chatter, and gave me comfits, and was wont to say to my father: "Maestro Giovanni, besides music, teach the boy those other arts which do you so much honour." To which my father answered: "I do not wish him to practise any art but playing and composing; for in this profession I hope to make him the greatest man of the world, if God prolongs his life." To these words one of the old counsellors made answer: "Ah! Maestro Giovanni, do what the Gonfalonier tells you! for why should he never become anything more than a good musician?"

Thus some time passed, until the Medici returned.[2] When they arrived, the Cardinal, who afterwards became Pope Leo, received my father very kindly. During their exile the scutcheons which were on the palace of the Medici had had their balls erased, and a great red cross painted over them, which was the bearing of the Com-

1 Piero Soderini was elected Gonfalonier of the Florentine Republic for life in the year 1502. After nine years of government, he was banished, and when he died, Machiavelli wrote the famous sneering epitaph upon him. See J. A. Symonds' *Renaissance in Italy*, vol. i. p. 297.

2 This was in 1512, when Lorenzo's two sons, Giuliano and Giovanni (afterwards Pope Leo X.), came back through the aid of a Spanish army, after the great battle at Ravenna.

mune.[3] Accordingly, as soon as they returned, the red cross was scratched out, and on the scutcheon with red balls and the golden field were painted in again, and finished with great beauty. My father, who possessed a simple vein of poetry, instilled in him by nature, together with a certain touch of prophecy, which was doubtless a divine gift in him, wrote these four verses under the said arms of the Medici, when they were uncovered to the view:—

These arms, which have so long from sight been laid
  Beneath the holy cross, that symbol meek,
  Now lift their glorious glad face, and seek
With Peter's sacred cloak to be arrayed.

This epigram was read by all Florence. A few days afterwards Pope Julius II. died. The Cardinal de' Medici went to Rome, and was elected Pope against the expectation of everybody. He reigned as Leo X., that generous and great soul. My father sent him his four prophetic verses. The Pope sent to tell him to come to Rome; for this would be to his advantage. But he had no will to go; and so, in lieu of reward, his place in the palace was taken from him by Jacopo Salviati, upon that man's election as Gonfalonier.[4] This was the reason why I commenced goldsmith; after which I spent part of my time in learning that art, and part in playing, much against my will.

VII

When my father spoke to me in the way I have above described, I entreated him to let me draw a certain fixed number of hours in the day; all the rest of my time I would give to music, only with the view of satisfying his desire. Upon this he said to me: "So then, you take no pleasure in playing?" To which I answered, "No;" because that art seemed too base in comparison with what I had in my own mind. My good father, driven to despair by this fixed idea of mine, placed me in the workshop of Cavaliere Bandinello's father, who was called Michel Agnolo, a goldsmith from Pinzi di Monte, and a master excellent in that craft.[1] He had no distinction of birth

[3] The Medicean arms were "or, six pellets gules, three, two, and one." The Florentine Commune bore, "argent a cross gules."

[4] Cellini makes a mistake here. Salviati married a daughter of Lorenzo de' Medici, and obtained great influence in Florence; but we have no record of his appointment to the office of Gonfalonier.

[1] Baccio Bandinello, the sculptor, and a great rival of Cellini's, as will appear in the ensuing pages, was born in 1487, and received the honour of knighthood from Clement VII. and Charles V. Posterity has confirmed Cellini's opinion of Bandinello as an artist; for his works are coarse, pretentious, and incapable of giving pleasure to any person of refined intelligence.

whatever, but was the son of a charcoal-seller. This is no blame to Bandinello, who has founded the honour of the family—if only he had done so honestly! However that may be, I have no cause now to talk about him. After I had stayed there some days, my father took me away from Michel Agnolo, finding himself unable to live without having me always under his eyes. Accordingly, much to my discontent, I remained at music till I reached the age of fifteen. If I were to describe all the wonderful things that happened to me up to that time, and all the great dangers to my own life which I ran, I should astound my readers; but, in order to avoid prolixity, and having very much to relate, I will omit these incidents.

When I reached the age of fifteen, I put myself, against my father's will, to the goldsmith's trade with a man called Antonio, son of Sandro, known commonly as Marcone the goldsmith. He was a most excellent craftsman and a very good fellow to boot, high-spirited and frank in all his ways. My father would not let him give me wages like the other apprentices; for having taken up the study of this art to please myself, he wished me to indulge my whim for drawing to the full. I did so willingly enough; and that honest master of mine took marvellous delight in my performances. He had an only son, a bastard, to whom he often gave his orders, in order to spare me. My liking for the art was so great, or, I may truly say, my natural bias, both one and the other, that in a few months I caught up the good, nay, the best young craftsmen in our business, and began to reap the fruits of my labours. I did not, however, neglect to gratify my good father from time to time by playing on the flute or cornet. Each time he heard me, I used to make his tears fall accompanied with deep-drawn sighs of satisfaction. My filial piety often made me give him that contentment, and induce me to pretend that I enjoyed the music too.

VIII

At this time, I had a brother, younger by two years, a youth of extreme boldness and fierce temper. He afterwards became one of the great soldiers in the school of that marvellous general Giovannino de' Medici, father of Duke Cosimo.[1] The boy was about fourteen,

1 Cellini refers to the famous Giovanni delle Bande Nere, who was killed in an engagement in Lombardy in November 1526, by the Imperialist troops marching to the sack of Rome. His son Cosimo, after the murder of Duke Alessandro, established the second Medicean dynasty in Florence.

and I two years older. One Sunday evening, just before nightfall, he happened to find himself between the gate San Gallo and the Porta a Pinti; in this quarter he came to duel with a young fellow of twenty or thereabouts. They both had swords; and my brother dealt so valiantly that, after having badly wounded him, he was upon the point of following up his advantage. There was a great crowd of people present, among whom were many of the adversary's kinsfolk. Seeing that the thing was going ill for their own man, they put hand to their slings, a stone from one of which hit my poor brother in the head. He fell to the ground at once in a dead faint. It so chanced that I had been upon the spot alone, and without arms; and I had done my best to get my brother out of the fray by calling to him: "Make off; you have done enough." Meanwhile, as luck would have it, he fell, as I have said, half dead to earth. I ran up at once, seized his sword, and stood in front of him, bearing the brunt of several rapiers and a shower of stones. I never left his side until some brave soldiers came from the gate San Gallo and rescued me from the raging crowd; they marvelled much, the while, to find such valour in so young a boy.

Then I carried my brother home for dead, and it was only with great difficulty that he came to himself again. When he was cured, the Eight, who had already condemned our adversaries and banished them for a term of years, sent us also into exile for six months at a distance of ten miles from Florence.[2] I said to my brother: "Come along with me;" and so we took leave of our poor father; and instead of giving us money, for he had none, he bestowed on us his blessing. I went to Siena, wishing to look up a certain worthy man called Maestro Francesco Castoro. On another occasion, when I had run away from my father, I went to this good man, and stayed some time with him, working at the goldsmith's trade until my father sent for me back. Francesco, when I reached him, recognised me at once, and gave me work to do. While thus occupied, he placed a house at my disposal for the whole time of my sojourn in Siena. Into this I moved, together with my brother, and applied myself to labour for the space of several months. My brother had acquired the rudiments of Latin, but was still so young that he could not yet relish the taste of virtuous employment, but passed his time in dissipation.

[2] The Eight, or Gli Otto, were a magistracy in Florence with cognizance of matters affecting the internal peace of the city.

IX

The Cardinal de' Medici, who afterwards became Pope Clement VII., had us recalled to Florence at the entreaty of my father.[1] A certain pupil of my father's, moved by his own bad nature, suggested to the Cardinal that he ought to send me to Bologna, in order to learn to play well from a great master there. The name of this master was Antonio, and he was in truth a worthy man in the musician's art. The Cardinal said to my father that, if he sent me there he would give me letters of recommendation and support. My father, dying with joy at such an opportunity, sent me off; and I being eager to see the world, went with good grace.

When I reached Bologna, I put myself under a certain Maestro Ercole del Piffero, and began to earn something by my trade. In the meantime I used to go every day to take my music lesson, and in a few weeks made considerable progress in that accursed art. However I made still greater in my trade of goldsmith; for the Cardinal having given me no assistance, I went to live with a Bolognese illuminator who was called Scipione Cavalletti (his house was in the street of our Lady del Baraccan); and while there I devoted myself to drawing and working for one Graziadio, a Jew, with whom I earned considerably.

At the end of six months I returned to Florence, where that fellow Pierino, who had been my father's pupil, was greatly mortified by my return. To please my father, I went to his house and played the cornet and the flute with one of his brothers, who was named Girolamo, several years younger than the said Piero, a very worthy young man, and quite the contrary of his brother. On one of those days my father came to Piero's house to hear us play, and in ecstasy at my performance exclaimed: "I shall yet make you a marvellous musician against the will of all or any one who may desire to prevent me." To this Piero answered, and spoke the truth: "Your Benvenuto will get much more honour and profit if he devotes himself to the goldsmith's trade than to this piping." These words made my father angry, seeing that I too had the same opinion as Piero, that he flew into a rage and cried out at him: "Well did I know that it was

1 This Cardinal and Pope was Giulio, a natural son of Giuliano, Lorenzo de' Medici's brother, who had been killed in the Pazzi conspiracy, year 1478. Giulio lived to become Pope Clement VII., to suffer the sack of Rome in 1527, and to make the concordat with Charles V. at Bologna in 1529-30, which settled for three centuries the destiny of Italy. We shall hear much more of him from Cellini in the course of this narrative.

you, *you* who put obstacles in the way of my cherished wish; you are the man who had me ousted from my place at the palace, paying me back with that black ingratitude which is the usual recompense of great benefits. I got you promoted, and you have got me cashiered; I taught you to play with all the little art you have, and you are preventing my son from obeying me; but bear in mind these words of prophecy: not years or months, I say, but only a few weeks will pass before this dirty ingratitude of yours shall plunge you into ruin." To these words answered Pierino and said: "Maestro Giovanni, the majority of men, when they grow old, go mad at the same time; and this has happened to you. I am not astonished at it, because most liberally have you squandered all your property, without reflecting that your children had need of it. I mind to do just the opposite, and to leave my children so much that they shall be able to succour yours." To this my father answered: "No bad tree ever bore good fruit; quite the contrary; and I tell you further that you are bad, and that your children will be mad and paupers, and will cringe for alms to my virtuous and wealthy sons." Thereupon we left the house, muttering words of anger on both sides. I had taken my father's part; and when we stepped into the street together, I told him I was quite ready to take vengeance for the insults heaped on him by that scoundrel, provided he permit me to give myself up to the art of design. He answered: "My dear son, I too in my time was a good draughtsman; but for recreation, after such stupendous labours, and for the love of me who am your father, who begat you and brought you up and implanted so many honourable talents in you, for the sake of recreation, I say, will not you promise sometimes to take in hand your flute and that seductive cornet, and to play upon them to your heart's content, inviting the delight of music?" I promised I would do so, and very willingly for his love's sake. Then my good father said that such excellent parts as I possessed would be the greatest vengeance I could take for the insults of his enemies.

Not a whole month had been completed after this scene before the man Pierino happened to be building a vault in a house of his, which he had in the Via dello Studio; and being one day in a ground-floor room above the vault which he was making, together with much company around him, he fell to talking about his old master, my father. While repeating the words which he had said to him concerning his ruin, no sooner had they escaped his lips than the floor where he was standing (either because the vault had been badly built, or rather though the sheer mightiness of God, who does not always pay on Saturday) suddenly gave way. Some of the stones and bricks of the vault, which fell with him, broke both his legs. The friends who were with him, remaining on the border of the broken vault, took no harm, but were astounded and full of wonder, especially because of the prophecy which he had just contemptuously repeated to them. When my father heard of this, he took his sword, and went to see the man. There, in the presence of his father, who was called Niccolaio da Volterra, a trumpeter of the Signory, he said. "O Piero, my dear pupil, I am sorely grieved at your mischance; but if you remember it was only a short time ago that I warned you of it; and as much as I then said will come to happen between your children and mine." Shortly afterwards, the ungrateful Piero died of that illness. He left a wife of bad character and one son, who after the lapse of some years came to me to beg for alms in Rome. I gave him something, as well because it is my nature to be charitable, as also because I recalled with tears the happy state which Pierino held when my father spake those words of prophecy, namely, that Pierino's children should live to crave succour from his own virtuous sons. Of this perhaps enough is now said; but let none ever laugh at the prognostications of any worthy man whom he has wrongfully insulted; because it is not he who speaks, nay, but the very voice of God through him.

X

All this while I worked as a goldsmith, and was able to assist my good father. His other son, my brother Cecchino, had, as I said before, been instructed in the rudiments of Latin letters. It was our father's wish to make me, the elder, a great musician and composer, and him, the younger, a great and learned jurist. He could not, however, put force upon the inclinations of our nature, which directed me to the arts of design, and my brother, who had a fine and graceful person, to the profession of arms. Cecchino, being still quite a lad, was returning from his first lesson in the school of the stupendous Giovannino de' Medici. On the day when he reached home, I happened to be absent; and he, being in want of proper clothes, sought out our sisters, who, unknown to my father, gave him a cloak and doublet of mine, both new and of good quality. I ought to say that, beside the aid I gave my father and my excellent and honest sisters,

I had bought those handsome c[illegible] out of my own savings. When I found I had been cheated, and my clothes taken from me, and my brother from whom I should have recovered them was gone, I asked my father why he suffered so great a wrong to be done me, seeing that I was always ready to assist him. He replied that I was his good son, but that the other, whom he thought to have lost, had been found again; also that it was a duty, nay, a precept from God Himself, that he who hath should give to him who hath not; and that for his sake I ought to bear this injustice, for God would increase me in all good things. I, like a youth without experience, retorted on my poor afflicted parent; and taking the miserable remnants of my clothes and money, went toward a gate of the city. As I did not know which gate would start me on the road to Rome, I arrived at Lucca, and from Lucca reached Pisa.

When I came to Pisa (I was about sixteen years of age at the time), I stopped near the middle bridge, by what is called the Fish-stone, at the shop of a goldsmith, and began attentively to watch what the master was about.[1] He asked me who I was, and what was my profession. I told him that I worked a little in the same trade as his own. This worthy man bade me come into his shop, and at once gave me work to do, and spoke as follows: "Your good appearance makes me believe you are a decent honest youth." Then he told me out gold, silver, and gems; and when the first day's work was finished, he took me in the evening to his house, where he dwelt respectably with his handsome wife and children. Thinking of the grief which my good father might be feeling for me, I wrote him that I was sojourning with a very excellent and honest man, called Maestro Ulivieri della Chiostra, and was working with him at many good things of beauty and importance. I bade him be of good cheer, for that I was bent on learning, and hoped by my acquirements to bring him back both profit and honour before long. My good father answered the letter at once in words like these: "My son, the love I bear you is so great, that if it were not for the honour of our family, which above all things I regard, I should immediately have set off for you; for indeed it seems like being without the light of my eyes, when I do not see you daily, as I used to do. I will make it my business to complete the training of my household up to virtuous honesty; do you make it yours to acquire excellence in your art; and I only

[1] The Fish-stone, or Pietra del Pesce, was the market on the quay where the fish brought from the sea up the Arno to Pisa used to be sold.

wish you to remember these four simple words, obey them, and never let them escape your memory:

> In whatever house you be,
> Steal not, and live honestly."

XI

This letter fell into the hands of my master Ulivieri, and he read it unknown to me. Afterwards he avowed that he had read it, and added: "So then, my Benvenuto, your good looks did not deceive me, as a letter from your father which has come into my hands gives me assurance, which proves him to be a man of notable honesty and worth. Consider yourself then to be at home here, and as though in your own father's house."

While I stayed at Pisa, I went to see the Campo Santo, and there I found many beautiful fragments of antiquity, that is to say, marble sarcophagi. In other parts of Pisa also I saw many antique objects, which I diligently studied whenever I had days or hours free from the labour of the workshop. My master, who took pleasure in coming to visit me in the little room which he had allotted me, observing that I spent all my time in studious occupations, began to love me like a father. I made great progress in the one year that I stayed there, and completed several fine and valuable things in gold and silver, which inspired me with a resolute ambition to advance in my art.

My father, in the meanwhile, kept writing piteous entreaties that I should return to him; and in every letter bade me not to lose the music he had taught me with such trouble. On this, I suddenly gave up all wish to go back to him; so much did I hate that accursed music; and I felt as though of a truth I were in paradise the whole year I stayed at Pisa, where I never played the flute.

At the end of the year my master Ulivieri had occasion to go to Florence, in order to sell certain gold and silver sweepings which he had;[1] and inasmuch as the bad air of Pisa had given me a touch of fever, I went with the fever hanging still about me, in my master's company, back to Florence. There my father received him most affectionately, and lovingly prayed him, unknown by me, not to insist on taking me again to Pisa. I was ill about two months, during

[1] I have translated *spazzature* by *sweepings*. It means all refuse of the precious metals left in the goldsmith's trays.

which time my father had me most kindly treated and cured, always repeating that it seemed to him a thousand years till I got well again, in order that he might hear me play a little. But when he talked to me of music, with his fingers on my pulse, seeing he had some acquaintance with medicine and Latin learning, he felt it change so much if he approached that topic, that he was often dismayed and left my side in tears. When I perceived how greatly he was disappointed, I bade one of my sisters bring me a flute; for though the fever never left me, that instrument is so easy that it did not hurt me to play upon it; and I used it with such dexterity of hand and tongue that my father coming suddenly upon me, blessed me a thousand times, exclaiming that while I was away from him I had made great progress, as he thought; and he begged me to go forwards, and not to sacrifice so fine an accomplishment.

XII

When I had recovered my health, I returned to my old friend Marcone, the worthy goldsmith, who put me in the way of earning money, with which I helped my father and our household. About that time there came to Florence a sculptor named Piero Torrigiani;[1] he arrived from England, where he had resided many years; and being intimate with my master, he daily visited his house; and when he saw my drawings and the things which I was making, he said: "I have come to Florence to enlist as many young men as I can; for I have undertaken to execute a great work for my king, and want some of my own Florentines to help me. Now your method of working and your designs are worthy rather of a sculptor than a goldsmith; and since I have to turn out a great piece of bronze, I will at the same time turn you into a rich and able artist." This man had a splendid person and a most arrogant spirit, with the air of a great soldier more than a sculptor, especially in regard to his vehement gestures and his resonant voice, together with a habit he had of knitting his brows, enough to frighten any man of courage. He kept talking every day about his gallant feats among those beasts of Englishmen.

[1] Torrigiani worked in fact for Henry VIII., and his monument to Henry VII. still exists in the Lady Chapel of Westminster Abbey. From England he went to Spain, where he modelled a statue of the Virgin for a great nobleman. Not receiving the pay he expected, he broke his work to pieces; for which act of sacrilege the Inquisition sent him to prison, where he starved himself to death in 1522. Such at least is the legend of his end.

In course of conversation he happened to mention Michel Agnolo Buonarroti, led thereto by a drawing I had made from a cartoon of that divinest painter.[2] This cartoon was the first masterpiece which Michel Agnolo exhibited, in proof of his stupendous talents. He produced it in competition with another painter, Lionardo da Vinci, who also made a cartoon; and both were intended for the council-hall in the palace of the Signory. They represented the taking of Pisa by the Florentines; and our admirable Lionardo had chosen to depict a battle of horses, with the capture of some standards, in as divine a style as could possibly be imagined. Michel Agnolo in his cartoon portrayed a number of foot-soldiers, who, the season being summer, had gone to bathe in Arno. He drew them at the very moment the alarm sounded, and the men all naked run to arms; so splendid in their action that nothing survives of ancient or of modern art that touches the same lofty point of excellence; and as I have already said, the design of the great Lionardo was itself most admirably beautiful. These two cartoons stood, one in the palace of the Medici, the other in the hall of the Pope. So long as they remained intact, they were the school of the world. Though the divine Michel Agnolo in later life finished that great chapel of Pope Julius,[3] he never rose half-way to the same pitch of power; his genius never afterwards attained to the force of those first studies.

XIII

Now let us return to Piero Torrigiani, who, with my drawing in his hand, spoke as follows: "This Buonarroti and I used, when we were boys, to go into the Church of the Carmine, to learn drawing from the chapel of Masaccio.[1] It was Buonarroti's habit to banter all who were drawing there; and one day, among others, when he was annoying me, I got more angry than usual, and clenching my fist, gave him such a blow on the nose, that I felt bone and cartilage go down like biscuit beneath my knuckles; and this mark of mine he will carry with him to the grave." [2] These words begat in me such

2 The cartoons to which Cellini here alludes were made by Michel Angelo and Lionardo for the decoration of the Sala del Gran Consiglio in the Palazzo Vecchio at Florence. Only the shadows of them remain to this day; a part of Michel Angelo's, engraved by Schiavonetti, and a transcript by Rubens from Lionardo's, called the Battle of the Standard.

3 The Sistine Chapel in the Vatican.

1 The Chapel of the Carmine, painted in fresco by Masaccio and some other artist, possibly Filippino Lippi, is still the most important monument of Florentine art surviving from the period preceding Raphael.

2 The profile portraits of Michel Angelo Buonarroti confirm this story. They show the bridge of his nose bent in an angle, as though it had been broken.

hatred of the man, since I was always gazing at the masterpieces of the divine Michel Agnolo, that although I felt a wish to go with him to England, I now could never bear the sight of him.

All the while I was at Florence, I studied the noble manner of Michel Agnolo, and from this I have never deviated. About that time I contracted a close and familiar friendship with an amiable lad of my own age, who was also in the goldsmith's trade. He was called Francesco, son of Filippo, and grandson of Fra Lippo Lippi, that most excellent painter.[3] Through intercourse together, such love grew up between us that, day or night, we never stayed apart. The house where we lived was still full of the fine studies which his father had made, bound up in several books of drawings by his hand, and taken from the best antiquities of Rome. The sight of these things filled me with passionate enthusiasm; and for two years or thereabouts we lived in intimacy. At that time I fashioned a silver bas-relief of the size of a little child's hand. It was intended for the clasp of a man's belt; for they were then worn as large as that. I carved on it a knot of leaves in the antique style, with figures of children and other masks of great beauty. This piece I made in the workshop of one Francesco Salimbene; and on it's being exhibited to the trade, the goldsmiths praised me as the best young craftsman of their art.

There was one Giovan Battista, surnamed Il Tasso, a wood-carver, precisely of my own age, who one day said to me that if I was willing to go to Rome, he should be glad to join me.[4] Now we had this conversation together immediately after dinner; and I being angry with my father for the same old reason of the music, said to Tasso: "You are a fellow of words, not deeds." He answered: "I too have come to anger with my mother; and if I had cash enough to take me to Rome, I would not turn back to lock the door of that wretched little workshop I call mine." To these words I replied that if that was all that kept him in Florence I had money enough in my pockets to bring us both to Rome. Talking thus and walking onwards, we found ourselves at the gate San Piero Gattolini without noticing that we had got there; whereupon I said: "Friend Tasso, this is

[3] Fra Filippo Lippi was a Carmelite monk, whose frescoes at Prato and Spoleto and oil-paintings in Florence and elsewhere are among the most genial works of the pre-Raphaelite Renaissance. Vasari narrates his love-adventures with Lucrezia Buti, and Robert Browning has drawn a clever portrait of him in his "Men and Women." His son, Filippo or Filippino, was also an able painter, some of whose best work survives in the Strozzi Chapel of S. Maria Novella at Florence, and in the Church of S. Maria Sopra Minerva at Rome.

[4] Tasso was an able artist, mentioned both by Vasari and Pietro Aretino. He stood high in the favour of Duke Cosimo de' Medici, who took his opinion on the work of other craftsmen.

God's doing that we have reached this gate without either you or me noticing that we were there; and now that I am here, it seems to me that I have finished half the journey." And so, being of one accord, we pursued our way together, saying, "Oh, what will our old folks say this evening?" We then made an agreement not to think more about them till we reached Rome. So we tied our aprons behind our backs, and trudged almost in silence to Siena. When we arrived at Siena, Tasso said (for he had hurt his feet) that he would not go farther, and asked me to lend him money to get back. I made answer: "I should not have enough left to go forward; you ought indeed to have thought of this on leaving Florence; and if is because of your feet that you shirk the journey, we will find a return horse for Rome, which will deprive you of the excuse." Accordingly I hired a horse; and seeing that he did not answer, I took my way toward the gate of Rome. When he knew that I was firmly resolved to go, muttering between his teeth, and limping as well as he could, he came on behind me very slowly and at a great distance. On reaching the gate, I felt pity for my comrade, and waited for him, and took him on the crupper, saying: "What would our friends speak of us to-morrow, if, having left for Rome, we had not pluck to get beyond Siena?" Then the good Tasso said I spoke the truth; and as he was a pleasant fellow, he began to laugh and sing; and in this way, always singing and laughing, we travelled the whole way to Rome. I had just nineteen years then, and so had the century.

When we reached Rome, I put myself under a master who was known as Il Firenzuola. His name was Giovanni, and he came from Firenzuola in Lombardy, a most able craftsman in large vases and big plate of that kind. I showed him part of the model for the clasp which I had made in Florence at Salimbene's. It pleased him exceedingly; and turning to one of his journeymen, a Florentine called Giannotto Giannotti, who had been several years with him, he spoke as follows: "This fellow is one of the Florentines who know something, and you are one of those who know nothing." Then I recognised the man, and turned to speak with him; for before he went to Rome, we often went to draw together, and had been very intimate comrades. He was so put out by the words his master flung at him, that he said he did not recognise me or know who I was; whereupon I got angry and cried out: "O Giannotto, you who were once my friend—for have we not been together in such and such places, and drawn, and ate, and drunk, and slept in company at your house in the country? I don't want you to bear witness on my behalf to this worthy man, your master, because I hope that my hands are such that without aid from you they will declare what sort of a fellow I am."

XIV

When I had thus spoken, Firenzuola, who was a man of hot spirit and brave, turned to Giannotto, and said to him: "You vile rascal, aren't you ashamed to treat a man who has been so intimate a comrade with you in this way?" And with the same movement of quick feeling, he faced round and said to me: "Welcome to my workshop; and do as you have promised; let your hands declare what man you are."

He gave me a very fine piece of silver plate to work on for a cardinal. It was a little oblong box, copied from the porphyry sarcophagus before the door of the Rotonda. Beside what I copied, I enriched it with so many elegant masks of my invention, that my master went about showing it through the art, and boasting that so good a piece of work had been turned out from his shop.[1] It was about half a cubit in size, and was so constructed as to serve for a saltcellar at table. This was the first earning that I touched at Rome, and part of it I sent to assist my good father; the rest I kept for my own use, living upon it while I went about studying the antiquities of Rome, until my money failed, and I had to return to the shop for work. Battista del Tasso, my comrade, did not stay long in Rome, but went back to Florence.

After undertaking some new commissions, I took it into my head, as soon as I had finished them, to change my master; I had indeed been worried into doing so by a certain Milanese, called Pagolo Arsago.[2] My first master, Firenzuola, had a great quarrel about this with Arsago, and abused him in my presence; whereupon I took up speech in defence of my new master. I said that I was born free, and free I meant to live, and that there was no reason to complain of him, far less of me, since some few crowns of wages were still due to me; also that I chose to go, like a free journeyman, where it pleased me, knowing I did wrong to no man. My new master then

[1] Cellini's use of the word *arte* for the *art* or *trade* of goldsmiths corresponds to "the art" as used by English writers early in this century. See Haydon's Autobiography, *passim.*

[2] The Italian is *sobbillato,* which might be also translated *inveigled* or *instigated.* But Varchi, the contemporary of Cellini, gives this verb the force of using pressure and boring on until somebody is driven to do something.

put in with his excuses, saying that he had not asked me to come, and that I should gratify him by returning with Firenzuola. To this I replied that I was not aware of wronging the latter in any way, and as I had completed his commissions, I chose to be my own master and not the man of others, and that he who wanted me must beg me of myself. Firenzuola cried: "I don't intend to beg you of yourself; I have done with you; don't show yourself again upon my premises." I reminded him of the money he owed me. He laughed me in the face; on which I said that if I knew how to use my tools in handicraft as well as he had seen, I could be quite as clever with my sword in claiming the just payment of my labour. While we were exchanging these words, an old man happened to come up, called Maestro Antonio, of San Marino. He was the chief among the Roman goldsmiths, and had been Firenzuola's master. Hearing what I had to say, which I took good care that he should understand, he immediately espoused my cause, and bade Firenzuola pay me. The dispute waxed warm, because Firenzuola was an admirable swordsman, far better than he was a goldsmith. Yet reason made itself heard; and I backed my cause with the same spirit, till I got myself paid. In course of time Firenzuola and I became friends, and at his request I stood godfather to one of his children.

XV

I went on working with Pagolo Arsago, and earned a good deal of money, the greater part of which I always sent to my good father. At the end of two years, upon my father's entreaty, I returned to Florence, and put myself once more under Francesco Salimbene, with whom I earned a great deal, and took continual pains to improve in my art. I renewed my intimacy with Francesco di Filippo; and though I was too much given to pleasure, owing to that accursed music, I never neglected to devote some hours of the day or night to study. At that time I fashioned a silver heart's-key (*chiavaquore*), as it was then called. This was a girdle three inches broad, which used to be made for brides, and was executed in half relief with some small figures in the round. It was a commission from a man called Raffaello Lapaccini. I was very badly paid; but the honour which it brought me was worth far more than the gain I might have justly made by it. Having at this time worked with many different persons in Florence, I had come to know some worthy men among the goldsmiths, as, for instance, Marcone, my first master; but I also met with others reputed honest, who did all they could to ruin me, and robbed me grossly. When I perceived this, I left their company, and held them for thieves and blackguards. One of the goldsmiths, called Giovanbattista Sogliani, kindly accommodated me with part of his shop, which stood at the side of the New Market near the Landi's bank. There I finished several pretty pieces, and made good gains, and was able to give my family much help. This roused the jealousy of the bad men among my former masters, who were called Salvadore and Michele Guasconti. In the guild of the goldsmiths they had three big shops, and drove a thriving trade. On becoming aware of their evil will against me, I complained to certain worthy fellows, and remarked that they ought to have been satisfied with the thieveries they practised on me under the cloak of hypocritical kindness. This coming to their ears, they threatened to make me sorely repent of such words; but I, who knew not what the colour of fear was, paid them little or no heed.

XVI

It chanced one day that I was leaning against a shop of one of these men, who called out to me, and began partly reproaching, partly bullying. I answered that had they done their duty by me, I should have spoken of them what one speaks of good and worthy men; but as they had done the contrary, they ought to complain of themselves and not of me. While I was standing there and talking, one of them, named Gherardo Guasconti, their cousin, having perhaps been put up to it by them, lay in wait till a beast of burden went by.[1] It was a load of bricks. When the load reached me, Gherardo pushed it so violently on my body that I was very much hurt. Turning suddenly round and seeing him laughing, I struck him such a blow on the temple that he fell down, stunned, like one dead. Then I faced round to his cousins, and said: "That's the way to treat cowardly thieves of your sort;" and when they wanted to make a move upon me, trusting to their numbers, I, whose blood was now well up, laid hands to a little knife I had, and cried: "If one of you comes out of the shop, let the other run for the confessor, because the doctor will have nothing to do here." These words so frightened

1 The Italian is *appostò che passassi una soma.* The verb *appostare* has the double meaning of lying in wait and arranging something on purpose. Cellini's words may mean, *caused a beast of burden to pass by.*

them that not one stirred to help their cousin. As soon as I had gone, the fathers and sons ran to the Eight, and declared that I had assaulted them in their shops with sword in hand, a thing which had never yet been seen in Florence. The magistrates had me summoned. I appeared before them; and they began to upbraid and cry out upon me—partly, I think, because they saw me in my cloak, while the others were dressed like citizens in mantle and hood;[2] but also because my adversaries had been to the houses of those magistrates, and had talked with all of them in private, while I, inexperienced in such matters, had not spoken to any of them, trusting in the goodness of my cause. I said that, having received such outrage and insult from Gherardo, and in my fury having only given him a box on the ear, I did not think I deserved such a vehement reprimand. I had hardly time to finish the word box, before Prinzivalle della Stufa,[3] who was one of the Eight, interrupted me by saying: "You gave him a blow, and not a box, on the ear." The bell was rung and we were all ordered out, when Prinzivalle spoke thus in my defence to his brother judges: "Mark, sirs, the simplicity of this poor young man, who has accused himself of having given a box on the ear, under the impression that this is of less importance than a blow; whereas a box on the ear in the New Market carries a fine of twenty-five crowns, while a blow costs little or nothing. He is a young man of admirable talents, and supports his poor family by his labour in great abundance; I would to God that our city had plenty of this sort, instead of the present dearth of them."

XVII

Among the magistrates were some Radical fellows with turned-up hoods, who had been influenced by the entreaties and the calumnies of my opponents, because they all belonged to the party of Fra Girolamo; and these men would have had me sent to prison and punished without too close a reckoning.[1] But the good Prinzivalle put a stop

2 Varchi says that a man who went about with only his cloak or cape by daytime, if he were not a soldier, was reputed an ill-liver. The Florentine citizens at this time still wore their ancient civil dress of the long gown and hood called *lucco*.

3 This man was an ardent supporter of the Medici, and in 1510 organized a conspiracy in their favour against the Gonfalonier Soderini.

1 Cellini calls these magistrates *arronzinati cappuccetti*, a term corresponding to our Roundheads. The democratic or anti-Medicean party in Florence at that time, who adhered to the republican principles of Fra Girolamo Savonarola, distinguished themselves by wearing the long tails of their hoods twisted up and turned round their heads. Cellini shows his Medicean sympathies by using this contemptuous term, and by the honourable mention he makes of Prinzivalle della Stufa.

to that. So they sentenced me to pay four measures of flour, which were to be given as alms to the nunnery of the Murate.[2] I was called in again; and he ordered me not to speak a word under pain of their displeasure, and to perform the sentence they had passed. Then, after giving me another sharp rebuke, they sent us to the chancellor; I muttering all the while, "It was a slap and not a blow," with which we left the Eight bursting with laughter. The chancellor bound us over upon bail on both sides; but only I was punished by having to pay the four measures of meal. Albeit just then I felt as though I had been massacred, I sent for one of my cousins, called Maestro Annibale, the surgeon, father of Messer Librodoro Librodori, desiring that he should go bail for me.[3] He refused to come, which made me so angry, that, fuming with fury and swelling like an asp, I took a desperate resolve. At this point one may observe how the stars do not so much sway as force our conduct. When I reflected on the great obligations which this Annibale owed my family, my rage grew to such a pitch that, turning wholly to evil, and being also by nature somewhat choleric, I waited till the magistrates had gone to dinner; and when I was alone, and observed that none of their officers were watching me, in the fire of my anger, I left the place, ran to my shop, seized a dagger and rushed to the house of my enemies, who were at home and shop together. I found them at table; and Gherardo, who had been the cause of the quarrel, flung himself upon me. I stabbed him in the breast, piercing doublet and jerkin through and through to the shirt, without however grazing his flesh or doing him the least harm in the world. When I felt my hand go in, and heard the clothes tear, I thought that I had killed him; and seeing him fall terror-struck to earth, I cried: "Traitors, this day is the day on which I mean to murder you all." Father, mother, and sisters, thinking the last day had come, threw themselves upon their knees, screaming out for mercy with all their might; but I perceiving that they offered no resistance, and that he was stretched for dead upon the ground, thought it too base a thing to touch them. I ran storming down the staircase; and when I reached the street, I found all the rest of the household, more than twelve persons; one of them had seized an iron shovel, another a thick iron pipe, one had an anvil, some of them hammers, and some cudgels. When I got among them, raging like a mad bull, I flung four or five

2 A convent of closely immured nuns.

3 The word I have translated *massacred* above is *assassinato*. It occurs frequently in Italian of this period, and indicates the extremity of wrong and outrage.

to the earth, and fell down with them myself, continually aiming my dagger now at one and now at another. Those who remained upright plied both hands with all their force, giving it me with hammers, cudgels, and anvil; but inasmuch as God does sometimes mercifully intervene, He so ordered that neither they nor I did any harm to one another. I only lost my cap, on which my adversaries seized, though they had run away from it before, and struck at it with all their weapons. Afterwards, they searched among their dead and wounded, and saw that not a single man was injured.

XVIII

I went off in the direction of Santa Maria Novella, and stumbling up against Fra Alessio Strozzi, whom by the way I did not know, I entreated this good friar for the love of God to save my life, since I had committed a great fault. He told me to have no fear; for had I done every sin in the world, I was yet in perfect safety in his little cell.

After about an hour, the Eight, in an extraordinary meeting, caused one of the most dreadful bans which ever were heard of to be published against me, announcing heavy penalties against who should harbour me or know where I was, without regard to place or to the quality of my protector. My poor afflicted father went to the Eight, threw himself upon his knees, and prayed for mercy for his unfortunate young son. Thereupon one of those Radical fellows, shaking the crest of his twisted hood, stood up and addressed my father with these insulting words:[1] "Get up from there, and begone at once, for to-morrow we shall send your son into the country with the lances."[2] My poor father had still the spirit to answer: "What God shall have ordained, that will you do, and not a jot or tittle more." Whereto the same man replied that for certain God had ordained as he had spoken. My father said: "The thought consoles me that you do not know for certain;" and quitting their presence, he came to visit me, together with a young man of my own age, called Pierro di Giovanni Landi—we loved one another as though we had been brothers.

1 *Un di queli arrovellati scotendo la cresto dello arronzinato cappuccio.* See above, p. 28. The democrats in Cellini's days were called at Florence *Arrabbiati* or *Arrovellati.* In the days of Savonarola this nickname had been given to the ultra-Medicean party or Palleschi.

2 *Lanciotti.* There is some doubt about this word. But it clearly means men armed with lances, at the disposal of the Signory.

Under his mantle the lad carried a first-rate sword and a splendid coat of mail; and when they found me, my brave father told me what had happened, and what the magistrates had said to him. Then he kissed me on the forehead and both eyes, and gave me his hearty blessing, saying: "May the power of goodness of God be your protection;" and reaching me the sword and armour, he helped me with his own hands to put them on. Afterwards he added: "Oh, my good son, with these arms in thy hand thou shalt either live or die." Pier Landi, who was present, kept shedding tears; and when he had given me ten golden crowns, I bade him remove a few hairs from my chin, which were the first down of my manhood. Frate Alessio disguised me like a friar and gave me a lay brother to go with me.[3] Quitting the convent, and issuing from the city by the gate of Prato, I went along the walls as far as the Piazza di San Gallo. Then I ascended the slope of Montui, and in one of the first houses there I found a man called Il Grassuccio, own brother to Messer Benedetto da Monte Varchi.[4] I flung off my monk's clothes, and became once more a man. Then we mounted two horses, which were waiting there for us, and went by night to Siena. Grassuccio returned to Florence, sought out my father, and gave him the news of my safe escape. In the excess of his joy, it seemed a thousand years to my father till he should meet that member of the Eight who had insulted him; and when he came across the man, he said: "See you, Antonio, that it was God who knew what had to happen to my son, and not yourself?" To which the fellow answered: "Only let him get another time into our clutches!" And my father: "I shall spend my time in thanking God that He has rescued him from that fate."

XIX

At Siena I waited for the mail to Rome, which I afterwards joined; and when we passed the Paglia, we met a courier carrying news of the new Pope, Clement VII. Upon my arrival in Rome, I went to work in the shop of the master-goldsmith Santi. He was dead; but a son of his carried on the business. He did not work himself, but entrusted all his commissions to a young man named Lucagnolo from Iesi, a country fellow, who while yet a child had come

[3] *Un converso,* an attendant on the monks.

[4] Benedetto da Monte Varchi was the celebrated poet, scholar, and historian of Florence, better known as Varchi. Another of his brothers was a physician of high repute at Florence. They continued throughout Cellini's life to live on terms of intimacy with him.

into Santi's service. This man was short but well proportioned, and was a more skilful craftsman than any one whom I had met with up to that time; remarkable for facility and excellent in design. He executed large plate only: that is to say, vases of the utmost beauty, basons, and such pieces.[1] Having put myself to work there, I began to make some candelabra for the Bishop of Salamanca, a Spaniard.[2] They were richly chased, so far as that sort of work admits. A pupil of Raffaello da Urbino called Gian Francesco, and commonly known as Il Fattore, was a painter of great ability; and being on terms of friendship with the Bishop, he introduced me to his favour, so that I obtained many commissions from that prelate, and earned considerable sums of money.[3]

During that time I went to draw, sometimes in Michel Agnolo's chapel, and sometimes in the house of Agostino Chigi of Siena, which contained many incomparable paintings by the hand of that great master Raffaello.[4] This I did on feast-days, because the house was then inhabited by Messer Gismondo, Agostino's brother. They plumed themselves exceedingly when they saw young men of my sort coming to study in their palaces. Gismondo's wife, noticing my frequent presence in that house—she was a lady as courteous as could be, and of surpassing beauty—came up to me one day, looked at my drawings, and asked me if I was a sculptor or a painter; to whom I said I was a goldsmith. She remarked that I drew too well for a goldsmith; and having made one of her waiting-maids bring a lily of the finest diamonds set in gold, she showed it to me, and bade me value it. I valued it at 800 crowns. Then she said that I had very nearly hit the mark, and asked me whether I felt capable of setting the stones really well. I said that I should much like to do so, and began before her eyes to make a little sketch for it, working all the better because of the pleasure I took in conversing with so lovely and agreeable a gentlewoman. When the sketch was finished, another Roman lady of great beauty joined us; she had been above, and now descending to the ground-floor, asked Madonna Porzia what she was doing there. She answered with a smile: "I am amusing myself

1 Cellini calls this *grosseria*.

2 Don Francesco de Bobadilla. He came to Rome in 1517, was shut up with Clement in the castle of S. Angelo in 1527, and died in 1529, after his return to Spain.

3 This painter, Gio. Francesco Penni, surnamed Il Fattore, aided Raphael in his Roman frescoes and was much beloved by him. Together with Giulio Romano he completed the imperfect Stanze of the Vatican.

4 Cellini here alludes to the Sistine Chapel and to the Villa Farnesina in Trastevere, built by the Sienese banker, Agostino Chigi. It was here that Raphael painted his Galatea and the whole fable of Cupid and Psyche.

by watching this worthy young man at his drawing; he is as good as he is handsome." I had by this time acquired a trifle of assurance, mixed, however, with some honest bashfulness; so I blushed and said: "Such as I am, lady, I shall ever be most ready to serve you." The gentlewoman, also slightly blushing, said: "You know well that I want you to serve me;" and reaching me the lily, told me to take it away; and gave me besides twenty golden crowns which she had in her bag, and added: "Set me the jewel after the fashion you have sketched, and keep for me the old gold in which it is now set." On this the Roman lady observed: "If I were in that young man's body, I should go off without asking leave." Madonna Porzia replied that virtues rarely are at home with vices, and that if I did such a thing, I should strongly belie my good looks of an honest man. Then turning round, she took the Roman lady's hand, and with a pleasant smile said: "Farewell, Benvenuto." I stayed on a short while at the drawing I was making, which was a copy of a Jove by Raffaello. When I had finished it and left the house, I set myself to making a little model of wax, in order to show how the jewel would look when it was completed. This I took to Madonna Porzia, whom I found with the same Roman lady. Both of them were highly satisfied with my work, and treated me so kindly that, being somewhat emboldened, I promised the jewel should be twice as good as the model. Accordingly I set hand to it, and in twelve days I finished it in the form of a fleur-de-lys, as I have said above, ornamenting it with little masks, children, and animals, exquisitely enamelled, whereby the diamonds which formed the lily were more than doubled in effect.

XX

While I was working at this piece, Lucagnolo, of whose ability I have before spoken, showed considerable discontent, telling me over and over again that I might acquire far more profit and honour by helping him to execute large plate, as I had done at first. I made him answer that, whenever I chose, I should always be capable of working at great silver pieces; but that things like that on which I was now engaged were not commissioned every day; and beside their bringing no less honour than large silver plate, there was also more profit to be made by them. He laughed me in the face, and said: "Wait and see, Benvenuto; for by the time that you have finished that work of yours, I will make haste to have finished this vase, which I took in hand when you did the jewel; and then experience shall teach you what profit I shall get from my vase, and what you will get from your ornament." I answered that I was very glad indeed to enter into such a competition with so good a craftsman as he was, because the end would show which of us was mistaken. Accordingly both the one and the other of us, with a scornful smile upon our lips, bent our heads in grim earnest to the work, which both were now desirous of accomplishing; so that after about ten days, each had finished his undertaking with great delicacy and artistic skill.

Lucagnolo's was a huge silver piece, used at the table of Pope Clement, into which he flung away bits of bone and the rind of divers fruits, while eating; an object of ostentation rather than necessity. The vase was adorned with two fine handles, together with many masks, both small and great, and masses of lovely foliage, in as exquisite a style of elegance as could be imagined; on seeing which I said it was the most beautiful vase that ever I set eyes on. Thinking he had convinced me, Lucagnolo replied: "Your work seems to me no less beautiful, but we shall soon perceive the difference between the two." So he took his vase and carried it to the Pope, who was very well pleased with it, and ordered at once that he should be paid at the ordinary rate of such large plate. Meanwhile I carried mine to Madonna Porzia, who looked at it with astonishment, and told me I had far surpassed my promise. Then she bade me ask for my reward whatever I liked; for it seemed to her my desert was so great that if I craved a castle she could hardly recompense me; but since that was not in her hands to bestow, she added laughing that I must beg what lay within her power. I answered that the greatest reward I could desire for my labour was to have satisfied her ladyship. Then, smiling in my turn, and bowing to her, I took my leave, saying I wanted no reward but that. She turned to the Roman lady and said: "You see that the qualities we discerned in him are companied by virtues, and not vices." They both expressed their admiration, and then Madonna Porzia continued: "Friend Benvenuto, have you never heard it said that when the poor give to the rich, the devil laughs?" I replied: "Quite true! and yet, in the midst of all his troubles, I should like this time to see him laugh;" and as I took my leave, she said that this time she had no will to bestow on him that favour.

When I came back to the shop, Lucagnolo had the money for his vase in a paper packet; and on my arrival he cried out: "Come and compare the price of your jewel with the price of my plate." I said that he must leave things as they were till the next day, because I hope that even as my work in its kind was not less excellent than his, so I should be able to show him quite an equal price for it.

XXI

On the day following, Madonna Porzia sent a major-domo of hers to my shop, who called me out, and putting into my hands a paper packet full of money from his lady, told me that she did not choose the devil should have his whole laugh out: by which she hinted that the money sent me was not the entire payment merited by my industry, and other messages were added worthy of so courteous a lady. Lucagnolo, who was burning to compare his packet with mine, burst into the shop; then in the presence of twelve journeymen and some neighbours, eager to behold the result of this competition, he seized his packet, scornfully exclaiming "Ou! ou!" three or four times, while he poured his money on the counter with a great noise. They were twenty-five crowns in giulios; and he fancied that mine would be four or five crowns *di moneta*.[1] I for my part, stunned and stifled by his cries, and by the looks and smiles of the bystanders, first peeped into my packet; then, after seeing that it contained nothing but gold, I retired to one end of the counter, and, keeping my eyes lowered and making no noise at all, I lifted it with both hands suddenly above my head, and emptied it like a mill hopper.[2] My coin was twice as much as his; which caused the onlookers, who had fixed their eyes on me with some derision, to turn round suddenly to him and say: "Lucagnolo, Benvenuto's pieces, being all of gold and twice as many as yours, make a far finer effect." I thought for certain that, what with jealousy and what with shame, Lucagnolo would have fallen dead upon the spot; and though he took the third part of my gain, since I was a journeyman (for such is the custom of the trade, two-thirds fall to the workman and one-third to the masters of the shop), yet inconsiderate envy had more power in him than avarice: it ought indeed to have worked quite the other way, he being a

1 *Scudi di giuli* and *scudi di moneta*. The *giulio* was a sliver coin worth 56 Italian centimes. The *scudi di moneta* was worth 10 *giulios*. Cellini was paid in golden crowns, which had a much higher value. The *scuda* and the *ducato* at this epoch were reckoned at 7 *lire*, the *lira* at 20 *soldi*.

2 The packet was funnel-shaped, and Cellini poured the coins out from the broad end.

peasant's son from Iesi. He cursed his art and those who taught it him, vowing that thenceforth he would never work at large plate, but give his whole attention to those brothel gewgaws, since they were so well paid. Equally enraged on my side, I answered, that every bird sang its own note; that he talked after the fashion of the hovels he came from; but that I dared swear that I should succeed with ease in making his lubberly lumber, while he would never be successful in my brothel gewgaws.[3] Thus I flung off in a passion, telling him that I would soon show him that I spoke truth. The bystanders openly declared against him, holding him for a lout, as indeed he was, and me for a man, as I had proved myself.

XXII

Next day, I went to thank Madonna Porzia, and told her that her ladyship had done the opposite of what she said she would; for that while I wanted to make the devil laugh, she had made him once more deny God. We both laughed pleasantly at this, and she gave me other commissions for fine and substantial work.

Meanwhile, I contrived, by means of a pupil of Raffaello da Urbino, to get an order from the Bishop of Salamanca for one of those great water-vessels called *acquereccia,* which are used for ornaments to place on sideboards. He wanted a pair made of equal size; and one of them he intrusted to Lucagnolo, the other to me. Giovan Francesco, the painter I have mentioned, gave us the design.[1] Accordingly I set hand with marvellous good-will to this piece of plate, and was accommodated with a part of his workshop by a Milanese named Maestro Giovan Piero della Tacca. Having made my preparations, I calculated how much money I should need for certain affairs of my own, and sent all the rest to assist my poor father.

It so happened that just when this was being paid to him in Florence, he stumbled upon one of those Radicals who were in the Eight at the time when I got into that little trouble there. It was the very man who had abused him so rudely, and who swore that I should certainly be sent into the country with the lances. Now this fellow had some sons of very bad morals and repute; wherefore my father said to him: "Misfortunes can happen to anybody, especially to men of choleric humour when they are in the right, even as it

[3] The two slang phrases translated above are *bordellerie* and *coglionerie.*
[1] That is, Il Fattore. See above, p. 32.

happened to my son; but let the rest of his life bear witness how virtuously I have brought him up. Would God, for your well-being, that your sons may act neither worse nor better toward you than mine do to me. God rendered me able to bring them up as I have done; and where my own power could not reach, 'twas He who rescued them, against your expectation, out of your violent hands." On leaving the man, he wrote me all this story, begging me for God's sake to practise music at times, in order that I might not lose the fine accomplishment which he had taught me with such trouble. The letter so overflowed with expressions of the tenderest fatherly affection, that I was moved to tears of filial piety, resolving, before he died, to gratify him amply with regard to music. Thus God grants us those lawful blessings which we ask in prayer, nothing doubting.

XXIII

While I was pushing forward Salamanca's vase, I had only one little boy as help, whom I had taken at the entreaty of friends, and half against my own will, to be my workman. He was about fourteen years of age, bore the name of Paulino, and was son to a Roman burgess, who lived upon the income of his property. Paulino was the best-mannered, the most honest, and the most beautiful boy I ever saw in my whole life. His modest ways and actions, together with his superlative beauty and his devotion to myself, bred in me as great an affection for him as a man's breast can hold. This passionate love led me oftentimes to delight the lad with music; for I observed that his marvellous features, which by complexion wore a tone of modest melancholy, brightened up, and when I took my cornet, broke into a smile so lovely and so sweet, that I do not marvel at the silly stories which the Greeks have written about the deities of heaven. Indeed, if my boy had lived in those times, he would probably have turned their heads still more.[1] He had a sister, named Faustina, more beautiful, I verily believe, than that Faustina about whom the old books gossip so. Sometimes he took me to their vineyard, and, so far as I could judge, it struck me that Paulino's good father would have welcomed me as a son-in-law. This affair led me to play more than I was used to do.

It happened at that time that one Giangiacomo of Cesena, a musi-

[1] *Gli Arebbe fatti più uscire de' gangheri;* would have taken them still more off the hinges.

cian in the Pope's band, and a very excellent performer, sent word through Lorenzo, the trumpeter of Lucca, who is now in our Duke's service, to inquire whether I was inclined to help them at the Pope's Ferragosto, playing soprano with my cornet in some motets of great beauty selected by them for that occasion.[2] Although I had the greatest desire to finish the vase I had begun, yet, since music has a wondrous charm of its own, and also because I wished to please my old father, I consented to join them. During eight days before the festival we practised two hours a day together; then on the first of August we went to the Belvedere, and while Pope Clement was at table, we played those carefully studied motets so well that his Holiness protested he had never heard music more sweetly executed or with better harmony of parts. He sent for Giangiacomo, and asked him where and how he had procured so excellent a cornet for soprano, and inquired particularly who I was. Giangiacomo told him my name in full. Whereupon the Pope said: "So, then, he is the son of Maestro Giovanni?" On being assured I was, the Pope expressed his wish to have me in his service with the other bandsmen. Giangiacomo replied: "Most blessed Father, I cannot pretend for certain that you will get him, for his profession, to which he devotes himself assiduously, is that of a goldsmith, and he works in it miraculously well, and earns by it far more than he could do by playing." To this the Pope added: "I am the better inclined to him now that I find him possessor of a talent more than I expected. See that he obtains the same salary as the rest of you; and tell him from me to join my service, and that I will find work enough by the day for him to do in his other trade." Then stretching out his hand, he gave him a hundred golden crowns of the Camera in a handkerchief, and said:[3] "Divide these so that he may take his share."

When Giangiacomo left the Pope, he came to us, and related in detail all that the Pope had said; and after dividing the money between the eight of us, and giving me my share, he said to me: "Now I am going to have you inscribed among our company." I replied: "Let the day pass; to-morrow I will give my answer." When I left them, I went meditating whether I ought to accept the invitation, inasmuch as I could not but suffer if I abandoned the noble studies of my art. The following night my father appeared to me in a dream, and begged me with tears of tenderest affection, for God's love and

2 The *Ferragosto* or *Feriæ Augusti* was a festival upon the first of August.
3 The Camera Apostolica was the Roman Exchequer.

his, to enter upon this engagement. Methought I answered that nothing would induce me to do so. In an instant he assumed so horrible an aspect as to frighten me out of my wits, and cried: "If you do not, you will have a father's curse; but if you do, may you be ever blessed by me!" When I woke, I ran, for very fright, to have myself inscribed. Then I wrote to my old father, telling him the news, which so affected him with extreme joy that a sudden fit of illness took him, and wellnigh brought him to death's door. In his answer to my letter, he told me that he too had dreamed nearly the same as I had.

XXIV

Knowing now that I had gratified my father's honest wish, I began to think that everything would prosper with me to a glorious and honourable end. Accordingly, I set myself with indefatigable industry to the completion of the vase I had begun for Salamanca. That prelate was a very extraordinary man, extremely rich, but difficult to please. He sent daily to learn what I was doing; and when his messenger did not find me at home, he broke into fury, saying that he would take the work out of my hands and give it to others to finish. This came of my slavery to that accursed music. Still I laboured diligently night and day, until, when I had brought my work to a point when it could be exhibited, I submitted it to the inspection of the Bishop. This so increased his desire to see it finished that I was sorry I had shown it. At the end of three months I had it ready, with little animals and foliage and masks, as beautiful as one could hope to see. No sooner was it done than I sent it by the hand of my workman, Paulino, to show that able artist Lucagnolo, of whom I have spoken above. Paulino, with the grace and beauty which belonged to him, spoke as follows: "Messer Lucagnolo, Benvenuto bids me say that he has sent to show you his promises and your lumber, expecting in return to see from you his gewgaws." This message given, Lucagnolo took up the vase, and carefully examined it; then he said to Paulino: "Fair boy, tell your master that he is a great and able artist, and that I beg him to be willing to have me for a friend, and not to engage in aught else." The mission of that virtuous and marvellous lad caused me the greatest joy; and then the vase was carried to Salamanca, who ordered it to be valued. Lucagnolo took part in the valuation, estimating and praising it far above my own opinion. Salamanca, lifting up the vase, cried like a true Spaniard:

"I swear by God that I will take as long in paying him as he has lagged in making it." When I heard this, I was exceedingly put out, and fell to cursing all Spain and every one who wished well to it.

Amongst other beautiful ornaments, this vase had a handle, made all of one piece, with most delicate mechanism, which, when a spring was touched, stood upright above the mouth of it. While the prelate was one day ostentatiously exhibiting my vase to certain Spanish gentlemen of his suite, it chanced that one of them, upon Monsignor's quitting the room, began roughly to work the handle, and as the gentle spring which moved it could not bear his loutish violence, it broke in his hand. Aware what mischief he had done, he begged the butler who had charge of the Bishop's plate to take it to the master who had made it, for him to mend, and promised to pay what price he asked, provided it was set to rights at once. So the vase came once more into my hands, and I promised to put it forthwith in order, which indeed I did. It was brought to me before dinner; and at twenty-two o'clock the man who brought it returned, all in a sweat, for he had run the whole way, Monsignor having again asked for it to show to certain other gentlemen.[1] The butler, then, without giving me time to utter a word, cried: "Quick, quick, bring the vase." I, who wanted to act at leisure, and not to give it up to him, said that I did not mean to be so quick. The serving-man got into such a rage that he made as though he would put one hand to his sword, while with the other he threatened to break the shop open. To this I put a stop at once with my own weapon, using therewith spirited language, and saying: "I am not going to give it to you! Go and tell Monsignor, your master, that I want the money for my work before I let it leave this shop." When the fellow saw he could not obtain it by swaggering, he fell to praying to me, as one prays to the Cross, declaring that if I would only give it up, he would take care I should be paid. These words did not make me swerve from my purpose; but I kept on saying the same thing. At last, despairing of success, he swore to come with Spaniards enough to cut me in pieces. Then he took to his heels; while I, who inclined to believe partly in their murderous attack, resolved that I would defend myself with courage. So I got an admirable little gun ready, which I used for shooting

1 The Italians reckoned time from sundown till sundown, counting twenty-four hours. Twenty-two o'clock was therefore two hours before nightfall. One hour of the night was one hour after nightfall, and so forth. By this system of reckoning, it is clear that the hours varied with the season of the year; and unless we know the exact month in which an event took place, we cannot translate any hour into terms of our own system.

game, and muttered to myself: "He who robs me of my property and labour may take my life too, and welcome." While I was carrying on this debate in my own mind, a crowd of Spaniards arrived, led by their major-domo, who, with the headstrong rashness of his race, bade them go in and take the vase and give me a good beating. Hearing these words, I showed them the muzzle of my gun, and prepared to fire, and cried in a loud voice: "Renegade Jews, traitors, is it thus that one breaks into houses and shops in our city of Rome? Come as many of you thieves as like, an inch nearer to this wicket, and I'll blow all their brains out with my gun." Then I turned the muzzle toward their major-domo, and making as though I would discharge it, called out: "And you big thief, who are egging them on, I mean to kill you first." He clapped spurs to the jennet he was riding, and took flight headlong. The commotion we were making stirred up all the neighbours, who came crowding round, together with some Roman gentlemen who chanced to pass, and cried: "Do but kill the renegades, and we will stand by you." These words had the effect of frightening the Spaniards in good earnest. They withdrew, and were compelled by the circumstances to relate the whole affair to Monsignor. Being a man of inordinate haughtiness, he rated the members of his household, both because they had engaged in such an act of violence, and also because, having begun, they had not gone through with it. At this juncture the painter, who had been concerned in the whole matter, came in, and the Bishop bade him go and tell me that if I did not bring the vase at once, he would make mincemeat of me;[2] but if I brought it, he would pay its price down. These threats were so far from terrifying me, that I sent him word I was going immediately to lay my case before the Pope.

In the meantime, his anger and my fear subsided; whereupon, being guaranteed by some Roman noblemen of high degree that the prelate would not harm me, and having assurance that I should be paid, I armed myself with a large poniard and my good coat of mail, and betook myself to his palace, where he had drawn up all his household. I entered, and Paulino followed with the silver vase. It was just like passing through the Zodiac, neither more nor less; for one of them had the face of the lion, another of the scorpion, a third of the crab. However, we passed onward to the presence of the rascally priest, who spouted out a torrent of such language as only priests and Spaniards have at their command. In return I never raised my

2 Lit., "the largest piece left of me should be my ears."

eyes to look at him, nor answered word for word. That seemed to augment the fury of his anger; and causing paper to be put before me, he commanded me to write an acknowledgment to the effect that I had been amply satisfied and paid in full. Then I raised my head, and said I should be very glad to do so when I had received the money. The Bishop's rage continued to rise; threats and recriminations were flung about; but at last the money was paid, and I wrote the receipt. Then I departed, glad at heart and in high spirits.

XXV

When Pope Clement heard the story—he had seen the vase before, but it was not shown him as my work—he expressed much pleasure and spoke warmly in my praise, publicly saying that he felt very favourably toward me. This caused Monsignor Salamanca to repent that he had hectored over me; and in order to make up our quarrel, he sent the same painter to inform me that he meant to give me large commissions. I replied that I was willing to undertake them, but that I should require to be paid in advance. This speech too came to Pope Clement's ears, and made him laugh heartily. Cardinal Cibo was in the presence, and the Pope narrated to him the whole history of my dispute with the Bishop.[1] Then he turned to one of his people, and ordered him to go on supplying me with work for the palace. Cardinal Cibo sent for me, and after some time spent in agreeable conversation, gave me the order for a large vase, bigger than Salamanca's. I likewise obtained commissions from Cardinal Cornaro, and many others of the Holy College, especially Ridolfi and Salviati; they all kept me well employed, so that I earned plenty of money.[2]

Madonna Porzia now advised me to open a shop of my own. This I did; and I never stopped working for that excellent and gentle lady, who paid me exceedingly well, and by whose means perhaps it was that I came to make a figure in the world.

I contracted close friendship with Signor Gabbriello Ceserino, at that time Gonfalonier of Rome, and executed many pieces for him. One, among the rest, is worthy of mention. It was a large golden medal to wear in the hat. I engraved upon it Leda with her swan; and being very well pleased with the workmanship, he said he should

1 Innocenzio Cibo Malaspina, Archbishop of Genoa, and nephew of Lorenza de' Medici. He was a prelate of vast wealth and a great patron of arts and letters.

2 Marco Cornaro was a brother of Caterina, the Queen of Cyprus. He obtained the hat in 1492. Niccolò Ridolfi was a nephew of Leo X. Giovanni Salviati, the son of Jacopo mentioned above, p. 13, was also a nephew of Leo X., who gave him the hat in 1517.

like to have it valued, in order that I might be properly paid. Now, since the medal was executed with consummate skill, the valuers of the trade set a far higher price on it than he had thought of. I therefore kept the medal, and got nothing for my pains. The same sort of adventures happened in this case as in that of Salamanca's vase. But I shall pass such matters briefly by, lest they hinder me from telling things of greater importance.

XXVI

Since I am writing my life, I must from time to time diverge from my profession in order to describe with brevity, if not in detail, some incidents which have no bearing on my career as artist. On the morning of Saint John's Day I happened to be dining with several men of our nation, painters, sculptors, goldsmiths, amongst the most notable of whom was Rosso and Gainfrancesco, the pupil of Raffaello.[1] I had invited them without restraint or ceremony to the place of our meeting, and they were all laughing and joking, as is natural when a crowd of men come together to make merry on so great a festival. It chanced that a light-brained swaggering young fellow passed by; he was a soldier of Rienzo da Ceri, who, when he heard the noise that we were making, gave vent to a string of opprobrious sarcasms upon the folk of Florence.[2] I, who was the host of those great artists and men of worth, taking the insult to myself, slipped out quietly without being observed, and went up to him. I ought to say that he had a punk of his there, and was going on with his stupid ribaldries to amuse her. When I met him, I asked if he was the rash fellow who was speaking evil of the Florentines. He answered at once: "I am that man." On this I raised my hand, struck him in the face, and said: "And I am *this* man." Then we each of us drew our swords with spirit; but the fray had hardly begun when a crowd of persons intervened, who rather took my part than not, hearing and seeing that I was in the right.

On the following day a challenge to fight with him was brought me, which I accepted very gladly, saying that I expected to complete

[1] St. John's Day was the great Florentine Festival, on which all the Guilds went in procession with pageants through the city. Of the Florentine painter, Il Rosso, or Maitre Roux, this is the first mention by Cellini. He went to France in 1534, and died an obscure death there in 1541.

[2] This Rienzo, Renzo, or Lorenzo da Ceri, was a captain of adventurers or Condottiere, who hired his mercenary forces to paymasters. He defended Crema for the Venetians in 1514, and conquered Urbino for the Pope in 1515. Afterwards he fought for the French in the Italian wars. We shall hear more of him again during the sack of Rome.

this job far quicker than those of the other art I practised. So I went at once to confer with a fine old man called Bevilacqua, who was reputed to have been the first sword of Italy, because he had fought more than twenty serious duels and had always come off with honour. This excellent man was a great friend of mine; he knew me as an artist and had also been concerned as intermediary in certain ugly quarrels between me and others. Accordingly, when he had learned my business, he answered with a smile: "My Benvenuto, if you had an affair with Mars, I am sure you would come out with honour, because through all the years that I have known you, I have never seen you wrongfully take up a quarrel." So he consented to be my second, and we repaired with sword in hand to the appointed place; but no blood was shed, for my opponent made the matter up, and I came with much credit out of the affair.[3] I will not add further particulars; for though they would be very interesting in their own way, I wish to keep both space and words for my art, which has been my chief inducement to write as I am doing, and about which I shall have only too much to say.

The spirit of honourable rivalry impelled me to attempt some other masterpiece, which should equal, or even surpass, the productions of that able craftsman, Lucagnolo, whom I have mentioned. Still I did not on this account neglect my own fine art of jewellery; and so both the one and the other wrought me much profit and more credit, and in both of them I continued to produce things of marked originality. There was at that time in Rome a very able artist of Perugia named Lautizio, who worked only in one department, where he was sole and unrivalled throughout the world.[4] You must know that at Rome every cardinal has a seal, upon which his title is engraved, and these seals are just as large as a child's hand of about twelve years of age; and, as I have already said, the cardinal's title is engraved upon the seal together with a great many ornamental figures. A well-made article of the kind fetches a hundred, or more than a hundred crowns. This excellent workman, like Lucagnolo, roused in me some honest rivalry, although the art he practised is far remote from the other branches of gold-smithery, and consequently Lautizio was not skilled in making anything but seals. I gave my mind to acquiring his craft also, although I found it very difficult; and, unrepelled by

[3] The Italian, *restando dal mio avversario,* seems to mean that Cellini's opponent proposed an accommodation, apologized, or stayed the duel at a certain point.

[4] See Cellini's Treatise *Oreficeria,* cap. vi., for more particulars about this artist.

the trouble which it gave me, I went on zealously upon the path of profit and improvement.

There was in Rome another most excellent craftsman of ability, who was a Milanese named Messer Caradosso.[5] He dealt in nothing but little chiselled medals, made of plates of metal, and such-like things. I have seen of his some paxes in half relief, and some Christs a palm in length wrought of the thinnest golden plates, so exquisitely done that I esteemed him the greatest master in that kind I had ever seen, and I envied him more than all the rest together. There were also other masters who worked at medals carved in steel, which may be called the models and true guides for those who aim at striking coins in the most perfect style. All these divers arts I set myself with unflagging industry to learn.

I must not omit the exquisite art of enamelling, in which I have never known any one excel save a Florentine, our countryman, called Amerigo.[6] I did not know him, but was well acquainted with his incomparable masterpieces. Nothing in any part of the world or by any craftman that I have seen, approached the divine beauty of their workmanship. To this branch too I devoted myself with all my strength, although it is extremely difficult, chiefly because of the fire, which after long time and trouble spent in other processes, has to be applied at last, and not unfrequently brings the whole to ruin. In spite of its great difficulties, it gave me so much pleasure that I looked upon them as recreation; and this came from the special gift which the God of nature bestowed on me, that is to say, a temperament so happy and of such excellent parts that I was freely able to accomplish whatever it pleased me to take in hand. The various departments of art which I have described are very different one from the other, so that a man who excels in one of them, if he undertakes the others, hardly ever achieves the same success; whereas I strove with all my power to become equally versed in all of them: and in the proper place I shall demonstrate that I attained my object.

XXVII

At that time, while I was still a young man of about twenty-three, there raged a plague of such extraordinary violence that many thou-

[5] His real name was Ambrogio Foppa. The nickname Caradosso is said to have stuck to him in consequence of a Spaniard calling him Bear's-face in his own tongue. He struck Leo X.'s coins; and we possess some excellent medallion portraits by his hand.

[6] For him, consult Cellini's *Oreficeria*.

sands died of it every day in Rome. Somewhat terrified at this calamity, I began to take certain amusements, as my mind suggested, and for a reason which I will presently relate. I had formed a habit of going on feast-days to the ancient buildings, and copying parts of them in wax or with the pencil; and since these buildings are all ruins, and the ruins house innumerable pigeons, it came into my head to use my gun against these birds. So then, avoiding all commerce with people, in my terror of the plague, I used to put a fowling-piece on my boy Pagolino's shoulder, and he and I went out alone into the ruins; and oftentimes we came home laden with a cargo of the fattest pigeons. I did not care to charge my gun with more than a single ball; and thus it was by pure skill in the art that I filled such heavy bags. I had a fowling-piece which I had made myself; inside and out it was as bright as any mirror. I also used to make a very fine sort of powder, in doing which I discovered secret processes, beyond any which have yet been found; and on this point, in order to be brief, I will give but one particular, which will astonish good shots of every degree. This is, that when I charged my gun with powder weighing one-fifth of the ball, it carried two hundred paces point-blank. It is true that the great delight I took in this exercise bid fair to withdraw me from my art and studies; yet in another way it gave me more than it deprived me of, seeing that each time I went out shooting I returned with greatly better health, because the open air was a benefit to my constitution. My natural temperament was melancholy, and while I was taking these amusements, my heart leapt up with joy, and I found that I could work better and with far greater mastery than when I spent my whole time in study and manual labour. In this way my gun, at the end of the game, stood me more in profit than in loss.

It was also the cause of my making acquaintance with certain hunters after curiosities, who followed in the track [1] of those Lombard peasants who used to come to Rome to till the vineyards at the proper season. While digging the ground, they frequently turned up antique medals, agates, chrysoprases, cornelians, and cameos; also sometimes jewels, as, for instance, emeralds, sapphires, diamonds, and rubies. The peasants used to sell things of this sort to the traders for a mere trifle; and I very often, when I met them, paid the latter several times as many golden crowns as they had given giulios for some object. Independently of the profit I made by this traffic, which was

[1] *Stavano alle velette.* Perhaps *lay in wait for.*

at least tenfold, it brought me also into agreeable relations with nearly all the cardinals of Rome. I will only touch upon a few of the most notable and rarest of these curiosities. There came into my hands, among many other fragments, the head of a dolphin about as big as a good-sized ballot-bean. Not only was the style of this head extremely beautiful, but nature had here far surpassed art; for the stone was an emerald of such good colour, that the man who bought it from me for tens of crowns sold it again for hundreds after setting it as a finger-ring. I will mention another kind of gem; this was a magnificent topaz; and here art equalled nature; it was as large as a hazel-nut, with the head of Minerva in a style of inconceivable beauty. I remember yet another precious stone, different from these; it was a cameo, engraved with Hercules binding Cerberus of the triple throat; such was its beauty and the skill of its workmanship, that our great Michel Agnolo protested he had never seen anything so wonderful. Among many bronze medals, I obtained one upon which was a head of Jupiter. It was the largest that had ever been seen; the head of the most perfect execution; and it had on the reverse side a very fine design of some little figures in the same style. I might enlarge at great length on this curiosity; but I will refrain for fear of being prolix.

XXVIII

As I have said above, the plague had broken out in Rome; but though I must return a little way upon my steps, I shall not therefore abandon the main path of my history. There arrived in Rome a surgeon of the highest renown, who was called Maestro Giacomo da Carpi.[1] This able man, in the course of his other practice, undertook the most desperate cases of the so-called French disease. In Rome this kind of illness is very partial to the priests, and especially to the richest of them. When, therefore, Maestro Giacomo had made his talents known, he professed to work miracles in the treatment of such cases by means of certain fumigations; but he only undertook a cure after stipulating for his fees, which he reckoned not by tens, but by hundreds of crowns. He was a great connoisseur in the arts of design. Chancing to pass one day before my shop, he saw a lot of

[1] Giacomo Berengario da Carpi was, in fact, a great physician, surgeon, and student of anatomy. He is said to have been the first to use mercury in the cure of syphilis, a disease which was devastating Italy after the year 1495. He amassed a large fortune, which, when he died at Ferrara about 1530, he bequeathed to the Duke there.

drawings which I had laid upon the counter, and among these were several designs for little vases in a capricious style, which I had sketched for my amusement. These vases were in quite a different fashion from any which had been seen up to that date. He was anxious that I should finish one or two of them for him in silver; and this I did with the fullest satisfaction, seeing they exactly suited my own fancy. The clever surgeon paid me very well, and yet the honour which the vases brought me was worth a hundred times as much; for the best craftsmen in the goldsmith's trade declared they had never seen anything more beautiful or better executed.

No sooner had I finished them than he showed them to the Pope; and the next day following he betook himself away from Rome. He was a man of much learning, who used to discourse wonderfully about medicine. The Pope would fain have had him in his service, but he replied that he would not take service with anybody in the world, and that whoso had need of him might come to seek him out. He was a person of great sagacity, and did wisely to get out of Rome; for not many months afterwards, all the patients he had treated grew so ill that they were a hundred times worse off than before he came. He would certainly have been murdered if he had stopped. He showed my little vases to several persons of quality; amongst others, to the most excellent Duke of Ferrara, and pretended that he had got them from a great lord in Rome, by telling this nobleman that if he wanted to be cured, he must give him those two vases; and that the lord had answered that they were antique, and besought him to ask for anything else which it might be convenient for him to give, provided only he would leave him those; but, according to his own account, Maestro Giacomo made as though he would not undertake the cure, and so he got them.

I was told this by Messer Alberto Bendedio in Ferrara, who with great ostentation showed me some earthenware copies he possessed of them.[2] Thereupon I laughed, and as I said nothing, Messer Alberto Bendedio, who was a haughty man, flew into a rage and said: "You are laughing at them, are you? And I tell you that during the last thousand years there has not been born a man capable of so much as copying them." I then, not caring to deprive them of so eminent a reputation, kept silence, and admired them with mute stupefaction. It was said to me in Rome by many great lords, some of whom were my friends, that the work of which I have been speaking was, in

2 See below, Book II. Chap. viii., for a full account of this incident at Ferrara.

their opinion of marvellous excellence and genuine antiquity; whereupon, emboldened by their praises, I revealed that I had made them. As they would not believe it, and as I wished to prove that I had spoken truth, I was obliged to bring evidence and to make new drawings of the vases; for my word alone was not enough, inasmuch as Maestro Giacomo had cunningly insisted upon carrying off the old drawings with him. By this little job I earned a fair amount of money.

XXIX

The plague went dragging on for many months, but I had as yet managed to keep it at bay; for though several of my comrades were dead, I survived in health and freedom. Now it chanced one evening that an intimate comrade of mine brought home to supper a Bolognese prostitute named Faustina. She was a very fine woman, but about thirty years of age; and she had with her a little serving-girl of thirteen or fourteen. Faustina belonging to my friend, I would not have touched her for all the gold in the world; and though she declared she was madly in love with me, I remained steadfast in my loyalty. But after they had gone to bed, I stole away the little serving-girl, who was quite a fresh maid, and woe to her if her mistress had known of it! The result was that I enjoyed a very pleasant night, far more to my satisfaction than if I had passed it with Faustina. I rose upon the hour of breaking fast, and felt tired, for I had travelled many miles that night, and was wanting to take food, when a crushing headache seized me; several boils appeared on my left arm, together with a carbuncle which showed itself just beyond the palm of the left hand where it joins the wrist. Everybody in the house was in a panic; my friend, the cow and the calf, all fled. Left alone there with my poor little prentice, who refused to abandon me, I felt stifled at the heart, and made up my mind for certain I was a dead man.

Just then the father of the lad went by, who was physician to the Cardinal Iacoacci,[1] and lived as member of that prelate's household.[2] The boy called out: "Come, father, and see Benvenuto; he is in bed with some trifling indisposition." Without thinking what my complaint might be, the doctor came up at once, and when he had felt my pulse, he saw and felt what was very contrary to his own wishes.

1 Probably Domenico Iacobacci, who obtained the hat in 1517.
2 *A sua provisione stava, i. e.*, he was in the Cardinal's regular pay.

Turning round to his son, he cried: "O traitor of a child, you've ruined me; how can I venture now into the Cardinal's presence?" His son made answer: "Why, father, this man my master is worth far more than all the cardinals in Rome." Then the doctor turned to me and said: "Since I am here, I will consent to treat you. But of one thing only I warn you, that if you have enjoyed a woman, you are doomed." To this I replied: "I did so this very night." He answered: "With whom, and to what extent?" [3] I said: "Last night, and with a girl in her earliest maturity." Upon this, perceiving that he had spoken foolishly, he made haste to add: "Well, considering the sores are so new, and have not yet begun to stink, and that the remedies will be taken in time, you need not be too much afraid, for I have good hopes of curing you." When he had prescribed for me and gone away, a very dear friend of mine, called Giovanni Rigogli, came in, who fell to commiserating my great suffering and also my desertion by my comrade, and said: "Be of good cheer, my Benvenuto, for I will never leave your side until I see you restored to health." I told him not to come too close, since it was all over with me. Only I besought him to be so kind as to take a considerable quantity of crowns, which were lying in a little box near my bed, and when God had thought fit to remove me from this world, to send them to my poor father, writing pleasantly to him, in the way I too had done, so far as that appalling season of the plague permitted.[4] My beloved friend declared that he had no intention whatsoever of leaving me, and that come what might, in life or death, he knew very well what was his duty toward a friend. And so we went on by the help of God: and the admirable remedies which I had used began to work a great improvement, and I soon came well out of that dreadful sickness.

The sore was still open, with a plug of lint inside it and a plaster above, when I went out riding on a little wild pony. He was covered with hair four fingers long, and was exactly as big as a well-grown bear; indeed he looked just like a bear. I rode out on him to visit the painter Rosso, who was then living in the country, toward Cività Vecchia, at a place of Count Anguillara's called Cervetera. I found my friend, and he was very glad to see me; whereupon I said: "I am come to do to you that which you did to me so many months ago."

3 *Quanto.* Perhaps we ought to read *quando—when?*

4 *Come ancora io avevo fatto secondo l'usanza che promettava quell' arrabiata stagione.* I am not sure that I have given the right sense in the text above. Leclanché interprets the words thus: "that I too had fared according to the wont of that appalling season," *i. e.,* had died of the plague. But I think the version in my sense is more true both to Italian and to Cellini's special style.

He burst out laughing, embraced and kissed me, and begged me for the Count's sake to keep quiet. I stayed in that place about a month, with much content and gladness, enjoying good wines and excellent food, and treated with the greatest kindness by the Count; every day I used to ride out alone along the seashore, where I dismounted, and filled my pockets with all sorts of pebbles, snail shells, and sea shells of great rarity and beauty.

On the last day (for after this I went there no more) I was attacked by a band of men, who had disguised themselves, and disembarked from a Moorish privateer. When they thought that they had run me into a certain passage, where it seemed impossible that I should escape from their hands, I suddenly mounted my pony, resolved to be roasted or boiled alive at that pass perilous, seeing I had little hope to evade one or the other of these fates;[5] but, as God willed, my pony, who was the same I have described above, took an incredibly wide jump, and brought me off in safety, for which I heartily thanked God. I told the story to the Count; he ran to arms; but we saw the galleys setting out to sea. The next day following I went back sound and with good cheer to Rome.

XXX

The plague had by this time almost died out, so that the survivors when they met together alive, rejoiced with much delight in one another's company. This led to the formation of a club of painters, sculptors, and goldsmiths, the best that were in Rome; and the founder of it was a sculptor with the name of Michel Agnolo.[1] He was a Sienese and a man of great ability, who could hold his own against any other workman in that art; but, above all, he was the most amusing comrade and the heartiest good fellow in the universe. Of all the members of the club, he was the eldest, and yet the youngest from the strength and vigour of his body. We often came together; at the very least twice a week. I must not omit to mention that our society counted Giulio Romano, the painter, and Gian Francesco, both of them celebrated pupils of the mighty Raffaello da Urbino.

After many and many merry meetings, it seemed good to our worthy president that for the following Sunday we should repair to

[5] *i. e.*, to escape either being drowned or shot.

[1] This sculptor came to Rome with his compatriot Baldassare Peruzzi, and was employed upon the monument of Pope Adrian VI., which he executed with some help from Tribolo.

supper in his house, and that each one of us should be obliged to bring with him his crow (such was the nickname Michel Agnolo gave to women in the club), and that whoso did not bring one should be sconced by paying a supper to the whole company. Those of us who had no familiarity with women of the town, were forced to purvey themselves at no small trouble and expense, in order to appear without disgrace at that distinguished feast of artists. I had reckoned upon being well provided with a young woman of considerable beauty, called Pantasilea, who was very much in love with me; but I was obliged to give her up to one of my dearest friends, called Il Bachiacca, who on his side had been, and still was, over head and ears in love with her.[2] This exchange excited a certain amount of lover's anger, because the lady, seeing I had abandoned her at Bachiacca's first entreaty, imagined that I held in slight esteem the great affection which she bore me. In course of time a very serious incident grew out of this misunderstanding, through her desire to take revenge for the affront I had put upon her; whereof I shall speak hereafter in the proper place.

Well, then, the hour was drawing nigh when we had to present ourselves before that company of men of genius, each with his own crow; and I was still unprovided; and yet I thought it would be stupid to fail of such a madcap bagatelle;[3] but what particularly weighed upon my mind was that I did not choose to lend the light of my countenance in that illustrious sphere to some miserable plume-plucked scarecrow. All these considerations made me devise a pleasant trick, for the increase of merriment and the diffusion of mirth in our society.

Having taken this resolve, I sent for a stripling of sixteen years, who lived in the next house to mine; he was the son of a Spanish coppersmith. This young man gave his time to Latin studies, and was very diligent in their pursuit. He bore the name of Diego, had a handsome figure, and a complexion of marvellous brilliancy; the outlines of his head and face were far more beautiful than those of the antique Antinous: I had often copied them, gaining thereby much honour from the works in which I used them. The youth had no acquaintances, and was therefore quite unknown; dressed very ill and

2 There were two artists at this epoch surnamed Bachiacca, the twin sons of Ubertino Verdi, called respectively Francesco and Antonio. Francesco was an excellent painter of miniature oil-pictures; Antonio the first embroiderer of his age. The one alluded to here is probably Francesco.

3 *Mancare di una sì pazza cosa.* The *pazza cosa* may be the supper-party or the *cornacchia.*

negligently; all his affections being set upon those wonderful studies of his. After bringing him to my house, I begged him to let me array him in a woman's clothes which I had caused to be laid out. He readily complied, and put them on at once, while I added new beauties to the beauty of his face by the elaborate and studied way in which I dressed his hair. In his ears I placed two little rings, set with two large and fair pearls; the rings were broken; they only clipped his ears, which looked as though they had been pierced. Afterwards I wreathed his throat with chains of gold and rich jewels, and ornamented his fair hands with rings. Then I took him in a pleasant manner by one ear, and drew him before a great looking-glass. The lad, when he beheld himself, cried out with a burst of enthusiasm: "Heavens! is that Diego?" I said: "That is Diego, from whom until this day I never asked for any kind of favour; but now I only beseech Diego to do me pleasure in one harmless thing; and it is this—I want him to come in those very clothes to supper with the company of artists whereof he has often heard me speak." The young man, who was honest, virtuous, and wise, checked his enthusiasm, bent his eyes to the ground, and stood for a short while in silence. Then with a sudden move he lifted up his face and said: "With Benvenuto I will go; now let us start."

I wrapped his head in a large kind of napkin, which is called in Rome a summer-cloth; and when we reached the place of meeting, the company had already assembled, and everybody came forward to greet me. Michel Agnolo had placed himself between Giulio and Giovan Francesco. I lifted the veil from the head of my beauty; and then Michel Agnolo, who, as I have already said, was the most humorous and amusing fellow in the world, laid his two hands, the one on Giulio's and the other on Gian Francesco's shoulders, and pulling them with all his force, made them bow down, while he, on his knees upon the floor, cried out for mercy, and called to all the folk in words like these: "Behold ye of what sort are the angels of paradise! for though they are called angels, here shall ye see that they are not all of the male gender." Then with a loud voice he added:

"Angel beauteous, angel best,
Save me thou, make thou me blest."

Upon this my charming creature laughed, and lifted the right hand and gave him a papal benediction, with many pleasant words to boot. So Michel Agnolo stood up, and said it was the custom to kiss the feet of the Pope and the cheeks of angels; and having done the latter to Diego, the boy blushed deeply, which immensely enhanced his beauty.

When this reception was over, we found the whole room full of sonnets, which every man of us had made and sent to Michel Agnolo. My lad began to read them, and read them all aloud so gracefully, that his infinite charms were heightened beyond the powers of language to describe. Then followed conversation and witty sayings, on which I will not enlarge, for that is not my business; only one clever word must be mentioned, for it was spoken by that admirable painter Giulio, who, looking round with meaning[4] in his eyes on the bystanders, and fixing them particularly upon the women, turned to Michel Agnolo and said: "My dear Michel Agnolo, your nickname of crow very well suits those ladies to-day, though I vow they are somewhat less fair than crows by the side of one of the most lovely peacocks which fancy could have painted."

When the banquet was served and ready, and we were going to sit down to table, Giulio asked leave to be allowed to place us. This being granted, he took the women by the hand, and arranged them all upon the inner side, with my fair in the centre; then he placed all the men on the outside and me in the middle, saying there was no honour too great for my deserts. As a background to the women, there was spread an espalier of natural jasmines in full beauty,[5] which set off their charms, and especially Diego's, to such great advantage, that words would fail to describe the effect. Then we all of us fell to enjoying the abundance of our host's well-furnished table. The supper was followed by a short concert of delightful music, voices joining in harmony with instruments; and forasmuch as they were singing and playing from the book, my beauty begged to be allowed to sing his part. He performed the music better than almost all the rest, which so astonished the company that Giulio and Michel Agnolo dropped their earlier tone of banter, exchanging it for well-weighed terms of sober heartfelt admiration.

After the music was over, a certain Aurelio Ascolano,[6] remarkable for his gift as an improvisatory poet, began to extol the women

4 *Virtuosamente.* Cellini uses the word *virtuoso* in many senses, but always more with reference to intellectual than moral qualities. It denotes genius, artistic ability, masculine force, &c.

5 *Un tessuto di gelsumini naturali e bellissimi. Tessuto* is properly something woven, a fabric; and I am not sure whether Cellini does not mean that the ladies had behind their backs a tapestry representing jasmines in a natural manner.

6 Probably Eurialo d'Ascoli, a friend of Caro, Molza, Aretino.

in choice phrases of exquisite compliment. While he was chanting, the two girls who had my beauty between them never left off chattering. One of them related how she had gone wrong; the other asked mine how it had happened with her, and who were her friends, and how long she had been settled in Rome, and many other questions of the kind. It is true that, if I chose to describe such laughable episodes, I could relate several odd things which then occurred through Pantasilea's jealousy on my account; but since they form no part of my design, I pass them briefly over. At last the conversation of those loose women vexed my beauty, whom we had christened Pomona for the nonce; and Pomona, wanting to escape from their silly talk, turned restlessly upon her chair, first to one side and then to the other. The female brought by Giulio asked whether she felt indisposed. Pomona answered, yes, she thought she was a month or so with a child; this gave them the opportunity of feeling her body and discovering the real sex of the supposed woman. Thereupon they quickly withdrew their hands and rose from table, uttering such gibing words as are commonly addressed to young men of eminent beauty. The whole room rang with laughter and astonishment, in the midst of which Michel Agnolo, assuming a fierce aspect, called out for leave to inflict on me the penance he thought fit. When this was granted, he lifted me aloft amid the clamour of the company, crying: "Long live the gentleman! long live the gentleman!" and added that this was the punishment I deserved for having played so fine a trick. Thus ended that most agreeable supper-party, and each of us returned to his own dwelling at the close of day.

XXXI

It would take too long to describe in detail all the many and divers pieces of work which I executed for a great variety of men. At present I need only say that I devoted myself with sustained diligence and industry to acquiring mastery in the several branches of art which I enumerated a short while back. And so I went on labouring incessantly at all of them; but since no opportunity has presented itself as yet for describing my most notable performances, I shall wait to report them in their proper place before very long. The Sienese sculptor, Michel Agnolo, of whom I have recently been speaking, was at that time making the monument of the late Pope Adrian. Giulio Romano went to paint for the Marquis of Mantua. The other members of the club betook themselves in different directions, each to his own business; so that our company of artists was well-nigh altogether broken up.

About this time there fell into my hands some little Turkish poniards; the handle as well as the blade of these daggers was made of iron, and so too was the sheath. They were engraved by means of iron implements with foliage in the most exquisite Turkish style, very neatly filled in with gold. The sight of them stirred in me a great desire to try my own skill in that branch, so different from the others which I practised; and finding that I succeeded to my satisfaction, I executed several pieces. Mine were far more beautiful and more durable than the Turkish, and this for divers reasons. One was that I cut my grooves much deeper and with wider trenches in the steel; for this is not usual in Turkish work. Another was that the Turkish arabesques are only composed of arum leaves with a few small sunflowers;[1] and though these have a certain grace, they do not yield so lasting a pleasure as the patterns which we use. It is true that in Italy we have several different ways of designing foliage; the Lombards, for example, construct very beautiful patterns by copying the leaves of briony and ivy in exquisite curves, which are extremely agreeable to the eye; the Tuscans and the Romans make a better choice, because they imitate the leaves of the acanthus, commonly called bear's-foot, with its stalks and flowers, curling in divers wavy lines; and into these arabesques one may excellently well insert the figures of little birds and different animals, by which the good taste of the artist is displayed. Some hints for creatures of this sort can be observed in nature among the wild flowers, as, for instance, in snapdragons and some few other plants, which must be combined and developed with the help of fanciful imaginings by clever draughtsmen. Such arabesques are called grotesques by the ignorant. They have obtained this name of grotesques among the moderns through being found in certain subterranean caverns in Rome by students of antiquity; which caverns were formerly chambers, hot-baths, cabinets for study, halls, and apartments of like nature. The curious discovering them in such places (since the level of the ground has gradually been raised while they have remained below, and since in Rome these vaulted rooms are commonly called grottoes), it has followed that the word grotesque is applied to the patterns I have mentioned. But this is not the right term for them, inasmuch as the ancients, who

1 *Gichero*, arum maculatum, and *clisia*, the sunflower.

delighted in composing monsters out of goats, cows, and horses, called these chimerical hybrids by the name of monsters; and the modern artificers of whom I speak, fashioned from the foliage which they copied monsters of like nature; for these the proper name is therefore monsters, and not grotesques. Well, then, I designed patterns of this kind, and filled them in with gold, as I have mentioned; and they were far more pleasing to the eye than the Turkish.

It chanced at that time that I lighted upon some jars or little antique urns filled with ashes, and among the ashes were some iron rings inlaid with gold (for the ancients also used that art), and in each of the rings was set a tiny cameo of shell. On applying to men of learning, they told me that these rings were worn as amulets by folk desirous of abiding with mind unshaken in any extraordinary circumstance, whether of good or evil fortune. Hereupon, at the request of certain noblemen who were my friends, I undertook to fabricate some trifling rings of this kind; but I made them of refined steel; and after they had been well engraved and inlaid with gold, they produced a very beautiful effect; and sometimes a single ring brought me more than forty crowns, merely in payment for my labour.

It was the custom at that epoch to wear little golden medals, upon which every nobleman or man of quality had some device or fancy of his own engraved; and these were worn in the cap. Of such pieces I made very many, and found them extremely difficult to work. I have already mentioned the admirable craftsman Caradosso, who used to make such ornaments; and as there were more than one figure on each piece, he asked at least a hundred gold crowns for his fee. This being so—not, however, because his prices were so high, but because he worked so slowly—I began to be employed by certain nobleman, for whom, among other things, I made a medal in competition with that great artist, and it had four figures, upon which I had expended an infinity of labour. These men of quality, when they compared my piece with that of the famous Caradosso, declared that mine was by far the better executed and more beautiful, and bade me ask what I liked as the reward of my trouble; for since I had given them such perfect satisfaction, they wished to do the like by me. I replied that my greatest reward and what I most desired was to have rivalled the masterpieces of so eminent an artist; and that if their lordships thought I had, I acknowledged myself to be most amply rewarded. With this I took my leave, and they immediately sent me such a very liberal present, that I was well content; indeed there grew in me so great a spirit to do well, that to this event I attributed what will afterwards be related of my progress.

XXXII

I shall be obliged to digress a little from the history of my art, unless I were to omit some annoying incidents which have happened in the course of my troubled career. One of these, which I am about to describe, brought me into the greatest risk of my life. I have already told the story of the artist's club, and of the farcical adventures which happened owing to the woman whom I mentioned, Pantasilea, the one who felt for me that false and fulsome love. She was furiously enraged because of the pleasant trick by which I brought Diego to our banquet, and she swore to be revenged on me. How she did do so is mixed up with the history of a young man called Luigi Pulci, who had recently come to Rome. He was the son of one of the pulcis, who had been beheaded for incest with his daughter; and the youth possessed extraordinary gifts for poetry together with sound Latin scholarship; he wrote well, was graceful in manners, and of surprising personal beauty; he had just left the service of some bishop, whose name I do not remember, and was thoroughly tainted with a very foul disease. While he was yet a lad and living in Florence, they used in certain places of the city to meet together during the nights of summer on the public streets; and he, ranking among the best of the improvisatori, sang there. His recitations were so admirable, that the divine Michel Agnolo Buonarroti, that prince of sculptors and of painters, went, wherever he heard that he would be, with the greatest eagerness and delight to listen to him. There was a man called Piloto, a goldsmith, very able in his art, who, together with myself, joined Buonarroti upon these occasions.[1] Thus acquaintance sprang up between me and Luigi Pulci; and so, after the lapse of many years he came, in the miserable plight which I have mentioned, to make himself known to me again in Rome, beseeching me for God's sake to help him. Moved to compassion by his great talents, by the love of my fatherland, and by my own natural tenderness of heart, I took him into my house, and had him medically treated in such wise that, being but a youth, he soon regained his health. While he was still pursu-

1 Piloto, of whom we shall hear more hereafter, was a prominent figure in the Florentine society of artists, and a celebrated practical joker. Vasari says that a young man of whom he had spoken ill murdered him. Lasca's Novelle, *Le Cene,* should be studied by those who seek an insight into this curious Bohemia of the sixteenth century.

ing his cure, he never omitted his studies, and I provided him with books according to the means at my disposal. The result was that Luigi, recognising the great benefits he had received from me, oftentimes with words and tears returned me thanks, protesting that if God should ever put good fortune in his way, he would recompense me for my kindness. To this I replied that I had not done for him as much as I desired, but only what I could, and that it was the duty of human beings to be mutually serviceable. Only I suggested that he should repay the service I had rendered him by doing likewise to some one who might have the same need of him as he had had of me. The young man in question began to frequent the Court of Rome, where he soon found a situation, and enrolled himself in the suite of a bishop, a man of eighty years, who bore the title of Gurgensis.[2] This bishop had a nephew called Messer Giovanni: he was a nobleman of Venice; and the said Messer Giovanni made show of marvellous attachment to Luigi Pulci's talents; and under the pretence of these talents, he brought him as familiar to himself as his own flesh and blood. Luigi having talked of me, and of his great obligations to me, with Messer Giovanni, the latter expressed a wish to make my acquaintance. Thus then it came to pass, that when I had upon a certain evening invited that woman Pantasilea to supper, and had assembled a company of men of parts who were my friends, just at the moment of our sitting down to table, Messer Giovanni and Luigi Pulci arrived, and after some complimentary speeches, they both remained to sup with us. The shameless strumpet, casting her eyes upon the young man's beauty, began at once to lay her nets for him; perceiving which, when the supper had come to an agreeable end, I took Luigi aside, and conjured him, by the benefits he said he owed me, to have nothing whatever to do with her. To this he answered: "Good heavens, Benvenuto! do you then take me for a madman?" I rejoined: "Not for a madman, but for a young fellow;" and I swore to him by God: "I do not give that woman the least thought; but for your sake I should be sorry if through her you came to break your neck." Upon these words he vowed and prayed to God, that, if ever he but spoke with her, he might upon the moment break his neck. I think the poor lad swore this oath to God with all his heart, for he did break his neck, as I shall presently relate. Messer Giovanni showed signs too evident of loving him in a dishonourable way; for we began to notice that Luigi had new suits of silk and velvet every

2 Girolamo Balbo, of the noble Venetian family, Bishop of Gurck, in Carinthia.

morning, and it was known that he abandoned himself altogether to bad courses. He neglected his fine talents, and pretended not to see or recognise me, because I had once rebuked him, and told him he was giving his soul to foul vices, which would make him break his neck, as he had vowed.

XXXIII

Now Messer Giovanni brought his favourite a very fine black horse, for which he paid 150 crowns. The beast was admirably trained to hand, so that Luigi could go daily to caracole around the lodgings of that prostitute Pantasilea. Though I took notice of this, I paid it no attention, only remarking that all things acted as their nature prompted; and meanwhile I gave my whole mind to my studies. It came to pass one Sunday evening that we were invited to sup together with the Sienese sculptor, Michel Agnolo, and the time of the year was summer. Bachiacca, of whom I have already spoken, was present at the party; and he had brought with him his old flame, Pantasilea. When we were at table, she sat between me and Bachiacca; but in the very middle of the banquet she rose, and excused herself upon the pretext of a natural need, saying she would speedily return. We, meanwhile, continued talking very agreeably and supping; but she remained an unaccountably long time absent. It chanced that, keeping my ears open, I thought I heard a sort of subdued tittering in the street below. I had a knife in hand, which I was using for my service at the table. The window was so close to where I sat, that, by merely rising, I could see Luigi in the street, together with Pantasilea; and I heard Luigi saying: "Oh, if that devil Benvenuto only saw us, shouldn't we just catch it!" She answered: "Have no fear; only listen to the noise they're making; we are the last thing they're thinking of." At these words, having made them both well out, I leaped from the window, and took Luigi by the cape; and certainly I should then have killed him with the knife I held, but that he was riding a white horse, to which he clapped spurs, leaving his cape in my grasp, in order to preserve his life. Pantasilea took to her heels in the direction of a neighbouring church. The company at supper rose immediately, and came down, entreating me in a body to refrain from putting myself and them to inconvenience for a strumpet. I told them that I should not have let myself be moved on her account, but that I was bent on punishing the infamous young man, who showed how little he regarded me. Accordingly I would not yield to the remonstrances of those ingenious and worthy men, but took my sword, and went alone toward Prati:—the house where we were supping, I should say, stood close to the Castello gate, which led to Prati.[1] Walking thus upon the road to Prati, I had gone far before the sun sank, and I re-entered Rome itself at a slow pace. Night had fallen; darkness had come on; but the gates of Rome were not yet shut.

Toward two hours after sunset, I walked along Pantasilea's lodging, with the intention, if Luigi Pulci were there, of doing something to the discontent of both. When I heard and saw that no one but a poor servant-girl called Canida was in the house, I went to put away my cloak and the scabbard of my sword, and then returned to the house, which stood behind the Banchi on the river Tiber. Just opposite stretched a garden belonging to an innkeeper called Romolo. It was enclosed by a thick hedge of thorns, in which I hid myself, standing upright, and waiting till the woman came back with Luigi. After keeping watch awhile there, my friend Bachiacca crept up to me; whether led by his own suspicions or by the advice of others, I cannot say. In a low voice he called out to me: "Gossip" (for so we used to name ourselves for fun); and then he prayed me for God's love, using the words which follow, with tears in the tone of his voice: "Dear gossip, I entreat you not to injure that poor girl; she at least has erred in no wise in this matter—no, not at all." When I heard what he was saying, I replied: "If you don't take yourself off now, at this first word I utter, I will bring my sword here down upon your head." Overwhelmed with fright, my poor gossip was suddenly taken ill with the colic, and withdrew to ease himself apart; indeed, he could not but obey the call. There was a glorious heaven of stars, which shed good light to see by. All of a sudden I was aware of the noise of many horses; they were coming toward me from the one side and the other. It turned out to be Luigi and Pantasilea, attended by a certain Messer Benvegnato of Perugia, who was chamberlain to Pope Clement, and followed by four doughty captains of Perugia, with some other valiant soldiers in the flower of youth; altogether reckoned, there were more than twelve swords. When I understood the matter, and saw not how to fly, I did my best to crouch into the hedge. But the thorns pricked and hurt me, goading me into madness like a bull; and

[1] The Porta Castello was the gate called after the Castle of S. Angelo. Prati, so far as I can make out, was an open space between the Borgo and the Bridge of S. Angelo. In order to get inside Rome itself, Cellini had to pass a second gate. His own lodging and Pantasilea's house were in the quarter of the Bianchi, where are now the Via Giulia and Via de' Banchi Vecchi.

I had half resolved to take a leap and hazard my escape. Just then Luigi, with his arm round Pantasilea's neck, was heard crying: "I must kiss you once again, if only to insult that traitor Benvenuto." At that moment, annoyed as I was by the prickles, and irritated by the young man's words, I sprang forth, lifted my sword on high, and shouted at the top of my voice: "You are all dead folk!" My blow descended on the shoulder of Luigi; but the satyrs who doted on him, had steeled his person round with coats of mail and such-like villainous defences; still the stroke fell with crushing force. Swerving aside, the sword hit Pantasilea full in nose and mouth. Both she and Luigi grovelled on the ground, while Bachiacca, with his breeches down to heels, screamed out and ran away. Then I turned upon the others boldly with my sword; and those valiant fellows, hearing a sudden commotion in the tavern, thought there was an army coming of a hundred men; and though they drew their swords with spirit, yet two horses which had taken fright in the tumult cast them into such disorder that a couple of the best riders were thrown, and the remainder took to flight. I, seeing that the affair was turning out well for me, ran as quickly as I could, and came off with honour from the engagement, not wishing to tempt fortune more than was my duty. During this hurly-burly, some of the soldiers and captains wounded themselves with their own arms; and Messer Benvegnato, the Pope's chamberlain, was kicked and trampled by his mule. One of the servants also, who had drawn his sword, fell down together with his master, and wounded him badly in the hand. Maddened by the pain, he swore louder than all the rest in his Perugian jargon, crying out: "By the body of God, I will take care that Benvegnato teaches Benvenuto how to live." He afterwards commissioned one of the captains who were with him (braver perhaps than the others, but with less aplomb, as being but a youth) to seek me out. The fellow came to visit me in the place of my retirement; that was the palace of a great Neapolitan nobleman, who had became acquainted with me in my art, and had besides taken a fancy to me because of my physical and mental aptitude for fighting, to which my lord himself was personally well inclined. So, then, finding myself made much of, and being precisely in my element, I gave such answer to the captain as I think must have made him earnestly repent of having come to look me up. After a few days, when the wounds of Luigi, and the strumpet, and the rest were healing, this great Neapolitan nobleman received overtures from Messer Benvegnato; for the prelate's anger had cooled, and he proposed to ratify a peace between me and Luigi and the soldiers, who had personally no quarrel with me, and only wished to make my acquaintance. Accordingly my friend the nobleman replied that he would bring me where they chose to appoint, and that he was very willing to effect a reconciliation. He stipulated that no words should be bandied about on either side, seeing that would be little to their credit; it was enough to go through the form of drinking together and exchanging kisses; he for his part undertook to do the talking, and promised to settle the matter to their honour. This arrangement was carried out. On Thursday evening my protector took me to the house of Messer Benvegnato, where all the soldiers who had been present at that discomfiture were assembled, and already seated at table. My nobleman was attended by thirty brave fellows, all well armed; a circumstance which Messer Benvegnato had not anticipated. When we came into the hall, he walking first, I following, he spake to this effect: "God save you, gentlemen; we have come to see you, I and Benvenuto, whom I love like my own brother; and we are ready to do whatever you propose." Messer Benvegnato, seeing the hall filled with such a crowd of men, called out: "It is only peace, and nothing else, we ask of you." Accordingly he promised that the governor of Rome and his catchploes should give me no trouble. Then we made peace, and I returned to my shop, where I could not stay an hour without that Neapolitan nobleman either coming to see me or sending for me.

Meanwhile Luigi Pulci, having recovered from his wound, rode every day upon the black horse which was so well trained to heel and bridle. One day, among others, after it had rained a little, and he was making his horse curvet just before Pantasilea's door, he slipped and fell, with the horse upon him. His right leg was broken short off in the thigh; and after a few days he died there in Pantasilea's lodgings, discharging thus the vow he registered so heartily to Heaven. Even so may it be seen that God keeps account of the good and the bad, and gives to each one what he merits.

XXXIV

The whole world was now in warfare.[1] Pope Clement had sent to get some troops from Giovanni de' Medici, and when they came,

[1] War had broken out in 1521 between Charles V. and Francis I., which disturbed all Europe and involved the States of Italy in serious complications. At the moment when this chapter opens, the Imperialist army under the Constable of Bourbon was marching upon Rome in 1527.

they made such disturbances in Rome, that it was ill living in open shops.[2] On this account I retired to a good snug house behind the Banchi, where I worked for all the friends I had acquired. Since I produced few things of much importance at that period, I need not waste time in talking about them. I took much pleasure in music and amusements of the kind. On the death of Giovanni de' Medici in Lombardy, the Pope, at the advice of Messer Jacopo Salviati, dismissed the five hands he had engaged; and when the Constable of Bourbon knew there were no troops in Rome, he pushed his army with the utmost energy up to the city. The whole of Rome upon this flew to arms. I happened to be intimate with Alessandro, the son of Piero del Bene, who, at the time when the Colonnesi entered Rome, had requested me to guard his palace.[3] On this more serious occasion, therefore, he prayed me to enlist fifty comrades for the protection of the said house, appointing me their captain, as I had been when the Colonnesi came. So I collected fifty young men of the highest courage, and we took up our quarters in his palace, with good pay and excellent appointments.

Bourbon's army had now arrived before the walls of Rome, and Alessandro begged me to go with him to reconnoitre. So we went with one of the stoutest fellows in our Company; and on the way a youth called Cecchino della Casa joined himself to us. On reaching the walls by the Campo Santo, we could see that famous army, which was making every effort to enter the town. Upon the ramparts where we took our station several young men were lying killed by the besiegers; the battle raged there desperately, and there was the densest fog imaginable. I turned to Alessandro and said: "Let us go home as soon as we can, for there is nothing to be done here; you see the enemies are mounting, and our men are in flight." Alessandro, in a panic, cried: "Would God that we had never come here!" and turned in maddest haste to fly. I took him up somewhat sharply with these words: "Since you have brought me here, I must perform some action worthy of a man;" and directing my arquebuse where I saw the thickest and most serried troop of fighting men, I aimed exactly at one

2 These troops entered Rome in October 1526. They were disbanded in March 1527.

3 Cellini here refers to the attack made upon Rome by the great Ghibelline house of Colonna, led by their chief captain, Pompeo, in September 1526. They took possession of the city and drove Clement into the Castle of S. Angelo, where they forced him to agree to terms favouring the Imperial cause. It was customary for Roman gentlemen to hire bravi for the defence of their palaces when any extraordinary disturbance was expected, as, for example, upon the vacation of the Papal Chair.

whom I remarked to be higher than the rest; the fog prevented me from being certain whether he was on horseback or on foot. Then I turned to Alessandro and Cecchino, and bade them discharge their arquebuses, showing them how to avoid being hit by the besiegers. When we had fired two rounds apiece, I crept cautiously up to the wall, and observing among the enemy a most extraordinary confusion, I discovered afterwards that one of our shots had killed the Constable of Bourbon; and from what I subsequently learned, he was the man whom I had first noticed above the heads of the rest.[4]

Quitting our position on the ramparts, we crossed the Campo Santo, and entered the city by St. Peter's; then coming out exactly at the church of Santo Agnolo, we got with the greatest difficulty to the great castle; for the generals Renzo di Ceri and Orazio Baglioni were wounding and slaughtering everybody who abandoned the defence of the walls.[5] By the time we had reached the great gate, part of the foemen had already entered Rome, and we had them in our rear. The castellan had ordered the portcullis to be lowered, in order to do which they cleared a little space, and this enabled us four to get inside. On the instant that I entered, the captain Pallone de' Medici claimed me as being of the Papal household, and forced me to abandon Allessandro, which I had to do, much against my will. I ascended to the keep, and at the same instant Pope Clement came in through the corridors into the castle; he had refused to leave the palace of St. Peter earlier, being unable to believe that his enemies would effect their entrance into Rome.[6] Having got into the castle in this way, I attached myself to certain pieces of artillery, which were under the command of a bombardier called Giuliano Fiorentino. Leaning there against the battlements, the unhappy man could see his poor house being sacked, and his wife and children outraged; fearing to strike his own folk, he dared not discharge the cannon, and flinging the

4 All historians of the sack of Rome agree in saying that Bourbon was shot dead while placing ladders against the outworks near the shop Cellini mentions. But the honour of firing the arquebuse which brought him down cannot be assigned to any one in particular. Very different stories were current on the subject. See Gregorovius, *Stadt Rom.*, vol. viii. p. 522.

5 For Renzo di Ceri see above, p. 44. Orazio Baglioni, of the semi-princely Perugian family, was a distinguished Condottiere. He subsequently obtained the captaincy of the Bande Nere, and died fighting near Naples in 1528. Orazio murdered several of his cousins in order to acquire the lordship of Perugia. His brother Malatesta undertook to defend Florence in the siege of 1530, and sold the city by treason to Clement.

6 Giovio, in his Life of the Cardinal Prospero Colonna, relates how he accompanied Clement in his flight from the Vatican to the castle. While passing some open portions of the gallery, he threw his violet mantle and cap of a Monsignore over the white stole of the Pontiff, for fear he might be shot at by the soldiers in the streets below.

burning fuse upon the ground, he wept as though his heart would break, and tore his cheeks with both his hands.[7] Some of the other bombardiers were behaving in like manner; seeing which, I took one of the matches, and got the assistance of a few men who were not overcome by their emotions. I aimed some swivels and falconets at points where I saw it would be useful, and killed with them a good number of the enemy. Had it not been for this, the troops who poured into Rome that morning, and were marching straight upon the castle, might possibly have entered it with ease, because the artillery was doing them no damage. I went on firing under the eyes of several cardinals and lords, who kept blessing me and giving me the heartiest encouragement. In my enthusiasm I strove to achieve the impossible; let it suffice that it was I who saved the castle that morning, and brought the other bombardiers back to their duty.[8] I worked hard the whole of that day; and when the evening came, while the army was marching into Rome through the Trastevere, Pope Clement appointed a great Roman nobleman named Antonio Santacroce to be captain of all the gunners. The first thing this man did was to come to me, and having greeted me with the utmost kindness, he stationed me with five fine pieces of artillery on the highest point of the castle, to which the name of the Angel specially belongs. This circular eminence goes round the castle, and surveys both Prati and the town of Rome. The captain put under my orders enough men to help in managing my guns, and having seen me paid in advance, he gave me rations of bread and a little wine, and begged me to go forward as I had begun. I was perhaps more inclined by nature to the profession of arms than to the one I had adopted, and I took such pleasure in its duties that I discharged them better than those of my own art. Night came, the enemy had entered Rome, and we who were in the castle (especially myself, who have always taken pleasure in extraordinary sights) stayed gazing on the indescribable scene of tumult and conflagration in the streets below. People who were anywhere else but where we were, could not have formed the least imagination of what it was. I will not, however, set myself to describe that tragedy, but will content myself with continuing the history of my own life and the circumstances which properly belong to it.

7 The short autobiography of Raffaello da Montelupo, a man in many respects resembling Cellini, confirms this part of our author's narrative. It is one of the most interesting pieces of evidence regarding what went on inside the castle during the sack of Rome. Montelupo was also a gunner, and commanded two pieces.

8 This is an instance of Cellini's exaggeration. He did more than yoeman's service, no doubt. But we cannot believe that, without him, the castle would have been taken.

XXXV

During the course of my artillery practice, which I never intermitted through the whole month passed by us beleaguered in the castle, I met with a great many very striking accidents, all of them worthy to be related. But since I do not care to be too prolix, or to exhibit myself outside the sphere of my profession, I will omit the larger part of them, only touching upon those I cannot well neglect, which shall be the fewest in number and the most remarkable. The first which comes to hand is this: Messer Antonio Santacroce had made me come down from the Angel, in order to fire on some houses in the neighbourhood, where certain of our besiegers had been seen to enter. While I was firing, a cannon shot reached me, which hit the angle of a battlement, and carried off enough of it to be the cause why I sustained no injury. The whole mass struck me in the chest and took my breath away. I lay stretched upon the ground like a dead man, and could hear what the bystanders were saying. Among them all, Messer Antonio Santacroce lamented greatly, exclaiming: "Alas, alas! we have lost the best defender that we had." Attracted by the uproar, one of my comrades ran up; he was called Gianfrancesco, and was a bandsman, but was far more naturally given to medicine than to music. On the spot he flew off, crying for a stoop of the very best Greek wine. Then he made a tile red-hot, and cast upon it a good handful of wormwood; after which he sprinkled the Greek wine; and when the wormwood was well soaked, he laid it on my breast, just where the bruise was visible to all. Such was the virtue of the wormwood that I immediately regained my scattered faculties. I wanted to begin to speak; but could not; for some stupid soldiers had filled my mouth with earth, imagining that by so doing they were giving me the sacrament; and indeed they were more like to have excommunicated me, since I could with difficulty come to myself again, the earth doing me more mischief than the blow. However, I escaped that danger, and returned to the rage and fury of the guns, pursuing my work there with all the ability and eagerness that I could summon.

Pope Clement, by this, had sent to demand assistance from the Duke of Urbino, who was with the troops of Venice; he commissioned the envoy to tell his Excellency that the Castle of S. Angelo would send up every evening three beacons from its summit accompanied by three discharges of the cannon thrice repeated, and that so long as this signal was continued, he might take for granted that the castle had not yielded. I was charged with lighting the beacons and firing the guns for this purpose; and all this while I pointed my artillery by day upon the places where mischief could be done. The Pope, in consequence, began to regard me with still greater favour, because he saw that I discharged my functions as intelligently as the task demanded. Aid from the Duke of Urbino never came; on which, as it is not my business, I will make no further comment.[1]

XXXVI

While I was at work upon that diabolical task of mine, there came from time to time to watch me some of the cardinals who were invested in the castle; and most frequently the Cardinal of Ravenna and the Cardinal de' Gaddi.[1] I often told them not to show themselves, since their nasty red caps gave a fair mark to our enemies. From neighbouring buildings, such as the Torre de' Bini, we ran great peril when they were there; and at last I had them locked off, and gained thereby their deep ill-will. I frequently received visits also from the general, Orazio Baglioni, who was very well affected toward me. One day while he was talking with me, he noticed something going forward in a drinking-place outside the Porta di Castello, which bore the name of Baccanello. This tavern had for sign a sun painted between two windows, of a bright red colour. The windows being closed, Signor Orazio concluded that a band of soldiers were carousing at table just between them and behind the sun. So he said to me. "Benvenuto, if you think that you could hit that wall an ell's breadth from the sun with your demi-cannon here, I believe you would be doing a good stroke of business, for there is a great commotion there, and men of much importance must probably be inside the house." I answered that I felt quite capable of hitting the sun in its centre, but that a barrel full of stones, which was standing close to the muzzle of the gun, might be knocked down by the shock of the discharge and the blast of the artillery. He rejoined: "Don't waste

1 Francesco Maria della Rovere, Duke of Urbino, commanded a considerable army as general of the Church, and was now acting for Venice. Why he effected no diversion while the Imperial troops were marching upon Rome, and why he delayed to relieve the city, was never properly explained. Folk attributed his impotent conduct partly to a natural sluggishness in warfare, and partly to his hatred for the house of Medici. Leo X. had deprived him of his dukedom, and given it to a Medicean prince. It is to this that Cellini probably refers in the cautious phrase which ends the chapter.

1 Benedetto Accolti of Arezzo, Archbishop of Ravenna in 1524, obtained the hat in 1527, three days before the sack of Rome. He was a distinguished man of letters. Niccolò Gaddi was created Cardinal on the same day as Accolti. We shall hear more of him in Cellini's pages.

time, Benvenuto. In the first place, it is not possible, where it is standing, that the cannon's blast should bring it down; and even if it were to fall, and the Pope himself was underneath, the mischief would not be so great as you imagine. Fire, then, only fire!" Taking no more thought about it, I struck the sun in the centre, exactly as I said I should. The cask was dislodged, as I predicted, and fell precisely between Cardinal Farnese and Messer Jacopo Salviati.[2] It might very well have dashed out the brains of both of them, except that just at that very moment Farnese was reproaching Salviati with having caused the sack of Rome, and while they stood apart from one another to exchange opprobrious remarks, my gabion fell without destroying them. When he heard the uproar in the court below, good Signor Orazio dashed off in a hurry; and I, thrusting my neck forward where the cask had fallen, heard some people saying: "It would not be a bad job to kill that gunner!" Upon this I turned two falconets toward the staircase, with mind resolved to let blaze on the first man who attempted to come up. The household of Cardinal Farnese must have received orders to go and do me some injury; accordingly I prepared to receive them, with a lighted match in hand. Recognising some who were approaching, I called out: "You lazy lubbers, if you don't pack off from there, and if but a man's child among you dares to touch the staircase, I have got two cannon loaded, which will blow you into powder. Go and tell the Cardinal that I was acting at the order of superior officers, and that what we have done and are doing is in defence of them priests,[3] and not to hurt them." They made away; and then came Signor Orazio Baglioni, running. I bade him stand back, else I'd murder him; for I knew very well who he was. He drew back a little, not without a certain show of fear, and called out: "Benvenuto, I am your friend!" To this I answered: "Sir, come up, but come alone, and then come as you like." The general, who was a man of mighty pride, stood still a moment, and then said angrily: "I have a good mind not to come up again, and to do quite the opposite of that which I intended toward you." I replied that just as I was put there to defend my neighbours, I was equally well able to defend myself too. He said that he was coming alone; and when he arrived at the top of the stairs, his features were more discomposed than I thought reasonable. So I kept my hand upon my sword, and stood eyeing him askance. Upon this

2 Alessandro Farnese, Dean of the Sacred College, and afterwards Pope Paul III. Of Giacopo Salviati we have already heard, p. 13.

3 *Loro preti.* Perhaps *their priests.*

he began to laugh, and the colour coming back into his face, he said to me with the most pleasant manner: "Friend Benvenuto, I bear you as great love as I have it in my heart to give; and in God's good time I will render you proof of this. Would to God you had killed those two rascals; for one of them is the cause of all this trouble, and the day perchance will come when the other will be found the cause of something even worse." He then begged me, if I should be asked, not to say that he was with me when I fired the gun; and for the rest bade me be of good cheer. The commotion which the affair made was enormous, and lasted a long while. However, I will not enlarge upon it further, only adding that I was within an inch of revenging my father on Messer Jacopo Salviati, who had grievously injured him, according to my father's complaints. As it was, unwittingly I gave the fellow a great fright. Of Farnese I shall say nothing here, because it will appear in its proper place how well it would have been if I had killed him.

XXXVII

I pursued my business of artilleryman, and every day performed some extraordinary feat, whereby the credit and the favour I acquired with the Pope was something indescribable. There never passed a day but what I killed one or another of our enemies in the besieging army. On one occasion the Pope was walking round the circular keep,[1] when he observed a Spanish Colonel in the Prati; he recognised the man by certain indications, seeing that this officer had formerly been in his service; and while he fixed his eyes on him, he kept talking about him. I, above by the Angel, knew nothing of all this, but spied a fellow down there, busying himself about the trenches with a javelin in his hand; he was dressed entirely in rose-colour; and so, studying the worst that I could do against him, I selected a gerfalcon which I had at hand; it is a piece of ordnance larger and longer than a swivel, and about the size of a demi-culverin. This I emptied, and loaded it again with a good charge of fine powder mixed with the coarser sort; then I aimed it exactly at the man in red, elevating prodigiously, because a piece of that calibre could hardly be expected to carry true at such a distance. I fired, and hit my man exactly in the middle. He had trussed his sword in front,[2] for swagger, after

1 The Mastio or main body of Hadrian's Mausoleum, which was converted into a fortress during the Middle Ages.

2 *S'aveva messo la spada dinanzi.* Perhaps *was bearing his sword in front of him.*

a way those Spaniards have; and my ball, when it struck him, broke upon the blade, and one could see the fellow cut in two fair halves. The Pope, who was expecting nothing of this kind, derived great pleasure and amazement from the sight, both because it seemed to him impossible that one should aim and hit the mark at such a distance, and also because the man was cut in two, and he could not comprehend how this should happen. He sent for me, and asked about it. I explained all the devices I had used in firing; but told him that why the man was cut in halves, neither he nor I could know. Upon my bended knees I then besought him to give me the pardon of his blessing for that homicide; and for all the others I had committed in the castle in the service of the Church. Thereat the Pope, raising his hand, and making a large open sign of the cross upon my face, told me that he blessed me, and that he gave me pardon for all murders I had ever perpetrated, or should ever perpetrate, in the service of the Apostolic Church. When I left him, I went aloft, and never stayed from firing to the utmost of my power; and few were the shots of mine that missed their mark. My drawing, and my fine studies in my craft, and my charming art of music, all were swallowed up in the din of that artillery; and if I were to relate in detail all the splendid things I did in that infernal work of cruelty, I should make the world stand by and wonder. But, not to be too prolix, I will pass them over. Only I must tell a few of the most remarkable, which are, as it were, forced in upon me.

To begin then: pondering day and night what I could render for my own part in defence of Holy Church, and having noticed that the enemy changed guard and marched past through the great gate of Santo Spirito, which was within a reasonable range, I thereupon directed my attention to that spot; but, having to shoot sideways, I could not do the damage that I wished, although I killed a fair percentage every day. This induced our adversaries, when they saw their passage covered by my guns, to load the roof of a certain house one night with thirty gabions, which obstructed the view I formerly enjoyed. Taking better thought than I had done of the whole situation, I now turned all my five pieces of artillery directly on the gabions, and waited till the evening hour, when they changed guard. Our enemies, thinking they were safe, came on at greater ease and in a closer body than usual; whereupon I set fire to my blow-pipes.[3] Not merely did I dash to pieces the gabions which stood in my way;

[3] *Soffioni*, the cannon being like tubes to blow a fire up.

but, what was better, by that one blast I slaughtered more than thirty men. In consequence of this manœuvre, which I repeated twice, the soldiers were thrown into such disorder, that being, moreover, encumbered with the spoils of that great sack, and some of them desirous of enjoying the fruits of their labour, they oftentimes showed a mind to mutiny and take themselves away from Rome. However, after coming to terms with their valiant captain, Gian di Urbino,[4] they were ultimately compelled, at their excessive inconvenience, to take another road when they changed guard. It cost them three miles of march, whereas before they had but half a mile. Having achieved this feat, I was entreated with prodigious favours by all the men of quality who were invested in the castle. This incident was so important that I thought it well to relate it, before finishing the history of things outside my art, the which is the real object of my writing: forsooth, if I wanted to ornament my biography with such matters, I should have far too much to tell. There is only one more circumstance which, now that the occasion offers, I propose to record.

XXXVIII

I shall skip over some intervening circumstances, and tell how Pope Clement, wishing to save the tiaras and the whole collection of the great jewels of the Apostolic Camera, had me called, and shut himself up together with me and the Cavalierino in a room alone.[1] This Cavalierino had been a groom in the stable of Filippo Strozzi; he was French, and a person of the lowest birth; but being a most faithful servant, the Pope had made him very rich, and confided in him like himself. So the Pope, the Cavaliere, and I, being shut up together, they laid before me the tiaras and jewels of the regalia; and his Holiness ordered me to take all the gems out of their gold settings. This I accordingly did; afterwards I wrapt them separately up in bits of paper and we sewed them into the linings of the Pope's and the Cavaliere's clothes. Then they gave me all the gold, which weighed about two hundred pounds, and bade me melt it down as secretly as I was able. I went up to the Angel, where I had my lodg-

4 This captain was a Spaniard, who played a very considerable figure in the war, distinguishing himself at the capture of Genoa and the battle of Lodi in 1522, and afterwards acting as Lieutenant-General to the Prince of Orange. He held Naples against Orazio Baglioni in 1528, and died before Spello in 1529.

1 This personage cannot be identified. The Filippo Strozzi mentioned as having been his master was the great opponent of the Medicean despotism, who killed himself in prison after the defeat of Montemurlo in 1539. He married in early life a daughter of Piero de' Medici.

ing, and could lock the door so as to be free from interruption. There I built a little draught-furnace of bricks, with a largish pot, shaped like an open dish, at the bottom of it; and throwing the gold upon the coals, it gradually sank through and dropped into the pan. While the furnace was working I never left off watching how to annoy our enemies; and as their trenches were less than a stone's-throw right below us, I was able to inflict considerable damage on them with some useless missiles,[2] of which there were several piles, forming the old munition of the castle. I chose a swivel and a falconet, which were both a little damaged in the muzzle, and filled them with the projectiles I have mentioned. When I fired my guns, they hurtled down like mad, occasioning all sorts of unexpected mischief in the trenches. Accordingly I kept these pieces always going at the same time that the gold was being melted down; and a little before vespers I noticed some one coming along the margin of the trench on muleback. The mule was trotting very quickly, and the man was talking to the soldiers in the trenches. I took the precaution of discharging my artillery just before he came immediately opposite; and so, making a good calculation, I hit my mark. One of the fragments struck him in the face; the rest were scattered on the mule, which fell dead. A tremendous uproar rose up from the trench; I opened fire with my other piece, doing them great hurt. The man turned out to be the Prince of Orange, who was carried through the trenches to a certain tavern in the neighbourhood, whither in a short while all the chief folk of the army came together.

When Pope Clement heard what I had done, he sent at once to call for me, and inquired into the circumstance. I related the whole, and added that the man must have been of the greatest consequence, because the inn to which they carried him had been immediately filled by all the chiefs of the army, so far at least as I could judge. The Pope, with a shrewd instinct, sent for Messer Antonio Santacroce, the nobleman who, as I have said, was chief and commander of the gunners. He bade him order all us bombardiers to point our pieces, which were very numerous, in one mass upon the house, and to discharge them all together upon the signal of an arquebuse being fired. He judged that if we killed the generals, the army, which was already almost on the point of breaking up, would take flight. God perhaps had heard the prayers they kept continually making, and meant to rid them in this manner of those impious scoundrels.

We put our cannon in order at the command of Santacroce, and

2 *Passatojacci.*

waited for the signal. But when Cardinal Orsini [3] became aware of what was going forward, he began to expostulate with the Pope, protesting that the thing by no means ought to happen, seeing they were on the point of concluding an accommodation, and that if the generals were killed, the rabble of the troops without a leader would storm the castle and complete their utter ruin. Consequently they could by no means allow the Pope's plan to be carried out. The poor Pope, in despair, seeing himself assassinated both inside the castle and without, said that he left them to arrange it. On this, our orders were countermanded; but I, who chafed against the leash,[4] when I knew that they were coming round to bid me stop from firing, let blaze one of my demi-cannons, and struck a pillar in the courtyard of the house, around which I saw a crowd of people clustering. This shot did such damage to the enemy that it was like to have made them evacuate the house. Cardinal Orsini was absolutely for having me hanged or put to death; but the Pope took up my cause with spirit. The high words that passed between them, though I well know what they were, I will not here relate, because I make no profession of writing history. It is enough for me to occupy myself with my own affairs.

XXXIX

After I had melted down the gold, I took it to the Pope, who thanked me cordially for what I had done, and ordered the Cavalierino to give me twenty-five crowns, apologising to me for his inability to give me more. A few days afterwards the articles of peace were signed. I went with three hundred comrades in the train of Signor Orazio Baglioni toward Perugia; and there he wished to make me captain of the company, but I was unwilling at the moment, saying that I wanted first to go and see my father, and to redeem the ban which was still in force against me at Florence. Signor Orazio told me that he had been appointed general of the Florentines; and Sir Pier Maria del Lotto, the envoy from Florence, was with him, to whom he specially recommended me as his man.[1]

In course of time I came to Florence in the company of several comrades. The plague was raging with indescribable fury. When I

3 Franciotto Orsini was educated in the household of his kinsman Lorenzo de' Medici. He followed the profession of arms, and married; but after losing his wife took orders, and received the hat in 1517.

4 *Io che non potevo stare alle mosse.*

1 Pier Maria di Lotto of S. Miniato was notary to the Florentine Signoria. He collected the remnants of the Bande Nere, and gave them over to Orazio Baglioni, who contrived to escape from S. Angelo in safety to Perugia.

reached home, I found my good father, who thought either that I must have been killed in the sack of Rome, or else that I should come back to him a beggar. However, I entirely defeated both these expectations; for I was alive, with plenty of money, a fellow to wait on me, and a good horse. My joy on greeting the old man was so intense, that, while he embraced and kissed me, I thought that I must die upon the spot. After I had narrated all the devilries of that dreadful sack, and had given him a good quantity of crowns which I had gained by my soldiering, and when we had exchanged our tokens of affection, he went off to the Eight to redeem my ban. It so happened that one of those magistrates who sentenced me, was now again a member of the board. It was the very man who had so inconsiderately told my father he meant to march me out into the country with the lances. My father took this opportunity of addressing him with some meaning words, in order to mark his revenge, relying on the favour which Orazio Baglioni showed me.

Matters standing thus, I told my father how Signor Orazio had appointed me captain, and that I ought to begin to think of enlisting my company. At these words the poor old man was greatly disturbed, and begged me for God's sake not to turn my thoughts to such an enterprise, although he knew I should be fit for this or yet a greater business, adding that his other son, my brother, was already a most valiant soldier, and that I ought to pursue the noble art in which I had laboured so many years and with such diligence of study. Although I promised to obey him, he reflected, like a man of sense, that if Signor Orazio came to Florence, I could not withdraw myself from military service, partly because I had passed my word, as well as for other reasons. He therefore thought of a good expedient for sending me away, and spoke to me as follows: "Oh, my dear son, the plague in this town is raging with immitigable violence, and I am always fancying you will come home infected with it. I remember, when I was a young man, that I went to Mantua, where I was very kindly received, and stayed there several years. I pray and command you, for the love of me, to pack off and go thither; and I would have you do this to-day rather than to-morrow."

XL

I had always taken pleasure in seeing the world; and having never been in Mantua, I went there very willingly. Of the money I had brought to Florence, I left the greater part with my good father, promising to help him wherever I might be, and confiding him to the care of my elder sister. Her name was Cosa; and since she never cared to marry, she was admitted as a nun in Santa Orsola; but she put off taking the veil, in order to keep house for our old father, and to look after my younger sister, who was married to one Bartolommeo, a surgeon. So then, leaving home with my father's blessing, I mounted my good horse, and rode off on it to Mantua.

It would take too long to describe that little journey in detail. The whole world being darkened over with plague and war, I had the greatest difficulty in reaching Mantua. However, in the end, I got there, and looked about for work to do, which I obtained from a Maestro Niccolo of Milan, goldsmith to the Duke of Mantua. Having thus settled down to work, I went after two days to visit Messer Giulio Romano, that most excellent painter, of whom I have already spoken, and my very good friend. He received me with the tenderest caresses, and took it very ill that I had not dismounted at his house. He was living like a lord, and executing a great work for the Duke outside the city gates, in a place called Del Te. It was a vast and prodigious undertaking, as may still, I suppose, be seen by those who go there.[1]

Messer Giulio lost no time in speaking of me to the Duke in terms of the warmest praise.[2] That Prince commissioned me to make a model for a reliquary, to hold the blood of Christ, which they have there, and say was brought them by Longinus. Then he turned to Giulio, bidding him supply me with a design for it. To this Giulio replied: "My lord, Benvenuto is a man who does not need other people's sketches, as your Excellency will be very well able to judge when you shall see his model." I set hand to the work, and made a drawing for the reliquary, well adapted to contain the sacred phial. Then I made a little waxen model of the cover. This was a seated Christ, supporting his great cross aloft with the left hand, while he seemed to lean against it, and with the fingers of his right hand he appeared to be opening the wound in his side. When it was finished, it pleased the Duke so much that he heaped favours on me, and gave me to understand that he would keep me in his service with such appointments as should enable me to live in affluence.

1 This is the famous Palazzo del Te, outside the walls of Mantua. It still remains the chief monument of Giulio Romano's versatile genius.

2 Federigo Gonzago was at this time Marquis of Mantua. Charles V. erected his fief into a duchy in 1530.

Meanwhile, I had paid my duty to the Cardinal his brother, who begged the Duke to allow me to make the pontifical seal of his most reverend lordship.[3] This I began; but while I was working at it I caught a quartan fever. During each access of this fever I was thrown into delirium, when I cursed Mantua and its master and whoever stayed there at his own liking. These words were reported to the Duke by the Milanese goldsmith, who had not omitted to notice that the Duke wanted to employ me. When the Prince heard the ravings of my sickness, he flew into a passion against me; and I being out of temper with Mantua, our bad feeling was reciprocal. The seal was finished after four months, together with several other little pieces I made for the Duke under the name of the Cardinal. His Reverence paid me well, and bade me return to Rome, to that marvellous city where we had made acquaintance.

I quitted Mantua with a good sum of crowns, and reached Governo, where the most valiant general Giovanni had been killed.[4] Here I had a slight relapse of fever, which did not interrupt my journey, and coming now to an end, it never returned on me again. When I arrived at Florence, I hoped to find my dear father, and knocking at the door, a hump-backed woman in a fury showed her face at the window; she drove me off with a torrent of abuse, screaming that the sight of me was a consumption to her. To this misshapen hag I shouted: "Ho! tell me, cross-grained hunchback, is there no other face to see here but your ugly visage?" "No, and bad luck to you." Whereto I answered in a loud voice: "In less than two hours may it[5] never vex us more!" Attracted by this dispute, a neighbour put her head out, from whom I learned that my father and all the people in the house had died of the plague. As I had partly guessed it might be so, my grief was not so great as it would otherwise have been. The woman afterwards told me that only my sister Liperata had escaped, and that she had taken refuge with a pious lady named Mona Andrea de' Bellacci.[6]

I took my way from thence to the inn, and met by accident a very dear friend of mine, Giovanni Rigogli. Dismounting at his house, we proceeded to the piazza, where I received intelligence that my

3 Ercole Gonzaga, created Cardinal in 1527. After the death of his brother, Duke Federigo, he governed Mantua for sixteen years as regent for his nephews, and became famous as a patron of arts and letters. He died at Trento in 1563 while presiding over the Council there, in the pontificate of Pius IV.

4 Giovanni de' Medici, surnamed Delle Bande Nere.

5 *i. e.*, your ugly visage.

6 Carpani states that between May and November 1527 about 40,000 persons died of plague in Florence.

brother was alive, and went to find him at the house of a friend of his called Bertino Aldobrandini. On meeting, we made demonstrations of the most passionate affection; for he had heard that I was dead, and I had heard that he was dead; and so our joy at embracing one another was extravagant. Then he broke out into a loud fit of laughter, and said: "Come, brother, I will take you where I'm sure you'd never guess! You must know that I have given our sister Liperata away again in marriage, and she holds it for absolutely certain that you are dead." On our way we told each other all the wonderful adventures we had met with; and when we reached the house where our sister dwelt, the surprise of seeing me alive threw her in into a fainting fit, and she fell senseless in my arms. Had not my brother been present, her speechlessness and sudden seizure must have made her husband imagine I was some one different from a brother—as indeed at first it did. Cecchino, however, explained matters, and busied himself in helping the swooning woman, who soon come to. Then, after shedding some tears for father, sister, husband, and a little son whom she had lost, she began to get supper ready; and during our merry meeting all that evening we talked no more about dead folk, but rather discoursed gaily about weddings. Thus, then, with gladness and great enjoyment we brought our supper-party to an end.

XLI

On the entreaty of my brother and sister, I remained at Florence, though my own inclination led me to return to Rome. The dear friend, also, who had helped me in some of my earlier troubles, as I have narrated (I mean Piero, son of Giovanni Landi)—he too advised me to make some stay in Florence; for the Medici were in exile, that is to say, Signor Ippolito and Signor Alessandro, who were afterwards respectively Cardinal and Duke of Florence; and he judged it would be well for me to wait and see what happened.[1]

At that time there arrived in Florence a Sienese, called Girolamo Marretti, who had lived long in Turkey and was a man of lively intellect. He came to my shop, and commissioned me to make a golden medal to be worn in the hat. The subject was to be Hercules wrench-

1 I may remind my readers that the three Medici of the ruling house were now illegitimate. Clement VII. was the bastard son of Giuliano, brother of Lorenzo the Magnificent. Ippolito, the Cardinal, was the bastard of Giuliano. Duke of Nemours, son of Lorenzo the Magnificent. Alessandro was the reputed bastard of Lorenzo, Duke of Urbino, grandson of Lorenzo the Magnificent. Alessandro became Duke of Florence, and after poisoning his cousin, Cardinal Ippolito, was murdered by a distant cousin, Lorenzino de' Medici. In this way the male line of Lorenzo the Magnificent was extinguished.

ing the lion's mouth. While I was working at this piece, Michel Agnolo Buonarroti came oftentimes to see it. I had spent infinite pains upon the design, so that the attitude of the figure and the fierce passion of the beast were executed in quite a different style from that of any craftsman who had hitherto attempted such groups. This, together with the fact that the special branch of art was totally unknown to Michel Agnolo, made the divine master give such praises to my work that I felt incredibly inspired for further effort. However, I found little else to do but jewel-setting; and though I gained more thus than in any other way, yet I was dissatisfied, for I would fain have been employed upon some higher task than that of setting precious stones.

Just then I met with Federigo Ginori, a young man of a very lofty spirit. He had lived some years in Naples, and being endowed with great charms of person and presence, had been the lover of a Neapolitan princess. He wanted to have a medal made, with Atlas bearing the world upon his shoulders, and applied to Michel Agnolo for a design. Michel Agnolo made this answer: "Go and find out a young goldsmith named Benvenuto; he will serve you admirably, and certainly he does not stand in need of sketches by me. However, to prevent your thinking that I want to save myself the trouble of so slight a matter, I will gladly sketch you something; but meanwhile speak to Benvenuto, and let him also make a model; he can then execute the better of the two designs." Federigo Ginori came to me, and told me what he wanted, adding thereto how Michel Agnolo had praised me, and how he had suggested I should make a waxen model while he undertook to supply a sketch. The words of that great man so heartened me, that I set myself to work at once with eagerness upon the model; and when I had finished it, a painter who was intimate with Michel Agnolo, called Giuliano Bugiardini, brought me the drawing of Atlas.[2] On the same occasion I showed Giuliano my little model in wax, which was very different from Michel Agnolo's drawing; and Federigo, in concert with Bugiardini, agreed that I should work upon my model. So I took it in hand, and when Michel Agnolo saw it, he praised me to the skies. This was a figure, as I have said, chiselled on a plate of gold; Atlas had the heaven upon his back, made out of a crystal ball, engraved with the zodiac upon a field of lapislazuli. The whole composition produced an indescribably fine

[2] This painter was the pupil of Bertoldo, a man of simple manners and of some excellence in his art. The gallery at Bologna has a fine specimen of his painting. Michel Agnolo delighted in his society.

effect; and under it ran the legend *Summa tulisse juvat!* [3] Federigo was so thoroughly well pleased that he paid me very liberally. Aluigi Alamanni was at that time in Florence. Federigo Ginori, who enjoyed his friendship, brought him often to my workshop, and through this introduction we became very intimate together.[4]

XLII

Pope Clement had now declared war upon the city of Florence, which thereupon was put in a state of defence; and the militia being organised in each quarter of the town, I too received orders to serve in my turn. I provided myself with a rich outfit, and went about with the highest nobility of Florence, who showed a unanimous desire to fight for the defence of our liberties. Meanwhile the speeches which are usual upon such occasions were made in every quarter; [1] the young men met together more than was their wont, and everywhere we had but one topic of conversation.

It happened one day, about noon, that a crowd of tall men and lusty young fellows, the first in the city, were assembled in my workshop, when a letter from Rome was put into my hands. It came from a man called Maestro Giacopino della Braca. His real name was Giacopo della Sciorina, but they called him della Barca in Rome, because he kept a ferry boat upon the Tiber between Ponte Sisto and Ponte Santo Agnolo. He was a person of considerable talent distinguished by his pleasantries and striking conversation, and he had formerly been a designer of patterns for the cloth-weavers in Florence. This man was intimate with the Pope, who took great pleasure in hearing him talk. Being one day engaged in conversation, they touched upon the sack and the defence of the castle. This brought me to the Pope's mind, and he spoke of me in the very highest terms, adding that if he knew where I was, he should be glad to get me back. Maestro Giacopo said I was in Florence; whereupon the Pope bade the man write and tell me to return to him. The letter I have mentioned was to the effect that I should do well if I resumed the service of Clement, and that this was sure to turn out to my advantage.

The young men who were present were curious to know what the letter contained · wherefore I concealed it as well as I could. After-

3 Cellini says *Summam.*

4 This was the agreeable didactic poet Luigi Alamanni, who had to fly from Florence after a conspiracy against Cardinal Giulio de' Medici in 1522. He could never reconcile himself to the Medicean tyranny, and finally took refuge in France, where he was honoured by François I. He died at Amboise in 1556.

1 *Feceri quelle orazioni.* It may mean "the prayers were offered up."

wards I wrote to Maestro Giacopo, begging him by no means, whether for good or evil, to write to me again. He however grew more obstinate in his officiousness, and wrote me another letter, so extravagantly worded, that if it had been seen, I should have got into serious trouble. The substance of it was that the Pope required me to come at once, wanting to employ me on work of the greatest consequence; also that if I wished to act aright, I ought to throw up everything, and not to stand against a Pope in the party of those hare-brained Radicals. This letter, when I read it, put me in such a fright, that I went to seek my dear friend Piero Landi. Directly he set eyes on me, he asked what accident had happened to upset me so. I told my friend that it was quite impossible for me to explain what lay upon my mind, and what was causing me this trouble; only I entreated him to take the keys I gave him, and to return the gems and gold in my drawers to such and such persons, whose names he would find inscribed upon my memorandum-book; next, I begged him to pack up the furniture of my house, and keep account of it with his usual loving-kindness; and in a few days he should hear where I was. The prudent young man, guessing perhaps pretty nearly how the matter stood, replied: "My brother, go your ways quickly; then write to me, and have no further care about your things." I did as he advised. He was the most loyal friend, the wisest, the most worthy, the most discreet, the most affectionate that I have ever known. I left Florence and went to Rome, and from there I wrote to him.

XLIII

Upon my arrival in Rome,[1] I found several of my former friends, by whom I was very well received and kindly entertained. No time was lost before I set myself to work at things which brought me profit, but were not notable enough to be described. There was a fine old man, a goldsmith, called Raffaello del Moro, who had considerable reputation in the trade, and was to boot a very worthy fellow. He begged me to consent to enter his workshop, saying he had some commissions of importance to execute, on which high profits might be looked for; so I accepted his proposal with good-will.

More than ten days had elapsed, and I had not presented myself

1 Cellini has been severely taxed for leaving Florence at this juncture and taking service under Pope Clement, the oppressor of her liberties. His own narrative admits some sense of shame. Yet we should remember that he never took any decided part in politics, and belonged to a family of Medicean sympathies. His father served Lorenzo and Piero; his brother was a soldier of Giovanni delle Bande Nere and Duke Alessandro. Many most excellent Florentines were convinced that the Medicean government was beneficial; and an artist had certainly more to expect from it than from the Republic.

to Maestro Giacopino della Barca. Meeting me one day by accident, he gave me a hearty welcome, and asked me how long I had been in Rome. When I told him I had been there about a fortnight, he took it very ill, and said that I showed little esteem for a Pope who had urgently compelled him to write three times for me. I, who had taken his persistence in the matter still more ill, made no reply, but swallowed down my irritation. The man, who suffered from a flux of words, began one of his long yarns, and went on talking, till at the last, when I saw him tired out, I merely said that he might bring me to the Pope when he saw fit. He answered that any time would do for him; and I, that I was always ready. So we took our way toward the palace. It was a Maundy Thursday; and when we reached the apartments of the Pope, he being known there and I expected, we were at once admitted.

The Pope was in bed, suffering from a slight indisposition, and he had with him Messer Jacopo Salviati and the Archbishop of Capua.[2] When the Pope set eyes on me, he was exceedingly glad. I kissed his feet, and then, as humbly as I could, drew near to him, and let him understand that I had things of consequence to utter. On this he waved his hand, and the two prelates retired to a distance from us. I began at once to speak: "Most blessed Father, from the time of the sack up to this hour, I have never been able to confess or to communicate, because they refuse me absolution. The case is this. When I melted down the gold and worked at the unsetting of those jewels, your Holiness ordered the Cavalierino to give me a modest reward for my labours, of which I received nothing, but on the contrary he rather paid me with abuse. When then I ascended to the chamber where I had melted down the gold, and washed the ashes, I found about a pound and a half of gold in tiny grains like millet-seeds; and inasmuch as I had not money enough to take me home respectably, I thought I would avail myself of this, and give it back again when opportunity should offer. Now I am here at the feet of your Holiness, who is the only true confessor. I entreat you to do me the favour of granting me indulgence, so that I may be able to confess and communicate, and by the grace of your Holiness regain the grace of my Lord God." Upon this the Pope, with a scarcely perceptible sigh, remembering perhaps his former trials, spoke as follows: "Benvenuto, I thoroughly believe what you tell me; it is in my power to absolve

[2] Nicolas Schomberg, a learned Dominican and disciple of Savonarola, made Archbishop of Capua in 1520. He was a faithful and able minister of Clement. Paul III. gave him his hat in 1535, and he died in 1537.

you of any unbecoming deed you may have done, and, what is more, I have the will. So, then, speak out with frankness and perfect confidence; for if you had taken the value of a whole tiara, I am quite ready to pardon you." Thereupon I answered: "I took nothing, most blessed Father, but what I have confessed; and this did not amount to the value of 140 ducats, for that was the sum I received from the Mint in Perugia, and with it I went home to comfort my poor old father." The Pope said: "Your father has been as virtuous, good, and worthy a man as was ever born, and you have not degenerated from him. I am very sorry that the money was so little; but such as you say it was, I make you a present of it, and give you my full pardon. Assure your confessor of this, if there is nothing else upon your conscience which concerns me. Afterwards, when you have confessed and communicated, you shall present yourself to me again, and it will be to your advantage."

When I parted from the Pope, Messer Giacopo and the Archbishop approached, and the Pope spoke to them in the highest terms imaginable about me; he said that he had confessed and absolved me; then he commissioned the Archbishop of Capua to send for me and ask if I had any other need beyond this matter, giving him full leave to absolve me amply, and bidding him, moreover, treat me with the utmost kindness.

While I was walking away with Maestro Giacopino, he asked me very inquisitively what was the close and lengthy conversation I had had with his Holiness. After he had repeated the question more than twice, I said that I did not mean to tell him, because they were matters with which he had nothing to do, and therefore he need not go on asking me. Then I went to do what had been agreed on with the Pope; and after the two festivals were over, I again presented myself before his Holiness. He received me even better than before, and said: "If you had come a little earlier to Rome, I should have commissioned you to restore my two tiaras, which were pulled to pieces in the castle. These, however, with the exception of the gems, are objects of little artistic interest; so I will employ you on a piece of the very greatest consequence, where you will be able to exhibit all your talents. It is a button for my priest's cope, which has to be made round like a trencher, and as big as a little trencher, one-third of a cubit wide. Upon this I want you to represent a God the Father in half-relief, and in the middle to set that magnificent big diamond, which you remember, together with several other gems of the greatest value.

Caradosso began to make me one, but did not finish it; I want yours to be finished quickly, so that I may enjoy the use of it a little while. Go, then, and make me a fine model." He had all the jewels shown me, and then I went off like a shot [3] to set myself to work.

XLIV

During the time when Florence was besieged, Federigo Ginori, for whom I made that medal of Atlas, died of consumption, and the medal came into the hands of Messer Luigi Alamanni, who, after a little while, took it to present in person to Francis, king of France, accompanied by some of his own finest compositions. The King was exceedingly delighted with the gift; whereupon Messer Luigi told his Majesty so much about my personal qualities, as well as my art, and spoke so favourably, that the King expressed a wish to know me.

Meanwhile I pushed my model for the button forward with all the diligence I could, constructing it exactly of the size which the jewel itself was meant to have. In the trade of the goldsmiths it roused considerable jealousy among those who thought that they were capable of matching it. A certain Micheletto had just come to Rome; [1] he was very clever at engraving cornelians, and was, moreover, a most intelligent jeweller, an old man of a great celebrity. He had been employed upon the Pope's tiaras; and while I was working at my model, he wondered much that I had not applied to him, being as he was a man of intelligence and of large credit with the Pope. At last, when he saw that I was not coming to him, he came to me, and asked me what I was about. "What the Pope has ordered me," I answered. Then he said: "The Pope has commissioned me to superintend everything which is being made for his Holiness." I only replied that I would ask the Pope, and then should know what answer I ought to give him. He told me that I should repent, and departing in anger, had an interview with all the masters of the art; they deliberated on the matter, and charged Michele with the conduct of the whole affair. As was to be expected from a person of his talents, he ordered more than thirty drawings to be made, all differing in their details, for the piece the Pope had commissioned.

Having already access to his Holiness's ear, he took into his counsel another jeweller, named Pompeo, a Milanese, who was in

[3] *Affusolato.* Lit., straight as a spindle.
[1] Vasari calls this eminent engraver of gems Micheline.

favour with the Pope, and related to Messer Traiano, the first chamberlain of the court;[2] these two together, then, began to insinuate that they had seen my model, and did not think me up to a work of such extraordinary import. The Pope replied that he would also have to see it, and that if he then found me unfit for the purpose, he should look around for one who was fit. Both of them put in that they had several excellent designs ready; to which the Pope made answer, that he was very pleased to hear it, but that he did not care to look at them till I had completed my model; afterwards, he would take them all into consideration at the same time.

After a few days I finished my model, and took it to the Pope one morning, when Messer Traiano made me wait till he had sent for Micheletto and Pompeo, bidding them make haste and bring their drawings. On their arrival we were introduced, and Micheletto and Pompeo immediately unrolled their papers, which the Pope inspected. The draughtsmen who had been employed were not in the jeweller's trade, and therefore, knew nothing about giving their right place to precious stones; and the jewellers, on their side, had not shown them how; for I ought to say that a jeweller, when he has to work with figures, must of necessity understand design, else he cannot produce anything worth looking at: and so it turned out that all of them had stuck that famous diamond in the middle of the breast of God the Father. The Pope, who was an excellent connoisseur, observing this mistake, approved of none of them; and when he had looked at about ten, he flung the rest down, and said to me, who was standing at a distance: "Now show me your model, Benvenuto, so that I may see if you have made the same mistake as those fellows." I came forward, and opened a little round box; whereupon one would have thought that a light from heaven had struck the Pope's eyes. He cried aloud: "If you had been in my own body, you could not have done it better, as this proves. Those men there have found the right way to bring shame upon themselves!" A crowd of great lords pressing round, the Pope pointed out the difference between my model and the drawings. When he had sufficiently commended it, the others standing terrified and stupid before him, he turned to me and said: "I am only afraid of one thing, and that is of the utmost consequence. Friend Benvenuto, wax is easy to work in; the real difficulty is to execute this in gold." To those words I answered without a moment's hesitation: "Most blessed Father, if I do not work it ten times better

2 Messer Traiano Alicorno.

than the model, let it be agreed beforehand that you pay me nothing." When they heard this, the noblemen made a great stir, crying out that I was promising too much. Among them was an eminent philosopher, who spoke out in my favour: "From the fine physiognomy and bodily symmetry which I observed in this young man, I predict that he will accomplish what he says, and think that he will even go beyond it." The Pope put in: "And this is my opinion also." Then he called his chamberlain, Messer Traiano, and bade him bring five hundred golden ducats of the Camera.

While we were waiting for the money, the Pope turned once more to gaze at leisure on the dexterous device I had employed for combining the diamond with the figure of God the Father. I had put the diamond exactly in the center of the piece; and above it God the Father was shown seated, leaning nobly in a sideways attitude,[3] which made a perfect composition, and did not interfere with the stone's effect. Lifting his right hand, he was in the act of giving the benediction. Below the diamond I had placed three children, who, with their arms upraised, were supporting the jewel. One of them, in the middle, was in full relief, the other two in half-relief. All around I set a crowd of cherubs, in divers attitude, adapted to the other gems. A mantle undulated to the wind around the figure of the Father, from the folds of which cherubs peeped out; and there were other ornaments besides which made a very beautiful effect. The work was executed in white stucco on a black stone. When the money came, the Pope gave it to me with his own hand, and begged me in the most winning terms to let him have it finished in his own days, adding that this should be to my advantage.

XLV

I took the money and the model home, and was in the utmost impatience to begin my work. After I had laboured diligently for eight days, the Pope sent word by one of his chamberlains, a very great gentleman of Bologna, that I was to come to him and bring what I had got in hand. On the way, the chamberlain, who was the most gentle-mannered person in the Roman court, told me that the Pope not only wanted to see what I was doing, but also intended to intrust me with another task of the highest consequence, which

[3] *In un certo bel modo svolto.* That means: turned aside, not fronting the spectator.

was, in fact, to furnish dies for the money of the Mint; and bade me arm myself beforehand with the answer I should give; in short, he wished me to be prepared, and therefore he had spoken. When we came into the presence, I lost no time in exhibiting the golden plate, upon which I had as yet carved nothing but my figure of God the Father; but this, though only in the rough, displayed a grander style than that of the waxen model. The Pope regarded it with stupefaction, and exclaimed: "From this moment forward I will believe everything you say." Then loading me with marks of favour, he added: "It is my intention to give you another commission, which, if you feel competent to execute it, I shall have no less at heart than this, or more." He proceeded to tell me that he wished to make dies for the coinage of his realm, and asked me if I had ever tried my hand at such things, and if I had the courage to attempt them. I answered that of courage for the task I had no lack, and that I had seen how dies were made, but that I had not ever made any. There was in the presence a certain Messer Tommaso, of Prato, his Holiness's Datary;[1] and this man, being a friend of my enemies, put in: "Most blessed Father, the favours you are showering upon this young man (and he by nature so extremely overbold) are enough to make him promise you a new world. You have already given him one great task, and now, by adding a greater, you are like to make them clash together." The Pope, in a rage, turned round on him, and told him to mind his own business. Then he commanded me to make the model for a broad doubloon of gold, upon which he wanted a naked Christ with his hands tied, and the inscription *Ecce Homo;* the reverse was to have a Pope and Emperor in the act together of propping up a cross which seemed to fall, and this legend: *Unus spiritus et una fides erat in eis.*

After the Pope had ordered this handsome coin, Bandinello the sculptor came up; he had not yet been made a knight; and, with his wonted presumption muffled up in ignorance, said: "For these goldsmiths one must make drawings for such fine things as that." I turned round upon him in a moment, and cried out that I did not want his drawings for my art, but that I hoped before very long to give his art some trouble by my drawings. The Pope expressed high satisfac-

1 His full name was Tommaso Cortese. The Papal Datario was the chief secretary of the office for requests, petitions, and patents. His title was derived from its being his duty to affix the *Datum Romæ* to documents. The fees of this office, which was also called Datario, brought in a large revenue to the Papacy.

tion at these words, and turning to me said: "Go then, my Benvenuto, and devote yourself with spirit to my service, and do not lend an ear to the chattering of these silly fellows."

So I went off, and very quickly made two dies of steel; then I stamped a coin in gold, and one Sunday after dinner took the coin and the dies to the Pope, who, when he saw the piece, was astonished and greatly gratified, not only because my work pleased him excessively, but also because of the rapidity with which I had performed it. For the further satisfaction and amazement of his holiness, I had brought with me all the old coins which in former times had been made by those able men who served Popes Giulio and Leo; and when I noticed that mine pleased him far better, I drew forth from my bosom a patent,[2] in which I prayed for the post of stamp-master [3] in the Mint. This place was worth six golden crowns a month, in addition to the dies, which were paid at the rate of a ducat for three by the Master of the Mint. The Pope took my patent and handed it to the Datary, telling him to lose no time in dispatching the business. The Datary began to put it in his pocket, saying: "Most blessed Father, your Holiness ought not to go so fast; these are matters which deserve some reflection." To this the Pope replied: "I have heard what you have got to say; give me here that patent." He took it, and signed it at once with his own hand; then, giving it back, added: "Now, you have no answer left; see that you dispatch it at once, for this is my pleasure; and Benvenuto's shoes are worth more than the eyes of all those other blockheads." So, having thanked his Holiness, I went back, rejoicing above measure, to my work.

XLVI

I was still working in the shop of Raffaello del Moro. This worthy man had a very beautiful young daughter, with regard to whom he had resigns on me; and I, becoming partly aware of his intentions, was very willing; but, while indulging such desires, I made no show of them: on the contrary, I was so discreet in my behaviour that I made him wonder. It so happened that the poor girl was attacked by a disorder in her right hand, which ate into the two bones belonging to the little finger and the next.[1] Owing to her father's careless-

[2] *Moto propio.* Cellini confuses his petition with the instrument, which he had probably drawn up ready for signature.

[3] *Maestro delle stampe della zecca, i. e.,* the artist who made the dies.

[1] *Ossicina che seguitano il dito,* &c. Probably metacarpal bones.

ness, she had been treated by an ignorant quack-doctor, who predicted that the poor child would be crippled in the whole of her right arm, if even nothing worse should happen. When I noticed the dismay of her father, I begged him not to believe all that this ignorant doctor had said. He replied that he had no acquaintance with physicians or with surgeons, and entreated me, if I knew of one, to bring him to the house.[2] I sent at once for a certain Maestro Giacomo of Perugia, a man of great skill in surgery, who examined the poor girl.[3] She was dreadfully frightened through having gained some inkling of the quack's predictions; whereas, my intelligent doctor declared that she would suffer nothing of consequence, and would be very well able to use her right hand; also that though the two last fingers must remain somewhat weaker than the others, this would be of no inconvenience at all to her. So he began his treatment; and after a few days, when he was going to extract a portion of the diseased bones, her father called for me, and begged me to be present at the operation. Maestro Giacomo was using some coarse steel instruments; and when I observed that he was making little way and at the same time was inflicting severe pain on the patient, I begged him to stop and wait half a quarter of an hour for me. I ran into the shop, and made a little scalping-iron of steel, extremely thin and curved; it cut like a razor. On my return, the surgeon used it, and began to work with so gentle a hand that she felt no pain, and in a short while the operation was over. In consequence of this service, and for other reasons, the worthy man conceived for me as much love, or more, as he had for two male children; and in the meanwhile he attended to the cure of his beautiful young daughter.

I was on terms of the closest intimacy with one Messer Giovanni Gaddi, who was a clerk of the Camera, and a great connoisseur of the arts, although he had no practical acquaintance with any.[4] In his household were a certain Messer Giovanni, a Greek of eminent learning, Messer Lodovico of Fano, no less distinguished as a man of letters, Messer Antonio Allegretti, and Messer Annibale Caro,[5] at

2 *Che gnene avviasse.*

3 Giacomo Rastelli was a native of Rimini, but was popularly known as of Perugia, since he had resided long in that city. He was a famous surgeon under several Popes until the year 1566, when he died at Rome, aged seventy-five.

4 Giovanni Gaddi of the Florentine family was passionately attached to men of art and letters. Yet he seems to have been somewhat disagreeable in personal intercourse; for even Annibale Caro, who owed much to his patronage, and lived for many years in his house, never became attached to him. We shall see how he treated Cellini during a fever.

5 Some poems of Allegretti's survive. He was a man of mark in the literary society of the age. Giovanni Greco may have been a Giovanni Vergezio, who presented Duke Cosimo with some Greek characters of exquisite finish. Lodovico da Fano is mentioned as an excellent Latin scholar. Annibale Caro was one of the most distinguished writers of Italian

that time in his early manhood. Messer Bastiano of Venice, a most excellent painter, and I were admitted to their society; and almost every day we met together in Messer Giovanni's company.[6]

Being aware of this intimacy, the worthy goldsmith Raffaello said to Messer Giovanni: "Good sir, you know me; now I want to marry my daughter to Benvenuto, and can think of no better intermediary than your worship. So I am come to crave your assistance, and to beg you to name for her such dowry from my estate as you may think suitable." The light-headed man hardly let my good friend finish what he had to say, before he put in quite at random: "Talk no more about it, Raffaello; you are farther from your object than January from mulberries." The poor man, utterly discouraged, looked about at once for another husband for his girl; while she and the mother and all the family lived on in a bad humour with me. Since I did not know the real cause of this—I imagined they were paying me with bastard coin for the many kindnesses I had shown them—I conceived the thought of opening a workshop of my own in their neighbourhood. Messer Giovanni told me nothing till the girl was married, which happened in a few months.

Meanwhile, I laboured assiduously at the work I was doing for the Pope, and also in the service of the Mint; for his Holiness had ordered another coin, of the value of two carlins, on which his own portrait was stamped, while the reverse bore a figure of Christ upon the waters, holding out his hand to S. Peter, with this inscription *Quare dubitasti?* My design won such applause that a certain secretary of the Pope, a man of the greatest talent, called Il Sanga,[7] was moved to this remark: "Your Holiness can boast of having a currency superior to any of the ancients in all their glory." The Pope replied: "Benvenuto, for his part, can boast of serving an emperor like me, who is able to discern his merit." I went on at my great piece in gold, showing it frequently to the Pope, who was very eager to see it, and each time expressed greater admiration.

XLVII

My brother, at this period, was also in Rome, serving Duke Alessandro, on whom the Pope had recently conferred the Duchy of

prose and verse in the later Renaissance. He spent the latter portion of his life in the service of the Farnesi.

[6] Messer Bastiano is the celebrated painter Sebastian del Piombo, born 1485, died 1547.

[7] Battista Sanga, a Roman, secretary to Gianmatteo Giberti, the good Archbishop of Verona, and afterwards to Clement VII. He was a great Latinist, and one of those ecclesiastics who earnestly desired a reform of the Church. He died, poisoned, at an early age.

Penna. This prince kept in his service a multitude of soldiers, worthy fellows, brought up to valour in the school of that famous general Giovanni de' Medici; and among these was my brother, whom the Duke esteemed as highly as the bravest of them. One day my brother went after dinner to the shop of a man called Baccino della Croce in the Banchi, which all those men-at-arms frequented. He had flung himself upon a settee, and was sleeping. Just then the guard of the Bargello passed by;[1] they were taking to prison a certain Captain Cisti, a Lombard, who had also been a member of Giovanni's troop, but was not in the service of the Duke. The captain, Cattivanza degli Strozzi, chanced to be in the same shop;[2] and when Cisti caught sight of him, he whispered: "I was bringing you those crowns I owed; if you want them, come for them before they go with me to prison." Now Cattivanza had a way of putting his neighbours to the push, not caring to hazard his own person. So, finding there around him several young fellows of the highest daring, more eager than apt for so serious an enterprise, he bade them catch up Captain Cisti and get the money from him, and if the guard resisted, overpower the men, provided they had pluck enough to do so.

The young men were but four, and all four of them without a beard. The first was called Bertino Aldobrandi, another Anguillotto of Lucca; I cannot recall the names of the rest. Bertino had been trained like a pupil by my brother; and my brother felt the most unbounded love for him. So then, off dashed the four brave lads, and came up with the guard of the Bargello—upwards of fifty constables, counting pikes, arquebuses, and two-handed-swords. After a few words they drew their weapons, and the four boys so harried the guard, that if Captain Cattivanza had but shown his face, without so much as drawing, they would certainly have put the whole pack to flight. But delay spoiled all; for Bertino received some ugly wounds and fell; at the same time, Anguillotto was also hit in the right arm, and being unable to use his sword, got out of the fray as well as he was able. The others did the same. Bertino Aldobrandi was lifted from the ground seriously injured.

1 The Bargello was the chief constable or sheriff in Italian towns. I shall call him Bargello always in my translation, since any English equivalent would be misleading. He did the rough work of policing the city, and was consequently a mark for all the men of spirit who disliked being kept in order. Giovio, in his Life of Cardinal Pompeo Colonna, quite gravely relates how it was the highest ambition of young Romans of spirit to murder the Bargello. He mentions, in particular, a certain Pietro Margano, who had acquired great fame and popularity by killing the Bargello of his day, one Cencio, in the Campo di Fiore. This man became an outlaw, and was favourably received by Cardinal Colonna, then at war with Clement VII.

2 His baptismal name was Bernardo. Cattivanza was a nickname. He fought bravely for Florence in the siege.

XLVIII

While these things were happening, we were all at table; for that morning we had dined more than an hour later than usual. On hearing the commotion, one of the old man's sons, the elder, rose from table to go and look at the scuffle. He was called Giovanni; and I said to him: "For Heaven's sake, don't go! In such matters one is always certain to lose, while there is nothing to be gained." His father spoke to like purpose: "Pray, my son, don't go!" But the lad, without heeding any one, ran down the stairs. Reaching the Banchi, where the great scrimmage was, and seeing Bertino lifted from the ground, he ran towards home, and met my brother Cecchino on the way, who asked what was the matter. Though some of the bystanders signed to Giovanni not to tell Cecchino, he cried out like a madman how it was that Bertino Aldobrandi had been killed by the guard. My poor brother gave vent to a bellow which might have been heard ten miles away. Then he turned to Giovanni: "Ah me! but could you tell me which of those men killed him for me?" Giovanni said, yes, that it was a man who had a big two-handed sword, with a blue feather in his bonnet. My poor brother rushed ahead, and having recognised the homicide by those signs, he threw himself with all his dash and spirit into the middle of the band, and before his man could turn on guard, ran him right through the guts, and with the sword's hilt thrust him to the ground. Then he turned upon the rest with such energy and daring, that his one arm was on the point of putting the whole band to flight, had it not been that, while wheeling round to strike an arquebusier, this man fired in self-defence, and hit the brave unfortunate young fellow above the knee of his right leg. While he lay stretched upon the ground, the constables scrambled off in disorder as fast as they were able, lest a pair to my brother should arrive upon the scene.

Noticing that the tumult was not subsided, I too rose from the table, and girding on my sword—for everybody wore one then—I went to the bridge of Sant' Agnolo, where I saw a group of several men assembled. On my coming up and being recognised by some of them, they gave way before me, and showed me what I least of all things wished to see, albeit I made mighty haste to view the sight. On

[1] *Oimè, saprestimi tu dire che di quelli me l'ha morto?* The *me* is so emphatic, that, though it makes poor English, I have preserved it in my version.

the instant I did not know Cecchino, since he was wearing a different suit of clothes from that in which I had lately seen him. Accordingly, he recognised me first, and said: "Dearest brother, do not be upset by my grave accident; it is only what might be expected in my profession: get me removed from here at once, for I have but few hours to live." They had acquainted me with the whole event while he was speaking, in brief words befitting such occasion. So I answered: "Brother, this is the greatest sorrow and the greatest trial that could happen to me in the whole course of my life. But be of good cheer; for before you lose sight of him who did the mischief, you shall see yourself revenged by my hand." Our words on both sides were to the purport, but of the shortest.

XLIX

The guard was now about fifty paces from us; for Maffio, their officer, had made some of them turn back to take up the corporal my brother killed. Accordingly, I quickly traversed that short space, wrapped in my cape, which I had tightened round me, and came up with Maffio, whom I should most certainly have murdered, for there were plenty of people round, and I had wound my way among them. With the rapidity of lightning, I had half drawn my sword from the sheath, when Berlinghier Berlinghieri, a young man of the greatest daring and my good friend, threw himself from behind upon my arms; he had four other fellows of like kidney with him, who cried out to Maffio: "Away with you, for this man here alone was killing you!" He asked: "Who is he?" and they answered: "Own brother to the man you see there." Without waiting to hear more, he made haste for Torre di Nona;[1] and they said: "Benvenuto, we prevented you against your will, but did it for your good; now let us go to succour him who must die shortly." Accordingly, we turned and went back to my brother, whom I had at once conveyed into a house. The doctors who were called in consultation, treated him with medicaments, but could not decide to amputate the leg, which might perhaps have saved him.

As soon as his wound had been dressed, Duke Alessandro appeared and most affectionately greeted him. My brother had not as yet lost consciousness; so he said to the Duke: "My lord, this only

[1] The Torre di Nona was one of the principal prisons in Rome, used especially for criminals condemned to death.

grieves me, that your Excellency is losing a servant than whom you may perchance find men more valiant in the profession of arms, but none more lovingly and loyally devoted to your service than I have been." The Duke bade him do all he could to keep alive; for the rest, he well knew him to be a man of worth and courage. He then turned to his attendants, ordering them to see that the brave young fellow wanted for nothing.

When he was gone, my brother lost blood so copiously, for nothing could be done to stop it, that he went off his head, and kept raving all the following night, with the exception that once, when they wanted to give him the communion, he said: "You would have done well to confess me before; now it is impossible that I should receive the divine sacrament in this already ruined frame; it will be enough if I partake of it by the divine virtue of the eyesight, whereby it shall be transmitted into my immortal soul, which only prays to Him for mercy and forgiveness." Having spoken thus, the host was elevated; but he straightway relapsed into the same delirious ravings as before, pouring forth a torrent of the most terrible frenzies and horrible imprecations that the mind of man could imagine; nor did he cease once all that night until the day broke.

When the sun appeared above our horizon, he turned to me and said: "Brother, I do not wish to stay here longer, for these fellows will end by making me do something tremendous, which may cause them to repent of the annoyance they have given me." Then he kicked out both his legs—the injured limb we had enclosed in a very heavy box—and made as though he would fling it across a horse's back. Turning his face round to me, he called out thrice—"Farewell, farewell!" and with the last word that most valiant spirit passed way.

At the proper hour, toward nightfall, I had him buried with due ceremony in the church of the Florentines; and afterwards I erected to his memory a very handsome monument of marble, upon which I caused trophies and banners to be carved. I must not omit to mention that one of his friends had asked him who the man was that had killed him, and if he could recognise him; to which he answered that he could, and gave his description. My brother, indeed, attempted to prevent this coming to my ears; but I got it very well impressed upon my mind, as will appear in the sequel.[2]

[2] Varchi, in his *Storia Florentina*, lib. xi., gives a short account of Cecchino Cellini's death in Rome, mentioning also Bertino Aldobrandi, in the attempt to revenge whom he lost his life.

L

Returning to the monument, I should relate that certain famous men of letters, who knew my brother, composed for me an epitaph, telling me that the noble young man deserved it. The inscription ran thus:—

"Francisco Cellino Florentino, qui quod in teneris annis ad Ioannem Medicem ducem plures victorias retulit et signifer fuït, facile documentum dedit quantæ fortitudinis et consilii vir futurus erat nì crudelis fati archibuso transfossus, quinto ætatis lustro jaceret, Benvenutus frater posuit. Obiit die xxvii *Maii* MD.XXIX."

He was twenty-five years of age; and since the soldiers called him Cecchino del Piffero,[1] his real name being Giovanfrancesco Cellini, I wanted to engrave the former, by which he was commonly known, under the armorial bearings of our family. This name then I had cut in fine antique characters, all of which were broken save the first and last. I was asked by the learned men who had composed that beautiful epitaph, wherefore I used these broken letters; and my answer was, because the marvellous framework of his body was spoiled and dead; and the reason why the first and last remained entire was, that the first should symbolise the great gift God had given him, namely, of a human soul, inflamed with his divinity, the which hath never broken, while the second represented the glorious renown of his brave actions. The thought gave satisfaction, and several persons have since availed themselves of my device. Close to the name I had the coat of us Cellini carved upon the stone, altering it in some particulars. In Ravenna, which is a most ancient city, there exist Cellini of our name in the quality of very honourable gentry, who bear a lion rampant or upon a field of azure, holding a lily gules in his dexter paw, with a label in chief and three little lilies or.[2] These are the true arms of the Cellini. My father showed me a shield as ours which had the paw only, together with the other bearings; but I should prefer to follow those of the Cellini of Ravenna, which I have described above. Now to return to what I caused to be engraved upon my brother's tomb: it was the lion's paw, but instead of a lily, I made the lion hold an axe, with the field of the

1 That is, Frank, the Fifer's son.

2 I believe Cellini meant here to write "on a chief argent a label of four points, and three lilies gules." He has tricked the arms thus in a MS. of the Palatine Library. See Leclanchè, p. 103; see also Piatti, vol. i. p. 233, and Plon, p. 2.

scutcheon quartered; and I put the axe in solely that I might not be unmindful to revenge him.

LI

I went on applying myself with the utmost diligence upon the gold-work for Pope Clement's button. He was very eager to have it, and used to send for me two or three times a week, in order to inspect it; and his delight in the work always increased. Often would he rebuke and scold me, as it were, for the great grief in which my brother's loss had plunged me and one day, observing me more downcast and out of trim than was proper, he cried aloud: "Benvenuto, oh! I did not know that you were mad. Have you only just learned that there is no remedy against death? One would think that you were trying to run after him." When I left the presence, I continued working at the jewel and the dies [1] for the Mint; but I also took to watching the arquebusier who shot my brother, as though he had been a girl I was in love with. The man had formerly been in the light cavalry, but afterwards had joined the arquebusiers as one of the Bargello's corporals; and what increased my rage was that he had used these boastful words: "If it had not been for me, who killed that brave young man, the least trifle of delay would have resulted in his putting us all to flight with great disaster." When I saw that the fever caused by always seeing him about was depriving me of sleep and appetite, and was bringing me by degrees to sorry plight, I overcame my repugnance to so low and not quite praiseworthy an enterprise, and made my mind up one evening to rid myself of the torment. The fellow lived in a house near a place called Torre Sanguigua, next door to the lodging of one of the most fashionable courtesans in Rome, named Signora Antea. It had just struck twenty-four, and he was standing at the house-door, with his sword in hand, having risen from supper. With great address I stole up to him, holding a large Pistojan dagger,[2] and dealt him a backhanded stroke, with which I meant to cut his head clean off; but as he turned round very suddenly, the blow fell upon the point of his left shoulder and broke the bone. He sprang up, dropped his sword, half-stunned with the great pain, and took to flight. I followed after,

1 *Ferri.* I have translated this word *dies;* but it seems to mean all the coining instruments, *stampe* or *conii* being the dies proper.

2 *Pugnal pistolese:* it came in time to mean a cutlass.

and in four steps caught him up, when I lifted my dagger above his head, which he was holding very low, and hit him in the back exactly at the juncture of the nape-bone and the neck. The poniard entered this point so deep into the bone, that, though I used all my strength to pull it out, I was not able. For just at that moment four soldiers with drawn swords sprang out from Antea's lodging, and obliged me to set hand to my own sword to defend my life. Leaving the poniard then, I made off, and fearing I might be recognised, took refuge in the palace of Duke Alessandro, which was between Piazza Navona and the Rotunda.[3] On my arrival, I asked to see the Duke; who told me that, if I was alone, I need only keep quiet and have no further anxiety, but to go on working at the jewel which the Pope had set his heart on, and stay eight days indoors. He gave this advice the more securely, because the soldiers had now arrived who interrupted the completion of my deed; they held the dagger in their hand, and were relating how the matter happened, and the great trouble they had to pull the weapon from the neck and head-bone of the man, whose name they did not know. Just then Giovan Bandini came up, and said to them:[4] "That poniard is mine, and I lent it to Benvenuto, who was bent on revenging his brother." The soldiers were profuse in their expressions of regret at having interrupted me, although my vengeance had been amply satisfied.

More than eight days elapsed, and the Pope did not send for me according to his custom. Afterwards he summoned me through his chamberlain, the Bolognese nobleman I have already mentioned, who let me, in his own modest manner, understand that his Holiness knew all, but was very well inclined toward me, and that I had only to mind my work and keep quiet. When we reached the presence, the Pope cast so menacing a glance towards me, that the mere look of his eyes made me tremble. Afterwards, upon examining my work his countenance cleared, and he began to praise me beyond measure, saying that I had done a vast amount in a short time. Then, looking me straight in the face, he added: "Now that you are cured, Benvenuto, take heed how you live."[5] I, who understood his meaning, promised that I would. Immediately upon this, I opened a very fine shop in the

3 That is, the Pantheon.

4 Bandini bears a distinguished name in Florentine annals. He served Duke Alessandro in affairs of much importance; but afterwards he betrayed the interests of his master, Duke Cosimo, in an embassy to Charles V. in 1543. It seems that he had then been playing into the hands of Filippo Strozzi, for which offence he passed fifteen years in a dungeon. See Varchi and Segni; also Montazio's *Prigionieri del Mastio di Volterra*, cap. vii.

5 This was the Pope's hint to Cellini that he was aware of the murder he had just committed.

Banchi, opposite Raffaello, and there I finished the jewel after the lapse of a few months.

LII

The Pope had sent me all those precious stones, except the diamond, which was pawned to certain Genoese bankers for some pressing need he had of money. The rest were in my custody, together with a model of the diamond. I had five excellent journeymen, and in addition to the great piece, I was engaged on several jobs; so that my shop contained property of much value in jewels, gems, and gold and silver. I kept a shaggy dog, very big and handsome, which Duke Alessandro gave me; the beast was capital as a retriever, since he brought me every sort of birds and game I shot, but he also served most admirably for a watchdog. It happened, as was natural at the age of twenty-nine, that I had taken into my service a girl of great beauty and grace, whom I used as a model in my art, and who was also complaisant of her personal favours to me. Such being the case, I occupied an apartment far away from my workmen's rooms, as well as from the shop; and this communicated by a little dark passage with the maid's bedroom. I used frequently to pass the night with her; and though I sleep as lightly as ever yet did man upon this earth, yet, after indulgence in sexual pleasure, my slumber is sometimes very deep and heavy.

So it chanced one night: for I must say that a thief, under the pretext of being a goldsmith, had spied on me, and cast his eyes upon the precious stones, and made a plan to steal them. Well, then, this fellow broke into the shop, where he found a quantity of little things in gold and silver. He was engaged in bursting open certain boxes to get at the jewels he had noticed, when my dog jumped upon him, and put him to much trouble to defend himself with his sword. The dog, unable to grapple with an armed man, ran several times through the house, and rushed into the rooms of the journeymen, which had been left open because of the great heat. When he found they paid no heed to his loud barking, he dragged their bed-clothes off; and when they still heard nothing, he pulled first one and then another by the arm till he roused them, and, barking furiously, ran before to show them where he wanted them to go. At last it became clear that they refused to follow; for the traitors, cross at being disturbed, threw stones and sticks at him; and this they could well do, for I had

ordered them to keep all night a lamp alight there; and in the end they shut their rooms tight; so the dog, abandoning all hope of aid from such rascals, set out alone again on his adventure. He ran down, and not finding the thief in the shop, flew after him. When he got at him, he tore the cape off his back. It would have gone hard with the fellow had he not called for help to certain tailors, praying them for God's sake to save him from a mad dog; and they, believing what he said, jumped out and drove the dog off with much trouble.

After sunrise my workmen went into the shop, and saw that it had been broken open and all the boxes smashed. They began to scream at the top of their voices: "Ah, woe is me! Ah, woe is me!" The clamour woke me, and I rushed out in a panic. Appearing thus before them, they cried out: "Alas to us! for we have been robbed by some one, who has broken and borne everything away!" These words wrought so forcibly upon my mind that I dared not go to my big chest and look if it still held the jewels of the Pope. So intense was the anxiety, that I seemed to lose my eyesight, and told them they themselves must unlock the chest, and see how many of the Pope's gems were missing. The fellows were all of them in their shirts; and when, on opening the chest, they saw the precious stones and my work with them, they took heart of joy and shouted: "There is no harm done; your piece and all the stones are here; but the thief has left us naked to the shirt, because last night, by reason of the burning heat, we took our clothes off in the shop and left them here." Recovering my senses, I thanked God, and said: "Go and get yourselves new suits of clothes; I will pay when I hear at leisure how the whole thing happened." What caused me the most pain, and made me lose my senses, and take fright—so contrary to my real nature—was the dread lest peradventure folk should fancy I had trumped a story of the robber up to steal the jewels. It had already been said to Pope Clement by one of his most trusted servants, and by others, that is, by Francesco del Nero, Zana de' Biliotti his accountant, the Bishop of Vasona, and several such men:[1] "Why, most blessed Father, do you confide gems to that vast value to a young fellow, who is all fire, more passionate for arms than for his art, and not yet thirty years of age?" The Pope asked in answer if any one of them knew that I had done aught to justify such suspicions. Whereto Francesco

[1] Of these people, we can trace the Bishop of Vasona. He was Girolamo Schio or Schedo, a native of Vicenza, the confidential agent and confessor of Clement VII., who obtained the See of Vaison in the county of Avignon in 1523, and died at Rome in 1533. His successor in the bishopric was Tomaso Cortesi, the Datary, mentioned above.

del Nero, his treasurer, replied:[2] "No, most blessed Father, because he has not as yet had an opportunity." Whereto the Pope rejoined: "I regard him as a thoroughly honest man; and if I saw with my own eyes some crime he had committed, I should not believe it." This was the man who[3] caused me the greatest torment, and who suddenly came up before my mind.

After telling the young men to provide themselves with fresh clothes, I took my piece, together with the gems, setting them as well as I could in their proper places, and went off at once with them to the Pope. Francesco del Nero had already told him something of the trouble in my shop, and had put suspicions in his head. So then, taking the thing rather ill than otherwise, he shot a furious glance upon me, and cried haughtily: "What have you come to do here? What is up?" "Here are all your precious stones, and not one of them is missing." At this the Pope's face cleared, and he said: "So then, you're welcome." I showed him the piece, and while he was inspecting it, I related to him the whole story of the thief and of my agony, and what had been my greatest trouble in the matter. During this speech, he oftentimes turned round to look me sharply in the eyes; and Francesco del Nero being also in the presence, this seemed to make him half sorry that he had not guessed the truth. At last, breaking into laughter at the long tale I was telling, he sent me off with these words: "Go, and take heed to be an honest man, as indeed I know that you are."

LIII

I went on working assiduously at the button, and at the same time laboured for the Mint, when certain pieces of false money got abroad in Rome, stamped with my own dies. They were brought at once to the Pope, who, hearing things against me, said to Giacopo Balducci, the Master of the Mint, "Take every means in your power to find the criminal; for we are sure that Benvenuto is an honest fellow." That traitor of a master, being in fact my enemy, replied: "Would God, most blessed Father, that it may turn out as you say; for we have some proofs against him." Upon this the Pope turned to the Governor of Rome, and bade him see he found the male-

[2] Varchi gives a very ugly account of this man, Francesco del Nero, who was nicknamed the *Crà del Piccadiglio*, in his History of Florence, book iii. "In the whole city of Florence there never was born, in my belief, a man of such irreligion or of such sordid avarice." Giovio confirms the statement.

[3] *Questo fu quello che.* This may be neuter: *This was the circumstance which.*

factor. During those days the Pope sent for me, and leading cautiously in conversation to the topic of the coins, asked me at the fitting moment: "Benvenuto, should you have the heart to coin false money?" To this I replied that I thought I could do so better than all the rascals who gave their minds to such vile work; for fellows who practise lewd trades of that sort are not capable of earning money, nor are they men of much ability. I, on the contrary, with my poor wits could gain enough to keep me comfortably; for when I set dies for the Mint, each morning before dinner I put at least three crowns into my pocket; this was the customary payment for the dies, and the Master of the Mint bore me a grudge, because he would have liked to have them cheaper; so then, what I earned with God's grace and the world's, sufficed me, and by coining false money I should not have made so much. The Pope very well perceived my drift; and whereas he had formerly given orders that they should see I did not fly from Rome, he now told them to look well about and have no heed of me, seeing he was ill-disposed to anger me, and in this way run the risk of losing me. The officials who received these orders were certain clerks of the Camera, who made the proper search, as was their duty, and soon found the rogue. He was a stamper in the service of the Mint, named Cesare Macherone, and a Roman citizen. Together with this man they detected a metal-founder of the Mint.[1]

LIV

On that very day, as I was passing through the Piazza Navona, and had my fine retriever with me, just when we came opposite the gate of the Bargello, my dog flew barking loudly inside the door upon a youth, who had been arrested at the suit of a man called Donnino (a goldsmith from Parma, and a former pupil of Caradosso), on the charge of having robbed him. The dog strove so violently to tear the fellow to pieces, that the constables were moved to pity. It so happened that he was pleading his own cause with boldness, and Donnino had not evidence enough to support the accusation; and what was more, one of the corporals of the guard, a Genoese, was a friend of the young man's father. The upshot was that, what with the dog and with those other circumstances, they were on the point of releasing their prisoner. When I came up, the dog had lost all fear of sword or staves, and was flying once more at the young

1 The word in Cellini is *ovolatore di zecca*.

man; so they told me if I did not call the brute off they would kill him. I held him back as well as I was able; but just then the fellow, in the act of readjusting his cape, let fall some paper packets from the hood, which Donnino recognised as his property. I too recognised a little ring; whereupon I called out: "This is the thief who broke into my shop and robbed it; and therefore my dog knows him;" then I loosed the dog, who flew again upon the robber. On this the fellow craved for mercy, promising to give back whatever he possessed of mine. When I had secured the dog, he proceeded to restore the gold and silver and the rings which he had stolen from me, and twenty-five crowns in addition. Then he cried once more to me for pity. I told him to make his peace with God, for I should do him neither good nor evil. So I returned to my business; and a few days afterwards, Cesare Macherone, the false coiner, was hanged in the Banchi opposite the Mint; his accomplice was sent to the galleys; the Genoese thief was hanged in the Campo di Fiore, while I remained in better repute as an honest man than I had enjoyed before.

LV

When I had nearly finished my piece, there happened that terrible inundation which flooded the whole of Rome.[1] I waited to see what would happen; the day was well-nigh spent, for the clocks struck twenty-two and the water went on rising formidably. Now the front of my house and shop faced the Banchi, but the back was several yards higher, because it turned toward Monte Giordano; accordingly, bethinking me first of my own safety and in the next place of my honour, I filled my pockets with the jewels, and gave the gold-piece into the custody of my workmen, and then descended barefoot from the back-windows, and waded as well as I could until I reached Monte Cavallo. There I sought out Messer Giovanni Gaddi, clerk of the Camera, and Bastiano Veneziano, the painter. To the former I confided the precious stones, to keep in safety: he had the same regard for me as though I had been his brother. A few days later, when the rage of the river was spent, I returned to my workshop, and finished the piece with such good fortune, through God's grace and my own great industry, that it was held to be the finest masterpiece which had been ever seen in Rome.[2]

1 This took place on the 8th and 9th October, 1530.

2 This famous masterpiece was preserved in the Castle of S. Angelo during the Papal Government of Rome. It was brought out on Christmas, Easter, and S. Peter's days.

When then I took it to the Pope, he was insatiable in praising me, and said: "Were I but a wealthy emperor, I would give my Benvenuto as much land as his eyes could survey; yet being nowadays but needy bankrupt potentates, we will at any rate give him bread enough to satisfy his modest wishes." I let the Pope run on to the end of his rhodomontade,[3] and then asked him for a mace-bearer's place which happened to be vacant. He replied that he would grant me something of far greater consequence. I begged his Holiness to bestow this little thing on me meanwhile by way of earnest. He began to laugh, and said he was willing, but that he did not wish me to serve, and that I must make some arrangement with the other mace-bearers to be exempted. He would allow them through me a certain favour, for which they had already petitioned, namely, the right of recovering their fees at law. This was accordingly done; and that mace-bearer's office brought me in little less than 200 crowns a year.[4]

LVI

I continued to work for the Pope, executing now one trifle and now another, when he commissioned me to design a chalice of exceeding richness. So I made both drawing and model for the piece. The latter was constructed of wood and wax. Instead of the usual top, I fashioned three figures of a fair size in the round; they represented Faith, Hope, and Charity. Corresponding to these, at the base of the cup, were three circular histories in bas-relief. One was the Nativity of Christ, the second the Resurrection, and the third S. Peter crucified head downwards; for thus I had received commission. While I had this work in hand, the Pope was often pleased to look at it; wherefore, observing that his Holiness had never thought again of giving me anything, and knowing that a post in the Piombo was vacant, I asked for this one evening. The good Pope, quite oblivious of his extravagances at the termination of the last piece, said to me: "That post in the Piombo is worth more than 800 crowns a year, so that if I gave it you, you would spend your time in scratching your paunch,[1] and your magnificent handicraft would be lost, and I should bear the blame." I replied at once as thus: "Cats of a good breed mouse better when they are fat than starving; and likewise honest

3 *Quella sua smania di parole.*
4 Cellini received this post among the Mazzieri (who walked like beadles before the Pope) on April 14, 1531. He resigned it in favour of Pietro Cornaro of Venice in 1535.
1 *Grattare il corpo,* which I have translated *scratch your paunch,* is equivalent *to twirl your thumbs.*

men who possess some talent, exercise it to far nobler purport when they have the wherewithal to live abundantly; wherefore princes who provide such folk with competences, let your Holiness take notice, are watering the roots of genius; for genius and talent, at their birth, come into this world lean and scabby; and your Holiness should also know that I never asked for the place with the hope of getting it. Only too happy I to have that miserable post of mace-bearer. On the other I built but castles in the air. Your Holiness will do well, since you do not care to give it me, to bestow it on a man of talent who deserves it, and not upon some fat ignoramus who will spend his time scratching his paunch, if I may quote your Holiness's own words. Follow the example of Pope Giulio's illustrious memory, who conferred an office of the same kind upon Bramante, that most admirable architect."

Immediately on finishing this speech, I made my bow, and went off in a fury. Then Bastiano Veneziano the painter approached, and said: "Most blessed Father, may your Holiness be willing to grant it to one who works assiduously in the exercise of some talent; and as your Holiness knows that I am diligent in my art, I beg that I may be thought worthy of it." The Pope replied: "That devil Benvenuto will not brook rebuke. I was inclined to give it him, but it is not right to be so haughty with a Pope. Therefore I do not well know what I am to do." The Bishop of Vasona then came up, and put in a word for Bastiano, saying: "Most blessed Father, Benvenuto is but young; and a sword becomes him better than a friar's frock. Let your Holiness give the place to this ingenious person Bastiano. Some time or other you will be able to bestow on Benvenuto a good thing, perhaps more suitable to him that this would be." Then the Pope turning to Messer Bartolommeo Valori, told him: "When next you meet Benvenuto, let him know from me that it was he who got that office in the Piombo for Bastiano the painter, and add that he may reckon on obtaining the next considerable place that falls; meanwhile let him look to his behaviour, and finish my commissions." [2]

The following evening, two hours after sundown, I met Messer Bartolommeo Valori [3] at the corner of the Mint; he was preceded

[2] The office of the Piombo in Rome was a bureau in which leaden seals were appended to Bulls and instruments of state. It remained for a long time in the hands of the Cistercians; but it used also to be conferred on laymen, among whom were Bremante and Sebastiano del Piombo. When the latter obtained it, he neglected his art and gave himself up to "scratching his paunch," as Cellini predicted.

[3] Bartolommeo or Baccio Valori, a devoted adherent of the Medici, played an im-

by two torches, and was going in haste to the Pope, who had sent for him. On my taking off my hat, he stopped and called me, and reported in the most friendly manner all the messages the Pope had sent me. I replied that I should complete my work with greater diligence and application than any I had yet attempted, but without the least hope of having any reward whatever from the Pope. Messer Bartolommeo reproved me, saying that this was not the way in which one ought to reply to the advances of a Pope. I answered that I should be mad to reply otherwise—mad if I based my hopes on such promises, being certain to get nothing. So I departed, and went off to my business.

Messer Bartolommeo must have reported my audacious speeches to the Pope, and more perhaps than I had really said; for his Holiness waited above two months before he sent to me, and during that while nothing would have induced me to go uncalled for to the palace. Yet he was dying with impatience to see the chalice, and commissioned Messer Ruberto Pucci to give heed to what I was about.[4] That right worthy fellow came daily to visit me, and always gave me some kindly word, which I returned. The time was drawing nigh now for the Pope to travel toward Bologna;[5] so at last, perceiving that I did not mean to come to him, he made Messer Ruberto bid me bring my work, that he might see how I was getting on. Accordingly, I took it; and having shown, as the piece itself proved, that the most important part was finished, I begged him to advance me five hundred crowns, partly on account, and partly because I wanted gold to complete the chalice. The Pope said: "Go on, go on at work till it is finished." I answered, as I took my leave, that I would finish it if he paid me the money. And so I went away.

LVII

When the Pope took his journey to Bologna, he left Cardinal Salviati as Legate of Rome, and gave him commission to push the work that I was doing forward, adding: "Benvenuto is a fellow who esteems his own great talents but slightly, and us less; look to it then

portant part in Florentine history. He was Clement's commissary to the Prince of Orange during the siege. Afterwards, feeling himself ill repaid for his services, he joined Filippo Strozzi in his opposition to the Medicean rule, and was beheaded in 1537, together with his son and a nephew.

4 Roberto Pucci was another of the devoted Medicean partisans who remained true to his colours. He sat among the forty-eight senators of Alessandro, and was made a Cardinal by Paul III. in 1534.

5 On November 18, 1532, Clement went to meet Charles V. at Bologna, where, in 1529, he had already given him the Imperial crown.

that you keep him always going, so that I may find the chalice finished on my return."

That beast of a Cardinal sent for me after eight days, bidding me bring the piece up. On this I went to him without the piece. No sooner had I shown my face, then he called out: "Where is that onion-stew of yours?[1] Have you got it ready?" I answered: "O most reverend Monsignor, I have not got my onion-stew ready, nor shall I make it ready, unless you give me onions to concoct it with." At these words, the Cardinal, who looked more like a donkey than a man, turned uglier by half than he was naturally; and wanting at once to cut the matter short, cried out: "I'll send you to a galley, and then perhaps you'll have the grace[2] to go on with your labour." The bestial manners of the man made me a beast too; and I retorted: "Monsignor, send me to the galleys when I've done deeds worthy of them; but for my present laches, I snap my fingers at your galleys: and what is more, I tell you that, just because of you, I will not set hand further to my piece. Don't send for me again, for I won't appear, no, not if you summon me by the police."

After this, the good Cardinal tried several times to let me know that I ought to go on working, and to bring him what I was doing to look at. I only told his messengers: "Say to Monsignor that he must send me onions, if he wants me to get my stew ready." Nor gave I ever any other answer; so that he threw up the commission in despair.

LVIII

The Pope came back from Bologna, and sent at once for me, because the Cardinal had written the worst he could of my affairs in his despatches. He was in the hottest rage imaginable, and bade me come upon the instant with my piece. I obeyed. Now, while the Pope was staying at Bologna, I had suffered from an attack of inflammation in the eyes, so painful that I scarce could go on living for the torment; and this was the chief reason why I had not carried out my work. The trouble was so serious that I expected for certain to be left without my eyesight; and I had reckoned up the sum on which I could subsist, if I were blind for life. Upon the way to the Pope, I turned over in my mind what I should put forward to excuse myself for not having been able to advance his work. I thought that while he was in-

1 *Cipollata.* Literally, a show of onions and pumpkins; metaphorically, a mess, gallimaufry.

2 *Arai di grazia di.* I am not sure whether I have given the right shade of meaning in the text above. It may mean: *You will be permitted.*

specting the chalice, I might tell him of my personal embarrassments. However, I was unable to do so; for when I arrived in the presence, he broke out coarsely at me: "Come here with your work; is it finished?" I displayed it; and his temper rising, he exclaimed: "In God's truth I tell thee, thou that makest it thy business to hold no man in regard, that, were it not for decency and order, I would have thee chucked together with thy work there out of windows." Accordingly, when I perceived that the Pope had become no better than a vicious beast, my chief anxiety was how I could manage to withdraw from his presence. So, while he went on bullying, I tucked the piece beneath my cape, and muttered under my breath: "The whole world could not compel a blind man to execute such things as these." Raising his voice still higher, the Pope shouted: "Come here; what say'st thou?" I stayed in two minds, whether or not to dash at full speed down the staircase; then I took my decision and threw myself upon my knees, shouting as loudly as I could, for he too had not ceased from shouting: "If an infirmity has blinded me, am I bound to go on working?" He retorted: "You saw well enough to make your way hither, and I don't believe one word of what you say." I answered, for I noticed he had dropped his voice a little: "Let your Holiness inquire of your physician, and you will find the truth out." He said: "So ho! softly; at leisure we shall hear if what you say is so." Then, perceiving that he was willing to give me hearing, I added: "I am convinced that the only cause of this great trouble which has happened to me is Cardinal Salviati; for he sent to me immediately after your Holiness's departure, and when I presented myself, he called my work a stew of onions, and told me he would send me to complete it in a galley; and such was the effect upon me of his knavish words, that in my passion I felt my face in flame, and so intolerable a heat attacked my eyes that I could not find my own way home. Two days, afterwards, cataracts fell on both my eyes; I quite lost my sight, and after your Holiness's departure I have been unable to work at all."

Rising from my knees, I left the presence without further license. It was afterwards reported to me that the Pope had said: "One can give commissions, but not the prudence to perform them. I did not tell the Cardinal to go so brutally about this business.[1] If it is true that he is suffering from his eyes, of which I shall get information through my doctor, one ought to make allowance for him." A great gentleman, intimate with the Pope, and a man of very distinguished

[1] *Che mettessi tanta mazza.*

parts, happened to be present. He asked who I was, using terms like these: "Most blessed Father, pardon if I put a question. I have seen you yield at one and the same time to the hottest anger I ever observed, and then to the warmest compassion; so I beg your Holiness to tell me who the man is; for if he is a person worthy to be helped, I can teach him a secret which may cure him of that infirmity." The Pope replied: "He is the greatest artist who was ever born in his own craft; one day, when we are together, I will show you some of his marvellous works, and the man himself to boot; and I shall be pleased if we can see our way toward doing something to assist him." Three days after this, the Pope sent for me after dinner-time, and I found that great noble in the presence. On my arrival, the Pope had my cope-button brought, and I in the meantime drew forth my chalice. The nobleman said, on looking at it, that he had never seen a more stupendous piece of work. When the button came, he was still more struck with wonder: and looking me straight in the face, he added. "The man is young, I trow, to be so able in his art, and still apt enough to learn much." He then asked me what my name was. I answered: "My name is Benvenuto." He replied: "And Benvenuto shall I be this day to you. Take flower-de-luces, stalk, blossom, root, together; then decoct them over a slack fire; and with the liquid bathe your eyes several times a day; you will most certainly be cured of that weakness; but see that you purge first, and then go forward with the lotion." The Pope gave me some kind words, and so I went away half satisfied.

LIX

It was true indeed that I had got the sickness; but I believe I caught it from that fine young servant-girl whom I was keeping when my house was robbed. The French disease, for it was that, remained in me more than four months dormant before it showed itself, and then it broke out over my whole body at one instant. It was not like what one commonly observes, but covered my flesh with certain blisters, of the size of six-pences, and rose-coloured. The doctors would not call it the French disease, albeit I told them why I thought it was that. I went on treating myself according to their methods, but derived no benefit. At last, then, I resolved on taking the wood, against the advice of the first physicians in Rome;[1] and I took it

[1] That is, Guiacum, called by the Italians *legno santo.*

with the most scrupulous discipline and rules of abstinence that could be thought of; and after a few days, I perceived in me a great amendment. The result was that at the end of fifty days I was cured and as sound as a fish in the water.

Some time afterwards I sought to mend my shattered health, and with this view I betook myself to shooting when the winter came in. That amusement, however, led me to expose myself to wind and water, and to staying out in marsh-lands; so that, after a few days, I fell a hundred times more ill than I had been before. I put myself once more under doctors' orders and attended to their directions, but grew always worse. When the fever fell upon me, I resolved on having recourse again to the wood; but the doctors forbade it, saying that if I took it with the fever on me, I should not have a week to live. However, I made my mind up to disobey their orders, observed the same diet as I had formerly adopted, and after drinking the decoction four days, was wholly rid of fever. My health improved enormously; and while I was following this cure, I went on always working at the models of the chalice. I may add that, during the time of that strict abstinence, I produced finer things and of more exquisite invention than at any other period of life. After fifty days my health was re-established, and I continued with the utmost care to keep it and confirm it. When at last I ventured to relax my rigid diet, I found myself as wholly free from those infirmities as though I had been born again. Although I took pleasure in fortifying the health I so much longed for, yet I never left off working; both the chalice and the Mint had certainly as much of my attention as was due to them and to myself.

LX

It happened that Cardinal Salviati, who, as I have related, entertained an old hostility against me, had been appointed Legate to Parma. In that city a certain Milanese goldsmith, named Tobbia, was taken up for false coining, and condemned to the gallows and the stake. Representations in his favour, as being a man of great ability, were made to the Cardinal, who suspended the execution of the sentence, and wrote to the Pope, saying the best goldsmith in the world had come into his hands, sentenced to death for coining false money, but that he was a good simple fellow, who could plead in his excuse that he had taken counsel with his confessor, and had received, as he said, from him permission to do this. Thereto he added: "If you send for this great artist to Rome, your Holiness will bring down the overweening arrogance of your favourite Benvenuto, and I am quite certain that Tobbia's work will please you far more than his." The Pope accordingly sent for him at once; and when the man arrived, he made us both appear before him, and commissioned each of us to furnish a design for mounting an unicorn's horn, the finest which had ever been seen, and which had been sold for 17,000 ducats of the Camera. The Pope meant to give it to King Francis; but first he wished it richly set in gold, and ordered us to make sketches for this purpose. When they were finished, we took them to the Pope. That of Tobbia was in the form of a candle-stick, the horn being stuck in it like a candle, and at the base of the piece he had introduced four little unicorns' head of a very poor design. When I saw the thing, I could not refrain from laughing gently in my sleeve. The Pope noticed this, and cried: "Here, show me your sketch!" It was a single unicorn's head, porportioned in size to the horn. I had designed the finest head imaginable; for I took it partly from the horse and partly from the stag, enriching it with fantastic mane and other ornaments. Accordingly, no sooner was it seen, then every one decided in my favour. There were, however, present at the competition certain Milanese gentlemen of the first consequence, who said: "Most blessed Father, your Holiness is sending this magnificent present into France; please to reflect that the French are people of no culture, and will not understand the excellence of Benvenuto's work; pyxes like this one of Tobbia's will suit their taste well, and these too can be finished quicker.[1] Benvenuto will devote himself to completing your chalice, and you will get two pieces done in the same time; moreover, this poor man, whom you have brought to Rome, will have the chance to be employed." The Pope, who was anxious to obtain his chalice, very willingly adopted the advice of the Milanese gentlefolk.

Next day, therefore, he commissioned Tobbia to mount the unicorn's horn, and sent his Master of the Wardrobe to bid me finish the chalice.[2] I replied that I desired nothing in the world more than to complete the beautiful work I had begun: and if the material had been anything but gold, I could very easily have done so myself; but

1 The word I have translated *pyxes* is *ciborii*, vessels for holding the Eucharist.

2 The Master of the Wardrobe was at that time Giovanni Aleotti. I need hardly remind my readers that *Guardaroba* or wardrobe was the apartment in a palace where arms, plate, furniture, and clothes were stored. We shall find, when we come to Cellini's service under Duke Cosimo, that princes spent much of their time in this place.

it being gold, his Holiness must give me some of the metal if he wanted me to get through with my work. To this the vulgar courtier answered: "Zounds! don't ask the Pope for gold, unless you mean to drive him into such a fury as will ruin you." I said: "Oh, my good lord, will your lordship please to tell me how one can make bread without flour? Even so without gold this piece of mine cannot be finished." The Master of the Wardrobe, having an inkling that I had made a fool of him, told me he should report all I had spoken to his Holiness; and this he did. The Pope flew into a bestial passion, and swore he would wait to see if I was so mad as not to finish. More than two months passed thus; and though I had declared I would not give a stroke to the chalice, I did not do so, but always went on working with the greatest interest. When he perceived I was not going to bring it, he began to display real displeasure, and protested he would punish me in one way or another.

A jeweller from Milan in the Papal service happened to be present when these words were spoken. He was called Pompeo, and was closely related to Messer Trajano, the most favoured servant of Pope Clement. The two men came, upon a common understanding, to him and said: "If your Holiness were to deprive Benvenuto of the Mint, perhaps he would take it into his head to complete the chalice." To this the Pope answered: "No; two evil things would happen: first, I should be ill served in the Mint, which concerns me greatly; and secondly, I should certainly not get the chalice." The two Milanese, observing the Pope indisposed towards me, at last so far prevailed that he deprived me of the Mint, and gave it to a young Perugian, commonly known as Fagiuolo.[3] Pompeo came to inform me that his Holiness had taken my place in the Mint away, and that if I did not finish the chalice, he would deprive me of other things besides. I retorted: "Tell his Holiness that he has deprived himself and not me of the Mint, and that he will be doing the same with regard to those other things of which he speaks; and that if he wants to confer the post on me again, nothing will induce me to accept it." The graceless and unlucky fellow went off like an arrow to find the Pope and report this conversation; he added also something of his own invention. Eight days later, the Pope sent the same man to tell me that he did not mean me to finish the chalice, and wanted to have it back precisely at the point to which I had already brought it. I told Pompeo:

[3] Vasari mentions a Girolamo Fagiuoli, who flourished at this period, but calls him a Bolognese.

"This thing is not like the Mint, which it was in his power to take away; but five hundred crowns which I received belong to his Holiness, and I am ready to return them; the piece itself is mine, and with it I shall do what I think best." Pompeo ran off to report my speech, together with some biting words which in my righteous anger I had let fly at himself.

LXI

After the lapse of three days, on a Thursday, there came to me two favourite Chamberlains of his Holiness; one of them is alive now, and a bishop; he was called Messer Pier Giovanni, and was an officer of the wardrobe; the other could claim nobler birth, but his name has escaped me. On arriving they spoke as follows: "The Pope hath sent us, Benvenuto; and since you have not chosen to comply with his request on easy terms, his commands now are that either you should give us up his piece, or that we should take you to prison." Thereupon I looked them very cheerfully in the face, replying: "My lords, if I were to give the work to his Holiness, I should be giving what is mine and not his, and at present I have no intention to make him this gift. I have brought it far forward with great labour, and do not want it to go into the hands of some ignorant beast who will destroy it with no trouble." While I spoke thus, the goldsmith Tobbia was standing by, who even presumptuously asked me for the models also of my work. What I retorted, in words worthy of such a rascal, need not here be repeated. Then, when those gentlemen, the Chamberlains, kept urging me to do quickly what I meant to do, I told them I was ready. So I took my cape up, and before I left the shop, I turned to an image of Christ, with solemn reverence and cap in hand, praying as thus: "O gracious and undying, just and holy our Lord, all the things thou doest are according to thy justice, which hath no peer on earth. Thou knowest that I have exactly reached the age of thirty, and that up to this hour I was never threatened with a prison for any of my actions. Now that it is thy will that I should go to prison, with all my heart I thank thee for this dispensation." Thereat I turned round to the two Chamberlains, and addressed them with a certain lowering look I have: "A man of my quality deserved no meaner catchpoles than your lordships: place me between you, and take me as your prisoner where you like." Those two gentlemen, with the most perfect manners, burst out laughing, and put me between them; and so we went off, talking pleasantly, until they brought me to the Governor of Rome, who was called Il Magalotto.[1] When I reached him (and the Procurator-Fiscal was with him, both waiting for me), the Pope's Chamberlains, still laughing, said to the Governor: "We give up to you this prisoner; now see you take good care of him. We are very glad to have acted in the place of your agents; for Benvenuto has told us that this being his first arrest, he deserved no catchpoles of inferior station then we are." Immediately on leaving us, they sought the Pope; and when they had minutely related the whole matter, he made at first as though he would give way to passion, but afterwards he put control upon himself and laughed, because there were then in the presence certain lords and cardinals, my friends, who had warmly espoused my cause.

Meanwhile, the Governor and the Fiscal were at me, partly bullying, partly expostulating, partly giving advice, and saying it was only reason that a man who ordered work from another should be able to withdraw it at his choice, and in any way which he thought best. To this I replied that such proceedings were not warranted by justice, neither could a Pope act thus; for that a Pope is not of the same kind as certain petty tyrant princes, who treat their folk as badly as they can, without regard to law or justice; and so a Vicar of Christ may not commit any of these acts of violence. Thereat the Governor, assuming his police-court style of threatening and bullying, began to say: "Benvenuto, Benvenuto, you are going about to make me treat you as you deserve." "You will treat me with honour and courtesy, if you wish to act as I deserve." Taking me up again, he cried: "Send for the work at once, and don't wait for a second order." I responded: "My lords, grant me the favour of being allowed to say four more words in my defence." The Fiscal, who was a far more reasonable agent of police than the Governor, turned to him and said: "Monsignor, suppose we let him say a hundred words, if he likes: so long as he gives up the work, that is enough for us." I spoke: "If any man you like to name had ordered a palace or a house to be built, he could with justice tell the master-mason: 'I do not want you to go on working at my house or palace;' and after paying him his labour, he would have the right to dismiss him. Likewise, if a nobleman gave commission for a jewel of a thousand crowns' value to be set, when he saw that the jeweller was not serving him according to

[1] Gregorio Magalotti was a Roman. The Procurator-Fiscal was then Benedetto Valenti. Magalotti is said to have discharged his office with extreme severity, and to have run great risks of his life in consequence.

his desire, he could say: 'Give me back my stone, for I do not want your work.' But in a case of this kind none of those considerations apply; there is neither house nor jewel here; nobody can command me further than that I should return the five hundred crowns which I have had. Therefore, monsignori, do everything you can do; for you will get nothing from me beyond the five hundred crowns. Go and say this to the Pope. Your threats do not frighten me at all; for I am an honest man, and stand in no fear of my sins." The Governor and Fiscal rose, and said they were going to the Pope, and should return with orders which I should soon learn to my cost. So I remained there under guard. I walked up and down a large hall, and they were about three hours away before they came back from the Pope. In that while the flower of our nation among the merchants came to visit me, imploring me not to persist in contending with a Pope, for this might be the ruin of me. I answered them that I had made my mind up quite well what I wished to do.

LXII

No sooner had the Governer returned, together with the Procurator, from the palace, than he sent for me, and spoke to this effect: "Benvenuto, I am certainly sorry to come back from the Pope with such commands as I have received; you must either produce the chalice on the instant, or look to your affairs." Then I replied that "inasmuch as I had never to that hour believed a holy Vicar of Christ could commit an unjust act, so I should like to see it before I did believe it; therefore do the utmost that you can." The Governor rejoined: "I have to report a couple of words more from the Pope to you, and then I will execute the orders given me. He says that you must bring your work to me here, and that after I have seen it put into a box and sealed, I must take it to him. He engages his word not to break the seal, and to return the piece to you untouched. But this much he wants to have done, in order to preserve his own honour in the affair." In return to this speech, I answered, laughing, that I would very willingly give up my work in the way he mentioned, because I should be glad to know for certain what a Pope's word was really worth.

Accordingly, I sent for my piece, and having had it sealed as described, gave it up to him. The Governor repaired again to the Pope, who took the box, according to what the Governor himself told me, and turned it several times about. Then he asked the Governor if he had seen the work; and he replied that he had, and that it had been sealed up in his presence, and added that it had struck him as a very admirable piece. Thereupon the Pope said: "You shall tell Benvenuto that Popes have authority to bind and loose things of far greater consequence than this;" and while thus speaking he opened the box with some show of anger, taking off the string and seals with which it was done up. Afterwards he paid it prolonged attention; and, as I subsequently heard, showed it to Tobbia the goldsmith, who bestowed much praise upon it. Then the Pope asked him if he felt equal to producing a piece in that style. On his saying yes, the Pope told him to follow it out exactly; then turned to the Governor and said: "See whether Benvenuto will give it up; for if he does, he shall be paid the value fixed on it by men of knowledge in this art; but if he is really bent on finishing it himself, let him name a certain time; and if you are convinced that he means to do it, let him have all the reasonable accommodations he may ask for." The Governor replied: "Most blessed Father, I know the violent temper of this young man; so let me have authority to give him a sound rating after my own fashion." The Pope told him to do what he liked with words, though he was sure he would make matters worse; and if at last he could do nothing else, he must order me to take the five hundred crowns to his jeweller, Pompeo.

The Governor returned, sent for me into his cabinet, and casting one of his catchpole's glances, began to speak as follows: "Popes have authority to loose and bind the whole world, and what they do is immediately ratified in heaven. Behold your box, then, which has been opened and inspected by his Holiness." I lifted up my voice at once, and said: "I thank God that now I have learned and can report what the faith of Popes is made of." Then the Governor launched out into brutal bullying words and gestures; but perceiving that they came to nothing, he gave up his attempt as desperate, and spoke in somewhat milder tones after this wise: "Benvenuto, I am very sorry that you are so blind to your own interest; but since it is so, go and take the five hundred crowns, when you think fit, to Pompeo." I took my piece up, went away, and carried the crowns to Pompeo on the instant. It is most likely that the Pope hàd counted on some want of money or other opportunity preventing me from bringing so considerable a sum at once, and was anxious in this way to repiece the broken thread of my obedience. When then he saw Pompeo coming to him with a smile upon his lips and the money in his hand, he soundly rated him, and lamented that the affair had turned out so. Then he said: "Go find Benvenuto in his shop, and treat him with all the courtesies of which your ignorant and brutal nature is capable, and tell him that if he is willing to finish that piece for a reliquary to hold the Corpus Domini when I walk in procession, I will allow him the conveniences he wants in order to complete it; provided only that he goes on working." Pompeo came to me, called me outside the shop, and heaped on me the most mawkish caresses of a donkey,[1] reporting everything the Pope had ordered. I lost no time in answering that "the greatest treasure I could wish for in the world was to regain the favour of so great a Pope, which had been lost to me, not indeed by my fault, but by the fault of my overwhelming illness and the wickedness of those envious men who take pleasure in making mischief; and since the Pope has plenty of servants, do not let him send you round again, if you value your life . . . nay, look well to your safety. I shall not fail, by night or day, to think and do everything I can in the Pope's service; and bear this well in mind, that when you have reported these words to his Holiness, you never in any way whatever meddle with the least of my affairs, for I will make you recognise your errors by the punishment they merit." The fellow related everything to the Pope, but in far more brutal terms than I had used; and thus the matter rested for a time while I again attended to my shop and business.

LXIII

Tobbia the goldsmith meanwhile worked at the setting and the decoration of the unicorn's horn. The Pope, moreover, commissioned him to begin the chalice upon the model he had seen in mine. But when Tobbia came to show him what he had done, he was very discontented, and greatly regretted that he had broken with me, blaming all the other man's works and the people who had introduced them to him; and several times Baccino della Croce came from him to tell me that I must not neglect the reliquary. I answered that I begged his Holiness to let me breathe a little after the great illness I had suffered, and from which I was not as yet wholly free, adding that I would make it clear to him that all the hours in which I could work should be spent in his service. I had indeed begun to make his portrait, and was executing a medal in secret. I fashioned the steel dies for

[1] *Le più isvenevole carezze d'asino.*

stamping this medal in my own house; while I kept a partner in my workshop, who had been my prentice and was called Felice.

At that time, as is the wont of young men, I had fallen in love with a Sicilian girl, who was exceedingly beautiful. On it becoming clear that she returned my affection, her mother perceived how the matter stood, and grew suspicious of what might happen. The truth is that I had arranged to elope with the girl for a year to Florence, unknown to her mother; but she, getting wind of this, left Rome secretly one night, and went off in the direction of Naples. She gave out that she was gone by Cività Vecchia, but she really went by Ostia. I followed them to Cività Vecchia, and did a multitude of mad things to discover her. It would be too long to narrate them all in detail; enough that I was on the point of losing my wits or dying. After two months she wrote to me that she was in Sicily, extremely unhappy. I meanwhile was indulging myself in all the pleasures man can think of, and had engaged in another love affair, merely to drown the memory of my real passion.

LXIV

It happened through a variety of singular accidents that I became intimate with a Sicilian priest, who was a man of very elevated genius and well instructed in both Latin and Greek letters. In the course of conversation one day we were led to talk about the art of necromancy; apropos of which I said: "Throughout my whole life I have had the most intense desire to see or learn something of this art." Thereto the priest replied: "A stout soul and a steadfast must the man have who sets himself to such an enterprise." I answered that of strength and steadfastness of soul I should have enough and to spare, provided I found the opportunity. Then the priest said: "If you have the heart to dare it, I will amply satisfy your curiosity." Accordingly we agreed upon attempting the adventure.

The priest one evening made his preparations, and bade me find a comrade, or not more than two. I invited Vincenzio Romoli, a very dear friend of mine, and the priest took with him a native of Pistoja, who also cultivated the black art. We went together to the Coliseum; and there the priest, having arrayed himself in necromancer's robes, began to describe circles on the earth with the finest ceremonies that can be imagined. I must say that he had made us bring precious perfumes and fire, and also drugs of fetid odour. When the preliminaries were completed, he made the entrance into the circle; and taking us by the hand, introduced us one by one inside it. Then he assigned our several functions; to the necromancer, his comrade, he gave the pentacle to hold; the other two of us had to look after the fire and the perfumes; and then he began his incantations. This lasted more than an hour and a half; when several legions appeared, and the Coliseum was all full of devils. I was occupied with the precious perfumes, and when the priest perceived in what numbers they were present, he turned to me and said: "Benvenuto, ask them something." I called on them to reunite me with my Sicilian Angelica. That night we obtained no answer; but I enjoyed the greatest satisfaction of my curiosity in such matters. The necromancer said that we should have to go a second time, and that I should obtain the full accomplishment of my request; but he wished me to bring with me a little boy of pure virginity.

I chose one of my shop-lads, who was about twelve years old, and invited Vincenzio Romoli again; and we also took a certain Agnolino Gaddi, who was a very intimate friend of both. When we came once more to the place appointed, the necromancer made just the same preparations, attended by the same and even more impressive details. Then he introduced us into the circle, which he had reconstructed with art more admirable and yet more wondrous ceremonies. Afterwards he appointed my friend Vincenzio to the ordering of the perfumes and the fire, and with him Agnolino Gaddi. He next placed in my hand the pentacle, which he bid me turn toward the points he indicated, and under the pentacle I held the little boy, my workman. Now the necromancer began to utter those awful invocations, calling by name on multitudes of demons who are captains of their legions, and these he summoned by the virtue and potency of God, the Uncreated, Living, and Eternal, in phrases of the Hebrew, and also of the Greek and Latin tongues, insomuch that in a short space of time the whole Coliseum was full of a hundredfold as many as had appeared upon the first occasion. Vincenzio Romoli, together with Agnolino, tended the fire and heaped on quantities of precious perfumes. At the advice of the necromancer, I again demanded to be reunited with Angelica. The sorcerer turned to me and said: "Hear you what they have replied; that in the space of one month you will be where she is?" Then once more he prayed me to stand firm by him, because the legions were a thousandfold more than he had summoned, and were the most dangerous of all the denizens of hell; and now that they had settled what I asked, it behoved us to be civil to them and dismiss them gently. On the other side, the boy, who was beneath the pentacle, shrieked out in terror that a million of the fiercest men were swarming round and threatening us. He said, moreover, that four huge giants had appeared, who were striving to force their way inside the circle. Meanwhile the necromancer, trembling with fear, kept doing his best with mild and soft persuasions to dismiss them. Vincenzio Romoli, who quaked like an aspen leaf, looked after the perfumes. Though I was quite as frightened as the rest of them, I tried to show it less, and inspired them all with marvellous courage; but the truth is that I had given myself up for dead when I saw the terror of the necromancer. The boy had stuck his head between his knees, exclaiming: "This is how I will meet death, for we are certainly dead men." Again I said to him: "These creatures are all inferior to us, and what you see is only smoke and shadow; so then raise your eyes." When he had raised them he cried out: "The whole Coliseum is in flames, and the fire is advancing on us;" then covering his face with his hands, he groaned again that he was dead, and that he could not endure the sight longer. The necromancer appealed for my support, entreating me to stand firm by him, and to have assafetida flung upon the coals; so I turned to Vincenzio Romoli, and told him to make the fumigation at once. While uttering these words I looked at Agnolino Gaddi, whose eyes were starting from their sockets in his terror, and who was more than half dead, and said to him: "Agnolo, in time and place like this we must not yield to fright, but do the utmost to bestir ourselves; therefore, up at once, and fling a handful of that assafetida upon the fire." Agnolo, at the moment when he moved to do this, let fly such a volley from his breech, that it was far more effectual than the assafetida.[1] The boy, roused by that great stench and noise, lifted his face a little, and hearing me laugh, he plucked up courage, and said the devils were taking to flight tempestuously. So we abode thus until the matin-bells began to sound. Then the boy told us again that but few remained, and those were at a distance. When the necromancer had concluded his ceremonies, he cut off his wizard's robe, and packed up a great bundle of books which he had brought with him; then, all together, we issued with him from the circle, huddling as close as we could to one another, especially the boy, who had got into the middle, and taken the necromancer by his gown and me by the cloak. All the while that we were going toward our

[1] *Fece una istrombazzata di coregge con tanta abundanzia di merda.*

houses in the Banchi, he kept saying that two of the devils he had seen in the Coliseum were gambolling in front of us, skipping now along roofs and now upon the ground. The necromancer assured me that, often as he had entered magic circles, he had never met with such a serious affair as this. He also tried to persuade me to assist him in consecrating a book, by means of which we should extract immeasurable wealth, since we could call up fiends to show us where treasures were, whereof the earth is full; and after this wise we should become the richest of mankind: love affairs like mine were nothing but vanities and follies without consequence. I replied that if I were a Latin scholar I should be very willing to do what he suggested. He continued to persuade me by arguing that Latin scholarship was of no importance, and that, if he wanted, he could have found plenty of good Latinists; but that he had never met with a man of soul so firm as mine, and that I ought to follow his counsel. Engaged in this conversation, we reached our homes, and each one of us dreamed all that night of devils.

LXV

As we were in the habit of meeting daily, the necromancer kept urging me to join in his adventure. Accordingly, I asked him how long it would take, and where we should have to go. To this he answered that we might get through with it in less than a month, and that the most suitable locality for the purpose was the hill country of Norcia;[1] a master of his in the art had indeed consecrated such a book quite close to Rome, at a place called the Badia di Farfa; but he had met with some difficulties there, which would not occur in the mountains of Norcia; the peasants also of that district are people to be trusted, and have some practice in these matters, so that at a pinch they are able to render valuable assistance.

This priestly sorcerer moved me so by his persuasions that I was well disposed to comply with his request; but I said I wanted first to finish the medals I was making for the Pope. I had confided what I was doing about them to him alone, begging him to keep my secret. At the same time I never stopped asking him if he believed that I should be reunited to my Sicilian Angelica at the time appointed; for the date was drawing near, and I thought it singular that I heard

1 This district of the Central Apennines was always famous for witches, poisoners, and so forth. The Farfa mentioned below is a village of the Sabine hills.

nothing about her. The necromancer told me that it was quite certain I should find myself where she was, since the devils never break their word and when they promise, as they did on that occasion; but he bade me keep my eyes open, and be on the look out against some accident which might happen to me in that connection, and put restraint upon myself to endure somewhat against my inclination, for he could discern a great and imminent danger in it: well would it be for me if I went with him to consecrate the book, since this would avert the peril that menaced me, and would make us both most fortunate.

I was beginning to hanker after the adventure more than he did; but I said that a certain Maestro Giovanni of Castel Bolognese had just come to Rome, very ingenious in the art of making medals of the sort I made in steel, and that I thirsted for nothing more than to compete with him and take the world by storm with some great masterpiece, which I hoped would annihilate all those enemies of mine by the force of genius and not the sword.[2] The sorcerer on his side went on urging: "Nay, prithee, Benvenuto, come with me and shun a great disaster which I see impending over you." However, I had made my mind up, come what would, to finish my medal, and we were now approaching the end of the month. I was so absorbed and enamoured by my work that I thought no more about Angelica or anything of that kind, but gave my whole self up to it.

LXVI

It happened one day, close on the hours of vespers, that I had to go at an unusual time for me from my house to my workshop; for I ought to say that the latter was in the Banchi, while I lived behind the Banchi, and went rarely to the shop; all my business there I left in the hands of my partner, Felice. Having stayed a short while in the workshop, I remembered that I had to say something to Alessandro del Bene. So I arose, and when I reached the Banchi, I met a man called Ser Benedetto, who was a great friend of mine. He was a notary, born in Florence, son of a blind man who said prayers about the streets for alms, and a Sienese by race. This Ser Benedetto had been very many years at Naples; afterwards he had settled in Rome, where he transacted business for some Sienese merchants of the Chigi.[1]

[2] Gio. Bernardi had been in the Duke of Ferrara's service. Giovio brought him to Rome, where he was patronised by the Cardinals Salviati and De' Medici. He made a famous medal of Clement VII., and was a Pontifical mace-bearer. He died at Faenza in 1555.

[1] The MS. has Figi; but this is probably a mistake of the amanuensis.

My partner had over and over again asked him for some moneys which were due for certain little rings confided to Ser Benedetto. That very day, meeting him in the Banchi, he demanded his money rather roughly, as his wont was. Benedetto was walking with his masters, and they, annoyed by the interruption, scolded him sharply, saying they would be served by somebody else, in order not to have to listen to such barking. Ser Benedetto did the best he could to excuse himself, swore that he had paid the goldsmith, and said he had no power to curb the rage of madmen. The Sienese took his words ill, and dismissed him on the spot. Leaving them, he ran like an arrow to my shop, probably to take revenge upon Felice. It chanced that just in the middle of the street we met. I, who had heard nothing of the matter, greeted him most kindly, according to my custom, to which courtesy he replied with insults. Then what the sorcerer had said flashed all at once upon my mind; and bridling myself as well as I was able, in the way he bade me, I answered: "Good brother Benedetto, don't fly into a rage with me, for I have done you no harm, nor do I know anything about these affairs of yours. Please go and finish what you have to do with Felice. He is quite capable of giving you a proper answer; but inasmuch as I know nothing about it, you are wrong to abuse me in this way especially as you are well aware that I am not the man to put up with insults." He retorted that I knew everything, and that he was the man to make me bear a heavier load than that, and that Felice and I were two great rascals. By this time a crowd had gathered round to hear the quarrel. Provoked by his ugly words, I stooped and took up a lump of mud—for it had rained—and hurled it with a quick and unpremeditated movement at his face. He ducked his head, so that the mud hit him in the middle of the skull. There was a stone in it with several sharp angles, one of which striking him, he fell stunned like a dead man: whereupon all the bystanders, seeing the great quantity of blood, judged that he was really dead.

LXVII

While he was still lying on the ground, and people were preparing to carry him away, Pompeo the jeweller passed by. The Pope had sent for him to give orders about some jewels. Seeing the fellow in such a miserable plight, he asked who had struck him; on which they told him: "Benvenuto did it, but the stupid creature brought it down upon himself." No sooner had Pompeo reached the Pope than he began to speak: "Most blessed Father, Benvenuto has this very moment murdered Tobbia; I saw it with my own eyes." On this the Pope in a fury ordered the Governor, who was in the presence, to take and hang me at once in the place where the homicide had been committed, adding that he must do all he could to catch me, and not appear again before him until he had hanged me.

When I saw the unfortunate Benedetto stretched upon the ground, I thought at once of the peril I was in, considering the power of my enemies, and what might ensue from this disaster. Making off, I took refuge in the house of Messer Giovanni Gaddi, clerk of the Camera, with the intention of preparing as soon as possible to escape from Rome. He, however, advised me not to be in such a hurry, for it might turn out perhaps that the evil was not so great as I imagined; and calling Messer Annibal Caro, who lived with him, bade him go for information.

While these arrangements were being made, a Roman gentleman appeared, who belonged to the household of Cardinal de' Medici, who had been sent by him.[1] Taking Messer Giovanni and me apart, he told us that the Cardinal had reported to him what the Pope said, and that there was no way of helping me out of the scrape; it would be best for me to shun the first fury of the storm by flight, and not to risk myself in any house in Rome. Upon this gentleman's departure, Messer Giovanni looked me in the face as though he were about to cry, and said: "Ah me! Ah woe is me! there is nothing I can do to aid you!" I replied: "By God's means, I shall aid myself alone; only I request you to put one of your horses at my disposal." They had already saddled a black Turkish horse, the finest and the best in Rome. I mounted with an arquebuse upon the saddle-bow, wound up in readiness to fire, if need were.[2] When I reached Ponte Sisto, I found the whole of the Bargello's guard there, both horse and foot. So, making a virtue of necessity, I put my horse boldly to a sharp trot, and with God's grace, being somehow unperceived by them, passed freely through. Then, with all the speed I could, I took the road to Palombara, a fief of my lord Giovanbatista Savello, whence I sent the horse

1 Ippolito de' Medici was a Cardinal, much against his natural inclination. When he went as Papal Legate to Hungary in 1532, he assumed the airs and style of a Condottiere. His jealousy of his cousin Alessandro led to his untimely death by poison in 1535.

2 The gun was an *arquebuso a ruola*, which had a wheel to cock it.

back to Messer Giovanni, without, however, thinking it well to inform him where I was.[3] Lord Giovanbatista, after very kindly entertaining me two days, advised me to remove and go towards Naples till the storm blew over. So, providing me with company, be set me on the way to Naples.

While travelling, I met a sculptor of my acquaintance, who was going to San Germano to finish the tomb of Piero de' Medici at Monte Cassino.[4] His name was Solosmeo, and he gave me the news that on the very evening of the fray, Pope Clement sent one of his chamberlains to inquire how Tobbia was getting on. Finding him at work, unharmed, and without even knowing anything about the matter, the messenger went back and told the Pope, who turned round to Pompeo and said: "You are a good-for-nothing rascal; but I promise you well that you have stirred a snake up which will sting you, and serve you right!" Then he addressed himself to Cardinal de' Medici, and commissioned him to look after me, adding that he should be very sorry to let me slip through his fingers. And so Solosmeo and I went on our way singing toward Monte Cassino, intending to pursue our journey thence in company toward Naples.

LXVIII

When Solosmeo had inspected his affairs at Monte Cassino, we resumed our journey; and having come within a mile of Naples, we were met by an innkeeper, who invited us to his house, and said he had been at Florence many years with Carlo Ginori;[1] adding, that if we put up at his inn, he would treat us most kindly, for the reason that we both were Florentines. We told him frequently that we did not want to go to him. However, he kept passing, sometimes in front and sometimes behind, perpetually repeating that he would have us stop at his hostelry. When this began to bore me, I asked if he could tell me anything about a certain Sicilian woman called Beatrice, who

3 A village in the Sabina, north of Tivoli. Giov. Battista Savelli, of a great Roman house, was a captain of cavalry in the Papal service after 1530. In 1540 he entered the service of Duke Cosimo, and died in 1553.

4 This sculptor was Antonio Solosmeo of Settignano. The monument erected to Piero de' Medici (drowned in the Garigliano, 1504) at Monte Cassino is by no means a brilliant piece of Florentine art. Piero was the exiled son of Lorenzo the Magnificent; and the Medici, when they regained their principality, erected this monument to his memory, employing Antonio da San Gallo, Francesco da San Gallo, and a Neapolitan, Matteo de' Quaranta. The work was begun in 1532. Solosmeo appears from this passage in Cellini to have taken the execution of it over.

1 A Gonfalonier of the Republic in 1527.

had a beautiful daughter named Angelica, and both were courtesans. Taking it into his head that I was jeering him, he cried out: "God send mischief to all courtesans and such as favour them!" Then he set spurs to his horse, and made off as though he was resolved to leave us. I felt some pleasure at having rid myself in so fair a manner of that ass of an innkeeper; and yet I was rather the loser than the gainer; for the great love I bore Angelica had come back to my mind, and while I was conversing, not without some lover's sighs, upon this subject with Solosmeo, we saw the man returning to us at a gallop. When he drew up, he said: "Two or perhaps three days ago a woman and a girl came back to a house in my neighbourhood; they had the names you mentioned, but whether they are Sicilians I cannot say." I answered: "Such power over me has that name of Angelica, that I am now determined to put up at your inn."

We rode on all together with mine host into the town of Naples, and descended at his house. Minutes seemed years to me till I had put my things in order, which I did in the twinkling of an eye; then I went to the house, which was not far from our inn, and found there my Angelica, who greeted me with infinite demonstrations of the most unbounded passion. I stayed with her from evenfall until the following morning, and enjoyed such pleasure as I never had before or since; but while drinking deep of this delight, it occurred to my mind how exactly on that day the month expired, which had been prophesied within the necromantic circle by the devils. So then let every man who enters into relation with those spirits weigh well the inestimable perils I have passed through!

LXIX

I happened to have in my purse a diamond, which I showed about among the goldsmiths; and though I was but young, my reputation as an able artist was so well known even at Naples that they welcomed me most warmly. Among others, I made acquaintance with a most excellent companion, a jeweller, Messer Domenico Fontana by name. This worthy man left his shop for the three days that I spent in Naples, nor ever quitted my company, but showed me many admirable monuments of antiquity in the city and its neighbourhood. Moreover, he took me to pay my respects to the Viceroy of Naples, who had let him know that he should like to see me. When I presented myself to his Excellency, he received me with much honour;[1] and while we were exchanging compliments, the diamond which I have mentioned caught his eye. He made me show it him, and prayed me, if I parted with it, to give him the refusal. Having taken back the stone, I offered it again to his Excellency, adding that the diamond and I were at his service. Then he said that the diamond pleased him well, but that he should be much better pleased if I were to stay with him; he would make such terms with me as would cause me to feel satisfied. We spoke many words of courtesy on both sides; and then coming to the merits of the diamond, his Excellency bade me without hesitation name the price at which I valued it. Accordingly I said that it was worth exactly two hundred crowns. He rejoined that in his opinion I had not overvalued it; but that since I had set it, and he knew me for the first artist in the world, it would not make the same effect when mounted by another hand. To this I said that I had not set the stone, and that it was not well set; its brilliancy was due to its own excellence; and that if I were to mount it afresh, I could make it show far better than it did. Then I put my thumb-nail to the angles of its facets, took it from the ring, cleaned it up a little, and handed it to the Viceroy. Delighted and astonished, he wrote me out a cheque[2] for the two hundred crowns I had demanded.

When I returned to my lodging, I found letters from the Cardinal de' Medici, in which he told me to come back post-haste to Rome, and to dismount without delay at the palace of his most reverend lordship. I read the letter to my Angelica, who begged me with tears of affection either to remain in Naples or to take her with me. I replied that if she was disposed to come with me, I would give up to her keeping the two hundred ducats I had received from the Viceroy. Her mother perceiving us in this close conversation, drew nigh and said: "Benvenuto, if you want to take my daughter to Rome, leave me a sum of fifteen ducats, to pay for my lying-in, and then I will travel after you." I told the old harridan that I would very gladly leave her thirty if she would give me my Angelica. We made the bargain, and Angelica entreated me to buy her a gown of black velvet, because the stuff was cheap at Naples. I consented to everything, sent for the velvet, settled its price and paid for it; then the old woman, who thought me over head and ears in love, begged for a gown of fine cloth for

1 The Spanish Viceroy was at this time Pietro Alvarez de Toledo, Marquis of Villafranca, and uncle of the famous Duke of Alva. He governed Naples for twenty years, from 1532 onwards.

2 *Mi fece una polissa.* A *polissa* was an order for money, practically identical with our *cheque*.

herself, as well as other outlays for her sons, and a good bit more money than I had offered. I turned to her with a pleasant air and said: "My dear Beatrice, are you satisfied with what I offered?" She answered that she was not; thereupon I said that what was not enough for her would be quite enough for me; and having kissed Angelica, we parted, she with tears, and I with laughter, and off at once I set for Rome.

LXX

I left Naples by night with my money in my pocket, and this I did to prevent being set upon or murdered, as is the way there; but when I came to Selciata,[1] I had to defend myself with great address and bodily prowess from several horsemen who came out to assassinate me. During the following days, after leaving Solosmeo at his work in Monte Cassino, I came one morning to breakfast at the inn of Adanagni;[2] and when I was near the house, I shot some birds with my arquebuse. An iron spike, which was in the lock of my musket, tore my right hand. Though the wound was not of any consequence, it seemed to be so, because it bled abundantly. Going into the inn, I put my horse up, and ascended to a large gallery, where I found a party of Neapolitan gentlemen just upon the point of sitting down to table; they had with them a young woman of quality, the loveliest I ever saw. At the moment when I entered the room, I was followed by a very brave young serving-man of mine holding a big partisan in his hand. The sight of us, our arms, and the blood, inspired those poor gentlemen with such terror, particularly as the place was known to be a nest of murderers, that they rose from table and called on God in a panic to protect them. I began to laugh, and said that God had protected them already, for that I was a man to defend them against whoever tried to do them harm. Then I asked them for something to bind up my wounded hand; and the charming lady took out a handkerchief richly embroidered with gold, wishing to make a bandage with it. I refused; but she tore the piece in half, and in the gentlest manner wrapt my hand up with her fingers. The company thus having regained confidence, we dined together very gaily; and when the meal was over, we all mounted and went off together. The gentlemen, however, were not as yet quite at their ease; so they left me in their

1 Ponte a Selice, between Capua and Aversa.

2 Anagni, where Boniface VIII. was outraged to the death by the French partisans of Philip le Bel.

cunning to entertain the lady, while they kept at a short distance behind. I rode at her side upon a pretty little horse of mine, making signs to my servant that he should keep somewhat apart, which gave us the opportunity of discussing things that are not sold by the apothecary.[3] In this way I journeyed to Rome with the greatest enjoyment I have ever had.

When I got to Rome, I dismounted at the palace of Cardinal de' Medici, and having obtained an audience of his most reverend lordship, paid my respects, and thanked him warmly for my recall. I then entreated him to secure me from imprisonment, and even from a fine if that were possible. The Cardinal was very glad to see me; told me to stand in no fear; then turned to one of his gentlemen, called Messer Pier Antonio Pecci of Siena, ordering him to tell the Bargello not to touch me.[4] He then asked him how the man was going on whose head I had broken with the stone. Messer Pier Antonio replied that he was very ill, and that he would probably be even worse; for when he heard that I was coming back to Rome, he swore he would die to serve me an ill turn. When the Cardinal heard that, he burst into a fit of laughter, and cried: "The fellow could not have taken a better way than this to make us know that he was born a Sienese." After that he turned to me and said: "For our reputation and your own, refrain these four or five days from going about in the Banchi; after that go where you like, and let fools die at their own pleasure."

I went home and set myself to finishing the medal which I had begun, with the head of Pope Clement and a figure of Peace on the reverse. The figure was a slender woman, dressed in very thin drapery, gathered at the waist, with a little torch in her hand, which was burning a heap of arms bound together like a trophy. In the background I had shown part of a temple, where was Discord chained with a load of fetters. Round about it ran a legend in these words: *Clauduntur belli portæ.*[5]

During the time that I was finishing this medal, the man whom I had wounded recovered, and the Pope kept incessantly asking for me. I, however, avoided visiting Cardinal de' Medici; for whenever I showed my face before him, his lordship gave me some commission of importance, which hindered me from working at my medal to the

3 *i. e.,* private and sentimental.
4 This Pecci passed into the service of Caterina de' Medici. In 1551 he schemed to withdraw Siena from the Spanish to the French cause, and was declared a rebel.
5 The medal was struck to celebrate the peace in Christendom between 1530 and 1536.

end. Consequently Messer Pier Carnesecchi, who was a great favourite of the Pope's, undertook to keep me in sight, and let me adroitly understand how much the Pope desired my services.[6] I told him that in a few days I would prove to his Holiness that his service had never been neglected by me.

LXXI

Not many days had passed before, my medal being finished, I stamped it in gold, silver, and copper. After I had shown it to Messer Pietro, he immediately introduced me to the Pope. It was on a day in April after dinner, and the weather very fine; the Pope was in the Belvedere. After entering the presence, I put my medals together with the dies of steel into his hand. He took them, and recognising at once their mastery of art, looked Messer Piero in the face and said: "The ancients never had such medals made for them as these."

While he and the others were inspecting them, taking up now the dies and now the medals in their hands, I began to speak as submissively as I was able: "If a greater power had not controlled the working of my inauspicious stars, and hindered that with which they violently menaced me, your Holiness, without your fault or mine, would have lost a faithful and loving servant. It must, most blessed Father, be allowed that in those cases where men are risking all upon one throw, it is not wrong to do as certain poor and simple men are wont to say, who tell us we must mark seven times and cut once.[1] Your Holiness will remember how the malicious and lying tongue of my bitter enemy so easily aroused your anger, that you ordered the Governor to have me taken on the spot and hanged; but I have no doubt that when you had become aware of the irreparable act by which you would have wronged yourself, in cutting off from you a servant such as even now your Holiness hath said he is, I am sure, I repeat, that, before God and the world, you would have felt no trifling twinges of remorse. Excellent and virtuous fathers, and masters of like quality, ought not to let their arm in wrath descend upon their sons and servants with such inconsiderate haste, seeing that subsequent repentance will avail them nothing. But now that God has

[6] Piero Carnesecchi was one of the martyrs of free-thought in Italy. He adopted Protestant opinions, and was beheaded and burned in Rome, August 1567.

[1] *Segnar sette e tagliar uno.* A proverb derived possibly from felling trees; or, as some commentators interpret, from the points made by sculptors on their marble before they block the statue out.

overruled the malign influences of the stars and saved me for your Holiness, I humbly beg you another time not to let yourself so easily be stirred to rage against me."

The Pope had stopped from looking at the medals and was now listening attentively to what I said. There were many noblemen of the greatest consequence present, which made him blush a little, as it were for shame; and not knowing how else to extricate himself from this entanglement, he said that he could not remember having given such an order. I changed the conversation in order to cover his embarrassment. His Holiness then began to speak again about the medals, and asked what method I had used to stamp them so marvellously, large as they were; for he had never met with ancient pieces of that size. We talked a little on this subject; but being not quite easy that I might not begin another lecture sharper than the last, he praised my medals, and said they gave him the greatest satisfaction, but that he should like another reverse made according to a fancy of his own, if it were possible to stamp them with two different patterns. I said that it was possible to do so. Then his Holiness commissioned me to design the history of Moses when he strikes the rock and water issues from it, with this motto: *Ut bibat populus.*[2] At last he added: "Go, Benvenuto; you will not have finished it before I have provided for your fortune." After I had taken leave, the Pope proclaimed before the whole company that he would give me enough to live on wealthily without the need of labouring for any one but him. So I devoted myself entirely to working out this reverse with the Moses on it.

LXXII

In the meantime the Pope was taken ill, and his physicians thought the case was dangerous. Accordingly my enemy began to be afraid of me, and engaged some Neapolitan soldiers to do to me what he was dreading I might do to him.[1] I had therefore much trouble to defend my poor life. In course of time, however, I completed the reverse; and when I took it to the Pope, I found him in bed in a most deplorable condition. Nevertheless, he received me with the greatest kindness, and wished to inspect the medals and the dies. He sent for spectacles and lights, but was unable to see anything

2 The medal commemorated a deep well sunk by Clement at Orvieto.

1 The meaning of this is, that if Clement died, Cellini would have had his opportunity of vengeance during the anarchy which followed a vacancy of the Papal See.

clearly. Then he began to fumble with his fingers at them, and having felt them a short while, he fetched a deep sigh, and said to his attendants that he was much concerned about me, but that if God gave him back his health he would make it all right.

Three days afterwards the Pope died, and I was left with all my labour lost; yet I plucked up courage, and told myself that these medals had won me so much celebrity, that any Pope who was elected would give me work to do, and peradventure bring me better fortune. Thus I encouraged and put heart into myself, and buried in oblivion all the injuries which Pompeo had done me. Then putting on my arms and girding my sword, I went to San Piero, and kissed the feet of the dead Pope, not without shedding tears. Afterwards I returned to the Banchi to look on at the great commotion which always happens on such occasions.

While I was sitting in the street with several of my friends, Pompeo went by, attended by ten men very well armed; and when he came just opposite, he stopped, as though about to pick a quarrel with myself. My companions, brave and adventurous young men, made signs to me to draw my sword; but it flashed through my mind that if I drew, some terrible mischief might result for persons who were wholly innocent. Therefore I considered that it would be better if I put my life to risk alone. When Pompeo had stood there time enough to say two Ave Marias, he laughed derisively in my direction; and going off, his fellows also laughed and wagged their heads, with many other insolent gestures. My companions wanted to begin the fray at once; but I told them hotly that I was quite able to conduct my quarrels to an end by myself, and that I had no need of stouter fighters than I was; so that each of them might mind his business. My friends were angry and went off muttering. Now there was among them my dearest comrade, named Albertaccio del Bene, own brother to Alessandro and Albizzo, who is now a very rich man in Lyons. He was the most redoubtable young man I ever knew, and the most high-spirited, and loved me like himself; and insomuch as he was well aware that my forbearance had not been inspired by want of courage, but by the most daring bravery, for he knew me down to the bottom of my nature, he took my words up and begged me to favour him so far as to associate him with myself in all I meant to do. I replied: "Dear Albertaccio, dearest to me above all men that live, the time will very likely come when you shall give me aid; but in this case, if you love me, do not attend to me, but look to your own business, and go at once like our other friends, for now there is no time to lose." These words were spoken in one breath.

LXXIII

In the meanwhile my enemies had proceeded slowly toward Chiavica, as the place was called, and had arrived at the crossing of several roads, going in different directions; but the street in which Pompeo's house stood was the one which leads straight to the Campo di Fiore. Some business or other made him enter the apothecary's shop which stood at the corner of Chiavica, and there he stayed a while transacting it. I had just been told that he had boasted of the insult which he fancied he had put upon me; but be that as it may, it was to his misfortune; for precisely when I came up to the corner, he was leaving the shop and his bravi had opened their ranks and received him in their midst. I drew a little dagger with a sharpened edge, and breaking the line of his defenders, laid my hands upon his breast so quickly and coolly, that none of them were able to prevent me. Then I aimed to strike him in the face; but fright made him turn his head round; and I stabbed him just beneath the ear. I only gave two blows, for he fell stone dead at the second. I had not meant to kill him; but as the saying goes, knocks are not dealt by measure. With my left hand I plucked back the dagger, and with my right hand drew my sword to defend my life. However, all those bravi ran up to the corpse and took no action against me; so I went back alone through Strada Giulia, considering how best to put myself in safety.

I had walked about three hundred paces, when Piloto the goldsmith, my very good friend, came up and said: "Brother, now that the mischief's done, we must see to saving you." I replied: "Let us go to Albertaccio del Bene's house; it is only a few minutes since I told him I should soon have need of him." When we arrived there, Albertaccio and I embraced with measureless affection; and soon the whole flower of the young men of the Banchi, of all nations except the Milanese, came crowding in; and each and all made proffer of their own life to save mine. Messer Luigi Rucellai also sent with marvellous promptitude and courtesy to put his services at my disposal, as did many other great folk of his station; for they all agreed in blessing my hands,[1] judging that Pompeo had done me too great

[1] *Tutti d' accordo mi benedissono le mani.* This is tantamount to approving Cellini's handiwork in murdering Pompeo.

and unforgivable an injury, and marvelling that I had put up with him so long.

LXXIV

Cardinal Cornaro, on hearing of the affair, despatched thirty soldiers, with as many partisans, pikes, and arquebuses, to bring me with all due respect to his quarters.[1] This he did unasked; whereupon I accepted the invitation, and went off with them, while more than as many of the young men bore me company. Meanwhile, Messer Traiano, Pompeo's relative and first chamberlain to the Pope, sent a Milanese of high rank to Cardinal de' Medici, giving him news of the great crime I had committed, and calling on his most reverend lordship to chastise me. The Cardinal retorted on the spot: "His crime would indeed have been great if he had not committed this lesser one; thank Messer Traiano from me for giving me this information of a fact of which I had not heard before." Then he turned and in presence of the nobleman said to the Bishop of Frullì,[2] his gentleman and intimate acquaintance: "Search diligently after my friend Benvenuto; I want to help and defend him; and whoso acts against him acts against myself." The Milanese nobleman went back, much disconcerted, while the Bishop of Frullì come to visit me at Cardinal Cornaro's palace. Presenting himself to the Cardinal, he related how Cardinal de' Medici had sent for Benvenuto, and wanted to be his protector. Now Cardinal Cornaro, who had the touchy temper of a bear, flew into a rage, and told the Bishop he was quite as well able to defend me as Cardinal de' Medici. The Bishop, in reply, entreated to be allowed to speak with me on some matters of his patron which had nothing to do with the affair. Cornaro bade him for that day make as though he had already talked with me.

Cardinal de' Medici was very angry. However, I went the following night, without Cornaro's knowledge, and under good escort, to pay him my respects. Then I begged him to grant me the favour of leaving me where I was, and told him of the great courtesy which Cornaro had shown me; adding that if his most reverend lordship suffered me to stay, I should gain one friend the more in my hour of need; otherwise his lordship might dispose of me exactly as he thought

1 This was Francesco, brother to Cardinal Marco Cornaro. He received the hat in 1528, while yet a layman, and the Bishopric of Brescia in 1531.

2 Forlì. The Bishop was Bernardo de' Medici.

best. He told me to do as I liked; so I returned to Cornaro's palace, and a few days afterwards the Cardinal Farnese was elected Pope.[3]

After he had put affairs of greater consequence in order, the new Pope sent for me, saying that he did not wish any one else to strike his coins. To these words of his Holiness a gentleman very privately acquainted with him, named Messer Latino Juvinale, made answer that I was in hiding for a murder committed on the person of one Pompeo of Milan, and set forth what could be argued for my justification in the most favourable terms.[4] The Pope replied: "I knew nothing of Pompeo's death, but plenty of Benvenuto's provocation; so let a safe-conduct be at once made out for him, in order that he may be placed in perfect security." A great friend of Pompeo's, who was also intimate with the Pope, happened to be there; he was a Milanese, called Messer Ambrogio.[5] This man said: "In the first days of your papacy it were not well to grant pardons of this kind." The Pope turned to him and answered: "You know less about such matters than I do. Know then that men like Benvenuto, unique in their profession, stand above the law; and how far more he, then, who received the provocation I have heard of?" When my safe conduct had been drawn out, I began at once to serve him, and was treated with the utmost favour.

LXXV

Messer Latino Juvinale came to call on me, and gave me orders to strike the coins of the Pope. This roused up all my enemies, who began to look about how they should hinder me; but the Pope, perceiving their drift, scolded them, and insisted that I should go on working. I took the dies in hand, designing a S. Paul, surrounded with this inscription: *Vas electionis.* This piece of money gave far more satisfaction than the models of my competitors; so that the Pope forbade any one else to speak to him of coins, since he wished me only to have to do with them. This encouraged me to apply myself with untroubled spirit to the task; and Messer Latino Juvinale, who had received such orders from the Pope, used to introduce me to his Holiness. I had it much at heart to recover the post of stamper to the Mint; but on this point the Pope took advice, and then told me

3 Paul III., elected October 13, 1534.

4 Latino Giovenale de' Manetti was a Latin poet and a man of humane learning, much esteemed by his contemporaries.

5 Ambrogio Recalcati. He was for many years the trusted secretary and diplomatic agent of Paul III.

I must first obtain pardon for the homicide, and this I should get at the holy Marie's day in August through the Caporioni of Rome.[1] I may say that it is usual every year on this solemn festival to grant the freedom of twelve outlaws to these officers. Meanwhile he promised to give me another safe-conduct, which should keep me in security until that time.

When my enemies perceived that they were quite unable to devise the means of keeping me out of the Mint, they resorted to another expedient. The deceased Pompeo had left three thousand ducats as dowry to an illegitimate daughter of his; and they contrived that a certain favourite of Signor Pier Luigi, the Pope's son, should ask her hand in marriage through the medium of his master.[2] Accordingly the match came off; but this fellow was an insignificant country lad, who had been brought up by his lordship; and, as folk said, he got but little of the money, since his lordship laid his hands on it and had the mind to use it. Now the husband of the girl, to please his wife, begged the prince to have me taken up; and he promised to do so when the first flush of my favour with the Pope had passed away. Things stood so about two months, the servant always suing for his wife's dower, the master putting him off with pretexts, but assuring the woman that he would certainly revenge her father's murder. I obtained an inkling of these designs; yet I did not omit to present myself pretty frequently to his lordship, who made show of treating me with great distinction. He had, however, decided to do one or other of two things—either to have me assassinated, or to have me taken up by the Bargello. Accordingly he commissioned a certain little devil of a Corsican soldier in his service to do the trick as cleverly as he could;[3] and my other enemies, with Messer Traiano at the head of them, promised the fellow a reward of one hundred crowns. He assured them that the job would be as easy as sucking a fresh egg. Seeing into their plot, I went about with my eyes open and with good attendance, wearing an under-coat and armlets of mail, for which I had obtained permission.

The Corsican, influenced by avarice, hoped to gain the whole sum

1 *Le sante Marie.* So the Feast of the Assumption is called at Florence, because devotion is paid on that day to the various images of the Virgin scattered through the town. The *Caporioni* of Rome were, like aldermen, wardens of the districts into which the city was divided.

2 Pier Luigi Farnese, Paul III.'s bastard, was successively created Gonfaloniere of the Church, Duke of Castro, Marquis of Novara, and finally Duke of Parma and Piacenza in 1545. He was murdered at Parma by his own courtiers in 1547. He was a man of infamous habits, quite unfit for the high dignities conferred on him.

3 *Che le facessi più netta che poteva.*

of money without risk, and imagined himself capable of carrying the matter through alone. Consequently, one day after dinner, he had me sent for in the name of Signor Pier Luigi. I went off at once, because his lordship had spoken of wanting to order several big silver vases. Leaving my home in a hurry, armed, however, as usual, I walked rapidly through Strada Giulia toward the Palazzo Farnese, not expecting to meet anybody at that hour of day. I had reached the end of the street and was making toward the palace, when, my habit being always to turn the corners wide, I observed the Corsican get up and take his station in the middle of the road. Being prepared, I was not in the least disconcerted; but kept upon my guard, and slackening pace a little, drew nearer toward the wall, in order to give the fellow a wide berth. He on his side came closer to the wall, and when we were now within a short distance of each other, I perceived by his gestures that he had it in his mind to do me mischief, and seeing me alone thus, thought he would succeed. Accordingly, I began to speak and said: "Brave soldier, if it had been night, you might have said you had mistaken me, but since it is full day, you know well enough who I am. I never had anything to do with you, and never injured you, but should be well disposed to do you service." He replied in a high-spirited way, without, however, making room for me to pass, that he did not know what I was saying. Then I answered: "I know very well indeed what you want, and what you are saying; but the job which you have taken in hand is more dangerous and difficult than you imagine, and may peradventure turn out the wrong way for you. Remember that you have to do with a man who would defend himself against a hundred; and the adventure you are on is not esteemed by men of courage like yourself." Meanwhile I also was looking black as thunder, and each of us had changed colour. Folk too gathered round us, for it had become clear that our words meant swords and daggers. He then, not having the spirit to lay hands on me, cried out: "We shall meet another time." I answered: "I am always glad to meet honest men and those who show themselves as such."

When we parted, I went to his lordship's palace, and found he had not sent for me. When I returned to my shop, the Corsican informed me, through an intimate friend of his and mine, that I need not be on my guard against him, since he wished to be my good brother; but that I ought to be much upon my guard against others, seeing I was in the greatest peril, for folk of much consequence had sworn to have my life. I sent to thank him, and kept the best lookout I could. Not many days after, a friend of mine informed me that Signor Pier Luigi had given strict orders that I should be taken that very evening. They told me this at twenty; whereupon I spoke with some of my friends, who advised me to be off at once. The order had been given for one hour after sunset; accordingly at twenty-three I left in the post for Florence. It seems that when the Corsican showed that he had not pluck enough to do the business as he promised, Signor Pier Luigi on his own authority gave orders to have me taken, merely to stop the mouth of Pompeo's daughter, who was always clamouring to know where her dower had gone to. When he was unable to gratify her in this matter of revenge on either of the two plans he had formed, he bethought him of another, which shall be related in its proper place.

LXXVI

I reached Florence in due course, and paid my respects to the Duke Alessandro, who greeted me with extraordinary kindness and pressed me to remain in his service. There was then at Florence a sculptor called Il Tribolino, and we were gossips, for I had stood godfather to his son.[1] In course of conversation he told me that a certain Giacopo del Sansovino, his first master, had sent for him; and whereas he had never seen Venice, and because of the gains he expected, he was very glad to go there.[2] On his asking me if I had ever been at Venice, I said no; this made him invite me to accompany him, and I agreed. So then I told Duke Alessandro that I wanted first to go to Venice, and that afterwards I would return to serve him. He exacted a formal promise to this effect, and bade me present myself before I left the city. Next day, having made my preparations, I went to take leave of the Duke, whom I found in the palace of the Pazzi, at that time inhabited by the wife and daughters of Signor Lorenzo Cibo.[3] Having sent word to his Excellency that I wished to set off for Venice with his good leave, Signor Cosimino

1 Niccolo de' Pericoli, a Florentine, who got the nickname of Tribolo in his boyhood, was a sculptor of some distinction. He worked on the bas-reliefs of San Petronio at Bologna, and helped Michel Agnolo da Siena to execute the tomb of Adrian VI. at Rome. Afterwards he was employed upon the sculpture of the Santa Casa at Loreto. He also made some excellent bronze-work for the Medicean villas at Cestello and Petraja. All through his life Tribolo served the Medici, and during the siege of Florence in 1530 he constructed a cork model of the town for Clement VII. Born 1485, died 1550.

2 This is the famous Giacopo Tatti, who took his artist's surname from his master, Andrea da Monte a Sansovino. His works at Florence, Rome, and Venice are justly famous. He died in 1570, aged ninety-three.

3 A brother of the Cardinal, and himself Marquis of Massa.

de' Medici, now Duke of Florence, returned with the answer that I must go to Niccolò de Monte Aguto, who would give me fifty golden crowns, which his Excellency bestowed on me in sign of his good-will, and afterwards I must return to serve him.

I got the money from Niccolò, and then went to fetch Tribolo, whom I found ready to start; and he asked me whether I had bound my sword. I answered that a man on horseback about to take a journey ought not to bind his sword. He said that the custom was so in Florence, since a certain Ser Maurizio then held office, who was capable of putting S. John the Baptist to the rack for any trifling peccadillo.[4] Accordingly one had to carry one's sword bound till the gates were passed. I laughed at this, and so we set off, joining the courier to Venice, who was nicknamed Il Lamentone. In his company we travelled through Bologna, and arrived one evening at Ferrara. There we halted at the inn of the Piazza, while Lamentone went in search of some Florentine exiles, to take them letters and messages from their wives. The Duke had given orders that only the courier might talk to them, and no one else, under penalty of incurring the same banishment as they had. Meanwhile, since it was a little past the hour of twenty-two, Tribolo and I went to see the Duke of Ferrara come back from Belfiore, where he had been at a jousting match. There we met a number of exiles, who stared at us as though they wished to make us speak to them. Tribolo, who was the most timorous man that I have ever known, kept on saying: "Do not look at them or talk to them, if you care to go back to Florence." So we stayed, and saw the Duke return; afterwards, when we regained our inn, we found Lamentone there. After nightfall there appeared Niccolò Benintendi, and his brother Piero, and another old man, whom I believe to have been Jacopo Nardi,[5] together with some young fellows, who began immediately to ask the courier news, each man of his own family in Florence.[6] Tribolo and I kept at a distance, in order to avoid speaking with them. After they had talked a while with Lamentone, Niccolò Benintendi [7] said: "I know those two men there very well; what's the reason they give themselves such

4 Ser Maurizio was entitled Chancellor, but really superintended the criminal magistracy of Florence. Varchi and Segni both speak of him as harsh and cruel in the discharge of his office.

5 Jacopo Nardi was the excellent historian of Florence, a strong anti-Medicean partisan, who was exiled in 1530.

6 I have translated the word *brigata* by *family* above, because I find Cellini in one of his letters alluding to his family as *la mia brigatina.*

7 Niccolò Benintendi, who had been a member of the Eight in 1529, was exiled by the Medici in 1530.

beastly airs, and will not talk to us?" Tribolo kept begging me to hold my tongue, while Lamentone told them that we had not the same permission as he had. Benintendi retorted it was idiotic nonsense, adding "Pox take them," and other pretty flowers of speech. Then I raised my head as gently as I could, and said: "Dear gentlemen, you are able to do us serious injury, while we cannot render you any assistance; and though you have flung words at us which we are far from deserving, we do not mean on that account to get into a rage with you." Thereupon old Nardi said that I had spoken like a worthy young man as I was. But Niccolò Benintendi shouted: "I snap my fingers at them and the Duke." [8] I replied that he was in the wrong toward us, since we had nothing to do with him or his affairs. Old Nardi took our part, telling Benintendi plainly that he was in the wrong, which made him go on muttering insults. On this I bade him know that I could say and do things to him which he would not like, and therefore he had better mind his business, and let us alone. Once more he cried out that he snapped his fingers at the Duke and us, and that we were all of us a heap of donkeys.[9] I replied by giving him the lie direct and drawing my sword. The old man wanting to be first upon the staircase, tumbled down some steps, and all the rest of them came huddling after him. I rushed onward, brandishing my sword along the walls with fury, and shouting: "I will kill you all!" but I took good care not to do them any harm, as I might too easily have done. In the midst of this tumult the inn-keeper screamed out; Lamentone cried, "For God's sake, hold!" some of them exclaimed, "Oh me, my head!" others, "Let me get out from here." In short, it was an indescribable confusion; they looked like a herd of swine. Then the host came with a light, while I withdrew upstairs and put my sword back in its scabbard. Lamentone told Niccolò Benintendi that he had behaved very ill. The host said to him: "It is as much as one's life is worth to draw swords here; and if the Duke were to know of your brawling, he would have you hanged. I will not do to you what you deserve; but take care you never show yourself again in my inn, or it will be the worse for you." Our host then came up to me, and when I began to make him my excuses, he would not suffer me to say a word, but told me that he knew I was entirely in the right, and bade me be upon my guard against those men upon my journey.

8 The Florentine slang is *Io ho in culo loro e il duca.*
9 *Un monte di asini.*

LXXVII

After we had supped, a barge-man appeared, and offered to take us to Venice. I asked if he would let us have the boat to ourselves; he was willing, and so we made our bargain. In the morning we rose early, and mounted our horses for the port, which is a few miles distant from Ferrara. On arriving there, we found Niccolò Benintendi's brother, with three comrades, waiting for me. They had among them two lances, and I had bought a stout pike in Ferrara. Being very well armed to boot, I was not at all frightened, as Tribolo was, who cried: "God help us! those fellows are waiting here to murder us." Lamentone turned to me and said: "The best that you can do is to go back to Ferrara, for I see that the affair is likely to be ugly; for Heaven's sake, Benvenuto, do not risk the fury of these mad beasts." To which I replied: "Let us go forward, for God helps those who have the right on their side; and you shall see how I will help myself. Is not this boat engaged for us?" "Yes," said Lamentone. "Then we will stay in it without them, unless my manhood has deserted me." I put spurs to my horse, and when I was within fifty paces, dismounted and marched boldly forward with my pike. Tribolo stopped behind, all huddled up upon his horse, looking the very image of frost. Lamentone, the courier, meanwhile, was swelling and snorting like the wind. That was his usual habit; but now he did so more than he was wont, being in doubt how this devilish affair would terminate. When I reached the boat, the master presented himself and said that those Florentine gentlemen wanted to embark in it with us, if I was willing. I answered: "The boat is engaged for us and no one else, and it grieves me to the heart that I am not able to have their company." At these words a brave young man of the Magalotti family spoke out: "Benvenuto, we will make you able to have it." To which I answered: "If God and my good cause, together with my own strength of body and mind, possess the will and the power, you shall not make me able to have what you say." So saying I leapt into the boat, and turning my pike's point against them, added: "I'll show you with this weapon that I am not able." Wishing to prove he was in earnest, Magalotti then seized his own and came toward me. I sprang upon the gunwale and hit him such a blow, that, if he had not tumbled backward, I must have pierced his body. His comrades, in lieu of helping him, turned to fly; and when I saw that I could kill him, instead of striking, I said: "Get up, brother; take your arms and go away. I have shown you that I cannot do what I do not want, and what I had the power to do I have not chosen to do." Then I called for Tribolo, the boatman, and Lamentone to embark; and so we got under way for Venice. When we had gone ten miles on the Po, we sighted those young men, who had got into a skiff and caught us up; and when they were alongside, that idiot Piero Benintendi sang out to me: "Go thy ways this time, Benvenuto; we shall meet in Venice." "Set out betimes then," I shouted, "for I am coming, and any man can meet me where he lists." In due course we arrived at Venice, when I applied to a brother of Cardinal Cornaro, begging him to procure for me the favour of being allowed to carry arms. He advised me to do so without hesitation, saying that the worst risk I ran was that I might lose my sword.

LXXVIII

Accordingly I girded on my sword, and went to visit Jacopo del Sansovino, the sculptor, who had sent for Tribolo. He received me most kindly, and invited us to dinner, and we stayed with him. In course of conversation with Tribolo, he told him that he had no work to give him at the moment, but that he might call again. Hearing this, I burst out laughing, and said pleasantly to Sansovino: "Your house is too far off from his, if he must call again." Poor Tribolo, all in dismay, exclaimed: "I have got your letter here, which you wrote to bid me come." Sansovino rejoined that men of his sort, men of worth and genius, were free to do that and greater things besides. Tribolo shrugged up his shoulders and muttered: "Patience, patience," several times. Thereupon, without regarding the copious dinner which Sansovino had given me, I took the part of my comrade Tribolo, for he was in the right. All the while at table Sansovino had never stopped chattering about his great achievements, abusing Michel Agnolo and the rest of his fellow-sculptors, while he bragged and vaunted himself to the skies. This had so annoyed me that not a single mouthful which I ate had tasted well; but I refrained from saying more than these two words: "Messer Jacopo, men of worth act like men of worth, and men of genius, who produce things beautiful and excellent, shine forth far better when other people praise them than when they boast so confidently of their own achievements." Upon this he and I rose from table blowing off the steam of our choler. The same day, happening to pass near the Rialto, I met Piero Benintendi in the company of some men; and perceiving that they were going to pick a quarrel with me, I turned into an apothecary's shop till the storm blew over. Afterwards I learned that the young Magalotti, to whom I showed that courtesy, had scolded them roundly; and thus the affair ended.

LXXIX

A few days afterwards we set out on our return to Florence. We lay one night at a place on this side Chioggia, on the left hand as you go toward Ferrara. Here the host insisted upon being paid before we went to bed, and in his own way; and when I observed that it was the custom everywhere else to pay in the morning, he answered: "I insist on being paid overnight, and in my own way." I retorted that men who wanted everything their own way ought to make a world after their own fashion, since things were differently managed here. Our host told me not to go on bothering his brains, because he was determined to do as he had said. Tribolo stood trembling with fear, and nudged me to keep quiet, lest they should do something worse to us; so we paid them in the way they wanted, and afterwards we retired to rest. We had, I must admit, the most capital beds, new in every particular, and as clean as they could be. Nevertheless I did not get one wink of sleep, because I kept on thinking how I could revenge myself. At one time it came into my head to set fire to his house; at another to cut the throats of four fine horses which he had in the stable; I saw well enough that it was easy for me to do all this; but I could not see how it was easy to secure myself and my companion. At last I resolved to put my things and my comrade's on board the boat; and so I did. When the towing-horses had been harnessed to the cable, I ordered the people not to stir before I returned, for I had left a pair of slippers in my bedroom. Accordingly I went back to the inn and called our host, who told me he had nothing to do with us, and that we might go to Jericho.[1] There was a ragged stable-boy about, half asleep, who cried out to me: "The master would not move to please the Pope, because he has got a wench in bed with him, whom he has been wanting this long while." Then he asked me for a tip, and I gave him a few Venetian coppers, and told him to make the barge-man wait

[1] *E che noi andassima al bordella.*

till I had found my slippers and returned. I went upstairs, took out a little knife as sharp as a razor, and cut the four beds that I found there into ribbons. I had the satisfaction of knowing I had done a damage of more than fifty crowns. Then I ran down to the boat with some pieces of the bed-covers [2] in my pouch, and bade the bargee start at once without delay. We had not gone far before my gossip Tribolo said that he had left behind some little straps belonging to his carpet-bag, and that he must be allowed to go back for them. I answered that he need not take thought for a pair of little straps, since I could make him as many big ones as he liked.[3] He told me I was always joking, but that he must really go back for his straps. Then he began ordering the bargee to stop, while I kept ordering him to go on. Meanwhile I informed my friend what kind of trick I had played our host, and showed him specimens of the bed-covers and other things, which threw him into such a quaking fright that he roared out to the bargee: "On with you, on with you, as quick as you can!" and never thought himself quite safe until we reached the gates of Florence.

When we arrived there, Tribolo said: "Let us bind our swords up, for the love of God; and play me no more of your games, I beg; for all this while I've felt as though my guts were in the saucepan." I made answer. "Gossip Tribolo, you need not tie your sword up, for you have never loosed it;" and this I said at random, because I never once had seen him act the man upon that journey. When he heard the remark, he looked at his sword and cried out: "In God's name, you speak true! Here it is tied, just as I arranged it before I left my house." My gossip deemed that I had been a bad travelling companion to him, because I resented affronts and defended myself against folk who would have done us injury. But I deemed that he had acted a far worse part with regard to me by never coming to my assistance at such pinches. Let him judge between us who stands by and has no personal interest in our adventures.

LXXX

No sooner had I dismounted than I went to visit Duke Alessandro, and thanked him greatly for his present of the fifty crowns, telling his Excellency that I was always ready to serve him according

2 *Sarge. Sergia* is interpreted *sopraccoperta del letto.*
3 The Italian for straps, *coregge,* has a double meaning, upon which Cellini plays.

to my abilities. He gave me orders at once to strike dies for his coinage; and the first I made was a piece of forty soldi, with the Duke's head on one side and San Cosimo and San Damiano on the other.[1] This was in silver, and it gave so much satisfaction that the Duke did not hesitate to say they were the best pieces of money in Christendom. The same said all Florence and every one who saw them. Consequently I asked his Excellency to make me appointments,[2] and to grant me the lodgings of the Mint. He bade me remain in his service, and promised he would give me more than I demanded. Meanwhile he said he had commissioned the Master of the Mint, a certain Carlo Acciaiuoli, and that I might go to him for all the money that I wanted. This I found to be true; but I drew my monies so discreetly, that I had always something to my credit, according to my account.

I then made dies for a giulio,[3] it had San Giovanni in profile, seated with a book in his hand, finer in my judgment than anything which I had done; and on the other side were the armorial bearings of Duke Alessandro. Next I made dies for half-giulios on which I struck the full face of San Giovanni in small. This was the first coin with a head in full face on so thin a piece of silver that had yet been seen. The difficulty of executing it is apparent only to the eyes of such as are past-masters in these crafts. Afterwards I made dies for the golden crowns; this crown had a cross upon one side with some little cherubim, and on the other side his Excellency's arms.

When I had struck these four sorts, I begged the Duke to make out my appointments and to assign me the lodgings I have mentioned, if he was contented with my service. He told me very graciously that he was quite satisfied, and that he would grant me my request. While we were thus talking, his Excellency was in his wardrobe, looking at a remarkable little gun that had been sent him out of Germany.[4] When he noticed that I too paid particular attention to this pretty instrument, he put it in my hands, saying that he knew how much pleasure I took in such things, and adding that I might choose for earnest of his promises an arquebuse to my own liking from the armoury, excepting only this one piece; he was well aware

1 These were the special patrons of the Medicean family, being physician-saints.

2 *Che mi fermassi una provvisione.*

3 The *giulio* was a coin of 56 Italian centimes or 8 Tuscan *crazie,* which in Florence was also called *barile* or *gabellotto,* because the sum had to be paid as duty on a barrel of wine.

4 See above, p. 110, for the right meaning of wardrobe.

that I should find things of greater beauty, and not less excellent, there. Upon this invitation, I accepted with thanks; and when he saw me looking round, he ordered his Master of the Wardrobe, a certain Pretino of Lucca, to let me take whatever I liked.[5] Then he went away with the most pleasant words at parting, while I remained, and chose the finest and best arquebuse I ever saw, or ever had, and took it back with me to home.

Two days afterward I brought some drawings which his Excellency had commissioned for gold-work he wanted to give his wife, who was at that time still in Naples.[6] I again asked him to settle my affairs. Then his Excellency told me that he should like me first to execute the die of his portrait in fine style, as I had done for Pope Clement. I began it in wax; and the Duke gave orders, while I was at work upon it, that whenever I went to take his portrait, I should be admitted. Perceiving that I had a lengthy piece of business on my hands, I sent for a certain Pietro Pagolo from Monte Ritondo, in the Roman district, who had been with me from his boyhood in Rome.[7] I found him with one Bernardonaccio,[8] a goldsmith, who did not treat him well; so I brought him away from there, and taught him minutely how to strike coins from those dies. Meanwhile, I went on making the Duke's portrait; and oftentimes I found him napping after dinner with that Lorenzino of his, who afterwards murdered him, and no other company; and much I marvelled that a Duke of that sort showed such confidence about his safety.[9]

LXXXI

It happened at this time Ottaviano de' Medici,[1] who to all appearances had got the government of everything in his own hands, favoured the old Master of the Mint against the Duke's will. This man was called Bastiano Cennini, an artist of the antiquated school, and of little skill in his craft.[2] Ottaviano mixed his stupid dies with

5 Messer Francesco of Lucca, surnamed Il Pretino.

6 Margaret of Austria, natural daughter to Charles V., was eventually married in 1536 to Alessandro de' Medici.

7 Pietro Pagolo Galleotti, much praised by Vasari for his artistic skill.

8 Perhaps Bernardo Sabatini.

9 This is the famous Tuscan Brutus who murdered Alessandro. He was descended from Lorenzo de' Medici, the brother of Cosimo, *Pater Patriæ*, and the uncle of Lorenzo the Magnificent.

1 This Ottaviano was not descended from either Cosimo or Lorenzo de' Medici, but from an elder, though less illustrious, branch of the great family. He married Francesca Salviati, the aunt of Duke Cosimo. Though a great patron of the arts and an intimate friend of M. A. Buonarroti, he was not popular, owing to his pride of place.

2 Cellini praises this man, however, in the preface to the *Oreficeria*.

mine in the coinage of crown-pieces. I complained of this to the Duke, who, when he saw how the matter stood, took it very ill, and said to me: "Go, tell this to Ottaviano de' Medici, and show him how it is."[8] I lost no time; and when I had pointed out the injury that had been done to my fine coins, he answered, like the donkey that he was: "We choose to have it so." I replied that it ought not to be so, and that I did not choose to have it so. He said: "And if the Duke likes to have it so?" I answered: "It would not suit me, for the thing is neither just nor reasonable." He told me to take myself off, and that I should have to swallow it in this way, even if I burst. Then I returned to the Duke, and related the whole unpleasant conversation between Ottaviano de' Medici and me, entreating his Excellency not to allow the fine coins which I had made for him to be spoiled, and begging for permission to leave Florence. He replied: "Ottaviano is too presuming: you shall have what you want; for this is an injury offered to myself."

That very day, which was a Thursday, I received from Rome a full safe-conduct from the Pope, with advice to go there at once and get the pardon of Our Lady's feast in mid-August, in order that I might clear myself from the penalties attaching to my homicide. I went to the Duke, whom I found in bed, for they told me he was suffering the consequence of a debauch. In little more than two hours I finished what was wanted for his waxen medal; and when I showed it to him, it pleased him extremely. Then I exhibited the safe-conduct sent me at the order of the Pope, and told him how his Holiness had recalled me to execute certain pieces of work; on this account I should like to regain my footing in the fair city of Rome, which would not prevent my attending to his medal. The Duke made answer half in anger: "Benvenuto, do as I desire: stay here; I will provide for your appointments, and will give you the lodgings in the Mint, with much more than you could ask for, because your requests are only just and reasonable. And who do you think will be able to strike the beautiful dies which you have made for me?" Then I said: "My lord, I have thought of everything, for I have here a pupil of mine, a young Roman whom I have taught the art; he will serve your Excellency very well till I return with your medal finished, to remain for ever in your service. I have in Rome a shop open, with journeymen and a pretty busi-

8 *Mostragnene.* This is perhaps equivalent to *mostraglielo.*

ness; as soon as I have got my pardon, I will leave all the devotion of Rome [4] to a pupil of mine there, and will come back, with your Excellency's good permission, to you." During this conversation, the Lorenzino de' Medici whom I have above mentioned was present, and no one else. The Duke frequently signed to him that he should join in pressing me to stay; but Lorenzino never said anything except: "Benvenuto, you would do better to remain where you are." I answered that I wanted by all means to regain my hold on Rome. He made no reply, but continued eyeing the Duke with very evil glances. When I had finished the medal to my liking, and shut it in its little box, I said to the Duke: "My lord, pray let me have your good-will, for I will make you a much finer medal than the one I made for Pope Clement. It is only reasonable that I should since that was the first I ever made. Messer Lorenzo here will give me some exquisite reverse, as he is a person learned and of the greatest genius." To these words Lorenzo suddenly made answer: "I have been thinking of nothing else but how to give you a reverse worthy of his Excellency." The Duke laughed a little, and looking at Lorenzo, said: "Lorenzo, you shall give him the reverse, and he shall do it here and shall not go away." Lorenzo took him up at once, saying: "I will do it as quickly as I can, and I hope to do something that shall make the whole world wonder." The Duke, who held him sometimes for a fool and sometimes for a coward, turned about in bed, and laughed at his bragging words. I took my leave without further ceremony, and left them alone together. The Duke, who did not believe that I was really going, said nothing further. Afterwards, when he knew that I was gone, he sent one of his servants, who caught me up at Siena, and gave me fifty golden ducats with a message from the Duke that I should take and use them for his sake, and should return as soon as possible; "and from Messer Lorenzo I have to tell you that he is preparing an admirable reverse for that medal which you want to make." I had left full directions to Petro Pagolo, the Roman above mentioned, how he had to use the dies; but as it was a very delicate affair, he never quite succeeded in employing them. I remained creditor to the Mint in a matter of more than seventy crowns on account of dies supplied by me.

[4] *Tutta la divozione di Roma.* It is not very clear what this exactly means. Perhaps "all the affection and reverence I have for the city of Rome," or merely "all my ties in Rome."

LXXXII

On the journey to Rome I carried with me that handsome arquebuse which the Duke gave me; and very much to my own pleasure, I used it several times by the way, performing incredible feats by means of it. The little house I had in Strada Giulia was not ready; so I dismounted at the house of Messer Giovanni Gaddi, clerk of the Camera, to whose keeping I had committed, on leaving Rome, many of my arms and other things I cared for. So I did not choose to alight at my shop, but sent for Felice, my partner, and got him to put my little dwelling forthwith into excellent order. The day following, I went to sleep there, after well providing myself with clothes and all things requisite, since I intended to go and thank the Pope next morning.

I had two young serving-lads, and beneath my lodgings lived a laundress who cooked extremely nicely for me. That evening I entertained several friends at supper, and having passed the time with great enjoyment, betook myself to bed. The night had hardly ended, indeed it was more than an hour before daybreak, when I heard a furious knocking at the house-door, stroke succeeding stroke without a moment's pause. Accordingly I called my elder servant, Cencio [1] (he was the man I took into the necromantic circle), and bade him to go and see who the madman was that knocked so brutally at that hour of the night. While Cencio was on this errand, I lighted another lamp, for I always keep one by me at night; then I made haste to pass an excellent coat of mail over my shirt, and above that some clothes which I caught up at random. Cencio returned, exclaiming: "Heavens, master! it is the Bargello and all his guard; and he says that if you do not open at once, he will knock the door down. They have torches, and a thousand things besides with them!" I answered: "Tell them that I am huddling my clothes on, and will come out to them in my shirt." Supposing it was a trap laid to murder me, as had before been done by Signor Pier Luigi, I seized an excellent dagger with my right hand, and with the left I took the safe-conduct; then I ran to the back-window, which looked out on gardens, and there I saw more than thirty constables; wherefore I knew that I could not escape upon that side. I made the two lads go in front, and told them to open the door exactly when I gave the word to do so. Then taking up an attitude of defence, with the dag-

[1] *i. e.,* Vincenzio Romoli.

ger in my right hand and the safe-conduct in my left, I cried to the lads: "Have no fear, but open!" The Bargello, Vittorio, and the officers sprang inside at once, thinking they could easily lay hands upon me; but when they saw me prepared in that way to receive them, they fell back, exclaiming: "We have a serious job on hand here!" Then I threw the safe-conduct to them, and said: "Read that! and since you cannot seize me, I do not mean that you shall touch me." The Bargello upon this ordered some of his men to arrest me, saying he would look to the safe-conduct later. Thereat I presented my arms boldly, calling aloud: "Let God defend the right! Either I shall escape your hands alive, or be taken a dead corpse!" The room was crammed with men; they made as though they would resort to violence; I stood upon my guard against them; so that the Bargello saw he would not be able to have me except in the way I said. Accordingly he called his clerk, and while the safe-conduct was being read, he showed by signs two or three times that he meant to have me secured by his officers; but this had no effect of shaking my determination. At last they gave up the attempt, threw my safe-conduct on the ground, and went away without their prize.

LXXXIII

When I returned to bed, I felt so agitated that I could not get to sleep again. My mind was made up to let blood as soon as day broke. However, I asked advice of Messer Gaddi, and he referred to a wretched doctor-fellow he employed,[1] who asked me if I had been frightened. Now, just consider what a judicious doctor this was, after I had narrated an occurrence of that gravity, to ask me such a question! He was an empty fribbler, who kept perpetually laughing about nothing at all. Simpering and sniggering, then, he bade me drink a good cup of Greek wine, keep my spirits up, and not be frightened. Messer Giovanni, however, said: "Master, a man of bronze or marble might be frightened in such circumstances. How much more one of flesh and blood!" The quack responded: "Monsignor, we are not all made after the same pattern; this fellow is no man of bronze or marble, but of pure iron." Then he gave one of his meaningless laughs, and putting his fingers on my wrist, said: "Feel here; this is not a man's pulse, but a lion's or a dragon's." At this, I, whose blood was thumping in my veins, probably far be-

[1] Possibly Bernardino Lilii of Todi.

yond anything which that fool of a doctor had learned from his Hippocrates or Galen, knew at once how serious was my situation; yet, wishing not to add to my uneasiness and to the harm I had already taken, I made show of being in good spirits. While this was happening, Messer Giovanni had ordered dinner, and we all of us sat down to eat in company. I remember that Messer Lodovico da Fano, Messer Antonio Allegretti, Messer Giovanni Greco, all of them men of the finest scholarship, and Messer Annibal Caro, who was then quite young, were present. At table the conversation turned entirely upon my act of daring. They insisted on hearing the whole story over and over again from my apprentice Cencio, who was a youth of superlative talent, bravery, and extreme personal beauty. Each time that he described my truculent behaviour, throwing himself into the attitudes I had assumed, and repeating the words which I had used, he called up some fresh detail to my memory. They kept asking him if he had been afraid; to which he answered that they ought to ask me if I had been afraid, because he felt precisely the same as I had.

All this chattering grew irksome to me; and since I still felt strongly agitated, I rose at last from table, saying that I wanted to go and get new clothes of blue silk and stuff for him and me; adding that I meant to walk in procession after four days at the feast of Our Lady, and meant Cencio to carry a white lighted torch on the occasion. Accordingly I took my leave, and had the blue cloth cut, together with a handsome jacket of blue sarcenet and a little doublet of the same; and I had a similar jacket and waistcoat made for Cencio.

When these things had been cut out, I went to see the Pope, who told me to speak with Messer Ambruogio; for he had given orders that I should execute a large piece of golden plate. So I went to find Messer Ambruogio, who had heard the whole of the affair of the Bargello, and had been in concert with my enemies to bring me back to Rome, and had scolded the Bargello for not laying hands on me. The man excused himself by saying that he could not do so in the face of the safe-conduct which I held. Messer Ambruogio now began to talk about the Pope's commission, and bade me make drawings for it, saying that the business should be put at once in train. Meanwhile the feast of Our Lady came round. Now it is the custom for those who get a pardon upon this occasion to give themselves up to prison; in order to avoid doing which I returned to the Pope, and told his Holiness that I was very unwilling to go to prison, and that I begged him to grant me the favour of a dispensation. The Pope answered that such was the custom, and that I must follow it. Thereupon I fell again upon my knees, and thanked him for the safe-conduct he had given me, saying at the same time that I should go back with it to serve my Duke in Florence, who was waiting for me so impatiently. On hearing this, the Pope turned to one of his confidential servants and said: "Let Benvenuto get his grace without the prison, and see that his *moto proprio* is made out in due form." As soon as the document had been drawn up, his Holiness signed it; it was then registered at the Capitol; afterwards, upon the day appointed, I walked in procession very honourably between two gentlemen, and so got clear at last.

LXXXIV

Four days had passed when I was attacked with violent fever attended by extreme cold; and taking to my bed, I made my mind up that I was sure to die. I had the first doctors of Rome called in, among whom was Francesco da Norcia, a physician of great age, and of the best repute in Rome.[1] I told them what I believed to be the cause of my illness, and said that I had wished to let blood, but that I had been advised against it; and if it was not too late, I begged them to bleed me now. Maestro Francesco answered that it would not be well for me to let blood then, but that if I had done so before, I should have escaped without mischief; at present they would have to treat the case with other remedies. So they began to doctor me as energetically as they were able, while I grew daily worse and worse so rapidly, that after eight days the physicians despaired of my life, and said that I might be indulged in any whim I had to make me comfortable. Maestro Francesco added: "As long as there is breath in him, call me at all hours; for no one can divine what Nature is able to work in a young man of this kind; moreover, if he should lose consciousness, administer these five remedies one after the other, and send for me, for I will come at any hour of the night; I would rather save him than any of the cardinals in Rome."

Every day Messer Giovanni Gaddi came to see me two or three times, and each time he took up one or other of my handsome fowling-pieces, coats of mail, or swords, using words like these:

1 Francesco Fusconi, physician to Popes Adrian VI., Clement VII., and Paul III.

"That is a handsome thing, that other is still handsomer;" and likewise with my models and other trifles, so that at last he drove me wild with annoyance. In his company came a certain Matio Franzesi [2] and this man also appeared to be waiting impatiently for my death, not indeed because he would inherit anything from me, but because he wished for what his master seemed to have so much at heart.

Felice, my partner, was always at my side, rendering the greatest services which it is possible for one man to give another. Nature in me was utterly debilitated and undone; I had not strength enough to fetch my breath back if it left me; and yet my brain remained as clear and strong as it had been before my illness. Nevertheless, although I kept my consciousness, a terrible old man used to come to my bedside, and make as though he would drag me by force into a huge boat he had with him. This made me call out to my Felice to draw near and chase that malignant old man away. Felice, who loved me most affectionately, ran weeping and crying: "Away with you, old traitor; you are robbing me of all the good I have in this world." Messer Giovanni Gaddi, who was present, then began to say: "The poor fellow is delirious, and has only a few hours to live." His fellow, Mattio Franzesi, remarked: "He has read Dante, and in the prostration of his sickness this apparition has appeared to him," [3] then he added laughingly: "Away with you, old rascal, and don't bother our friend Benvenuto." When I saw that they were making fun of me, I turned to Messer Gaddi and said: "My dear master, know that I am not raving, and that it is true that this old man is really giving me annoyance; but the best that you can do for me would be to drive that miserable Mattio from my side, who is laughing at my affliction; afterwards if your lordship deigns to visit me again, let me beg you to come with Messer Antonio Allegretti, or with Messer Annibal Caro, or with some other of your accomplished friends, who are persons of quite different intelligence and discretion from that beast." Thereupon Messer Giovanni told Mattio in jest to take himself out of his sight for ever; but because Mattio went on laughing, the joke turned to earnest, for Messer Giovanni would not look upon him again, but sent for Messer Antonio Allegretti, Messer Ludovico, and Messer Annibal Caro. On the arrival of these worthy men, I was greatly comforted, and talked

[2] Franzesi was a clever Italian poet. His burlesque *Capitoli* are printed with those of Berni and others.

[3] *Inferno*, iii., the verses about Charon.

reasonably with them awhile, not however without frequently urging Felice to drive the old man away. Messer Ludovico asked me what it was I seemed to see, and how the man was shaped. While I portrayed him accurately in words, the old man took me by the arm and dragged me violently towards him. This made me cry out for aid, because he was going to fling me under hatches in his hideous boat. On saying that last word, I fell into a terrible swoon, and seemed to be sinking down into the boat. They say that during that fainting-fit I flung myself about and cast bad words at Messer Giovanni Gaddi, to wit, that he came to rob me, and not from any motive of charity, and other insults of the kind, which caused him to be much ashamed. Later on, they say I lay still like one dead; and after waiting by me more than an hour, thinking I was growing cold, they left me for dead. When they returned home, Mattio Franzesi was informed, who wrote to Florence to Messer Bendetto Varchi, my very dear friend, that they had seen me die at such and such an hour of the night. When he heard the news, that most accomplished man and my dear friend composed an admirable sonnet upon my supposed but not real death, which shall be reported in its proper place.

More than three long hours passed, and yet I did not regain consciousness. Felice having used all the remedies prescribed by Maestro Francesco, and seeing that I did not come to, ran post-haste to the physician's door, and knocked so loudly that he woke him up, and made him rise, and begged him with tears to come to the house, for he thought that I was dead. Whereto Maestro Francesco, who was a very choleric man, replied: "My son, of what use do you think I should be if I came? If he is dead, I am more sorry than you are. Do you imagine that if I were to come with my medicine I could blow breath up through his guts[4] and bring him back to life for you?" But when he saw that the poor young fellow was going away weeping, he called him back and gave him an oil with which to anoint my pulses and my heart, telling him to pinch my little fingers and toes very tightly, and to send at once to call him if I should revive. Felice took his way, and did as Maestro Francesco had ordered. It was almost bright day when, thinking they would have to abandon hope, they gave orders to have my shroud made and to wash me. Suddenly I regained consciousness, and called out to Felice to drive away the old man on the moment, who kept tor-

[4] *Io gli possa soffiare in culo.*

menting me. He wanted to send for Maestro Francesco, but I told him not to do so, but to come close up to me, because that old man was afraid of him and went away at once. So Felice drew near to the bed; I touched him, and it seemed to me that the infuriated old man withdrew; so I prayed him not to leave me for a second.

When Maestro Francesco appeared, he said it was his dearest wish to save my life, and that he had never in all his days seen greater force in a young man than I had. Then he sat down to write, and prescribed for me perfumes, lotions, unctions, plasters, and a heap of other precious things. Meanwhile I came to life again by the means of more than twenty leeches applied to my buttocks, but with my body bore through, bound, and ground to powder. Many of my friends crowded in to behold the miracle of the resuscitated dead man, and among them people of the first importance.

In their presence I declared that the small amount of gold and money I possessed, perhaps some eight hundred crowns, what with gold, silver, jewels, and cash, should be given by my will to my poor sister in Florence, called Mona Liperata; all the remainder of my property, armour and everything besides, I left to my dearest Felice, together with fifty golden ducats, in order that he might buy mourning. At those words Felice flung his arms around my neck, protesting that he wanted nothing but to have me as he wished alive with him. Then I said: "If you want me alive, touch me as you did before, and threaten the old man, for he is afraid of you." At these words some of the folk were terrified, knowing that I was not raving, but talking to the purpose and with all my wits. Thus my wretched malady went dragging on, and I got but little better. Maestro Francesco, that most excellent man, came four or five times a day; Messer Giovanni Gaddi, who felt ashamed, did not visit me again. My brother-in-law, the husband of my sister, arrived; he came from Florence for the inheritance; but as he was a very worthy man, he rejoiced exceedingly to have found me alive. The sight of him did me a world of good, and he began to caress me at once, saying he had only come to take care of me in person; and this he did for several days. Afterwards I sent him away, having almost certain hope of my recovery. On this occasion he left the sonnet of Messer Benedetto Varchi, which runs as follows: [5]—

[5] This sonnet is so insipid, so untrue to Cellini's real place in art, so false to the far from saintly character of the man, that I would rather have declined translating it, had I not observed it to be a good example of that technical and conventional insincerity which was invading Italy at this epoch. Varchi was really sorry to hear the news of Cellini's death; but for his genuine emotion he found spurious vehicles of utterance. Cellini, mean-

"Who shall, Mattio, yield our pain relief?
Who shall forbid the sad expense of tears?
Alas! 'tis true that in his youthful years
Our friend hath flown, and left us here to grief.

He hath gone up to heaven, who was the chief
Of men renowned in art's immortal spheres;
Among the mighty dead he had no peers,
Nor shall earth see his like, in my belief.

O gentle sprite! if love still sway the blest,
Look down on him thou here didst love, and view
These tears that mourn my loss, not thy great good.

There dost thou gaze on His beatitude
Who made our universe, and findest true
The form of Him thy skill for men expressed."

LXXXV

My sickness had been of such a very serious nature that it seemed impossible for me to fling it off. That worthy man Maestro Francesco da Norcia redoubled his efforts, and brought me every day fresh remedies, trying to restore strength to my miserable unstrung frame. Yet all these endeavours were apparently insufficient to overcome the obstinacy of my malady, so that the physicians were in despair and at their wits' ends what to do. I was tormented by thirst, but had abstained from drinking for many days according to the doctors' orders. Felice, who thought he had done wonders in restoring me, never left my side. That old man ceased to give so much annoyance, yet sometimes he appeared to me in dreams.

One day Felice had gone out of doors, leaving me under the care of a young apprentice and a servant-maid called Beatrice. I asked the apprentice what had become of my lad Cencio, and what was the reason why I had never seen him in attendance on me. The boy replied that Cencio had been far more ill than I was, and that he was even at death's door. Felice had given them orders not to speak to me of this. On hearing the news, I was exceedingly distressed; then I called the maid Beatrice, a Pistojan girl, and asked her to bring me a great crystal water-cooler which stood near, full of clear and fresh water. She ran at once, and brought it to me full; I told her to put it to my lips, adding that if she let me take a draught ac-

while, had a right to prize it, since it revealed to him what friendship was prepared to utter after his decease.

cording to my heart's content, I would give her a new gown. This maid had stolen from me certain little things of some importance, and in her fear of being detected, she would have been very glad if I had died. Accordingly she allowed me twice to take as much as I could of the water, so that in good earnest I swallowed more than a flask full.[1] I then covered myself, and began to sweat, and fell into a deep sleep. After I had slept about an hour, Felice came home and asked the boy how I was getting on. He answered: "I do not know. Beatrice brought him that cooler full of water, and he has drunk almost the whole of it. I don't know now whether he is alive or dead." They say that my poor friend was on the point of falling to the ground, so grieved was he to hear this. Afterwards he took an ugly stick and began to beat the serving-girl with all his might, shouting out: "Ah! traitress, you have killed him for me then?" While Felice was cudgelling and she screaming, I was in a dream; I thought the old man held ropes in his hand, and while he was preparing to bind me, Felice had arrived and struck him with an axe, so that the old man fled exclaiming: "Let me go, and I promise not to return for a long while." Beatrice in the meantime had run into my bedroom shrieking loudly. This woke me up, and I called out: "Leave her alone; perhaps, when she meant to do me harm, she did me more good than you were able to do with all your efforts. She may indeed have saved my life; so lend me a helping hand, for I have sweated; and be quick about it." Felice recovered his spirits, dried and made me comfortable; and I, being conscious of a great improvement in my state, began to reckon on recovery.

When Maestro Francesco appeared and saw my great improvement, and the servant-girl in tears, and the prentice running to and fro, and Felice laughing, all this disturbance made him think that something extraordinary must have happened, which had been the cause of my amendment. Just then the other doctor, Bernardino, put in his appearance, who at the beginning of my illness had refused to bleed me. Maestro Francesco, that most able man, exclaimed: "Oh, power of Nature! She knows what she requires, and the physicians know nothing." That simpleton, Maestro Bernardino, made answer, saying: "If he had drunk another bottle he would have been cured upon the spot." Maestro Francesco da Norcia, a man of age and great authority, said: "That would have been a terrible misfortune, and would to God that it may fall on you!" Afterwards

1 *Un fiasco,* holding more than a quart.

he turned to me and asked if I could have drunk more water. I answered: "No, because I had entirely quenched my thirst." Then he turned to Maestro Bernardino, and said: "Look you how Nature has taken precisely what she wanted, neither more nor less. In like manner she was asking for what she wanted when the poor young man begged you to bleed him. If you knew that his recovery depended upon his drinking two flasks of water, why did you not say so before? You might then have boasted of his cure." At these words the wretched quack sulkily departed, and never showed his face again.

Maestro Francesco then gave orders that I should be removed from my room and carried to one of the hills there are in Rome. Cardinal Cornaro, when he heard of my improvement, had me transported to a place of his on Monte Cavallo. That very evening I was taken with great precautions in a chair, well wrapped up and protected from the cold. No sooner had I reached the place than I began to vomit, during which there came from my stomach a hairy worm about a quarter of a cubit in length: the hairs were long, and the worm was very ugly, speckled of divers colours, green, black, and red. They kept and showed it to the doctor, who said he had never seen anything of the sort before, and afterwards remarked to Felice: "Now take care of your Benvenuto, for he is cured. Do not permit him any irregularities; for though he has escaped this time, another disorder now would be the death of him. You see his malady has been so grave, that if we had brought him the extreme unction, we might not have been in time. Now I know that with a little patience and time he will live to execute more of his fine works." Then he turned to me and said: "My Benvenuto, be prudent, commit no excesses, and when you are quite recovered, I beg you to make me a Madonna with your own hand, and I will always pay my devotions to it for your sake." This I promised to do, and then asked him whether it would be safe for me to travel so far as to Florence. He advised me to wait till I was stronger, and till we could observe how Nature worked in me.

LXXXVI

When eight days had come and gone, my amendment was so slight that life itself became almost a burden to me; indeed I had been more than fifty days in that great suffering. So I made my mind up, and prepared to travel. My dear Felice and I went toward Florence in a pair of baskets;[1] and as I had not written, when I reached my sister's house, she wept and laughed over me all in one breath. That day many friends came to see me; among others Pier Landi, who was the best and dearest friend I ever had. Next day there came a certain Niccolò da Monte Aguto, who was also a very great friend of mine. Now he had heard the Duke say: "Benvenuto would have done much better to die, because he is come to put his head into a noose, and I will never pardon him." Accordingly when Niccolò arrived, he said to me in desperation: "Alas! my dear Benvenuto, what have you come to do here? Did you not know what you have done to displease the Duke? I have heard him swear that you were thrusting your head into a halter." Then I replied: "Niccolò, remind his Excellency that Pope Clement wanted to do as much to me before, and quite as unjustly; tell him to keep his eye on me, and give me time to recover; then I will show his Excellency that I have been the most faithful servant he will ever have in all his life; and forasmuch as some enemy must have served me this bad turn through envy, let him wait till I get well; for I shall then be able to give such an account of myself as will make him marvel."

This bad turn had been done me by Giorgetto Vassellario of Arezzo,[2] the painter; perchance in recompense for many benefits conferred on him. I had harboured him in Rome and provided for his costs, while he had turned my whole house upside down; for the man was subject to a species of dry scab, which he was always in the habit of scratching with his hands. It happened, then, that sleeping in the same bed as an excellent workman, named Manno, who was in my service, when he meant to scratch himself, he tore the skin from one of Manno's legs with his filthy claws, the nails of which he never used to cut. The said Manno left my service, and was resolutely bent on killing him. I made the quarrel up, and afterwards got Giorgio into Cardinal de' Medici's household, and continually helped him. For these deserts, then, he told Duke Alessandro that I had abused his Excellency, and had bragged I meant to be the first to leap upon the walls of Florence with his foes the exiles. These words, as I afterwards learned, had been put into Vasari's

1 *Un paio di ceste,* a kind of litter, here described in the plural, because two of them were perhaps put together. I have thought it best to translate the phrase literally. From a letter of Varchi to Bembo, we learn that Cellini reached Florence, November 9, 1535.

2 This is the famous Giorgio Vasari, a bad painter and worse architect, but dear to all lovers of the arts for his anecdotic work upon Italian artists.

lips by that excellent fellow[3] Ottaviano de' Medici, who wanted to revenge himself for the Duke's irritation against him, on account of the coinage and my departure from Florence. I, being innocent of the crime falsely ascribed to me, felt no fear whatever. Meanwhile that able physician Francesco da Monte Varchi attended to my cure with great skill. He had been brought by my very dear friend Luca Martini, who passed the larger portion of the day with me.[4]

LXXXVII

During this while I had sent my devoted comrade Felice back to Rome, to look after our business there. When I could raise my head a little from the bolster, which was at the end of fifteen days, although I was unable to walk upon my feet, I had myself carried to the palace of the Medici, and placed upon the little upper terrace. There they seated me to wait until the Duke went by. Many of my friends at court came up to greet me, and expressed surprise that I had undergone the inconvenience of being carried in that way, while so shattered by illness; they said that I ought to have waited till I was well, and then to have visited the Duke. A crowd of them collected, all looking at me as a sort of miracle; not merely because they had heard that I was dead, but far more because I had the look of a dead man. Then publicly, before them all, I said how some wicked scoundrel had told my lord the Duke that I had bragged I meant to be the first to scale his Excellency's walls, and also that I had abused him personally; wherefore I had not the heart to live or die till I had purged myself of that infamy, and found out who the audacious rascal was who had uttered such calumnies against me. At these words a large number of those gentlemen came round, expressing great compassion for me; one said one thing, one another, and I told them I would never go thence before I knew who had accused me. At these words Maestro Agostino, the Duke's tailor, made his way through all those gentlemen, and said: "If that is all you want to know, you shall know it at this very moment."

Giorgio the painter, whom I have mentioned, happened just then to pass, and Maestro Agostino exclaimed: "There is the man who accused you; now you know yourself if it be true or not." As fiercely as I could, not being able to leave my seat, I asked Giorgio if it

[3] *Galantuomo*, used ironically.
[4] Luca Martini was a member of the best literary society in his days, and the author of some famous burlesque pieces.

was true that he had accused me. He denied that it was so, and that he had ever said anything of the sort. Maestro Agostino retorted: "You gallows-bird! don't you know that I know it for most certain?" Giorgio made off as quickly as he could, repeating that he had not accused me. Then, after a short while, the Duke came by; whereupon I had myself raised up before his Excellency, and he halted. I told him that I had come there in that way solely in order to clear my character. The Duke gazed at me, and marvelled I was still alive; afterwards he bade me take heed to be an honest man and regain my health.

When I reached home, Niccolò da Monte Aguto came to visit me, and told me that I had escaped one of the most dreadful perils in the world, quite contrary to all his expectations, for he had seen my ruin written with indelible ink; now I must make haste to get well, and afterwards take French leave, because my jeopardy came from a quarter and a man who was able to destroy me. He then said, "Beware," and added: "What displeasure have you given to that rascal Ottaviano de' Medici?" I answered that I had done nothing to displease him, but that he had injured me; and told him all the affair about the Mint. He repeated: "Get hence as quickly as you can, and be of good courage, for you will see your vengeance executed sooner than you expect." I paid the best attention to my health, gave Pietro Pagolo advice about stamping the coins, and then went off upon my way to Rome without saying a word to the Duke or anybody else.

LXXXVIII

When I reached Rome, and had enjoyed the company of my friends awhile, I began the Duke's medal. In a few days I finished the head in steel, and it was the finest work of the kind which I had ever produced. At least once every day there came to visit me a sort of blockhead named Messer Francesco Soderini.[1] When he saw what I was doing, he used frequently to exclaim: "Barbarous wretch! you want then to immortalise that ferocious tyrant! You have never made anything so exquisite, which proves you our inveterate foe and their devoted friend; and yet the Pope and he have had it twice in mind to hang you without any fault of yours. That was the Father and the Son; now beware of the Holy Ghost." It

1 He had been banished in 1530 as a foe to the Medicean house.

was firmly believed that Duke Alessandro was the son of Pope Clement. Messer Francesco used also to say and swear by all his saints that, if he could, he would have robbed me of the dies for that medal. I responded that he had done well to tell me so, and that I would take such care of them that he should never see them more.

I now sent to Florence to request Lorenzino that he would send me the reverse of the medal. Niccoló da Monte Aguto, to whom I had written, wrote back, saying that he had spoken to that mad melancholy philosopher Lorenzino for it; he had replied that he was thinking night and day of nothing else, and that he would finish it as soon as he was able. Nevertheless, I was not to set my hopes upon his reverse, but I had better invent one out of my own head, and when I had finished it, I might bring it without hesitation to the Duke, for this would be to my advantage.

I composed the design of a reverse which seemed to me appropriate, and pressed the work forward to my best ability. Not being, however, yet recovered from that terrible illness, I gave myself frequent relaxation by going out on fowling expeditions with my friend Felice. This man had no skill in my art; but since we were perpetually day and night together, everybody thought he was a first-rate craftsman. This being so, as he was a fellow of much humour, we used often to laugh together about the great credit he had gained. His name was Felice Guadagni (Gain), which made him say in jest: "I should be called Felice Gain-little if you had not enabled me to acquire such credit that I can call myself Gain-much." I replied that there are two ways of gaining: the first is that by which one gains for one's self, the second that by which one gains for others; so I praised him much more for the second than the first, since he had gained for me my life.

We often held such conversations; but I remember one in particular on the day of Epiphany, when we were together near La Magliana. It was close upon nightfall, and during the day I had shot a good number of ducks and geese; then, as I had almost made my mind up to shoot no more that time, we were returning briskly toward Rome. Calling to my dog by his name, Barucco, and not seeing him in front of me, I turned round and noticed that the well-trained animal was pointing at some geese which had settled in a ditch. I therefore dismounted at once, got my fowling-piece ready, and at a very long range brought two of them down with a single ball. I never used to shoot with more than one ball, and was usually able to hit my mark at two hundred cubits, which cannot be done by other ways of loading. Of the two geese, one was almost dead, and the other, though badly wounded, was flying lamely. My dog retrieved the one and brought it to me; but noticing that the other was diving down into the ditch, I sprang forward to catch it. Trusting to my boots, which came high up the leg, I put one foot forward; it sank in the oozy ground; and so, although I got the goose, the boot of my right leg was full of water. I lifted my foot and let the water run out; then, when I had mounted, we made haste for Rome. The cold, however, was very great, and I felt my leg freeze, so that I said to Felice: "We must do something to help this leg, for I don't know how to bear it longer." The good Felice, without a word, leapt from his horse, and gathering some thistles and bits of stick, began to build a fire. I meanwhile was waiting, and put my hands among the breast-feathers of the geese, and felt them very warm. So I told him not to make the fire, but filled my boot with the feathers of the goose, and was immediately so much comforted that I regained vitality.

LXXXIX

We mounted, and rode rapidly toward Rome; and when we had reached a certain gently rising ground—night had already fallen—looking in the direction of Florence, both with one breath exclaimed in the utmost astonishment: "O God of heaven! what is that great thing one sees there over Florence?" It resembled a huge beam of fire, which sparkled and gave out extraordinary lustre.

I said to Felice: "Assuredly we shall hear to-morrow that something of vast importance has happened in Florence." As we rode into Rome, the darkness was extreme; and when we came near the Banchi and our own house, my little horse was going in an amble at a furious speed. Now that day they had thrown a heap of plaster and broken tiles in the middle of the road, which neither my horse nor myself perceived. In his fiery pace the beast ran up it; but on coming down upon the other side he turned a complete somersault. He had his head between his legs, and it was only through the power of God himself that I escaped unhurt. The noise we made brought the neighbours out with lights; but I had already jumped to my feet; and so, without remounting, I ran home, laughing to have come unhurt out of an accident enough to break my neck.

On entering the house, I found some friends of mine there, to whom, while we were supping together, I related the adventures of the day's chase and the diabolical apparition of the fiery beam which we had seen. They exclaimed: "What shall we hear to-morrow which this portent has announced?" I answered: "Some revolution must certainly have occurred in Florence." So we supped agreeably; and late the next day there came the news to Rome of Duke Alessandro's death.[1] Upon this many of my acquaintances came to me and said: "You were right in conjecturing that something of great importance had happened at Florence." Just then Francesco Soderini appeared jogging along upon a wretched mule he had, and laughing all the way like a madman. He said to me: "This is the reverse of that vile tyrant's medal which your Lorenzino de' Medici promised you." Then he added: "You wanted to immortalise the dukes for us; but we mean to have no more dukes;" and thereupon he jeered me, as though I had been the captain of the factions which made dukes. Meanwhile a certain Baccio Bettini,[2] who had an ugly big head like a bushel, came up and began to banter me in the same way about dukes, calling out: "We have dis-duked them, and won't have any more of them; and you were for making them immortal for us!" with many other tiresome quips of the same kind. I lost my patience at this nonsense, and said to them. "You blockheads! I am a poor goldsmith, who serve whoever pays me; and you are jeering me as though I were a party-leader. However, this shall not make me cast in your teeth the insatiable greediness, idiotcy, and good-for-nothingness of your predecessors. But this one answer I will make to all your silly railleries; that before two or three days at the longest have passed by, you will have another duke, much worse perhaps than he who now has left you." [3]

The following day Bettini came to my shop and said: "There is no need to spend money in couriers, for you know things before they happen. What spirit tells them to you?" Then he informed me that Cosimo de' Medici, the son of Signor Giovanni, was made Duke; but that certain conditions had been imposed at his election, which would hold him back from kicking up his heels at his own pleasure. I now had my opportunity for laughing at them, and saying: "Those men of Florence have set a young man upon a mettlesome horse;

1 Alessandro was murdered by his cousin Lorenzino at Florence on the 5th of January 1537.

2 Bettini was an intimate friend of Buonarroti and a considerable patron of the arts.

3 This exchange of ironical compliments testifies to Cellini's strong Medicean leanings, and also to the sagacity with which he judged the political situation.

next they have buckled spurs upon his heels, and put the bridle freely in his hands, and turned him out upon a magnificent field, full of flowers and fruits and all delightful things; next they have bidden him not to cross certain indicated limits: now tell me, you, who there is that can hold him back, whenever he has but the mind to cross them? Laws cannot be imposed on him who is the master of the law." So they left me alone, and gave me no further annoyance.[4]

XC

I now began to attend to my shop, and did some business, not however of much moment, because I had still to think about my health, which was not yet established after that grave illness I had undergone. About this time the Emperor returned victorious from his expedition against Tunis, and the Pope sent for me to take my advice concerning the present of honour it was fit to give him.[1] I answered that it seemed to me most appropriate to present his Imperial Majesty with a golden crucifix, for which I had almost finished an ornament quite to the purpose, and which would confer the highest honour upon his Holiness and me. I had already made three little figures of gold in the round, about a palm high; they were those which I had begun for the chalice of Pope Clement, representing Faith, Hope, and Charity. To these I added in wax what was wanting for the basement of the cross. I carried the whole to the Pope, with the Christ in wax, and many other exquisite decorations which gave him complete satisfaction. Before I took leave of his Holiness, we had agreed on every detail, and calculated the price of the work.

This was one evening four hours after nightfall, and the Pope had ordered Messer Latino Juvenale to see that I had money paid to me next morning. This Messer Latino, who had a pretty big dash of the fool in his composition, bethought him of furnishing the Pope with a new idea, which was, however, wholly of his own invention. So he altered everything which had been arranged; and next morning, when I went for the money, he said with his usual brutal arrogance: "It is our part to invent, and yours to execute; before

4 Cellini only spoke the truth on this occasion; for Cosimo soon kicked down the ladder which had lifted him to sovereignty, and showed himself the absolute master of Florence. Cosimo was elected Duke upon the 9th of January 1537.

1 Cellini returns to the year 1535, when Charles V. arrived in November from Tunis.

I left the Pope last night we thought of something far superior." To these first words I answered, without allowing him to proceed farther: "Neither you nor the Pope can think of anything better than a piece of which Christ plays a part; so you may go on with your courtier's nonsense till you have no more to say."

Without uttering one word, he left me in a rage, and tried to get the work given to another goldsmith. The Pope, however, refused, and sent for me at once, and told me I had spoken well, but that they wanted to make use of a Book of Hours of Our Lady, which was marvellously illuminated, and had cost the Cardinal de' Medici more than two thousand crowns. They thought that this would be an appropriate present to the Empress, and that for the Emperor they would afterwards make what I had suggested, which was indeed a present worthy of him; but now there was no time to lose, since the Emperor was expected in Rome in about a month and a half. He wanted the book to be enclosed in a case of massive gold, richly worked, and adorned with jewels valued at about six thousand crowns. Accordingly, when the jewels and the gold were given me, I began the work, and driving it briskly forward, in a few days brought it to such beauty that the Pope was astonished, and showed me the most distinguished signs of favour, conceding at the same time that that beast Juvenale should have nothing more to do with me.

I had nearly brought my work to its completion when the Emperor arrived, and numerous triumphal arches of great magnificence were erected in his honour. He entered Rome with extraordinary pomp, the description of which I leave to others, since I mean to treat of those things only which concern myself.[2] Immediately after his arrival, he gave the Pope a diamond which he had bought for twelve thousand crowns. This diamond the Pope committed to my care, ordering me to make a ring to the measure of his Holiness's finger; but first he wished me to bring the book in the state to which I had advanced it. I took it accordingly, and he was highly pleased with it; then he asked my advice concerning the apology which could be reasonably made to the Emperor for the unfinished condition of my work. I said that my indisposition would furnish a sound excuse, since his Majesty, seeing how thin and pale I was, would very readily believe and accept it. To this the Pope replied that he approved of the suggestion, but that I should add on the part of

2 The entry into Rome took place April 6. 1536.

his Holiness, when I presented the book to the Emperor, that I made him the present of myself. Then he told me in detail how I had to behave, and the words I had to say. These words I repeated to the Pope, asking him if he wished me to deliver them in that way. He replied: "You would acquit yourself to admiration if you had the courage to address the Emperor as you are addressing me." Then I said that I had the courage to speak with far greater ease and freedom to the Emperor, seeing that the Emperor was clothed as I was, and that I should seem to be speaking to a man formed like myself; this was not the case when I addressed his Holiness, in whom I beheld a far superior deity, both by reason of his ecclesiastical adornments, which shed a certain aureole about him, and at the same time because of his Holiness's dignity of venerable age; all these things inspired in me more awe than the Imperial Majesty. To these words the Pope responded: "Go, my Benvenuto; you are a man of ability; do us honour, and it will be well for you."

XCI

The Pope ordered out two Turkish horses, which had belonged to Pope Clement, and were the most beautiful that ever came to Christendom. Messer Durante,[1] his chamberlain, was bidden to bring them through the lower galleries of the palace, and there to give them to the Emperor, repeating certain words which his Holiness dictated to him. We both went down together, and when we reached the presence of the Emperor, the horses made their entrance through those halls with so much spirit and such a noble carriage that the Emperor and every one were struck with wonder. Thereupon Messer Durante advanced in so graceless a manner, and delivered his speech with so much of Brescian lingo, mumbling his words over in his mouth, that one never saw or heard anything worse; indeed the Emperor could not refrain from smiling at him. I meanwhile had already uncovered my piece; and observing that the Emperor had turned his eyes towards me with a very gracious look, I advanced at once and said: "Sacred Majesty, our most holy Father, Pope Paolo, sends this book of the Virgin as a present to your Majesty, the which is written in a fair clerk's hand, and illuminated by the greatest master who ever professed that art; and this rich cover of gold and jewels is unfinished, as you here behold it, by reason

[1] Messer Durante Duranti, Prefect of the Camera under Paul III., who gave him the hat in 1544, and the Bishopric of Brescia afterwards.

of my illness: wherefore his Holiness, together with the book, presents me also, and attaches me to your Majesty in order that I may complete the work; nor this alone, but everything which you may have it in your mind to execute so long as life is left me, will I perform at your service." Thereto the Emperor responded: "The book is acceptable to me, and so are you; but I desire you to complete it for me in Rome; when it is finished, and you are restored to health, bring it me and come to see me." Afterwards, in course of conversation, he called me by my name, which made me wonder, because no words had been dropped in which my name occurred; and he said that he had seen that fastening of Pope Clement's cope, on which I had wrought so many wonderful figures. We continued talking in this way a whole half hour, touching on divers topics artistic and agreeable; then, since it seemed to me that I had acquitted myself with more honour than I had expected, I took the occasion of a slight lull in the conversation to make my bow and to retire. The Emperor was heard to say: "Let five hundred golden crowns be given at once to Benvenuto." The person who brought them up asked who the Pope's man was who had spoken to the Emperor. Messer Durante came forward and robbed me of my five hundred crowns. I complained to the Pope, who told me not to be uneasy, for he knew how everything had happened, and how well I had conducted myself in addressing the Emperor, and of the money I should certainly obtain my share.

XCII

When I returned to my shop, I set my hand with diligence to finishing the diamond ring, concerning which the four first jewellers of Rome were sent to consult with me. This was because the Pope had been informed that the diamond had been set by the first jeweller of the world in Venice; he was called Maestro Miliano Targhetta; and the diamond being somewhat thin, the job of setting it was too difficult to be attempted without great deliberation. I was well pleased to receive these four jewellers, among whom was a man of Milan called Gaio. He was the most presumptuous donkey in the world, the one who knew least and who thought he knew most; the others were very modest and able craftsmen. In the presence of us all this Gaio began to talk, and said: "Miliano's foil should be preserved, and to do that, Benvenuto, you shall doff your cap;[1] for just as giving diamonds a tint is the most delicate and difficult thing in the jeweller's art, so is Miliano the greatest jeweller that ever lived, and this is the most difficult diamond to tint." I replied that it was all the greater glory for me to compete with so able a master in such an excellent profession. Afterwards I turned to the other jewellers and said: "Look here! I am keeping Miliano's foil, and I will see whether I can improve on it with some of my own manufacture; if not, we will tint it with the same you see here." That ass Gaio exclaimed that if I made a foil like that he would gladly doff his cap to it. To which I replied: "Supposing then I make it better, it will deserve two bows." "Certainly so," said he; and I began to compose my foils.

I took the very greatest pains in mixing the tints, the method of doing which I will explain in the proper place.[2] It is certain that the diamond in question offered more difficulties than any others which before or afterwards have come into my hands, and Miliano's foil was made with true artistic skill. However, that did not dismay me; but having sharpened my wits up, I succeeded not only in making something quite as good, but in exceeding it by far. Then, when I saw that I had surpassed him, I went about to surpass myself, and produced a foil by new processes which was a long way better than what I had previously made. Thereupon I sent for the jewellers; and first I tinted the diamond with Miliano's foil: then I cleaned it well and tinted it afresh with my own. When I showed it to the jewellers, one of the best among them, who was called Raffael del Moro, took the diamond in his hand and said to Gaio: "Benvenuto has outdone the foil of Miliano." Gaio, unwilling to believe it, took the diamond and said: "Benvenuto, this diamond is worth two thousand ducats more than with the foil of Miliano." I rejoined: "Now that I have surpassed Miliano, let us see if I can surpass myself." Then I begged them to wait for me a while, went up into a little cabinet, and having tinted the diamond anew unseen by them, returned and showed it to the jewellers. Gaio broke out at once: "This is the most marvellous thing that I have ever seen in the course of my whole lifetime. The stone is worth upwards of eighteen thousand crowns, whereas we valued it barely twelve thousand." The

1 In the *Oreficeria* Cellini gives an account of how these foils were made and applied. They were composed of paste, and coloured so as to enhance the effect of precious stones, particularly diamonds.

2 *Oreficeria*, cap. i.

other jewellers turned to him and said: "Benvenuto is the glory of our art, and it is only due that we should doff our caps to him and to his foils." Then Gaio said: "I shall go and tell the Pope, and I mean to procure for him one thousand golden crowns for the setting of this diamond." Accordingly he hurried to the Pope and told him the whole story; whereupon his Holiness sent three times on that day to see if the ring was finished.

At twenty-three o'clock I took the ring to the palace; and since the doors were always open to me, I lifted the curtain gently, and saw the Pope in private audience with the Marchese del Guasto.[3] The Marquis must have been pressing something on the Pope which he was unwilling to perform; for I heard him say. "I tell you, no; it is my business to remain neutral, and nothing else." I was retiring as quickly as I could, when the Pope himself called me back; so I entered the room, and presented the diamond ring, upon which he drew me aside, and the Marquis retired to a distance. While looking at the diamond, the Pope whispered to me: "Benvenuto, begin some conversation with me on a subject which shall seem important, and do not stop talking so long as the Marquis remains in this room." Then he took to walking up and down, and the occasion making for my advantage, I was very glad to discourse with him upon the methods I had used to tint the stone. The Marquis remained standing apart, leaning against a piece of tapestry; and now he balanced himself about on one foot, now on the other. The subject I had chosen to discourse upon was of such importance, if fully treated, that I could have talked about it at least three hours. The Pope was entertained to such a degree that he forgot the annoyance of the Marquis standing there. I seasoned what I had to say with that part of natural philosophy which belongs to our profession; and so having spoken for near upon an hour, the Marquis grew tired of waiting, and went off fuming. Then the Pope bestowed on me the most familiar caresses which can be imagined, and exclaimed: "Have patience, my dear Benvenuto, for I will give you a better reward for your virtues than the thousand crowns which Gaio tells me your work is worth."

On this I took my leave; and the Pope praised me in the presence of his household, among whom was the fellow Latino Juvenale, whom I have previously mentioned. This man, having become my

3 Alfonson d'Avalos, successor and heir to the famous Ferdinando d'Avalos, Marquis of Pescara. He acted for many years as Spanish Viceroy of Milan.

enemy, assiduously strove to do me hurt; and noticing that the Pope talked of me with so much affection and warmth, he put in his word: "There is no doubt at all that Benvenuto is a person of very remarkable genius; but while every one is naturally bound to feel more goodwill for his own countrymen than for others, still one ought to consider maturely what language it is right and proper to use when speaking of a Pope. He has had the audacity to say that Pope Clement indeed was the handsomest sovereign that ever reigned, and no less gifted; only that luck was always against him: and he says that your Holiness is quite the opposite; that the tiara seems to weep for rage upon your head; that you look like a truss of straw with clothes on, and that there is nothing in you except good luck." These words, reported by a man who knew most excellently how to say them, had such force that they gained credit with the Pope. Far from having uttered them, such things had never come into my head. If the Pope could have done so without losing credit, he would certainly have taken fierce revenge upon me; but being a man of great tact and talent, he made a show of turning it off with a laugh. Nevertheless he harboured in his heart a deep vindictive feeling against me, of which I was not slow to be aware, since I had no longer the same easy access to his apartments as formerly, but found the greatest difficulty in procuring audience. As I had now for many years been familiar with the manners of the Roman court, I conceived that some one had done me a bad turn; and on making dexterous inquiries, I was told the whole, but not the name of my calumniator. I could not imagine who the man was; had I but found him out, my vengeance would not have been measured by troy weight.[4]

XCIII

I went on working at my book, and when I had finished it I took it to the Pope, who was in good truth unable to refrain from commending it greatly. I begged him to send me with it to the Emperor, as he had promised. He replied that he would do what he thought fit, and that I had performed my part of the business. So he gave orders that I should be well paid. These two pieces of work on which I had spent upwards of two months, brought me in five hundred crowns: for the diamond I was paid one hundred and fifty crowns

[4] *Io ne arei fatte vendette a misura di carbone.*

and no more; the rest was given me for the cover of the book, which, however, was worth more than a thousand, being enriched with multitudes of figures, arabesques, enamellings, and jewels. I took what I could get and made my mind up to leave Rome without permission. The Pope meanwhile sent my book to the Emperor by the hand of his grandson Signor Sforza.[1] Upon accepting it, the Emperor expressed great satisfaction, and immediately asked for me. Young Signor Sforza, who had received his instructions, said that I had been prevented by illness from coming. All this was reported to me.

My preparations for the journey into France were made; and I wished to go alone, but was unable on account of a lad in my service called Ascanio. He was of very tender age, and the most admirable servant in the world. When I took him he had left a former master, named Francesco, a Spaniard and a goldsmith. I did not much like to take him, lest I should get into a quarrel with the Spaniard, and said to Ascanio: "I do not want to have you, for fear of offending your master." He contrived that his master should write me a note informing me that I was free to take him. So he had been with me some months; and since he came to us both thin and pale of face, we called him "the little old man;" indeed I almost thought he was one, partly because he was so good a servant, and partly because he was so clever that it seemed unlikely he should have such talent at thirteen years, which he affirmed his age to be. Now to go back to the point from which I started, he improved in person during those few months, and gaining in flesh, became the handsomest youth in Rome. Being the excellent servant which I have described, and showing marvellous aptitude for our art, I felt a warm and fatherly affection for him, and kept him clothed as if he had been my own son. When the boy perceived the improvement he had made, he esteemed it a good piece of luck that he had come into my hands; and he used frequently to go and thank his former master, who had been the cause of his prosperity. Now this man had a handsome young woman to wife, who said to him: "Surgetto" (that was what they called him when he lived with them), "what have you been doing to become so handsome?" Ascanio answered: "Madonna Francesca, it is my master who has made me so handsome, and far more good to boot." In her petty spiteful way she

[1] Sforza Sforza, son of Bosio, Count of Santa Fiore, and of Costanza Farnese, the Pope's natural daughter. He was a youth of sixteen at this epoch.

took it very ill that Ascanio should speak so; and having no reputation for chastity, she contrived to caress the lad more perhaps than was quite seemly, which made me notice that he began to visit her more frequently than his wont had been.

One day Ascanio took to beating one of our little shopboys, who, when I came home from out of doors, complained to me with tears that Ascanio had knocked him about without any cause. Hearing this, I said to Ascanio: "With cause or without cause, see you never strike any one of my family, or else I'll make you feel how I can strike myself." He bandied words with me, which made me jump on him and give him the severest drubbing with both fists and feet that he had ever felt. As soon as he escaped my clutches, he ran away without cape or cap, and for two days I did not know where he was, and took no care to find him. After that time a Spanish gentleman, called Don Diego, came to speak to me. He was the most generous man in the world. I had made, and was making, some things for him, which had brought us well acquainted. He told me that Ascanio had gone back to his old master, and asked me, if I thought it proper, to send him the cape and cap which I had given him. Thereupon I said that Francesco had behaved badly, and like a low-bred fellow; for if he had told me, when Ascanio first came back to him, that he was in his house, I should very willingly have given him leave; but now that he had kept him two days without informing me, I was resolved he should not have him; and let him take care that I do not set eyes upon the lad in his house. This message was reported by Don Diego, but it only made Francesco laugh. The next morning I saw Ascanio working at some trifles in wire at his master's side. As I was passing he bowed to me, and his master almost laughed me in the face. He sent again to ask through Don Diego whether I would not give Ascanio back the clothes he had received from me; but if not, he did not mind, and Ascanio should not want for clothes. When I heard this, I turned to Don Diego and said: "Don Diego, sir, in all your dealings you are the most liberal and worthy man I ever knew, but that Francesco is quite the opposite of you; he is nothing better than a worthless and dishonoured renegade. Tell him from me that if he does not bring Ascanio here himself to my shop before the bell for vespers, I will assuredly kill him; and tell Ascanio that if he does not quit that house at the hour appointed for his master, I will treat him much in the same way." Don Diego made no answer, but went and inspired such terror in Francesco that he knew not what to do with himself. Ascanio meanwhile had gone to find his father, who had come to Rome from Tagliacozzo, his birthplace; and this man also, when he heard about the row, advised Francesco to bring Ascanio back to me. Francesco said to Ascanio: "Go on your own account, and your father shall go with you." Don Diego put in: "Francesco, I foresee that something very serious will happen; you know better than I do what a man Benvenuto is; take the lad back courageously, and I will come with you." I had prepared myself, and was pacing up and down the shop waiting for the bell to vespers; my mind was made up to do one of the bloodiest deeds which I had ever attempted in my life. Just then arrived Don Diego, Francesco, Ascanio, and his father, whom I did not know. When Ascanio entered, I gazed at the whole company with eyes of rage, and Francesco, pale as death, began as follows: "See here, I have brought back Ascanio, whom I kept with me, not thinking that I should offend you." Ascanio added humbly: "Master, pardon me; I am at your disposal here, to do whatever you shall order." Then I said: "Have you come to work out the time you promised me?" He answered yes, and that he meant never to leave me. Then I turned and told the shopboy he had beaten to hand him the bundle of clothes, and said to him: "Here are all the clothes I gave you: take with them your discharge, and go where you like." Don Diego stood astonished at this, which was quite the contrary of what he had expected; while Ascanio with his father besought me to pardon and take him back. On my asking who it was who spoke for him, he said it was his father; to whom, after many entreaties, I replied: "Because you are his father, for your sake I will take him back."

XCIV

I had formed the resolution, as I said a short while back, to go toward France; partly because I saw that the Pope did not hold me in the same esteem as formerly, my faithful service having been besmirched by lying tongues; and also because I feared lest those who had the power might play me some worse trick. So I was determined to seek better fortune in a foreign land, and wished to leave Rome without company or license. On the eve of my projected departure, I told my faithful friend Felice to make free use of all my effects during my absence; and in the case of my not returning, left him everything I possessed. Now there was a Perugian workman in my employ, who had helped me on those commissions from the Pope; and after paying his wages, I told him he must leave my service. He begged me in reply to let him go with me, and said he would come at his own charges; if I stopped to work for the King of France, it would certainly be better for me to have Italians by me, and in particular such persons as I knew to be capable of giving me assistance. His entreaties and arguments persuaded me to take him on the journey in the manner he proposed. Ascanio, who was present at this debate, said, half in tears: "When you took me back, I said I wished to remain with you my lifetime, and so I have it in my mind to do." I told him that nothing in the world would make me consent; but when I saw that the poor lad was preparing to follow on foot, I engaged a horse for him too, put a small valise upon the crupper, and loaded myself with far more useless baggage than I should otherwise have taken.[1]

From home I travelled to Florence, from Florence to Bologna, from Bologna to Venice, and from Venice to Padua. There my dear friend Albertaccio del Bene made me leave the inn for his house; and next day I went to kiss the hand of Messer Pietro Bembo, who was not yet a Cardinal.[2] He received me with marks of the warmest affection which could be bestowed on any man; then turning to Albertaccio, he said: "I want Benvenuto to stay here, with all his followers, even though they be a hundred men; make then your mind up, if you want Benvenuto also, to stay here with me, for I do not mean elsewise to let you have him." Accordingly I spent a very pleasant visit at the house of that most accomplished gentleman. He had a room prepared for me which would have been too grand for a cardinal, and always insisted on my taking my meals beside him. Later on, he began to hint in very modest terms that he should greatly like me to take his portrait. I, who desired nothing in the world more, prepared some snow-white plaster in a little box, and set to work at once. The first day I spent two hours on end at my modelling, and blocked out the fine head of that eminent man with so much grace of manner that his lordship was fairly astounded. Now, though he was a man of profound erudition and without a rival in poetry, he understood nothing at all about my art; this made

1 He left Rome, April 1, 1537.

2 I need hardly say that this is the Bembo who ruled over Italian literature like a dictator from the reign of Leo X. onwards. He was of a noble Venetian house; Paul III. made him Cardinal in 1539. He died, aged seventy-seven, in 1547.

him think that I had finished when I had hardly begun, so that I could not make him comprehend what a long time it took to execute a thing of that sort thoroughly. At last I resolved to do it as well as I was able, and to spend the requisite time upon it; but since he wore his beard short after the Venetian fashion, I had great trouble in modelling a head to my own satisfaction. However, I finished it, and judged it about the finest specimen I had produced in all the points pertaining to my art. Great was the astonishment of Messer Pietro, who conceived that I should have completed the waxen model in two hours and the steel in ten, when he found that I employed two hundred on the wax, and then was begging for leave to pursue my journey toward France. This threw him into much concern, and he implored me at least to design the reverse for his medal, which was to be a Pegasus encircled with a wreath of myrtle. I performed my task in the space of some three hours, and gave it a fine air of elegance. He was exceedingly delighted, and said: "This horse seems to me ten times more difficult to do than the little portrait on which you have bestowed so much pains. I cannot understand what made it such a labour." All the same, he kept entreating me to execute the piece in steel, exclaiming: "For Heaven's sake, do it; I know that, if you choose, you will get it quickly finished." I told him that I was not willing to make it there, but promised without fail to take it in hand wherever I might stop to work.

While this debate was being carried on I went to bargain for three horses which I wanted on my travels; and he took care that a secret watch should be kept over my proceedings, for he had vast authority in Padua; wherefore, when I proposed to pay for the horses, which were to cost five hundred ducats, their owner answered: "Illustrious artist, I make you a present of the three horses." I replied: "It is not you who give them me; and from the generous donor I cannot accept them, seeing I have been unable to present him with any specimen of my craft." The good fellow said that, if I did not take them, I should get no other horses in Padua, and should have to make my journey on foot. Upon that I returned to the magnificent Messer Pietro, who affected to be ignorant of the affair, and only begged me with marks of kindness to remain in Padua. This was contrary to my intention, for I had quite resolved to set out; therefore I had to accept the three horses, and with them we began our journey.

XCV

I chose the route through the Grisons, all other passes being unsafe on account of war. We crossed the mountains of the Alba and Berlina; it was the 8th of May, and the snow upon them lay in masses.[1] At the utmost hazard of our lives we succeeded in surmounting those two Alpine ridges; and when they had been traversed, we stopped at a place which, if I remember rightly, is called Valdistà. There we took up quarters, and at nightfall there arrived a Florentine courier named Busbacca. I had heard him mentioned as a man of character and able in his profession, but I did not know that he had forfeited that reputation by his rogueries. When he saw me in the hostelry, he addressed me by my name, said he was going on business of importance to Lyons, and entreated me to lend him money for the journey. I said I had no money to lend, but that if he liked to join me, I would pay his expenses as far as Lyons. The rascal wept, and wheedled me with a long story, saying: "If a poor courier employed on affairs of national consequence has fallen short of money, it is the duty of a man like you to assist him." Then he added that he was carrying things of the utmost importance from Messer Filippo Strozzi;[2] and showing me a leather case for a cup he had with him, whispered in my ear that it held a goblet of silver which contained jewels to the value of many thousands of ducats, together with letters of vast consequence, sent by Messer Filippo Strozzi. I told him that he ought to let me conceal the jewels about his own person, which would be much less dangerous than carrying them in the goblet; he might give that up to me, and, its value being probably about ten crowns, I would supply him with twenty-five on the security. To these words the courier replied that he would go with me, since he could not do otherwise, for to give up the goblet would not be to his honour.

Accordingly we struck the bargain so; and taking horse next morning, came to a lake between Valdistate and Vessa; it is fifteen miles long when one reaches Vessa. On beholding the boats upon that lake I took fright; because they are of pine, of no great size and no great thickness, loosely put together, and not even pitched. If I had not

1 I have retained Cellini's spelling of names upon this journey. He passed the Bernina and Albula mountains, descended the valley of the Rhine to Wallenstadt, travelled by Weesen and probably Glarus to Lachen and Zurich, thence to Solothurn, Lausanne, Geneva, Lyons.

2 Filippo Strozzi was leader of the anti-Medicean party, now in exile. He fell into the hands of Duke Cosimo on the 1st of August in this year, 1537.

seen four German gentlemen, with their four horses, embarking in one of the same sort as ours, I should never have set my foot in it; indeed I should far more likely have turned tail; but when I saw their hare-brained recklessness, I took it into my head that those German waters would not drown folk, as ours do in Italy. However, my two young men kept saying to me: "Benvenuto, it is surely dangerous to embark in this craft with four horses." I replied: "You cowards, do you not observe how those four gentlemen have taken boat before us, and are going on their way with laughter? If this were wine, as indeed 'tis water, I should say that they were going gladly to drown themselves in it; but as it is but water, I know well that they have no more pleasure than we have in drowning there." The lake was fifteen miles long and about three broad; on one side rose a mountain very tall and cavernous, on the other some flat land and grassy. When we had gone about four miles, it began to storm upon the lake, and our oarsmen asked us to help in rowing; this we did awhile. I made gestures and directed them to land us on the farther shore; they said it was not possible, because there was not depth of water for the boat, and there were shoals there, which would make it go to pieces and drown us all; and still they kept on urging us to help them. The boatmen shouted one to the other, calling for assistance. When I saw them thus dismayed, my horse being an intelligent animal, I arranged the bridle on his neck and took the end of the halter with my left hand. The horse, like most of his kind, being not devoid of reason, seemed to have an instinct of my intention; for having turned his face towards the fresh grass, I meant that he should swim and draw me after him. Just at that moment a great wave broke over the boat. Ascanio shrieked out: "Mercy, my father; save me," and wanted to throw himself upon my neck. Accordingly, I laid hand to my little dagger, and told them to do as I had shown them, seeing that the horses would save their lives as well as I too hoped to escape with mine by the same means; but that if he tried to jump on me, I should kill him. So we went forward several miles in this great peril of our lives.

XCVI

When we had reached the middle of the lake, we found a little bit of level ground where we could land, and I saw that those four German gentlemen had already come to shore there; but on our wishing to disembark, the boatmen would hear nothing of it. Then I said to my young men: "Now is the time to show what stuff we are made of; so draw your swords, and force these fellows to put us on shore." This we did, not however without difficulty, for they offered a stubborn resistance. When at last we got to land, we had to climb that mountain for two miles, and it was more troublesome than getting up a ladder. I was completely clothed in mail, with big boots, and a gun in my hand; and it was raining as though the fountains of the heavens were opened. Those devils, the German gentlemen, leading their little horses by the bridle, accomplished miracles of agility; but our animals were not up to the business, and we burst with the fatigue of making them ascend that hill of difficulty. We had climbed a little way, when Ascanio's horse, an excellent beast of Hungarian race, made a false step. He was going a few paces before the courier Busbacca to whom Ascanio had given his lance to carry for him. Well, the path was so bad that the horse stumbled, and went on scrambling backwards, without being able to regain his footing, till he stuck upon the point of the lance, which that rogue of a courier had not the wit to keep out of his way. The weapon passed right through his throat; and when my other workman went to help him, his horse also, a black-coloured animal, slipped towards the lake, and held on by some shrub which offered but a slight support. This horse was carrying a pair of saddle-bags, which contained all my money and other valuables. I cried out to the young man to save his own life, and let the horse go to the devil. The fall was more than a mile of precipitous descent above the waters of the lake. Just below the place our boatmen had taken up their station; so that if the horse fell, he would have come precisely on them. I was ahead of the whole company, and we waited to see the horse plunge headlong; it seemed certain that he must go to perdition. During this I said to my young men: "Be under no concern; let us save our lives, and give thanks to God for all that happens. I am only distressed for that poor fellow Busbacca, who tied his goblet and his jewels to the value of several thousands of ducats on the horse's saddle-bow, thinking that the safest place. My things are but a few hundred crowns, and I am in no fear whatever, if only I get God's protection." Then Busbacca cried out: "I am not sorry for my own loss, but for yours." "Why," said I to him, "are you sorry for my trifles, and not for all that property of yours?" He answered. "I will tell you in God's name; in these circumstances and at the point of peril we have reached, truth must be spoken. I know that yours are crowns, and are so in good sooth; but that case in which I said I had so many jewels and other lies, is all full of caviare." On hearing this I could not hold from laughing; my young men laughed too; and he began to cry. The horse extricated itself by a great effort when we had given it up for lost. So then, still laughing, we summoned our forces, and bent ourselves to making the ascent. The four German gentlemen, having gained the top before us, sent down some folk who gave us aid. Thus at length we reached our lodging in the wilderness. Here, being wet to the skin, tired out, and famished, we were most agreeably entertained; we dried ourselves, took rest, and satisfied our hunger, while certain wild herbs were applied to the wounded horse. They pointed out to us the plant in question, of which the hedges were full; and we were told that if the wound was kept continually plugged with its leaves, the beast would not only recover, but would serve us just as if it had sustained no injury. We proceeded to do as they advised. Then having thanked those gentlemen, and feeling ourselves entirely refreshed, we quitted the place, and travelled onwards, thanking God for saving us from such great perils.

XCVII

We reached a town beyond Vessa, where we passed the night, and heard a watchman through all the hours singing very agreeably; for all the houses of that city being built of pine wood, it was the watchman's only business to warn folk against fire. Busbacca's nerves had been quite shaken by the day's adventures; accordingly, each hour when the watchman sang, he called out in his sleep: "Ah God, I am drowning!" That was because of the fright he had had; and besides, he had got drunk in the evening, because he would sit boozing with all the Germans who were there; and sometimes he cried: "I am burning," and sometimes: "I am drowning;" and at other times he thought he was in hell, and tortured with that caviare suspended round his throat.

This night was so amusing, that it turned all our troubles into laughter. In the morning we rose with very fine weather, and went to dine in a smiling little place called Lacca. Here we obtained excellent entertainment, and then engaged guides, who were returning to a town called Surich. The guide who attended us went along the dyked bank of a lake; there was no other road; and the dyke itself was covered with water, so that the reckless fellow slipped, and fell together with his horse beneath the water. I, who was but a few steps behind him, stopped my horse, and waited to see the donkey get out of the water. Just as if nothing had happened, he began to sing again, and made signs to me to follow. I broke away upon the right hand, and got through some hedges, making my young men and Busbacca take that way. The guide shouted in German that if the folk of those parts saw me they would put me to death. However, we passed forward, and escaped that other storm.

So we arrived at Surich, a marvellous city, bright and polished like a little gem. There we rested a whole day, then left betimes one morning, and reached another fair city called Solutorno. Thence we came to Usanna, from Usanna to Ginevra, from Ginevra to Lione, always singing and laughing. At Lione I rested four days, and had much pleasant intercourse with some of my friends there; I was also repaid what I had spent upon Busbacca; afterwards I set out upon the road to Paris. This was a delightful journey, except that when we reached Palissa [1] a band of venturers tried to murder us,[2] and it was only by great courage and address that we got free from them. From that point onward we travelled to Paris without the least trouble in the world. Always singing and laughing, we arrived safely at our destination.

XCVIII

After taking some repose in Paris, I went to visit the painter Rosso, who was in the King's service. I thought to find in him one of the sincerest friend I had in the world, seeing that in Rome I had done him the greatest benefits which one man can confer upon another. As these may be described briefly, I will not here omit their mention, in order to expose the shamelessness of such ingratitude. While he was in Rome, then, being a man given to back-biting, he spoke so ill of Raffaello da Urbino's works, that the pupils of the latter were quite resolved to murder him. From this peril I saved him by keeping a close watch upon him day and night. Again, the evil things said by Rosso against San Gallo,[1] that excellent architect, caused the latter to get work taken from him which he had previously

1 La Palice.
2 Cellini, in the narrative of his second French journey, explains that these *venturieri* were a notable crew of very daring brigands in the Lyonese province.
1 Antonio da San Gallo, one of the best architects of the later Renaissance.

procured for him from Messer Agnolo da Cesi; and after this San Gallo used his influence so strenuously against him that he must have been brought to the verge of starvation, had not I pitied his condition and lent him some scores of crowns to live upon. So then, not having been repaid, and knowing that he held employment under the King, I went, as I have said, to look him up. I did not merely expect him to discharge his debt, but also to show me favour and assist in placing me in that great monarch's service.

When Rosso set eyes on me, his countenance changed suddenly, and he exclaimed: "Benvenuto, you have taken this long journey at great charges to your loss; especially at this present time, when all men's thoughts are occupied with war, and not with the bagatelles of our professsion." I replied that I had brought money enough to take me back to Rome as I had come to Paris, and that this was not the proper return for the pains I had endured for him, and that now I began to believe what Maestro Antonio da San Gallo said of him. When he tried to turn the matter into jest on this exposure of his baseness, I showed him a letter of exchange for five hundred crowns upon Ricciardo del Bene. Then the rascal was ashamed, and wanted to detain me almost by force; but I laughed at him, and took my leave in the company of a painter whom I found there. This man was called Sguazzella:[2] he too was a Florentine; and I went to lodge in his house, with three horses and three servants, at so much per week. He treated me very well, and was even better paid by me in return.

Afterwards I sought audience of the King, through the introduction of his treasurer, Messer Giuliano Buonaccorti.[3] I met, however, with considerable delays, owing, as I did not then know, to the strenuous exertions Rosso made against my admission to his Majesty. When Messer Giuliano became aware of this, he took me down at once to Fontana Bilio,[4] and brought me into the presence of the King, who granted me a whole hour of very gracious audience. Since he was then on the point of setting out for Lyons, he told Messer Giuliano to take me with him, adding that on the journey we could discuss some works of art his Majesty had it in his head to execute. Accordingly, I followed the court; and on the way I entered into close relations with the Cardinal of Ferrara, who had not at that

2 A pupil of Andrea del Sarto, who went with him to France and settled there.
3 A Florentine exile mentioned by Varchi.
4 Fontainebleau. Cellini always writes it as above.

period obtained the hat.[5] Every evening I used to hold long conversations with the Cardinal, in the course of which his lordship advised me to remain at an abbey of his in Lyons, and there to abide at ease until the King returned from this campaign, adding that he was going on to Grenoble, and that I should enjoy every convenience in the abbey.

When we reached Lyons I was already ill, and my lad Ascanio had taken a quartan fever. The French and their court were both grown irksome to me, and I counted the hours till I could find myself again in Rome. On seeing my anxiety to return home, the Cardinal gave me money sufficient for making him a silver bason and jug. So we took good horses, and set our faces in the direction of Rome, passing the Simplon, and travelling for some while in the company of certain Frenchmen; Ascanio troubled by his quartan, and I by a slow fever which I found it quite impossible to throw off. I had, moreover, got my stomach out of order to such an extent, that for the space of four months, as I verily believed, I hardly ate one whole loaf of bread in the week; and great was my longing to reach Italy, being desirious to die there rather than in France.

XCIX

When we had crossed the mountains of the Simplon, we came to a river near a place called Indevedro.[1] It was broad and very deep, spanned by a long narrow bridge without ramparts. That morning a thick white frost had fallen; and when I reached the bridge, riding before the rest, I recognised how dangerous it was, and bade my servants and young men dismount and lead their horses. So I got across without accident, and rode on talking with one of the Frenchmen, whose condition was that of a gentleman. The other, who was a scrivener, lagged a little way behind, jeering the French gentleman and me because we had been so frightened by nothing at all as to give ourselves the trouble of walking. I turned round, and seeing him upon the middle of the bridge, begged him to come gently, since the place was very dangerous. The fellow, true to his French nature, cried out in French that I was a man of poor spirit, and that there was no danger whatsoever. While he spoke these words and urged his horse forward, the animal suddenly slipped over the bridge, and

5 Ippolito d'Este, son of Alfonso, Duke of Ferrara; Archbishop of Milan at the age of fifteen; Cardinal in 1539; spent a large part of his life in France.

1 Probably the Doveria in the Valdivedro.

fell with legs in air close to a huge rock there was there. Now God is very often merciful to madmen; so the two beasts, human and equine, plunged together into a deep wide pool, where both of them went down below the water. On seeing what had happened, I set off running at full speed, scrambled with much difficulty on to the rock, and dangling over from it, seized the skirt of the scrivener's gown and pulled him up, for he was still submerged beneath the surface. He had drunk his bellyful of water, and was within an ace of being drowned. I then, beholding him out of danger, congratulated the man upon my having been the means of rescuing his life. The fellow to this answered me in French, that I had done nothing; the important things to save were his writings, worth many scores of crowns; and these words he seemed to say in anger, dripping wet and spluttering the while. Thereupon, I turned round to our guides, and ordered them to help the brute, adding that I would see them paid. One of them with great address and trouble set himself to the business, and picked up all the fellow's writings, so that he lost not one of them: the other guide refused to trouble himself by rendering any assistance.

I ought here to say that we had made a purse up, and that I performed the part of paymaster. So, when we reached the place I mentioned, and had dined, I drew some coins from the common purse and gave them to the guide who helped to draw him from the water. Thereupon the fellow called out that I might pay them out of my own pocket; he had no intention of giving the man more than what had been agreed on for his services as guide. Upon this I retorted with insulting language. Then the other guide, who had done nothing, came up and demanded to be rewarded also. I told him that the one who had borne the cross deserved the recompense. He cried out that he would presently show me a cross which should make me repent. I replied that I would light a candle at that cross, which should, I hoped, make him to be the first to weep his folly. The village we were in lay on the frontier between Venice and the Germans. So the guide ran off to bring the folk together, and came, followed by a crowd, with a boar-spear in his hand. Mounted on my good steed, I lowered the barrel of my arquebuse, and turning to my comrades, cried: "At the first shot I shall bring that fellow down; do you likewise your duty, for these are highway robbers, who have used this little incident to contrive our murder." The innkeeper at whose house we had dined called one of the leaders, an imposing old man, and begged him to put a stop to the disorder, saying: "This is a most courageous young man; you may cut him to pieces, but he will certainly kill a lot of you, and perhaps will escape your hands after doing all the mischief he is able." So matters calmed down: and the old man, their leader, said to me: "Go in peace; you would not have much to boast of against us, even if you had a hundred men to back you." I recognised the truth of his words, and had indeed made up my mind to die among them; therefore, when no further insults were cast at me, I shook my head and exclaimed: "I should certainly have done my utmost to prove I am no statue, but a man of flesh and spirit." Then we resumed our journey; and that evening, at the first lodging we came to, settled our accounts together. There I parted for ever from that beast of a Frenchman, remaining on very friendly terms with the other, who was a gentleman. Afterwards I reached Ferrara, with my three horses and no other company.

Having dismounted, I went to court in order to pay my reverence to the Duke, and gain permission to depart next morning to Loreto. When I had waited until two hours after nightfall, his Excellency appeared. I kissed his hands; he received me with much courtesy, and ordered that water should be brought for me to wash my hands before eating. To this compliment I made a pleasant answer: "Most excellent lord, it is now more than four months that I have eaten only just enough to keep life together; knowing therefore that I could not enjoy the delicacies of your royal table, I will stay and talk with you while your Excellency is supping; in this way we should both have more pleasure than if I were to sup with you." Accordingly, we entered into conversation, and prolonged it for the next three hours. At that time I took my leave, and when I got back to the inn, found a most excellent meal ready; for the Duke had sent me the plates from his own banquet, together with some famous wine. Having now fasted two full hours beyond my usual hour for supping, I fell to with hearty appetite; and this was the first time since four months that I felt the power or will to eat.

C

Leaving Ferrara in the morning, I went to Santa Maria at Loreto; and thence, having performed my devotions, pursued the journey to Rome. There I found my most faithful Felice, to whom I abandoned my old shop with all its furniture and appurtenances, and opened another, much larger and roomier, next to Sugherello, the perfumer. I thought for certain that the great King Francis would not have remembered me. Therefore I accepted commissions from several noblemen; and in the meanwhile began the bason and jug ordered by the Cardinal Ferrara. I had a crowd of workmen, and many large affairs on hand in gold and silver.

Now the arrangement I had made with that Perugian workman[1] was that he should write down all the monies which had been disbursed on his account, chiefly for clothes and divers other sundries; and these, together with the costs of travelling, amounted to about seventy crowns. We agreed that he should discharge the debt by monthly payments of three crowns; and this he was well able to do, since he gained more than eight through me. At the end of two months the rascal decamped from my shop, leaving me in the lurch with a mass of business on my hands, and saying that he did not mean to pay me a farthing more. I was resolved to seek redress, but allowed myself to be persuaded to do so by the way of justice. At first I thought of lopping off an arm of his; and assuredly I should have done so, if my friends had not told me that it was a mistake, seeing I should lose my money and perhaps Rome too a second time, forasmuch as blows cannot be measured, and that with the agreement I held of his I could at any moment have him taken up. I listened to their advice, though I should have liked to conduct the affair more freely. As a matter of fact, I sued him before the auditor of the Camera, and gained my suit; in consequence of that decree, for which I waited several months, I had him thrown into prison. At the same time I was overwhelmed with large commissions; among others, I had to supply all the ornaments of gold and jewels for the wife of Signor Gierolimo Orsino, father of Signor Paolo, who is now the son-in-law of our Duke Cosimo.[2] These things I had nearly finished; yet others of the greatest consequence were always coming in. I employed eight work-people, and worked day and night together with them, for the sake alike of honour and of gain.

1 In his *Ricordi* Cellini calls the man Girolamo Pascucci.

2 He was Duke of Bracciano, father of Duke Paolo, who married Isabella de' Medici, and murdered her before his second marriage with Vittoria Accoramboni. See my *Renaissance in Italy*, vol. vi.

CI

While I was engaged in prosecuting my affairs with so much vigour, there arrived a letter sent post-haste to me by the Cardinal of Ferrara, which ran as follows:—

"Benvenuto, our dear friend,—During these last days the most Christian King here made mention of you, and said that he should like to have you in his service. Whereto I answered that you had promised me, whenever I sent for you to serve his Majesty, that you would come at once. His Majesty then answered: 'It is my will that provision for his journey, according to his merits, should be sent him;' and immediately ordered his Admiral to make me out an order for one thousand golden crowns upon the treasurer of the Exchequer. The Cardinal de' Gaddi, who was present at this conversation, advanced immediately, and told his Majesty that it was not necessary to make these dispositions, seeing that he had sent you money enough, and that you were already on the journey. If then, as I think probable, the facts are quite contrary to those assertions of Cardinal Gaddi, reply to me without delay upon the receipt of this letter; for I will undertake to gather up the fallen thread, and have the promised money given you by this magnanimous King."

Now let the world take notice, and all the folk that dwell on it, what power malignant stars with adverse fortune exercise upon us human beings! I had not spoken twice in my lifetime to that little simpleton of a Cardinal de' Gaddi; nor do I think that he meant by this bumptiousness of his to do me any harm, but only, through lightheadedness and senseless folly, to make it seem as though he also held the affairs of artists, whom the King was wanting, under his own personal supervision, just as the Cardinal of Ferrara did. But afterwards he was so stupid as not to tell me anything at all about the matter; elsewise, it is certain that my wish to shield a silly mannikin from reproach, if only for our country's sake, would have made me find out some excuse to mend the bungling of his foolish self-conceit.

Immediately upon the receipt of Cardinal Ferrara's letter, I answered that about Cardinal de' Gaddi I knew absolutely nothing, and that even if he had made overtures of that kind to me, I should not have left Italy without informing his most reverend lordship. I also said that I had more to do in Rome than at any previous time; but that if his most Christian Majesty made sign of wanting me, one word of his, communicated by so great a prince as his most reverend lordship, would suffice to make me set off upon the spot, leaving all other concerns to take their chance.

After I had sent my letter, that traitor, the Perugian workman, devised a piece of malice against me, which succeeded at once, owing to the avarice of Pope Paolo da Farnese, but also far more to that of his bastard, who was then called Duke of Castro.[1] The fellow in question informed one of Signor Pier Luigi's secretaries that, having been with me as workman several years, he was acquainted with all my affairs, on the strength of which he gave his word to Signor Pier Luigi that I was worth more than eighty thousand ducats, and that the greater part of this property consisted in jewels, which jewels belonged to the Church, and that I had stolen them in Castel Sant' Angelo during the sack of Rome, and that all they had to do was to catch me on the spot with secrecy.

It so happened that I had been at work one morning, more than three hours before daybreak, upon the trousseau of the bride I mentioned; then, while my shop was being opened and swept out, I put my cape on to go abroad and take the air. Directing my steps along the Strada Giulia, I turned into Chiavica, and at this corner Crespino, the Bargello, with all his constables, made up to me, and said: "You are the Pope's prisoner." I answered: "Crespino, you have mistaken your man." "No," said Crespino, "you are the artist Benvenuto, and I know you well, and I have to take you to the Castle of Sant' Angelo, where lords go, and men of accomplishments, your peers." Upon that four of his under-officers rushed on me, and would have seized by force a dagger which I wore, and some rings I carried on my finger; but Crespino rebuked them: "Not a man of you shall touch him: it is quite enough if you perform your duty, and see that he does not escape me." Then he came up, and begged me with words of courtesy to surrender my arms. While I was engaged in doing this, it crossed my mind that exactly on that very spot I had assassinated Pompeo. They took me straightway to the castle, and locked me in an upper chamber in the keep. This was the first time that I ever smelt a prison up to the age I then had of thirty-seven years.

CII

Signor Pier Luigi, the Pope's son, had well considered the large sum for which I stood accused; so he begged the reversion of it from

[1] He had been invested with the Duchy of Castro in 1537.

his most holy father, and asked that he might have the money made out to himself. The Pope granted this willingly, adding that he would assist in its recovery. Consequently, after having kept me eight whole days in prison, they sent me up for examination, in order to put an end if possible to the affair. I was summoned into one of the great halls of the papal castle, a place of much dignity. My examiners were, first, the Governor of Rome, called Messer Benedetto Conversini of Pistoja,[1] who afterwards became Bishop of Jesi; secondly, the Procurator-Fiscal, whose name I have forgotten;[2] and, thirdly, the judge in criminal cases, Messer Benedetto da Cagli. These three men began at first to question me in gentle terms, which afterwards they changed to words of considerable harshness and menace, apparently because I said to them: "My lords, it is more than half-an-hour now since you have been pestering me with questions about fables and such things, so that one may truly say you are chattering or prattling; by chattering I mean talking without reason, by prattling I mean talking nonsense: therefore I beg you to tell me what it really is you want of me, and to let me hear from your lips reasonable speech, and not jabberings or nonsense." In reply to these words of mine, the Governor, who was a Pistojan, could no longer disguise his furious temper, and began: "You talk very confidently, or rather far too arrogantly; but let me tell you that I will bring your pride down lower than a spaniel by the words of reason you shall hear from me; these will be neither jabberings nor nonsense, as you have it, but shall form a chain of arguments to answer which you will be forced to tax the utmost of your wits." Then he began to speak as follows: "We know for certain that you were in Rome at the time when this unhappy city was subject to the calamity of the sack; at that time you were in this Castle of Sant' Angelo, and were employed as bombardier. Now since you are a jeweller and goldsmith by trade, Pope Clement, being previously acquainted with you, and having by him no one else of your profession, called you into his secret counsels, and made you unset all the jewels of his tiaras, mitres, and rings; afterwards, having confidence in you, he ordered you to sew them into his clothes. While thus engaged, you sequestered, unknown to his Holiness, a portion of them, to the value of eighty thousand crowns. This has been told us by one of your workmen, to whom you disclosed the matter in your braggadocio way. Now, we

1 Bishop of Forlimpopoli in 1537, and of Jesi in 1540.
2 Benedetto Valenti.

tell you frankly that you must find the jewels, or their value in money: after that we will release you."

CIII

When I heard these words, I could not hold from bursting into a roar of laughter; then, having laughed a while, I said: "Thanks be to God that on this first occasion, when it has pleased His Divine Majesty to imprison me, I should not be imprisoned for some folly, as the wont is usually with young men. If what you say were the truth, I run no risk of having to submit to corporal punishment, since the authority of the law was suspended during that season. Indeed, I could excuse myself by saying that, like a faithful servant, I had kept back treasure to that amount for the sacred and holy Apostolic Church, waiting till I could restore it to a good Pope, or else to those who might require it of me; as, for instance, you might, if this were verily the case." When I had spoken so far, the furious Governor would not let me conclude my argument, but exclaimed in a burst of rage: "Interpret the affair as you like best, Benvenuto; it is enough for us to have found the property which we had lost; be quick about it, if you do not want us to use other measures than words." Then they began to rise and leave the chamber; but I stopped them, crying out: "My lords, my examination is not over; bring that to an end, and go then where you choose." They resumed their seats in a very angry temper, making as though they did not mean to listen to a word I said, and at the same time half relieved,[1] as though they had discovered all they wanted to know. I then began my speech, to this effect: "You are to know, my lords, that it is now some twenty years since I first came to Rome, and I have never been sent to prison here or elsewhere." On this that catchpole of a Governor called out: "And yet you have killed men enough here!" I replied: "It is you that say it, and not I; but if some one came to kill you, priest as you are, you would defend yourself, and if you killed him, the sanctity of law would hold you justified. Therefore let me continue my defence, if you wish to report the case to the Pope, and to judge me fairly. Once more I tell you that I have been a sojourner in this marvellous city Rome for nigh on twenty years, and here I have exercised my art in matters of vast importance. Knowing that this is the seat of Christ, I entertained the reasonable

1 *Sollevati.* It may mean *half-risen from their seats.*

belief that when some temporal prince sought to inflict on me a mortal injury, I might have recourse to this holy chair and to this Vicar of Christ, in confidence that he would surely uphold my cause. Ah me! whither am I now to go? What prince is there who will protect me from this infamous assassination? Was it not your business, before you took me up, to find out what I had done with those eighty thousand ducats? Was it not your duty to inspect the record of the jewels, which have been carefully inscribed by this Apostolic Camera through the last five hundred years? If you had discovered anything missing on that record, then you ought to have seized all my books together with myself. I tell you for a certainty that the registers, on which are written all the jewels of the Pope and the regalia, must be perfectly in order; you will not find there missing a single article of value which belonged to Pope Clement that has not been minutely noted. The one thing of the kind which occurs to me is this: When that poor man Pope Clement wanted to make terms with those thieves of the Imperial army, who had robbed Rome and insulted the Church, a certain Cesare Iscatinaro, if I rightly remember his name, came to negotiate with him;[2] and having nearly concluded the agreement, the Pope in his extremity, to show the man some mark of favour, let fall a diamond from his finger, which was worth about four thousand crowns, and when Iscatinaro stooped to pick it up, the Pope told him to keep it for his sake. I was present at these transactions: and if the diamond of which I speak be missing, I have told you where it went; but I have the firmest conviction that you will find even this noted upon the register. After this you may blush at your leisure for having done such cruel injustice to a man like me, who has performed so many honourable services for the apostolic chair. I would have you know that, but for me, the morning when the Imperial troops entered the Borgo, they would without let or hindrance have forced their way into the castle. It was I who, unrewarded for this act, betook myself with vigour to the guns which had been abandoned by the cannoneers and soldiers of the ordnance. I put spirit into my comrade Raffaello da Montelupo, the sculptor, who had also left his post and hid himself all frightened in a corner, without stirring foot or finger; I woke his courage up, and he and I alone together slew so many of the enemies that the

2 Gio. Bartolommeo di Gattinara. Raffaello da Montelupo, in his Autobiography, calls him Cattinaro, and relates how "when he came one day into the castle to negotiate a treaty, he was wounded in the arm by one of our arquebusiers." This confirms what follows above.

soldiers took another road. I it was who shot at Iscatinaro when I saw him talking to Pope Clement without the slightest mark of reverence, nay, with the most revolting insolence, like the Lutheran and infidel he was. Pope Clement upon this had the castle searched to find and hang the man who did it. I it was who wounded the Prince of Orange in the head down there below the trenches of the castle. Then, too, how many ornaments of silver, gold, and jewels, how many models and coins, so beautiful and so esteemed, have I not made for Holy Church! Is this then the presumptuous priestly recompense you give a man who has served and loved you with such loyalty, with such mastery of art? Oh, go and report the whole that I have spoken to the Pope; go and tell him that his jewels are all in his possession; that I never received from the Church anything but wounds and stonings at that epoch of the sack; that I never reckoned upon any gain beyond some small remuneration from Pope Paolo, which he had promised me. Now at last I know what to think of his Holiness and you his Ministers."

While I was delivering this speech, they sat and listened in astonishment. Then exchanging glances one with the other, and making signs of much surprise, they left me. All three went together to report what I had spoken to the Pope. The Pope felt some shame, and gave orders that all the records of the jewels should be diligently searched. When they had ascertained that none were missing, they left me in the castle without saying a word more about it. Signor Pier Luigi felt also that he had acted ill; and to end the affair, they set about to contrive my death.

CIV

During the agitations of this time which I have just related, King Francis received news of how the Pope was keeping me in prison, and with what injustice. He had sent a certain gentleman of his, named Monsignor di Morluc, as his ambassador to Rome;[1] to him therefore he now wrote, claiming me from the Pope as the man of his Majesty. The Pope was a person of extraordinary sense and ability, but in this affair of mine he behaved weakly and unintelligently; for he made answer to the King's envoy that his Majesty need pay me no attention, since I was a fellow who gave much trouble by fighting;

[1] Jean de Montluc, brother of the celebrated Marshal, Bishop of Valence, a friend of Margaret of Navarre, and, like her, a protector of the Huguenots. He negotiated the election of the Duke of Anjou to the throne of Poland.

therefore he advised his Majesty to leave me alone, adding that he kept me in prison for homicides and other deviltries which I had played. To this the King sent answer that justice in his realm was excellently maintained; for even as his Majesty was wont to shower rewards and favours upon men of parts and virtue, so did he ever chastise the troublesome. His Holiness had let me go, not caring for the service of the said Benvenuto, and the King, when he saw him in his realm, most willingly adopted him; therefore he now asked for him in the quality of his own man. Such a demand was certainly one of the most honourable marks of favour which a man of my sort could desire; yet it proved the source of infinite annoyance and hurt to me. The Pope was roused to such fury by the jealous fear he had lest I should go and tell the whole world how infamously I had been treated, that he kept revolving ways in which I might be put to death without injury to his own credit.

The castellan of Sant' Angelo was one of our Florentines, called Messer Giorgio, a knight of the Ugolini family.[2] This worthy man showed me the greatest courtesy, and let me go free about the castle on parole. He was well aware how greatly I had been wronged; and when I wanted to give security for leave to walk about the castle, he replied that though he could not take that, seeing the Pope set too much importance upon my affair, yet he would frankly trust my word, because he was informed by every one what a worthy man I was. So I passed my parole, and he granted me conveniences for working at my trade. I then, reflecting that the Pope's anger against me must subside, as well because of my innocence as because of the favour shown me by the King, kept my shop in Rome open, while Ascanio, my prentice, came to the castle and brought me things to work at. I could not indeed do much, feeling myself imprisoned so unjustly; yet I made a virtue of necessity, and bore my adverse fortune with as light a heart as I was able.

I had secured the attachment of all the guards and many soldiers of the castle. Now the Pope used to come at times to sup there, and on those occasions no watch was kept, but the place stood open like an ordinary palace. Consequently, while the Pope was there, the prisoners used to be shut up with great precautions; none such, however, were taken with me, who had the license to go where I liked, even at those times, about its precincts. Often then those soldiers

2 It is only known of this man that he was a Knight of Jerusalem, and had been Commendatore of Prato in 1511.

told me that I ought to escape, and that they would aid and abet me, knowing as they did how greatly I had been wronged. I answered that I had given my parole to the castellan, who was such a worthy man, and had done me such kind offices. One very brave and clever soldier used to say to me: "My Benvenuto, you must know that a prisoner is not obliged, and cannot be obliged, to keep faith, any more than aught else which befits a free man. Do what I tell you; escape from that rascal of a Pope and that bastard his son, for both are bent on having your life by villainy." I had, however, made my mind up rather to lose my life than to break the promise I had given that good man the castellan. So I bore the extreme discomforts of my situation, and had for companion of misery a friar of the Palavisina house, who was a very famous preacher.[3]

CV

This man had been arrested as a Lutheran. He was an excellent companion; but, from the point of view of his religion, I found him the biggest scoundrel in the world, to whom all kind of vices were acceptable. His fine intellectual qualities won my admiration; but I hated his dirty vices, and frankly taxed him with them. This friar kept perpetually reminding me that I was in no wise bound to observe faith with the castellan, since I had become a prisoner. I replied to these arguments that he might be speaking the truth as a friar, but that as a man he spoke the contrary; for every one who called himself a man, and not a monk, was bound to keep his word under all circumstances in which he chanced to be. I therefore, being a man, and not a monk, was not going to break the simple and loyal word which I had given. Seeing then that he could not sap my honour by the subtle and ingenious sophistries he so eloquently developed, the friar hit upon another way of tempting me. He allowed some days to pass, during which he read me the sermons of Fra Jerolimo Savonarola; and these he expounded with such lucidity and learning that his comment was even finer than the text. I remained in ecstasies of admiration; and there was nothing in the world I would not have done for him, except, as I have said, to break my promised word. When he saw the effect his talents had produced upon my mind, he thought of yet another method. Cautiously he began to ask what means I should have taken, supposing my jailers had locked me

[3] Cellini means Pallavicini. Nothing seems to be known about him, except that his imprisonment is mentioned in a letter of Caro's under date 1540.

up, in order to set the dungeon doors open and effect my flight. I then, who wanted to display the sharpness of my own wits to so ingenious a man, replied that I was quite sure of being able to open the most baffling locks and bars, far more those of our prison, to do which would be the same to me as eating a bit of new cheese. In order then to gain my secret, the friar now made light of these assertions, averring that persons who have gained some credit by their abilities, are wont to talk big things which, if they had to put their boasts in action, would speedily discredit them, and much to their dishonour. Himself had heard me speak so far from the truth, that he was inclined to think I should, when pushed to proof, end in a dishonourable failure. Upon this, feeling myself stung to the quick by that devil of a friar, I responded that I always made a practice of promising in words less than I could perform in deeds; what I had said about the keys was the merest trifle; in a few words I could make him understand that the matter was as I had told it; then, all too heedlessly, I demonstrated the facility with which my assertions could be carried into act. He affected to pay little attention; but all the same he learned my lesson well by heart with keen intelligence.

As I have said above, the worthy castellan let me roam at pleasure over the whole fortress. Not even at night did he lock me in, as was the custom with the other prisoners. Moreover, he allowed me to employ myself as I liked best, with gold or silver or with wax according to my whim. So then I laboured several weeks at the bason ordered by Cardinal Ferrara, but the irksomeness of my imprisonment bred in me a disgust for such employment, and I took to modelling in wax some little figures of my fancy, for mere recreation. Of the wax which I used, the friar stole a piece; and with this he proceeded to get false keys made, upon the method I had heedlessly revealed to him. He had chosen for his accomplice a registrar named Luigi, a Paduan, who was in the castellan's service. When the keys were ordered, the locksmith revealed their plot; and the castellan who came at times to see me in my chamber, noticing the wax which I was using, recognised it at once and exclaimed: "It is true that this poor fellow Benvenuto has suffered a most grievous wrong; yet he ought not to have dealt thus with me, for I have ever strained my sense of right to show him kindness. Now I shall keep him straitly under lock and key, and shall take good care to do him no more service." Accordingly, he had me shut up with disagreeable circumstances, among the worst of which were the words flung at me by some of his devoted servants, who were indeed extremely fond of me, but now, on this occasion, cast in my teeth all the kind offices the castellan had done me; they came, in fact, to calling me ungrateful, light, and disloyal. One of them in particular used those injurious terms more insolently than was decent; whereupon I, being convinced of my innocence, retorted hotly that I had never broken faith, and would maintain these words at the peril of my life, and that if he or any of his fellows abused me so unjustly, I would fling the lie back in his throat. The man, intolerant of my rebuke rushed to the castellan's room, and brought me the wax with the model of the keys. No sooner had I seen the wax than I told him that both he and I were in the right; but I begged him to procure for me an audience with the castellan, for I meant to explain frankly how the matter stood, which was of far more consequence than they imagined. The castellan sent for me at once, and I told him the whole course of events. This made him arrest the friar, who betrayed the registrar, and the latter ran a risk of being hanged. However, the castellan hushed the affair up, although it had reached the Pope's ears; he saved his registrar from the gallows, and gave me the same freedom as I had before.

CVI

When I saw how rigorously this affair was prosecuted, I began to think of my own concerns, and said: "Supposing another of these storms should rise, and the man should lose confidence in me, I should then be under no obligation to him, and might wish to use my wits a little, which would certainly work their end better than those of that rascally friar." So I began to have new sheets of a coarse fabric brought me, and did not send the dirty ones away. When my servants asked for them, I bade them hold their tongues, saying I had given the sheets to some of those poor soldiers; and if the matter came to knowledge, the wretched fellows ran risk of the galleys. This made my young men and attendants, especially Felice, keep the secret of the sheets in all loyalty. I meanwhile set myself to emptying a straw mattress, the stuffing of which I burned, having a chimney in my prison. Out of the sheets I cut strips, the third of a cubit in breadth; and when I had made enough in my opinion to clear the great height of the central keep of Sant' Angelo, I told my servants that I had given away what I wanted; they must now bring me others of a finer fabric, and I would always send back the dirty ones. This affair was presently forgotten.

Now my workpeople and serving-men were obliged to close my shop at the order of the Cardinals Santi Quattro [1] and Cornaro, who told me openly that the Pope would not hear of setting me at large, and that the great favours shown me by King Francis had done far more harm than good. It seems that the last words spoken from the King by Monsignor di Morluc had been to this effect, namely, that the Pope ought to hand me over to the ordinary judges of the court; if I had done wrong, he could chastise me; but otherwise, it was but reason that he should set me at liberty. This message so irritated the Pope that he made his mind up to keep me a prisoner for life. At the same time, the castellan most certainly did his utmost to assist me.

When my enemies perceived that my shop was closed, they lost no opportunity of taunting and reviling those servants and friends of mine who came to visit me in prison. It happened on one occasion that Ascanio, who came twice a day to visit me, asked to have a jacket cut out for him from a blue silk vest of mine I never used. I had only worn it once, on the occasion when I walked in procession. I replied that these were not the times nor was I in the place to wear such clothes. The young man took my refusal of this miserable vest so ill that he told me he wanted to go home to Tagliacozzo. All in a rage, I answered that he could not please me better than by taking himself off; and he swore with passion that he would never show his face to me again. When these words passed between us, we were walking round the keep of the castle. It happened that the castellan was also taking the air there; so just when we met his lordship Ascanio said: "I am going away; farewell for ever!" I added: "For ever, is my wish too; and thus in sooth shall it be. I shall tell the sentinels not to let you pass again!" Then, turning to the castellan, I begged him with all my heart to order the guards to keep Ascanio out, adding: "This little peasant comes here to add to my great trouble; I entreat you, therefore, my lord, not to let him enter any more." The castellan was much grieved, because he knew him to be a lad of marvellous talents; he was, moreover, so fair of person that every one who once set eyes on him seemed bound to love him beyond measure.

The boy went away weeping. That day he had with him a small scimitar, which it was at times his wont to carry hidden beneath his

1 Antonio Pucci, a Florentine, Cardinal de' Quattro Santi Coronati.

clothes. Leaving the castle then, and having his face wet with tears, he chanced to meet two of my chief enemies, Jeronimo the Perugian,[2] and a certain Michele, goldsmiths both of them. Michele, being Jeronimo's friend and Ascanio's enemy, called out: "What is Ascanio crying for? Perhaps his father is dead; I mean that father in the castle!" Ascanio answered on the instant: "He is alive, but you shall die this minute." Then, raising his hand, he struck two blows with the scimitar, both at the fellow's head; the first felled him to earth, the second lopped three fingers off his right hand, though it was aimed at his head. He lay there like a dead man. The matter was at once reported to the Pope, who cried in a great fury: "Since the King wants him to be tried, go and give him three days to prepare his defence!" So they came, and executed the commission which the Pope had given them.

The excellent castellan went off upon the spot to his Holiness, and informed him that I was no accomplice in the matter, and that I had sent Ascanio about his business. So ably did he plead my cause that he saved my life from this impending tempest. Ascanio meanwhile escaped to Tagliacozzo, to his home there, whence he wrote begging a thousand times my pardon, and acknowledging his wrong in adding troubles to my grave disaster; but protesting that if through God's grace I came out from the prison, he meant never to abandon me. I let him understand that he must mind his art, and that if God set me at large again I would certainly recall him.

CVII

The castellan was subject to a certain sickness, which came upon him every year and deprived him of his wits. The sign of its approach was that he kept continually talking, or rather jabbering, to no purpose. These humours took a different shape each year; one time he thought he was an oil-jar; another time he thought he was a frog, and hopped about as frogs do; another time he thought he was dead, and then they had to bury him; not a year passed but he got some such hypochondriac notions into his head. At this season he imagined that he was a bat, and when he went abroad to take the air, he used to scream like bats in a high thin tone; and then he would flap his hands and body as though he were about to fly. The doctors, when they saw the fit was coming on him, and his old serv-

2 *i. e.,* Girolamo Pascucci.

ants, gave him all the distractions they could think of; and since they had noticed that he derived much pleasure from my conversation, they were always fetching me to keep him company. At times the poor man detained me for four or five stricken hours without ever letting me cease talking. He used to keep me at his table, eating opposite to him, and never stopped chatting and making me chat; but during those discourses I contrived to make a good meal. He, poor man, could neither eat nor sleep; so that at last he wore me out. I was at the end of my strength; and sometimes when I looked at him, I noticed that his eyeballs were rolling in a frightful manner, one looking one way and the other in another.

He took it into his head to ask me whether I had ever had a fancy to fly. I answered that it had always been my ambition to do those things which offer the greatest difficulties to men, and that I had done them; as to flying, the God of Nature had gifted me with a body well suited for running and leaping far beyond the common average, and that with the talents I possessed for manual art I felt sure I had the courage to try flying. He then inquired what methods I should use; to which I answered that, taking into consideration all flying creatures, and wishing to imitate by art what they derived from nature, none was so apt a model as the bat. No sooner had the poor man heard the name bat, which recalled the humour he was suffering under, than he cried out at the top of his voice: "He says true—he says true; the bat's the thing—the bat's the thing!" Then he turned to me and said: "Benvenuto, if one gave you the opportunity, should you have the heart to fly?" I said if he would set me at liberty, I felt quite up to flying down to Prati, after making myself a pair of wings out of waxed linen. Thereupon he replied: "I too should be prepared to take flight; but since the Pope has bidden me guard you as though you were his own eyes, and I know you a clever devil who would certainly escape, I shall now have you locked up with a hundred keys in order to prevent you slipping through my fingers." I then began to implore him, and remind him that I might have fled, but that on account of the word which I had given him I would never have betrayed his trust: therefore I begged him for the love of God, and by the kindness he had always shown me, not to add greater evils to the misery of my present situation. While I was pouring out these entreaties, he gave strict orders to have me bound and taken and locked up in prison. On seeing that it could not be helped, I told him before all his servants: "Lock me well up, and keep good watch on me; for I shall certainly contrive to escape." So they took and confined me with the utmost care.

CVIII

I then began to deliberate upon the best way of making my escape. No sooner had I been locked in, than I went about exploring my prison; and when I thought I had discovered how to get out of it, I pondered the means of descending from the lofty keep, for so the great round central tower is called. I took those new sheets of mine, which, as I have said already, I had cut in strips and sewn together; then I reckoned up the quantity which would be sufficient for my purpose. Having made this estimate and put all things in order, I looked out a pair of pincers which I had abstracted from a Savoyard belonging to the guard of the castle. This man superintended the casks and cisterns; he also amused himself with carpentering. Now he possessed several pairs of pincers, among which was one both big and heavy. I then, thinking it would suit my purpose, took it and hid it in my straw mattress. The time had now come for me to use it; so I began to try the nails which kept the hinges of my door in place.[1] The door was double, and the clinching of the nails could not be seen; so that when I attempted to draw one out, I met with the greatest trouble; in the end, however, I succeeded. When I had drawn the first nail, I bethought me how to prevent its being noticed. For this purpose I mixed some rust, which I had scraped from old iron, with a little wax, obtaining exactly the same colour as the heads of the long nails which I had extracted. Then I set myself to counterfeit these heads and place them on the holdfasts; for each nail I extracted I made a counterfeit in wax. I left the hinges attached to their door-posts at top and bottom by means of some of the same nails that I had drawn; but I took care to cut these and replace them lightly, so that they only just supported the irons of the hinges.

All this I performed with the greatest difficulty, because the castellan kept dreaming every night that I had escaped, which made him send from time to time to inspect my prison. The man who came had the title and behaviour of a catchpoll. He was called Bozza, and used always to bring with him another of the same sort, named Giovanni and nicknamed Pedignone; the latter was a soldier, and

1 The door seems to have been hung upon hinges with plates nailed into the posts. Cellini calls these plates *bandelle*.

Bozza a serving-man. Giovanni never entered my prison without saying something offensive to me. He came from the district of Prato, and had been an apothecary in the town there. Every evening he minutely examined the holdfasts of the hinges and the whole chamber, and I used to say: "Keep a good watch over me, for I am resolved by all means to escape." These words bred a great enmity between him and me, so that I was obliged to use precautions to conceal my tools, that is to say, my pincers and a great big poniard and other appurtenances. All these I put away together in my mattress, where I also kept the strips of linen I had made. When day broke, I used immediately to sweep my room out; and though I am by nature a lover of cleanliness, at that time I kept myself unusually spick and span. After sweeping up, I made my bed as daintily as I could, laying flowers upon it, which a Savoyard used to bring me nearly every morning. He had the care of the cistern and the casks, and also amused himself with carpentering; it was from him I stole the pincers which I used in order to draw out the nails from the holdfasts of the hinges.

CIX

Well, to return to the subject of my bed; when Bozza and Pedignone came, I always told them to give it a wide berth, so as not to dirty and spoil it for me. Now and then, just to irritate me, they would touch it lightly, upon which I cried: "Ah, dirty cowards! I'll lay my hand on one of your swords there, and will do you a mischief that will make you wonder. Do you think you are fit to touch the bed of a man like me? When I chastise you I shall not heed my own life, for I am certain to take yours. Let me alone then with my troubles and my tribulations, and don't give me more annoyance than I have already; if not, I shall make you see what a desperate man is able to do." These words they reported to the castellan, who gave them express orders never to go near my bed, and when they came to me, to come without swords, but for the rest to keep a watchful guard upon me.

Having thus secured my bed from meddlers, I felt as though the main point was gained; for there lay all things needful to my venture. It happened on the evening of a certain feast-day that the castellan was seriously indisposed; his humours grew extravagant; he kept repeating that he was a bat, and if they heard that Benvenuto had flown away, they must let him go to catch me up, since he could fly by night most certainly as well or better than myself; for it was thus he argued: "Benvenuto is a counterfeit bat, but I am a real one; and since he is committed to my care, leave me to act; I shall be sure to catch him." He had passed several nights in this frenzy, and had worn out all his servants, whereof I received full information through divers channels, but especially from the Savoyard, who was my friend at heart.

On the evening of that feast-day, then, I made my mind up to escape, come what might; and first I prayed most devoutly to God, imploring His Divine Majesty to protect and succour me in that so perilous a venture. Afterwards I set to work at all the things I needed, and laboured the whole of the night. It was two hours before daybreak when at last I removed those hinges with the greatest toil; but the wooden panel itself and the bolt too offered such resistance that I could not open the door; so I had to cut into the wood; yet in the end I got it open, and shouldering the strips of linen which I had rolled up like bundles of flax upon two sticks, I went forth and directed my steps toward the latrines of the keep. Spying from within two tiles upon the roof, I was able at once to clamber up with ease. I wore a white doublet with a pair of white hose and a pair of half boots, into which I had stuck the poniard I have mentioned.

After scaling the roof, I took one end of my linen roll and attached it to a piece of antique tile which was built into the fortress wall; it happened to jut out scarcely four fingers. In order to fix the band, I gave it the form of a stirrup. When I had attached it to that piece of tile, I turned to God and said: "Lord God, give aid to my good cause; you know that it is good; you see that I am aiding myself." Then I let myself go gently by degrees, supporting myself with the sinews of my arms, until I touched the ground. There was no moonshine, but the light of a fair open heaven. When I stood upon my feet on solid earth, I looked up at the vast height which I had descended with such spirit, and went gladly away, thinking I was free. But this was not the case; for the castellan on that side of the fortress had built two lofty walls, the space between which he used for stable and henyard; the place was barred with thick iron bolts outside. I was terribly disgusted to find there was no exit from this trap; but while I paced up and down debating what to do, I stumbled on a long pole which was covered up with straw. Not without great trouble I succeeded in placing it against the wall, and then swarmed up it by the force of my arms until I reached the top. But since the wall ended in a sharp ridge, I had not strength enough to drag the pole up after me. Accordingly I made my mind up to use a portion of the second roll of linen which I had there; the other was left hanging from the keep of the castle. So I cut a piece off, tied it to the pole, and clambered down the wall, enduring the utmost toil and fatigue. I was quite exhausted, and had, moreover, flayed the inside of my hands, which bled freely. This compelled me to rest awhile, and I bathed my hands in my own urine. When I thought that my strength was recovered, I advanced quickly toward the last rampart, which faces toward Prati. There I put my bundle of linen lines down upon the ground, meaning to fasten them round a battlement, and descend the lesser as I had the greater height. But no sooner had I placed the linen, than I became aware behind me of a sentinel, who was going the rounds. Seeing my designs interrupted and my life in peril, I resolved to face the guard. This fellow, when he noticed my bold front, and that I was marching on him with weapon in hand, quickened his pace and gave me a wide berth. I had left my lines some little way behind; so I turned with hasty steps to regain them; and though I came within sight of another sentinel, he seemed as though he did not choose to take notice of me. Having found my lines and attached them to the battlement, I let myself go. On the descent, whether it was that I thought I had really come to earth and relaxed my grasp to jump, or whether my hands were so tired that they could not keep their hold, at any rate I fell, struck my head in falling, and lay stunned for more than an hour and a half, so far as I could judge.

It was just upon daybreak, when the fresh breeze which blows an hour before the sun revived me; yet I did not immediately recover my senses, for I thought my head had been cut off and fancied that I was in purgatory. With time, little by little, my faculties returned, and I perceived that I was outside the castle, and in a flash remembered all my adventures. I was aware of the wound in my head before I knew my leg was broken; for I put my hands up, and withdrew them covered with blood. Then I searched the spot well, and judged and ascertained that I had sustained no injury of consequence there; but when I wanted to stand up, I discovered that my right leg was broken three inches above the heel. Not even this dismayed me: I drew forth my poniard with its scabbard; the latter had a metal point ending in a large ball, which had caused the fracture of my leg; for the bone, coming into violent contact with the ball, and not being able to bend, had snapped at that point. I threw the sheath away, and with the poniard cut a piece of the linen which I had left. Then I bound my leg up as well as I could, and crawled on all fours with the poniard in my hand toward the city gate. When I reached it, I found it shut; but I noticed a stone just beneath the door which did not appear to be very firmly fixed. This I attempted to dislodge; after setting my hands to it, and feeling it move, it easily gave way, and I drew it out. Through the gap thus made I crept into the town.

CX

I had crawled more than five hundred paces from the place where I fell, to the gate by which I entered. No sooner had I got inside than some mastiff dogs set upon me and bit me badly. When they returned to the attack and worried me, I drew my poniard and wounded one of them so sharply that he howled aloud, and all the dogs, according to their nature, ran after him. I meanwhile made the best way I could on all fours toward the church of the Trespontina.

On arriving at the opening of the street which leads to Sant' Agnolo, I turned off in the direction of San Piero; and now the dawn had risen over me, and I felt myself in danger. When therefore I chanced to meet a water-carrier driving his donkey laden with full buckets, I called the fellow, and begged him to carry me upon his back to the terrace by the steps of San Piero, adding: "I am an unfortunate young man, who, while escaping from a window in a love-adventure, have fallen and broken my leg. The place from which I made my exit is one of great importance; and if I am discovered, I run risk of being cut to pieces; so for heaven's sake lift me quickly, and I will give you a crown of gold." Saying this, I clapped my hand to my purse, where I had a good quantity. He took me up at once, hitched me on his back, and carried me to the raised terrace by the steps to San Piero. There I bade him leave me, saying he must run back to his donkey.

I resumed my march, crawling always on all fours, and making for the palace of the Duchess, wife of Duke Ottavio and daughter of the Emperor.[1] She was his natural child, and had been married to

[1] Margaret of Austria, who married Ottaviano Farnese in November 1538, after Alessandro's murder.

Duke Alessandro. I chose her house for refuge, because I was quite certain that many of my friends, who had come with that great princess from Florence, were tarrying there; also because she had taken me into favour through something which the castellan had said in my behalf. Wishing to be of service to me, he told the Pope that I had saved the city more than a thousand crowns of damage, caused by heavy rain on the occasion when the Duchess made her entrance into Rome. He related how he was in despair, and how I put heart into him, and went on to describe how I had pointed several large pieces of artillery in the direction where the clouds were thickest, and whence a deluge of water was already pouring; then, when I began to fire, the rain stopped, and at the fourth discharge the sun shone out; and so I was the sole cause of the festival succeeding, to the joy of everybody. On hearing this narration the Duchess said: "That Benvenuto is one of the artists of merit, who enjoyed the goodwill of my late husband, Duke Alessandro, and I shall always hold them in mind if an opportunity comes of doing such men service." She also talked of me to Duke Ottavio. For these reasons I meant to go straight to the house of her Excellency, which was a very fine palace situated in Borgio Vecchio.

I should have been quite safe from recapture by the Pope if I could have stayed there; but my exploits up to this point had been too marvellous for a human being, and God was unwilling to encourage my vainglory; accordingly, for my own good, He chastised me a second time worse even than the first. The cause of this was that while I was crawling on all fours up those steps, a servant of Cardinal Cornaro recognised me. His master was then lodging in the palace; so the servant ran up to his room and woke him, crying: "Most reverend Monsignor, your friend Benvenuto is down there; he has escaped from the castle, and is crawling on all fours, streaming with blood; to all appearances he has broken a leg, and we don't know whither he is going." The Cardinal exclaimed at once: "Run and carry him upon your back into my room here." When I arrived, he told me to be under no apprehension, and sent for the first physicians of Rome to take my case in hand. Among them was Maestro Jacomo of Perugia, a most excellent and able surgeon. He set the bone with dexterity, then bound the limb up, and bled me with his own hand. It happened that my veins were swollen far beyond their usual size, and he too wished to make a pretty wide incision; accordingly the blood sprang forth so copiously, and spurted with such force into his face, that he had to abandon the operation. He regarded this as a very bad omen, and could hardly be prevailed upon to undertake my cure. Indeed, he often expressed a wish to leave me, remembering that he ran no little risk of punishment for having treated my case, or rather for having proceeded to the end with it. The Cardinal had me placed in a secret chamber, and went off immediately to beg me from the Pope.

CXI

During this while all Rome was in an uproar; for they had observed the bands of linen fastened to the great keep of the castle, and folk were running in crowds to behold so extraordinary a thing. The castellan had gone off into one of his worst fits of frenzy; in spite of all his servants, he insisted upon taking his flight also from the tower, saying that no one could recapture me except himself if he were to fly after me. Messer Ruberto Pucci, the father of Messer Pandolfo,[1] having heard of the great event, went in person to inspect the place; afterwards he came to the palace, where he met with Cardinal Cornaro, who told him exactly what had happened, and how I was lodged in one of his own chambers, and already in the doctor's hands. These two worthy men went together, and threw themselves upon their knees before the Pope; but he, before they could get a word out, cried aloud: "I know all that you want of me." Messer Ruberto Pucci then began: "Most blessed Father, we beg you for Heaven's grace to give us up that unfortunate man; surely his great talents entitle him to exceptional treatment; moreover, he has displayed such audacity, blent with so much ingenuity, that his exploit might seem superhuman. We know not for what crimes your Holiness has kept him so long in prison; however, if those crimes are too exorbitant, your Holiness is wise and holy, and may your will be done unquestioned; still, if they are such as can be condoned, we entreat you to pardon him for our sake." The Pope, when he heard this, felt shame, and answered: "I have kept him in prison at the request of some of my people, since he is a little too violent in his behaviour; but recognising his talents, and wishing to keep him near our person, we had intended to treat him so well that he should have no reason to return to France. I am very sorry to hear of his bad accident; tell him to mind his health, and when he is recovered, we will make it up to him for all his troubles."

1 See above, p. 105.

Those two excellent men returned and told me the good news they were bringing from the Pope. Meanwhile the nobility of Rome, young, old, and all sorts, came to visit me. The castellan, out of his mind as he was, had himself carried to the Pope; and when he was in the presence of his Holiness, began to cry out, and to say that if he did not send me back to prison, he would do him a great wrong. "He escaped under parole which he gave me; woe is me that he has flown away when he promised not to fly!" The Pope said, laughing: "Go, go; for I will give him back to you without fail." The castellan then added, speaking to the Pope: "Send the Governor to him to find out who helped him to escape; for if it is one of my men, I will hang him from the battlement whence Benvenuto leaped." On his departure the Pope called the Governor, and said, smiling: "That is a brave fellow, and his exploit is something marvellous; all the same, when I was a young man, I also descended from the fortress at that very spot." In so saying the Pope spoke the truth: for he had been imprisoned in the castle for forging a brief at the time when he was abbreviator *di Parco Majoris.*[2] Pope Alexander kept him confined for some length of time; and afterwards, his offence being of too ugly a nature, had resolved on cutting off his head. He postponed the execution, however, till after Corpus Domini; and Farnese, getting wind of the Pope's will, summoned Pietro Chiavelluzzi with a lot of horses, and managed to corrupt some of the castle guards with money. Accordingly, upon the day of Corpus Domini, while the Pope was going in procession, Farnese got into a basket and was let down by a rope to the ground. At that time the outer walls had not been built around the castle; only the great central tower existed; so that he had not the same enormous difficulty that I met with in escaping; moreover, he had been imprisoned justly, and I against all equity. What he wanted was to brag before the Governor of having in his youth been spirited and brave; and it did not occur to him that he was calling attention to his own huge rogueries. He said then: "Go and tell him to reveal his accomplice without apprehension to you, be the man who he may be, since I have pardoned him; and this you may assure him without reservation."

2 The Collegium Abbreviatorum di Parco Majori consisted of seventy-two members. It was established by Pius II. Onofrio Panvinio tells this story of Paul III.'s imprisonment and escape, but places it in the Papacy of Innocent VIII. See *Vita Pauli III.*, in continuation of Platina.

CXII

So the Governor came to see me. Two days before he had been made Bishop of Jesi;[1] and when he entered he said: "Friend Benvenuto, although my office is wont to frighten men, I come to set your mind at rest, and to do this I have full authority from his Holiness's own lips, who told me how he also escaped from Sant' Angelo, but had many aids and much company, else he would not have been able to accomplish it. I swear by the sacraments which I carry on my person (for I was consecrated Bishop two days since) that the Pope has set you free and pardoned you, and is very sorry for your accident. Attend to your health, and take all things for the best; for your imprisonment, which you certainly underwent without a shadow of guilt, will have been for your perpetual welfare. Henceforward you will tread down poverty, and will have to go back to France, wearing out your life in this place and in that. Tell me then frankly how the matter went, and who rendered you assistance; afterwards take comfort, repose, and recover." I began at the beginning, and related the whole story exactly as it had happened, giving him the most minute countersigns, down to the water-carrier who bore me on his back. When the Governor had heard the whole, he said: "Of a surety these are too great exploits for one man alone; no one but you could have performed them." So he made me reach my hand forth, and said: "Be of good courage and comfort your heart, for by this hand which I am holding you are free, and if you live, shall live in happiness." While thus conversing with me, he had kept a whole heap of great lords and noblemen waiting, who were come to visit me, saying one to the other: "Let us go to see this man who works miracles." So, when he departed, they stayed by me, and one made me offers of kindness, and another made me presents.

While I was being entertained in this way, the Governor returned to the Pope, and reported all that I had said. As chance would have it, Signor Pier Luigi, the Pope's son, happened to be present, and all the company gave signs of great astonishment. His Holiness remarked: "Of a truth this is a marvellous exploit." Then Pier Luigi began to speak as follows: "Most blessed Father, if you set that man free, he will do something still more marvellous, because

[1] Cellini confuses Jesi with Forlimpopoli. See above, p. 188, note.

he has by far too bold a spirit. I will tell you another story about him which you do not know. That Benvenuto of yours, before he was imprisoned, came to words with a gentleman of Cardinal Santa Fiore,[2] about some trifle which the latter had said to him. Now Benvenuto's retort was so swaggeringly insolent that it amounted to throwing down a cartel. The gentleman referred the matter to the Cardinal, who said that if he once laid hands on Benvenuto he would soon clear his head of such folly. When the fellow heard this, he got a little fowling-piece of his ready, with which he is accustomed to hit a penny in the middle; accordingly, one day when the Cardinal was looking out of a window, Benvenuto's shop being under the palace of the Cardinal, he took his gun and pointed it upon the Cardinal. The Cardinal, however, had been warned, and presently withdrew. Benvenuto, in order that his intention might escape notice, aimed at a pigeon which was brooding high up in a hole of the palace, and hit it exactly in the head—a feat one would have thought incredible. Now let your Holiness do what you think best about him; I have discharged my duty by saying what I have. It might even come into his head, imagining that he had been wrongly imprisoned, to fire upon your Holiness. Indeed he is too truculent, by far too confident in his own powers. When he killed Pompeo, he gave him two stabs with a poniard in the throat, in the midst of ten men who were guarding him; then he escaped, to their great shame, and yet they were no inconsiderable persons."

CXIII

While these words were being spoken, the gentleman of Santa Fiore with whom I had that quarrel was present, and confirmed to the Pope what had been spoken by his son. The Pope swelled with rage, but said nothing. I shall now proceed to give my own version of the affair, truly and honestly.

This gentleman came to me one day, and showed me a little gold ring which had been discoloured by quicksilver, saying at the same time: "Polish up this ring for me, and be quick about it." I was engaged at the moment upon jewel-work of gold and gems of great importance: besides, I did not care to be ordered about so haughtily by a man I had never seen or spoken to; so I replied that I did not

2 Ascanio Sforza, son of Boslo, Count of Santa Fiore, and grandson of Paul III. He got the hat in 1534, at the age of sixteen.

happen to have by me the proper tool for cleaning up his ring,[1] and that he had better go to another goldsmith. Without further provocation he retorted that I was a donkey; whereupon I said that he was not speaking the truth; that I was a better man than he in every respect, but that if he kept on irritating me I would give him harder kicks than any donkey could. He related the matter to the Cardinal, and painted me as black as the devil in hell. Two days afterwards I shot a wild pigeon in a cleft high up behind the palace. The bird was brooding in that cleft, and I had often seen a goldsmith named Giovan Francesca della Tacca, from Milan, fire at it; but he never hit it. On the day when I shot it, the pigeon scarcely showed its head, being suspicious because it had been so often fired at. Now this Giovan Francesco and I were rivals in shooting wildfowl; and some gentlemen of my acquaintance, who happened to be at my shop, called my attention, saying: "Up there is Giovan Francesco della Tacca's pigeon, at which he has so often fired; look now, the poor creature is so frightened that it hardly ventures to put its head out." I raised my eyes, and said: "That morsel of its head is quite enough for me to shoot it by, if it only stays till I can point my gun." The gentlemen protested that even the man who invented firearms could not hit it. I replied: "I bet a bottle of that excellent Greek wine Palombo the host keeps, that if it keeps quiet long enough for me to point my good Broccardo (so I used to call my gun), I will hit it in that portion of its head which it is showing." So I aimed my gun, elevating my arms, and using no other rest, and did what I had promised, without thinking of the Cardinal or any other person; on the contrary, I held the Cardinal for my very good patron. Let the world, then, take notice, when Fortune has the will to ruin a man, how many divers ways she takes! The Pope, swelling with rage and grumbling, remained revolving what his son had told him.

CXIV

Two days afterwards the Cardinal Cornaro went to beg a bishopric from the Pope for a gentleman of his called Messer Andrea Centano. The Pope, in truth, had promised him a bishopric; and this being now vacant, the Cardinal reminded him of his word. The

[1] Cellini calls it *isvivatoio*. It is properly *avvivatoio*, a sort of brass rod with a wooden handle

Pope acknowledged his obligation, but said that he too wanted a favour from his most reverend lordship, which was that he would give up Benvenuto to him. On this the Cardinal replied: "Oh, if your Holiness has pardoned him and set him free at my disposal, what will the world say of you and me?" The Pope answered: "I want Benvenuto, you want the bishopric; let the world say what it chooses." The good Cardinal entreated his Holiness to give him the bishopric, and for the rest to think the matter over, and then to act according as his Holiness decided. The Pope, feeling a certain amount of shame at so wickedly breaking his word, took what seemed a middle course: "I will send for Benvenuto, and in order to gratify the whim I have, will put him in those rooms which open on my private garden; there he can attend to his recovery, and I will not prevent any of his friends from coming to visit him. Moreover, I will defray his expenses until this caprice of mine has left me."

The Cardinal came home, and sent the candidate for this bishopric on the spot to inform me that the Pope was resolved to have me back, but that he meant to keep me in a ground-floor room in his private garden, where I could receive the visits of my friends, as I had done in his own house. I implored this Messer Andrea to ask the Cardinal not to give me up to the Pope, but to let me act on my own account. I would have myself wrapped up in a mattress, and carried to a safe place outside Rome; for if he gave me up to the Pope, he would certainly be sending me to death. It is believed that when the Cardinal heard my petition he was not ill-disposed to grant it; but Messer Andrea, wanting to secure the bishopric, denounced me to the Pope, who sent at once and had me lodged in the ground-floor chamber of his private garden. The Cardinal sent me word not to eat the food provided for me by the Pope; he would supply me with provisions; meanwhile I was to keep my spirits up, for he would work in my cause till I was set free. Matters being thus arranged, I received daily visits and generous offers from many great lords and gentlemen. Food came from the Pope, which I refused to touch, only eating that which came from Cardinal Cornaro; and thus I remained awhile.

I had among my friends a young Greek of the age of twenty-five years. He was extremely active in all physical exercises, and the best swordsman in Rome; rather poor-spirited, however, but loyal to the backbone; honest, and ready to believe what people told him.

He had heard it said that the Pope made known his intention of compensating me for all I had gone through. It is true that the Pope began by saying so, but he ended by saying quite the opposite. I then determined to confide in the young Greek, and said to him: "Dearest brother, they are plotting my ruin; so now the time has come to help me. Do they imagine, when they heap those extraordinary favours on me, that I am not aware they are done to betray me?" The worthy young man answered: "My Benvenuto, they say in Rome that the Pope has bestowed on you an office with an income of five hundred crowns; I beseech you therefore not to let those suspicions deprive you of so great a windfall." All the same I begged him with clasped hands to aid me in escaping from that place, saying I knew well that a Pope of that sort, though he could do me much good if he chose, was really studying secretly, and to save appearances, how he might best destroy me; therefore we must be quick and try to save me from his clutches. If my friend would get me out of that place by the means I meant to tell him, I should always regard him as the saviour of my life, and when occasion came would lay it down for him with gladness. The poor young man shed tears, and cried: "Oh, my dear brother, though you are bringing destruction on your head, I cannot but fulfil your wishes; so explain your plan, and I will do whatever you may order, albeit much against my will." Accordingly we came to an agreement, and I disclosed to him the details of my scheme, which was certain to have succeeded without difficulty. When I hoped that he was coming to execute it, he came and told me that for my own good he meant to disobey me, being convinced of the truth of what he had heard from men close to the Pope's person, who understood the real state of my affairs. Having nothing else to rely upon, I remained in despair and misery. This passed on the day of Corpus Domini 1539.

CXV

After my conversation with the Greek, the whole day wore away, and at night there came abundant provisions from the kitchen of the Pope; the Cardinal Cornaro also sent good store of viands from his kitchen; and some friends of mine being present when they arrived, I made them stay to supper, and enjoyed their society, keeping my leg in splints beneath the bed-clothes. An hour after nightfall they left me; and two of my servants, having made me comfortable for the night, went to sleep in the ante-chamber. I had a dog, black as a mulberry, one of those hairy ones, who followed me admirably when I went out shooting, and never left my side. During the night he lay beneath my bed, and I had to call out at least three times to my servant to turn him out, because he howled so fearfully. When the servants entered, the dog flew at them and tried to bite them. They were frightened, and thought he must be mad, because he went on howling. In this way we passed the first four hours of the night. At the stroke of four the Bargello came into my room with a band of constables. Then the dog sprang forth and flew at them with such fury, tearing their capes and hose, that in their fright they fancied he was mad. But the Bargello, like an experienced person, told them: "It is the nature of good dogs to divine and foretell the mischance coming on their masters. Two of you take sticks and beat the dog off; while the others strap Benvenuto on this chair; then carry him to the place you wot of." It was, as I have said, the night after Corpus Domini, and about four o'clock.

The officers carried me, well shut up and covered, and four of them went in front, making the few passengers who were still abroad get out of the way. So they bore me to Torre di Nona, such is the name of the place, and put me in the condemned cell. I was left upon a wretched mattress under the care of a guard, who kept all night mourning over my bad luck, and saying to me: "Alas! poor Benvenuto, what have you done to those great folk?" I could now form a very good opinion of what was going to happen to me, partly by the place in which I found myself, and also by what the man had told me.[1] During a portion of that night I kept racking my brains what the cause could be why God thought fit to try me so, and not being able to discover it, I was violently agitated in my soul. The guard did the best he could to comfort me; but I begged him for the love of God to stop talking, seeing I should be better able to compose myself alone in quiet. He promised to do as I asked; and then I turned my whole heart to God, devoutly entreating Him to deign to take me into His kingdom. I had, it is true, murmured against my lot, because it seemed to me that, so far as human laws go, my departure from the world in this way would be too unjust; it is true also that I had committed homicides, but His Vicar had called me from my native city and pardoned me by the authority

1 Cellini thought he was going to have his throat cut. And indeed the Torre di Nona was a suspicious place, it being one of the worst criminal prisons in Rome.

he had from Him and from the laws; and what I had done had all been done in defence of the body which His Majesty had lent me; so I could not admit that I deserved death according to the dispensation under which man dwells here; but it seemed that what was happening to me was the same as what happens to unlucky people in the street, when a stone falls from some great height upon their head and kills them; this we see clearly to be the influence of the stars; not indeed that the stars conspire to do us good or evil, but the effect results from their conjunctions, to which we are subordinated. At the same time I know that I am possessed of free-will, and if I could exert the faith of a saint, I am sure that the angels of heaven would bear me from this dungeon and relieve me of all my afflictions; yet inasmuch as God has not deemed me worthy of such miracles, I conclude that those celestial influences must be wreaking their malignity upon me. In this long struggle of the soul I spent some time; then I found comfort, and fell presently asleep.

CXVI

When the day dawned, the guard woke me up and said: "Oh, unfortunate but worthy man, you have no more time to go on sleeping, for one is waiting here to give you evil news." I answered: "The sooner I escape from this earthly prison, the happier shall I be; especially as I am sure my soul is saved, and that I am going to an undeserved death. Christ, the glorious and divine, elects me to the company of His disciples and friends, who, like Himself, were condemned to die unjustly. I too am sentenced to an unjust death, and I thank God with humility for this sign of grace. Why does not the man come forward who has to pronounce my doom?" The guard replied: "He is too grieved for you, and sheds tears." Then I called him by his name of Messer Benedetto da Cagli,[1] and cried: "Come forward, Messer Benedetto, my friend, for now, I am resolved and in good frame of mind; far greater glory is it for me to die unjustly than if I had deserved this fate. Come forward, I beg, and let me have a priest, in order that I may speak a couple of words with him. I do not indeed stand in need of this, for I have already made my heart's confession to my Lord God; yet I should like to observe the ordinances of our Holy Mother Church; for though she has done me this abominable wrong, I pardon her with all my soul. So come,

[1] It will be remembered that Benedetto da Cagli was one of Cellini's three examiners during his first imprisonment in S. Angelo.

friend Messer Benedetto, and despatch my business before I lose control over my better instincts."

After I had uttered these words, the worthy man told the guard to lock the door, because nothing could be done without his presence. He then repaired to the house of Signor Pier Luigi's wife, who happened to be in company with the Duchess of whom I spoke above.[2] Presenting himself before them both, he spoke as follows: "My most illustrious mistress, I entreat you for the love of God to tell the Pope that he must send some one else to pronounce sentence upon Benvenuto and perform my office; I renounce the task, and am quite decided not to carry it through." Then, sighing, he departed with the strongest signs of inward sorrow. The Duchess, who was present, frowned and said: "So this is the fine justice dealt out here in Rome by God's Vicar! The Duke, my late husband, particularly esteemed this man for his good qualities and eminent abilities; he was unwilling to let him return to Rome, and would gladly have kept him close to his own person." Upon this she retired, muttering words of indignation and displeasure. Signor Pier Luigi's wife, who was called Signora Jerolima, betook herself to the Pope, and threw herself upon her knees before him in the presence of several cardinals. She pleaded my cause so warmly that she woke the Pope to shame; whereupon he said: "For your sake we will leave him quiet; yet you must know that we had no ill-will against him." These words he spoke because of the cardinals who were around him, and had listened to the eloquence of that brave-spirited lady.

Meanwhile I abode in extreme discomfort, and my heart kept thumping against my ribs. Not less was the discomfort of the men appointed to discharge the evil business of my execution; but when the hour for dinner was already past, they betook themselves to their several affairs, and my meal was also served me. This filled with a glad astonishment, and I exclaimed: "For once truth has been stronger than the malice of the stars! I pray God, therefore, that, if it be His pleasure, He will save me from this fearful peril." Then I fell to eating with the same stout heart for my salvation as I had previously prepared for my perdition. I dined well, and afterwards remained without seeing or hearing any one until an hour after nightfall. At that time the Bargello arrived with a large part of his

2 The wife of Pier Luigi Farnese was Jeronima, daughter of Luigi Orsini, Count of Pitigliano.

guard, and had me replaced in the chair which brought me on the previous evening to the prison. He spoke very kindly to me, bidding me be under no apprehension; and bade his constables take good care not to strike against my broken leg, but to treat me as though I were the apple of their eye. The men obeyed, and brought me to the castle whence I had escaped; then, when we had mounted to the keep, they left me shut up in a dungeon opening upon a little court there is there.

CXVII

The castellan, meanwhile, ill and afflicted as he was, had himself transported to my prison, and exclaimed: "You see that I have recaptured you!" "Yes," said I, "but you see that I escaped, as I told you I would. And if I had not been sold by a Venetian Cardinal, under Papal guarantee, for the price of a bishopric, the Pope a Roman and a Farnese (and both of them have scratched with impious hands the face of the most sacred laws), you would not have recovered me. But now that they have opened this vile way of dealing, do you the worst you can in your turn; I care for nothing in the world." The wretched man began shouting at the top of his voice: "Ah, woe is me; woe is me! It is all the same to this fellow whether he lives or dies, and behold, he is more fiery than when he was in health. Put him down there below the garden, and do not speak to me of him again, for he is the destined cause of my death."

So I was taken into a gloomy dungeon below the level of a garden, which swam with water, and was full of big spiders and many venomous worms. They flung me a wretched mattress of coarse hemp, gave me no supper, and locked four doors upon me. In that condition I abode until the nineteenth hour of the following day. Then I received food, and I requested my jailers to give me some of my books to read. None of them spoke a word, but they referred my prayer to the unfortunate castellan, who had made inquiries concerning what I said. Next morning they brought me an Italian Bible which belonged to me, and a copy of the Chronicles of Giovanni Villani.[1] When I asked for certain other of my books, I was told that I could have no more, and that I had got too many already.

[1] This mention of an Italian Bible shows that we are still in the days before the Council of Trent.

Thus, then, I continued to exist in misery upon that rotten mattress, which in three days soaked up water like a sponge. I could hardly stir because of my broken leg; and when I had to get out of bed to obey a call of nature, I crawled on all fours with extreme distress, in order not to foul the place I slept in. For one hour and a half each day I got a little glimmering of light, which penetrated that unhappy cavern through a very narrow aperture. Only for so short a space of time could I read; the rest of the day and night I abode in darkness, enduring my lot, nor ever without meditations upon God and on our human frailty. I thought it certain that a few more days would put an end of my unlucky life in that sad place and in that miserable manner. Nevertheless, as well as I was able, I comforted my soul by calling to mind how much more painful it would have been, on passing from this life, to have suffered that unimaginable horror of the hangman's knife. Now, being as I was, I should depart with the anodyne of sleepiness, which robbed death of half its former terrors. Little by little I felt my vital forces waning, until at last my vigorous temperament had become adapted to that purgatory. When I felt it quite acclimatised, I resolved to put up with all those indescribable discomforts so long as it held out.

CXVIII

I began the Bible from the commencement, reading and reflecting on it so devoutly, and finding in it such deep treasures of delight, that, if I had been able, I should have done naught else but study it. However, light was wanting; and the thought of all my troubles kept recurring and gnawing at me in the darkness, until I often made my mind up to put an end somehow to my own life. They did not allow me a knife, however, and so it was no easy matter to commit suicide. Once, notwithstanding, I took and propped a wooden pole I found there, in position like a trap. I meant to make it topple over on my head, and it would certainly have dashed my brains out; but when I had arranged the whole machine, and was approaching to put it in motion, just at the moment of my setting my hand to it, I was seized by an invisible power and flung four cubits from the spot, in such a terror that I lay half dead. Like that I remained from dawn until the nineteenth hour, when they brought my food. The jailers must have visited my cell several times without my taking notice of them; for when at last I heard them, Captain Sandrino

Monaldi [1] had entered, and I heard him saying: "Ah, unhappy man! behold the end to which so rare a genius has come!" Roused by these words, I opened my eyes, and caught sight of priests with long gowns on their backs, who were saying: "Oh, you told us he was dead!" Bozza replied: "Dead I found him, and therefore I told you so." Then they lifted me from where I lay, and after shaking up the mattress, which was now as soppy as a dish of maccaroni, they flung it outside the dungeon. The castellan, when these things were reported to him, sent me another mattress. Thereafter, when I searched my memory to find what could have diverted me from that design of suicide, I came to the conclusion that it must have been some power divine and my good guardian angel.

CXIX

During the following night there appeared to me in dreams a marvellous being in the form of a most lovely youth, who cried, as though he wanted to reprove me: "Knowest thou who lent thee that body, which thou wouldst have spoiled before its time?" I seemed to answer that I recognized all things pertaining to me as gifts from the God of nature. "So, then," he said, "thou hast contempt for His handiwork, through this thy will to spoil it? Commit thyself unto His guidance, and lose not hope in His great goodness!" Much more he added, in words of marvellous efficacy, the thousandth part of which I cannot now remember.

I began to consider that the angel of my vision spoke the truth. So I cast my eyes around the prison, and saw some scraps of rotten brick, with the fragments of which, rubbing one against the other, I composed a paste. Then, creeping on all fours, as I was compelled to go, I crawled up to an angle of my dungeon door, and gnawed a splinter from it with my teeth. Having achieved this feat, I waited till the light came on my prison; that was from the hour of twenty and a half to twenty-one and a half. When it arrived, I began to write, the best I could, on some blank pages in my Bible, and rebuked the regents of my intellectual self for being too impatient to endure this life; they replied to my body with excuses drawn from all that they had suffered; and the body gave them hope of better fortune. To this effect, then, by way of dialogue, I wrote as follows:—

[1] A Florentine, banished in 1530 for having been in arms against the Medici.

Benvenuto in the body.

Afflicted regents of my soul!
  Ah, cruel ye! have ye such hate of life?

The Spirits of his soul.

If Heaven against you roll,
  Who stands for us? who saves us in the strife?
  Let us, O let us go toward better life!

Benvenuto.

Nay, go not yet awhile!
  Ye shall be happier and lighter far—
  Heaven gives this hope—than ye were ever yet!

The Spirits.

We will remain some little while,
  If only by great God you promised are
  Such grace that no worse woes on us be set.

After this I recovered strength; and when I had heartened up myself, I continued reading in the Bible, and my eyes became so used to that darkness that I could now read for three hours instead of the bare hour and a half I was able to employ before.

With profound astonishment I dwelt upon the force of God's Spirit in those men of great simplicity, who believed so fervently that He would bring all their heart's desire to pass. I then proceeded to reckon in my own case too on God's assistance, both because of His divine power and mercy, and also because of my own innocence; and at all hours, sometimes in prayer and sometimes in communion with God, I abode in those high thoughts of Him. There flowed into my soul so powerful a delight from these reflections upon God, that I took no further thought for all the anguish I had suffered, but rather spent the day in singing psalms and divers other compositions on the theme of His divinity.

I was greatly troubled, however, by one particular annoyance: my nails had grown so long that I could not touch my body without wounding it; I could not dress myself but what they turned inside or out, to my great torment. Moreover, my teeth began to perish in my mouth. I became aware of this because the dead teeth being pushed out by the living ones, my gums were gradually perforated, and the points of the roots pierced through the tops of their cases.

When I was aware of this, I used to pull one out, as though it were a weapon from a scabbard, without any pain or loss of blood. Very many of them did I lose in this way. Nevertheless, I accommodated myself to these new troubles also; at times I sang, at times I prayed, and at times I wrote by means of the paste of brick-dust I have described above. At this time I began composing a Capitolo in praise of my prison, relating in it all the accidents which had befallen me.[1] This poem I mean to insert in its proper place.

CXX

The good castellan used frequently to send messengers to find out secretly what I was doing. So it happened on the last day of July that I was rejoicing greatly by myself alone while I bethought me of the festival they keep in Rome upon the 1st of August; and I was saying to myself: "In former years I kept the feast among the pleasures and the frailties of the world; this year I shall keep it in communion with God. Oh, how far more happy am I thus than I was then!" The persons who heard me speak these words reported them to the castellan. He was greatly annoyed, and exclaimed: "Ah, God! that fellow lives and triumphs in his infinite distress, while I lack all things in the midst of comfort, and am dying only on account of him! Go quickly, and fling him into that deepest of the subterranean dungeons where the preacher Foiano was starved to death.[1] Perhaps when he finds himself in such ill plight he will begin to droop his crest."

Captain Sandrino Monaldi came at once into my prison with about twenty of the castellan's servants. They found me on my knees; and I did not turn at their approach, but went on paying my orisons before a God the Father, surrounded with angels, and a Christ arising victorious from the grave, which I had sketched upon the wall with a little piece of charcoal I had found covered up with earth. This was after I had lain four months upon my back in bed with my leg

[1] Capitolo is the technical name for a copy of verses in *terza rima* on a chosen theme. Poems of this kind, mostly burlesque or satirical, were very popular in Cellini's age. They used to be written on trifling or obscene subjects in a mock-heroic style. Berni stamped the character of high art upon the species, which had long been in use among the unlettered vulgar. See for further particulars Symonds' *Renaissance in Italy,* vol. v. chap. xiv.

[1] Fra Benedetto da Foiano had incurred the wrath of Pope Clement VII. by preaching against the Medici in Florence. He was sent to Rome and imprisoned in a noisome dungeon of S. Angelo in the year 1530, where Clement made him perish miserably by diminishing his food and water daily till he died. See Varchi's *Storia Fiorentina,* lib. xii. chap. 4.

broken, and had so often dreamed that angels came and ministered to me, that at the end of those four months the limb became as sound as though it never had been fractured. So then these fellows entered, all in armour, as fearful of me as though I were a poison-breathing dragon. The captain spoke as follows: "You must be aware that there are many of us here, and our entrance has made a tumult in this place, yet you do not turn round." When I heard these words, I was well able to conceive what greater harm might happen to me, but being used and hardened to misfortune, I said to them: "Unto this God who supports me, to Him in heaven I have turned my soul, my contemplation, and all my vital spirits; to you I have turned precisely what belongs to you. What there is of good in me, you are not worthy to behold, nor can you touch it. Do then to that which is under your control all the evil you are able." The captain, in some alarm, and not knowing what I might be on the point of doing, said to four of his tallest fellows: "Put all your arms aside." When they had done so, he added: "Now upon the instant leap on him, and secure him well. Do you think he is the devil, that so many of us should be afraid of him? Hold him tight now, that he may not escape you." Seized by them with force and roughly handled, and anticipating something far worse than what afterwards happened, I lifted my eyes to Christ and said: "Oh, just God, Thou paidest all our debts upon that high-raised cross of Thine; wherefore then must my innocence be made to pay the debts of whom I do not even know? Nevertheless, Thy will be done." Meanwhile the men were carrying me away with a great lighted torch; and I thought that they were about to throw me down the oubliette of Sammabo. This was the name given to a fearful place which had swallowed many men alive; for when they are cast into it, they fall to the bottom of a deep pit in the foundations of the castle. This did not, however, happen to me; wherefore I thought that I had made a very good bargain when they placed me in that hideous dungeon I have spoken of, where Fra Foiano died of hunger, and left me there without doing me further injury.

When I was alone, I began to sing a *De profundis clamavi,* a *Miserere,* and *In te Domine speravi.* During the whole of that first day of August I kept festival with God, my heart rejoicing ever in the strength of hope and faith. On the second day they drew me from that hole, and took me back again to the prison where I had drawn those representations of God. On arriving there, the sight of them filled me with such sweetness and such gladness that I wept abundantly. On every day that followed, the castellan sent to know what I was doing and saying. The Pope, who had heard the whole history (and I must add that the doctors had already given the castellan over), spoke as follows: "Before my castellan dies I will let him put that Benvenuto to death in any way he likes, for he is the cause of his death, and so the good man shall not die unrevenged." On hearing these words from the mouth of Duke Pier Luigi, the castellan replied: "So, then, the Pope has given me Benvenuto, and wishes me to take my vengeance on him? Dismiss the matter from your mind, and leave me to act." If the heart of the Pope was ill-disposed against me, that of the castellan was now at the commencement savage and cruel in the extreme. At this juncture the invisible being who had diverted me from my intention of suicide, came to me, being still invisible, but with a clear voice, and shook me, and made me rise, and said to me. "Ah me! my Benvenuto, quick, quick, betake thyself to God with thy accustomed prayers, and cry out loudly, loudly!" In a sudden consternation I fell upon my knees, and recited several of my prayers in a loud voice; after this I said *Qui habitat in adjutorio;* then I communed a space with God; and in an instant the same clear and open voice said to me: "Go to rest, and have no further fear!" The meaning of this was, that the castellan, after giving the most cruel orders for my death, suddenly countermanded them, and said: "Is not this Benvenuto the man whom I have so warmly defended, whom I know of a surety to be innocent, and who has been so greatly wronged? Oh, how will God have mercy on me and my sins if I do not pardon those who have done me the greatest injuries? Oh, why should I injure a man both worthy and innocent, who has only done me services and honour? Go to! instead of killing him, I give him life and liberty: and in my will I'll have it written that none shall demand of him the heavy debt for his expenses here which he would elsewhere have to pay." This the Pope heard, and took it very ill indeed.

CXXI

I meanwhile continued to pray as usual, and to write my Capitolo, and every night I was visited with the gladdest and most pleasant dreams that could be possibly imagined. It seemed to me while dreaming that I was always in the visible company of that being whose voice and touch, while he was still invisible, I had so often felt. To him I made but one request, and this I urged most earnestly, namely, that he would bring me where I could behold the sun. I told him that this was the sole desire I had, and that if I could but see the sun once only, I should die contented. All the disagreeable circumstances of my prison had become, as it were, to me friendly and companionable; not one of them gave me annoyance. Nevertheless, I ought to say that the castellan's parasites, who were waiting for him to hang me from the battlement whence I had made my escape, when they saw that he had changed his mind to the exact opposite of what he previously threatened, were unable to endure the disappointment. Accordingly, they kept continually trying to inspire me with the fear of imminent death by means of various terrifying hints. But, as I have already said, I had become so well acquainted with troubles of this sort that I was incapable of fear, and nothing any longer could disturb me; only I had that one great longing to behold the sphere of the sun, if only in a dream.

Thus then, while I spent many hours a day in prayer with deep emotion of the spirit toward Christ, I used always to say: "Ah, very Son of God! I pray Thee by Thy birth, by Thy death upon the cross, and by Thy glorious resurrection, that Thou wilt deign to let me see the sun, if not otherwise, at least in dreams. But if Thou wilt grant me to behold it with these mortal eyes of mine, I engage myself to come and visit Thee at Thy holy sepulchre." This vow and these my greatest prayers to God I made upon the 2nd of October in the year 1539. Upon the following morning, which was the 3rd of October, I woke at daybreak, perhaps an hour before the rising of the sun. Dragging myself from the miserable lair in which I lay, I put some clothes on, for it had begun to be cold; then I prayed more devoutly than ever I had done in the past, fervently imploring Christ that He would at least grant me the favour of knowing by divine inspiration what sin I was so sorely expiating; and since His Divine Majesty had not deemed me worthy of beholding the sun even in a dream I besought Him to let me know the cause of my punishment.

CXXII

I had barely uttered these words, when that invisible being, like a whirlwind, caught me up and bore me away into a large room, where he made himself visible to my eyes in human form, appearing like a young man whose beard is just growing, with a face of indescribable beauty, but austere, not wanton. He bade me look around the room, and said: "The crowd of men thou seest in this place are all those who up to this day have been born and afterwards have died upon the earth." Thereupon I asked him why he brought me hither, and he answered: "Come with me and thou shalt soon behold." In my hand I had a poniard, and upon my back a coat of mail; and so he led me through that vast hall, pointing out the people who were walking by innumerable thousands up and down, this way and that. He led me onward, and went forth in front of me through a little low door into a place which looked like a narrow street; and when he drew me after him into the street, at the moment of leaving the hall, behold I was disarmed and clothed in a white shirt, with nothing on my head, and I was walking on the right hand of my companion. Finding myself in this condition, I was seized with wonder, because I did not recognise the street; and when I lifted my eyes, I discerned that the splendour of the sun was striking on a wall, as it were a house-front, just above my head. Then I said: "Oh, my friend! what must I do in order to be able to ascend so high that I may gaze upon the sphere of the sun himself?" He pointed out some huge stairs which were on my right hand, and said to me: "Go up thither by thyself." Quitting his side, I ascended the stairs backwards, and gradually began to come within the region of the sunlight. Then I hastened my steps, and went on, always walking backwards as I have described, until I discovered the whole sphere of the sun. The strength of his rays, as is their wont, first made me close my eyes; but becoming aware of my misdoing, I opened them wide, and gazing steadfastly at the sun, exclaimed: "Oh, my sun, for whom I have so passionately yearned! Albeit your rays may blind me, I do not wish to look on anything again but this!" So I stayed awhile with my eyes fixed steadily on him; and after a brief space I beheld in one moment the whole might of those great burning rays fling themselves upon the left side of the sun; so that the orb remained quite clear without its rays, and I was able to contemplate it with vast delight. It seemed to me something marvellous that the rays should be removed in that manner. Then I reflected that divine grace it was which God had granted me that morning, and cried aloud: "Oh, wonderful Thy power! oh, glorious Thy virtue! How far greater is the grace which Thou art granting me than that which I expected!" The sun without his rays appeared to me to be a bath of the purest molten gold, neither more nor less. While I stood contemplating this wondrous thing, I noticed that the middle of the sphere began to swell, and the swollen surface grew, and suddenly a Christ upon the cross formed itself out of the same substance as the sun. He bore the aspect of divine benignity, with such fair grace that the mind of man could not conceive the thousandth part of it; and while I gazed in ecstasy, I shouted: "A miracle! a miracle! O God! O clemency Divine! O immeasurable Goodness! what is it Thou hast deigned this day to show me!" While I was gazing and exclaiming thus, the Christ moved toward that part where his rays were settled, and the middle of the sun once more bulged out as it had done before; the boss expanded, and suddenly transformed itself into the shape of a most beautiful Madonna, who appeared to be sitting enthroned on high, holding her child in her arms with an attitude of the greatest charm and a smile upon her face. On each side of her was an angel, whose beauty far surpasses man's imagination. I also saw within the rondure of the sun, upon the right hand, a figure robed like a priest; this turned its back to me, and kept its face directed to the Madonna and the Christ. All these things I beheld, actual, clear, and vivid, and kept returning thanks to the glory of God as loud as I was able. The marvellous apparition remained before me little more than half a quarter of an hour: then it dissolved, and I was carried back to my dark lair.

I began at once to shout aloud: "The virtue of God hath deigned to show me all His glory, the which perchance no mortal eye hath ever seen before. Therefore I know surely that I am free and fortunate and in the grace of God; but you miscreants shall be miscreants still, accursed, and in the wrath of God. Mark this, for I am certain of it, that on the day of All Saints, the day upon which I was born in 1500, on the first of November, at four hours after nightfall, on that day which is coming you will be forced to lead me from this gloomy dungeon; less than this you will not be able to do, because I have seen it with these eyes of mine and in that throne of God. The priest who kept his face turned to God and his back to me, that priest was S. Peter, pleading my cause, for the shame he felt that such foul wrongs should be done to Christians in his own house. You may go and tell it to whom you like; for none on earth has the power to do me harm henceforward; and tell that lord who keeps me here, that if he will give me wax or paper and the means of portraying this glory of God which was revealed to me, most assuredly shall I convince him of that which now perhaps he holds in doubt."

CXXIII

The physicians gave the castellan no hope of his recovery, yet he remained with a clear intellect, and the humours which used to afflict him every year had passed away. He devoted himself entirely to the care of his soul, and his conscience seemed to smite him, because he felt that I had suffered and was suffering a grievous wrong. The Pope received information from him of the extraordinary things which I related; in answer to which his Holiness sent word—as one who had no faith either in God or aught beside—that I was mad, and that he must do his best to mend his health. When the castellan received this message, he sent to cheer me up, and furnished me with writing materials and wax, and certain little wooden instruments employed in working wax, adding many words of courtesy, which were reported by one of his servants who bore me good-will. This man was totally the opposite of that rascally gang who had wished to see me hanged. I took the paper and the wax, and began to work; and while I was working I wrote the following sonnet addressed to the castellan:—

"If I, my lord, could show to you the truth,
Of that Eternal Light to me by Heaven
In this low life revealed, you sure had given
More heed to mine than to a monarch's sooth.

Ah! could the Pastor of Christ's flock in ruth
Believe how God this soul with sight hath shriven
Of glory unto which no weight hath striven
Ere he escaped earth's cave of care uncouth;

The gates of Justice, holy and austere,
Would roll asunder, and rude impious Rage
Fall chained with shrieks that should assail the skies.

Had I but light, ah me! my art should rear
A monument of Heaven's high equipage!
Nor should my misery bear so grim a guise."

CXXIV

On the following day, when the servant of the castellan who was my friend brought me my food, I gave him this sonnet copied out in writing. Without informing the other ill-disposed servants who were my enemies, he handed it to the castellan. At that time this worthy man would gladly have granted me my liberty, because he fancied that the great wrong done to me was a main cause of his death. He took the sonnet, and having read it more than once, exclaimed: "These are neither the words nor the thoughts of a madman, but rather of a sound and worthy fellow." Without delay he ordered his secretary to take it to the Pope, and place it in his own hands, adding a request for my deliverance.

While the secretary was on his way with my sonnet to the Pope, the castellan sent me lights for day and night, together with all the conveniences one could wish for in that place. The result of this was that I began to recover from my physical depression, which had reached a very serious degree.

The Pope read the sonnet several times. Then he sent word to the castellan that he meant presently to do what would be pleasing to him. Certainly the Pope had no unwillingness to release me then; but Signor Pier Luigi, his son, as it were in the Pope's despite, kept me there by force.

The death of the castellan was drawing near; and while I was engaged in drawing and modelling that miracle which I had seen, upon the morning of All Saints' day he sent his nephew, Piero Ugolini, to show me certain jewels. No sooner had I set eyes on them than I exclaimed: "This is the countersign of my deliverance!" Then the young man, who was not a person of much intelligence, began to say: "Never think of that, Benvenuto!" I replied: "Take your gems away, for I am so treated here that I have no light to see by except what this murky cavern gives, and that is not enough to test the quality of precious stones. But, as regards my deliverance from this dungeon, the day will not end before you come to fetch me out. It shall and must be so, and you will not be able to prevent it." The man departed, and had me locked in; but after he had remained away two hours by the clock, he returned without armed men, bringing only a couple of lads to assist my movements; so after this fashion he conducted me to the spacious rooms which I had previously occupied (that is to say, in 1538), where I obtained all the conveniences I asked for.

CXXV

After the lapse of a few days, the castellan, who now believed that I was at large and free, succumbed to his disease and departed this life. In his room remained his brother, Messer Antonio Ugolini, who had informed the deceased governor that I was duly released. From what I learned, this Messer Antonio received commission from the Pope to let me occupy that commodious prison until he had decided what to do with me.

Messer Durante of Brescia, whom I have previously mentioned, engaged the soldier (formerly druggist of Prato) to administer some deadly liquor in my food;[1] the poison was to work slowly, producing its effect at the end of four or five months. They resolved on mixing pounded diamond with my victuals. Now the diamond is not a poison in any true sense of the word, but its incomparable hardness enables it, unlike ordinary stones, to retain very acute angles. When every other stone is pounded, that extreme sharpness of edge is lost; their fragments becoming blunt and rounded. The diamond alone preserves its trenchant qualities; wherefore, if it chances to enter the stomach together with food, the peristaltic motion[2] needful to digestion brings it into contact with the coats of the stomach and the bowels, where it sticks, and by the action of fresh food forcing it farther inwards, after some time perforates the organs. This eventually causes death. Any other sort of stone or glass mingled with the food has not the power to attach itself, but passes onward with the victuals. Now Messer Durante entrusted a diamond of trifling value to one of the guards; and it is said that a certain Lione, a goldsmith of Arezzo, my great enemy, was commissioned to pound it.[3] The man happened to be very poor, and the diamond was worth perhaps some scores of crowns. He told the guard that the dust he gave him back was the diamond in question properly ground down. The morning when I took it, they mixed it with all I had to eat; it was a Friday, and I had it in salad, sauce, and pottage. That morning I ate heartily, for I had fasted on the previous evening; and this day was a festival. It is true that I felt

1 For Messer Durante, see above, p. 166. For the druggist of Prato employed as a warder in S. Angelo, see above, p. 199.

2 *In quel girare che e' fanno e' cibi.* I have for the sake of clearness used the technical phrase above.

3 The name of Leone Leoni is otherwise known as a goldsmith and bronze-caster. He made the tomb for Giangiacomo de' Medici, Il Medighino, in the Cathedral of Milan.

the victuals scrunch beneath my teeth; but I was not thinking about knaveries of this sort. When I had finished, some scraps of salad remained upon my plate, and certain very fine and glittering splinters caught my eye among these remnants. I collected them, and took them to the window, which let a flood of light into the room; and while I was examining them, I remembered that the food I ate that morning had scrunched more than usual. On applying my senses strictly to the matter, the verdict of my eyesight was that they were certainly fragments of pounded diamond. Upon this I gave myself up without doubt as dead, and in my sorrow had recourse with pious heart to holy prayers. I had resolved the question, and thought that I was doomed. For the space of a whole hour I prayed fervently to God, returning thanks to Him for so merciful a death. Since my stars had sentenced me to die, I thought it no bad bargain to escape from life so easily. I was resigned, and blessed the world and all the years which I had passed in it. Now I was returning to a better kingdom with the grace of God, the which I thought I had most certainly acquired.

While I stood revolving these thoughts in my mind, I held in my hand some flimsy particles of the reputed diamond, which of a truth I firmly believed to be such. Now hope is immortal in the human breast; therefore I felt myself, as it were, lured onward by a gleam of idle expectation. Accordingly, I took up a little knife and a few of those particles, and placed them on an iron bar of my prison. Then I brought the knife's point with a slow strong grinding pressure to bear upon the stone, and felt it crumble. Examining the substance with my eyes, I saw that it was so. In a moment new hope took possession of my soul, and I exclaimed: "Here I do not find my true foe, Messer Durante, but a piece of bad soft stone, which cannot do me any harm whatever!" Previously I had been resolved to remain quiet and to die in peace; now I revolved other plans; but first I rendered thanks to God and blessed poverty; for though poverty is oftentimes the cause of bringing men to death, on this occasion it had been the very cause of my salvation. I mean in this way: Messer Durante, my enemy, or whoever it was, gave a diamond to Lione to pound for me of the worth of more than a hundred crowns; poverty induced him to keep this for himself, and to pound for me a greenish beryl of the value of two carlins, thinking perhaps, because it also was a stone, that it would work the same effect as the diamond.

CXXVI

At this time the Bishop of Pavia, brother of the Count of San Secondo, and commonly called Monsignor de' Rossi of Parma, happened to be imprisoned in the castle for some troublesome affairs at Pavia.[1] Knowing him to be my friend, I thrust my head out of the hole in my cell, and called him with a loud voice, crying that those thieves had given me a pounded diamond with the intention of killing me. I also sent some of the splinters which I had preserved, by the hand of one of his servants, for him to see. I did not disclose my discovery that the stone was not a diamond, but told him that they had most assuredly poisoned me, after the death of that most worthy man the castellan. During the short space of time I had to live, I begged him to allow me one loaf a day from his own stores, seeing that I had resolved to eat nothing which came from them. To this request he answered that he would supply me with victuals.

Messer Antonio, who was certainly not cognisant of the plot against my life, stirred up a great noise, and demanded to see the pounded stone, being also persuaded that it was a diamond; but on reflection that the Pope was probably at the bottom of the affair, he passed it over lightly after giving his attention to the incident.

Henceforth I ate the victuals sent me by the Bishop, and continued writing my Capitolo on the prison, into which I inserted daily all the new events which happened to me, point by point. But Messer Antonio also sent me food; and he did this by the hand of that Giovanni of Prato, the druggist, then soldier in the castle, whom I have previously mentioned. He was a deadly foe of mine, and was the man who had administered the powdered diamond. So I told him that I would partake of nothing he brought me unless he tasted it before my eyes.[2] The man replied that Popes have their meat tasted. I answered: "Noblemen are bound to taste the meat for Popes; in like measure, you, soldier, druggist, peasant from Prato, are bound to taste the meat for a Florentine of my station." He retorted with coarse words, which I was not slow to pay back in kind.

Now Messer Antonio felt a certain shame for his behaviour; he had it also in his mind to make me pay the costs which the late castellan, poor man, remitted in my favour. So he hunted out an-

1 Gio. Girolamo de' Rossi, known in literature as a poet and historian of secondary importance.

2 *Me ne faceva la credenza.*

other of his servants, who was my friend, and sent me food by this man's hands. The meat was tasted for me now with good grace, and no need for altercation. The servant in question told me that the Pope was being pestered every day by Monsignor di Morluc, who kept asking for my extradition on the part of the French King. The Pope, however, showed little disposition to give me up; and Cardinal Farnese, formerly my friend and patron, had declared that I ought not to reckon on issuing from that prison for some length of time.[3] I replied that I should get out in spite of them all. The excellent young fellow besought me to keep quiet, and not to let such words of mine be heard, for they might do me some grave injury; having firm confidence in God, it was my duty to await His mercy, remaining in the meanwhile tranquil. I answered that the power and goodness of God are not bound to stand in awe before the malign forces of iniquity.

CXXVII

A few days had passed when the Cardinal of Ferrara arrived in Rome. He went to pay his respects to the Pope, and the Pope detained him up to supper-time. Now the Pope was a man of great talent for affairs, and he wanted to talk at his ease with the Cardinal about French politics. Everybody knows that folk, when they are feasting together, say things which they would otherwise retain. This therefore happened. The great King Francis was most frank and liberal in all his dealings, and the Cardinal was well acquainted with his temper. Therefore the latter could indulge the Pope beyond his boldest expectations. This raised his Holiness to a high pitch of merriment and gladness, all the more because he was accustomed to drink freely once a week, and went indeed to vomit after his indulgence. When, therefore, the Cardinal observed that the Pope was well disposed, and ripe to grant favours, he begged for me at the King's demand, pressing the matter hotly, and proving that his Majesty had it much at heart. Upon this the Pope laughed aloud; he felt the moment for his vomit at hand; the excessive quantity of wine which he had drunk was also operating; so he said: "On the spot, this instant, you shall take him to your house." Then, having given express orders to this purpose, he rose from table. The Cardinal immediately sent for me, before Signor Pier Luigi could get wind of

[3] This was the Cardinal Alessandro, son of Pier Luigi Farnese.

the affair; for it was certain that he would not have allowed me to be loosed from prison.

The Pope's mandatary came together with two great gentlemen of the Cardinal's, and when four o'clock of the night was passed, they removed me from my prison, and brought me into the presence of the Cardinal, who received me with indescribable kindness. I was well lodged, and left to enjoy the comforts of my situation.

Messer Antonio, the old castellan's brother, and his successor in the office, insisted on extracting from me the costs for food and other fees and perquisites claimed by sheriffs and such fry, paying no heed to his predecessor's will in my behalf. This affair cost me several scores of crowns; but I paid them, because the Cardinal told me to be well upon my guard if I wanted to preserve my life, adding that had he not extracted me that evening from the prison, I should never have got out. Indeed, he had already been informed that the Pope greatly regretted having let me go.

CXXVIII

I am now obliged to take a step backwards, in order to resume the thread of some events which will be found in my Capitolo. While I was sojourning those few days in the chamber of the Cardinal, and afterwards in the Pope's private garden, there came among my other friends to visit me a cashier of Messer Bindo Altoviti, who was called Bernardo Galluzzi. I had entrusted to him a sum of several hundred crowns, and the young man sought me out in the Pope's garden, expressing his wish to give back this money to the uttermost farthing. I answered that I did not know where to place my property, either with a dearer friend or in a place that seemed to me more safe. He showed the strongest possible repugnance to keeping it, and I was, as it were, obliged to force him. Now that I had left the castle for the last time, I discovered that poor Bernardo Galluzzi was ruined, whereby I lost my money. Now while I was still imprisoned in that dungeon, I had a terrible dream, in which it seemed to me that words of the greatest consequence were written with a pen upon my forehead; the being who did this to me repeated at least three times that I should hold my tongue and not report the words to any one. When I awoke I felt that my forehead had been meddled with. In my Capitolo upon the prison I have related many incidents of this sort. Among others, it was told me (I not knowing what I then prophesied) how everything which afterwards happened to Signor Pier Luigi would take place, so clearly and so circumstantially that I am under the persuasion it was an angel from heaven who informed me. I will not omit to relate another circumstance also, which is perhaps the most remarkable which has ever happened to any one. I do so in order to justify the divinity of God and of His secrets, who deigned to grant me that great favour; for ever since the time of my strange vision until now an aureole of glory (marvellous to relate) has rested on my head. This is visible to every sort of men to whom I have chosen to point it out; but those have been very few. This halo can be observed above my shadow in the morning from the rising of the sun for about two hours, and far better when the grass is drenched with dew. It is also visible at evening about sunset. I became aware of it in France at Paris; for the air in those parts is so much freer from mist, that one can see it there far better manifested than in Italy, mists being far more frequent among us. However, I am always able to see it and to show it to others, but not so well as in the country I have mentioned.

Now I will set forth the Capitolo I wrote in prison, and in praise of the said prison; after that I will follow the course of the good and evil things which have happened to me from time to time; and I mean also to relate what happens in the future.

THIS CAPITOLO I WRITE TO LUCA MARTINI, ADDRESSING HIM IN IT AS WILL APPEAR.[1]

Whoso would know the power of God's dominion,
And how a man resembles that high good,
Must lie in prison, is my firm opinion:

On grevious thoughts and cares of home must brood,
Oppressed with carking pains in flesh and bone,
Far from his native land full many a rood.

If you would fain by worthy deeds be known,
Seek to be prisoned without cause, lie long,
And find no friend to listen to your moan.

See that men rob you of your all by wrong;
Add perils to your life; be used with force,
Hopeless of help, by brutal foes and strong.

1 Cellini's Capitolo in Praise of the Prison is clearly made up of pieces written, as described above, in the dungeon of S. Angelo, and of passages which he afterwards composed to bring these pieces into a coherent whole. He has not displayed much literary skill in the redaction, and I have been at pains to preserve the roughness of the original.

Be driven at length to some mad desperate course;
  Burst from your dungeon, leap the castle wall;
  Recaptured, find the prison ten times worse.

Now listen, Luca, to the best of all!
  Your leg's been broken; you've been bought and sold;
  Your dungeon's dripping; you've no cloak or shawl.

Never one friendly word; your victuals cold
  Are brought with sorry news by some base groom
  Of Prato—soldier now—druggist of old.

Mark well how Glory steeps her sons in gloom!
  You have no seat to sit on, save the stool:
  Yet were you active from your mother's womb.

The knave who serves hath orders strict and cool
  To list no word you utter, give you naught,
  Scarcely to ope the door; such is their rule.

These toys hath Glory for her nursling wrought!
  No paper, pens, ink, fire, or tools of steel,
  To exercise the quick brain's teeming thought.

Alack that I so little can reveal!
  Fancy one hundred for each separate ill:
  Full space and place I've left for prison weal!

But now my former purpose to fulfil,
  And sing the dungeon's praise with honour due—
  For this angelic tongues were scant of skill.

Here never languish honest men and true
  Except by placemen's fraud, misgovernment,
  Jealousies, anger, or some spiteful crew.

To tell the truth whereon my mind is bent,
  Here man knows God, nor ever stints to pray,
  Feeling his soul with hell's fierce anguish rent.

Let one be famed as bad as mortal may,
  Send him in jail two sorry years to pine,
  He'll come forth holy, wise, beloved alway.

Here soul, flesh, clothes their substance gross refine;
  Each bulky lout grows light like gossamere;
  Celestial thrones before purged eyeballs shine.

I'll tell thee a great marvel! Friend, give ear!
The fancy took me on one day to write:
Learn now what shifts one may be put to here.

My cell I search, prick brows and hair upright,
Then turn me toward a cranny in the door,
And with my teeth a splinter disunite;

Next find a piece of brick upon the floor,
Crumble a part therefore to powder small,
And form a paste by sprinkling water o'er.[2]

Then, then came Poesy with fiery call
Into my carcass, by the way methought:
Whence bread goes forth—there was none else at all.

Now to return unto my primal thought:
Who wills to know what weal awaits him, must
First learn the ill that God for him hath wrought.

The jail contains all arts in act and trust;
Should you but hanker after surgeon's skill,
'Twill draw the spoiled blood from your veins adust.

Next there is something in itself that will
Make you right eloquent, a bold brave spark,
Big with high-soaring thoughts for good and ill.

Blessed is the man who lies in dungeon dark,
Languishing many a month, then takes his flight
Of war, truce, peace he knows, and tells the mark.

Needs be that all things turn to his delight;
The jail has crammed his brain so full of wit,
They'll dance no morris to upset the wight.

Perchance thou'lt urge: "Think how thy life did flit;
Nor is it true the jail can teach thee lore,
To fill thy breast and heart with strength of it!"

Nay, for myself I'll ever praise it more:
Yet would I like one law passed—that the man
Whose acts deserve it should not escape this score.

Whoso hath gotten the poor folk in ban,
I'd make him learn those lessons of the jail;
For then he'd know all a good ruler can:

2 The Italian is *acqua morta;* probably a slang phrase for urine.

He'd act like men who weigh by reason's scale,
Nor dare to swerve from truth and right aside,
Nor would confusion in the realm prevail.

While I was bound in prison to abide,
Foison of priests, friars, soldiers I could see;
But those who best deserved it least I spied.

Ah! could you know what rage came over me,
When for such rogues the jail relaxed her hold!
This makes one weep that one was born to be!

I'll add no more. Now I'm become fine gold,
Such gold as none flings lightly to the wind,
Fit for the best work eyes shall e'er behold.

Another point hath passed into my mind
Which I've not told thee, Luca; where I wrote
Was in the book of one our kith and kind.[3]

There down the margins I was wont to note
Each torment grim that crushed me like a vice:
The paste my hurrying thoughts could hardly float.

To make an O, I dipped the splinter thrice
In that thick mud; worse woe could scarcely grind
Spirits in hell debarred from Paradise.

Seeing I'm not the first by fraud confined,
This I'll omit; and once more seek the cell
Wherein I rack for rage both heart and mind.

I praise it more than other tongues will tell;
And, for advice to such as do not know,
Swear that without it none can labour well.

Yet oh! for one like Him I learned but now,
Who'd cry to me as by Bethesda's shore:
Take thy clothes, Benvenuto, rise and go!

Credo I'd sing, Salve reginas pour
And Paternosters; alms I'd then bestow
Morn after morn on blind folk, lame, and poor.

Ah me! how many a time my cheek must grow
Blanched by those lilies! Shall I then forswear
Florence and France through them for evermore?[4]

[3] *Un nostro parente.* He says above that he wrote the Capitolo on the leaves of his Bible.
[4] Here he begins to play upon the lilies, which were arms of the Farnesi, of Florence, and of France.

If to the hospital I come, and fair
Find the Annunziata limned, I'll fly:
Else shall I show myself a brute beast there.[5]

These words flout not Her worshipped sanctity,
Nor those Her lilies, glorious, holy, pure,
The which illumine earth and heaven high!

But for I find at every coign obscure
Base lilies which spread hooks where flowers should blow
Needs must I fear lest these to ruin lure.[6]

To think how many walk like me in woe!
Born what, how slaved to serve that hateful sign!
Souls lively, graceful, like to gods below!

I saw that lethal heraldry decline
From heaven like lightning among people vain;
Then on the stone I saw strange lustre shine.

The castle's bell must break ere I with strain
Thence issued; and these things Who speaketh true
In heaven on earth, to me made wondrous plain.[7]

Next I beheld a bier of sombre hue
Adorned with broken lilies; crosses, tears;
And on their beds a lost woe-stricken crew.[8]

I saw the Death who racks our souls with fears;
This man and that she menaced, while she cried:
"I clip the folk who harm thee with these shears!"

That worthy one then on my brow wrote wide
With Peter's pen words which—for he bade shun
To speak them thrice—within my breast I hide.[9]

Him I beheld who drives and checks the sun,
Clad with its splendour 'mid his court on high,
Seld-seen by mortal eyes, if e're by one.[10]

Then did a solitary sparrow cry
Loud from the keep; hearing which note, I said:
"He tells that I shall live and you must die!"

5 Gabriel holds the lily in Italian paintings when he salutes the Virgin Mary with *Ave Virgo!*
6 That is, he finds everywhere in Italy the arms of the Farnesi.
7 Allusion to his prevision of the castellan's death.
8 Allusion to his prevision of Pier Luigi Farnese's murder.
9 Allusion to the angel who visited him in prison.

I sang, and wrote my hard case, head by head,
Asking from God pardon and aid in need,
For now I felt mine eyes outworn and dead.

Ne'er lion, tiger, wolf, or bear knew greed
Hungrier than that man felt for human blood;
No viper with more venomous fang did feed.[11]

The cruel chief was he of robbers' brood,
Worst of the worst among a gang of knaves;
Hist! I'll speak soft lest I be understood!

Say, have ye seen catchpolls, the famished slaves,
In act a poor man's homestead to distrain,
Smashing down Christs, Madonnas, with their staves?

So on the first of August did that train
Dislodge me to a tomb more foul, more cold:—
"November damns and dooms each rogue to pain!"[12]

I at mine ears a trumpet had which told
Truth; and each word to them I did repeat,
Reckless, if but grief's load from me were rolled.

They, when they saw their final hope retreat,
Gave me a diamond, pounded, no fair ring,
Deeming that I must die if I should eat.

That villian churl whose office 'twas to bring
My food, I bade taste first; but meanwhile thought:
"Not here I find my foe Durante's sting!"

Yet erst my mind unto high God I brought
Beseeching Him to pardon all my sin,
And spoke a Miserere sorrow-fraught.

Then when I gained some respite from that din
Of troubles, and had given my soul to God,
Contented better realms and state to win,

I saw along the path which saints have trod,
From heaven descending, glad, with glorious palm,
An angel: clear he cried, "Upon earth's sod

10 Allusion to his vision of the sun in the dungeon.
11 An invective against Pier Luigi Farnese.
12 Allusion to the prophetic words he flung at the officers who took him to Foiano's dungeon.

Live longer! Through Him who heard thy psalm,
  Those foes shall perish, each and all, in strife,
  While thou remainest happy, free, and calm,
Blessed by our Sire in heaven on earth for life!’[2]

SECOND BOOK

I

I REMAINED for some time in the Cardinal of Ferrara's palace, very well regarded in general by everybody, and much more visited even than I had previously been. Everybody was astonished that I should have come out of prison and have been able to live through such indescribable afflictions;[1] and while I was recovering my breath and endeavouring to resume the habit of my art, I had great pleasure in re-writing the Capitolo. Afterwards, with a view to re-establishing my strength, I determined to take a journey of a few days for change of air. My good friend the Cardinal gave me permission and lent me horses; and I had two young Romans for my companions, one of them a craftsman in my trade, the other only a comrade in our journey. We left Rome, and took the road to Tagliacozzo, intending to visit my pupil Ascanio, who lived there. On our arrival, I found the lad, together with his father, brothers, sisters, and step-mother. I was entertained by them two days with indescribable kindness; then I turned my face towards Rome, taking Ascanio with me. On the road we fell to conversing about our art, which made me die of impatience to get back and recommence my labours.

Having reached Rome, I got myself at once in readiness to work, and was fortunate enough to find again a silver basin which I had begun for the Cardinal before I was imprisoned. Together with this basin I had begun a very beautiful little jug; but this had been stolen, with a great quantity of other valuable articles. I set Pagolo, whom I have previously mentioned, to work upon the basin. At the same time I recommenced the jug, which was designed with round figures and bas-reliefs. The basin was executed in a similar style, with round figures and fishes in bas-relief. The whole had such richness and good keeping, that every one who beheld it expressed astonishment at the force of the design and beauty of invention, and also at the delicacy[2] with which these young men worked.

1 This assertion is well supported by contemporary letters of Caro and Alamanni.
2 *Pulitezza.* This indicates precision, neatness, cleanness of execution.

The Cardinal came at least twice a day to see me, bringing with him Messer Luigi Alamanni and Messer Gabriel Cesano;[3] and here we used to pass an hour or two pleasantly together. Notwithstanding I had very much to do, he kept giving me fresh commissions. Among others, I had to make his pontifical seal of the size of the hand of a boy of twelve. On it I engraved in intaglio two little histories, the one of San Giovanni preaching in the wilderness, the other of Sant' Ambrogio expelling the Arians[4] on horseback with a lash in his hand. The fire and correctness of design of this piece, and its nicety of workmanship, made every one say that I had surpassed the great Lautizio, who ranked alone in this branch of the profession. The Cardinal was so proud of it that he used to compare it complacently with the other seals of the Roman cardinals, which were nearly all from the hand of Lautizio.

II

In addition to these things the Cardinal ordered me to make the model for a salt-cellar; but he said he should like me to leave the beaten track pursued by such as fabricated these things. Messer Luigi, apropos of this salt-cellar, made an eloquent description of his own idea; Messer Gabriello Cesano also spoke exceedingly well to the same purpose. The Cardinal, who was a very kindly listener, showed extreme satisfaction with the designs which these two able men of letters had described in words. Then he turned to me and said: "My Benvenuto, the design of Messer Luigi and that of Messer Gabriello please me both so well that I know not how to choose between them; therefore I leave the choice to you, who will have to execute the work." I replied as follows: "It is apparent, my lords, of what vast consequence are the sons of kings and emperors, and what a marvellous brightness of divinity appears in them; nevertheless, if you ask some poor humble shepherd which he loves best, those royal children or his sons, he will certainly tell you that he loves his own sons best. Now I too have a great affection for the children which I bring forth from my art; consequently the first which I will show you, most reverend monsignor my good master, shall be of my own making and invention. There are many things beautiful enough in words which do not match together well when executed by an artist." Then I

3 The name of Cesano is well known in the literary correspondence of those times.
4 It will be remembered that the Cardinal was Archbishop of Milan.

turned to the two scholars and said: "You have spoken, I will do." Upon this Messer Luigi Alamanni smiled, and added a great many witty things, with the greatest charm of manner, in my praise; they became him well, for he was handsome of face and figure, and had a gentle voice. Messer Gabriello Cesano was quite the opposite, as ugly and displeasing as the other was agreeable; accordingly he spoke as he looked.

Messer Luigi had suggested that I should fashion a Venus with Cupid, surrounded by a crowd of pretty emblems, all in proper keeping with the subject. Messer Gabriello proposed that I should model an Amphitrite, the wife of Neptune, together with those Tritons of the sea, and many such-like fancies, good enough to describe in words, but not to execute in metal.

I first laid down an oval framework, considerably longer than half a cubit—almost two-thirds, in fact; and upon this ground, wishing to suggest the interminglement of land and ocean, I modelled two figures, considerably taller than a palm in height, which were seated with their legs interlaced, suggesting those lengthier branches of the sea which run up into the continents. The sea was a man, and in his hand I placed a ship, elaborately wrought in all its details, and well adapted to hold a quantity of salt. Beneath him I grouped the four sea-horses, and in his right hand he held his trident. The earth I fashioned like a woman, with all the beauty of form, the grace, and charm of which my art was capable. She had a richly decorated temple firmly based upon the ground at one side; and here her hand rested. This I intended to receive the pepper. In her other hand I put a cornucopia, overflowing with all the natural treasures I could think of. Below this goddess, in the part which represented earth, I collected the fairest animals that haunt our globe. In the quarter presided over by the deity of ocean, I fashioned such choice kinds of fishes and shells as could be properly displayed in that small space. What remained of the oval I filled in with luxuriant ornamentation.

Then I waited for the Cardinal; and when he came, attended by the two accomplished gentlemen, I produced the model I had made in wax. On beholding it, Messer Gabriel Cesano was the first to lift his voice up, and to cry: "This is a piece which it will take the lives of ten men to finish: do not expect, most reverend monsignor, if you order it, to get it in your lifetime. Benvenuto, it seems, has chosen to display his children in a vision, but not to give them to the touch, as we did when we spoke of things that could be carried out.

while he has shown nothing beyond the bounds of possibility." Messer Alamanni took my side; but the Cardinal said he did not care to undertake so important an affair. Then I turned to them and said: "Most reverend monsignor, and you, gentlemen, fulfilled with learning; I tell you that I hope to complete this piece for whosoever shall be destined to possess it;[1] and each one of you shall live to see it executed a hundred times more richly than the model. Indeed, I hope that time will be left me to produce far greater things than this." The Cardinal replied in heat: "Unless you make it for the King, to whom I mean to take you, I do not think that you will make it for another man alive." Then he showed me letters in which the King, under one heading, bade him return as soon as possible, bringing Benvenuto with him. At this I raised my hands to heaven, exclaiming: "Oh, when will that moment come, and quickly?" The Cardinal bade me put myself in readiness, and arrange the affairs I had in Rome. He gave me ten days for these preparations.

III

When the time came to travel, he gave me a fine and excellent horse. The animal was called Tornon, because it was a gift from the Cardinal Tornon.[1] My apprentices, Pagolo and Ascanio, were also furnished with good mounts.

The Cardinal divided his household, which was very numerous, into two sections. The first, and the more distinguished, he took with him, following the route of Romagna, with the object of visiting Madonna del Loreto, and then making for Ferrara, his own home. The other section he sent upon the road to Florence. This was the larger train; it counted a great multitude, including the flower of his horse. He told me that if I wished to make the journey without peril, I had better go with him, otherwise I ran some risk of my life. I expressed my inclination to his most reverend lordship to travel in his suite. But, having done so, since the will of Heaven must be accomplished, it pleased God to remind me of my poor sister, who had suffered greatly from the news of my misfortunes. I also remembered my cousins, who were nuns in Viterbo, the one abbess and the other camerlinga,[2] and who had therefore that rich convent

1 *A chi l'arà avere.* For whomsoever it is going to belong to.
1 This was the famous François de Tournon, made Cardinal in 1530, and employed as minister by François I.
2 This official in a convent was the same as cellarer or superintendent of the cellar and provisions.

under their control. They too had endured sore tribulations for my sake, and to their fervent prayers I firmly believed that I owed the grace of my deliverance by God. Accordingly, when these things came into my mind, I decided for the route to Florence. I might have travelled free of expense with the Cardinal or with that other train of his, but I chose to take my own way by myself. Eventually I joined company with a very famous clockmaker, called Maestro Cherubino, my esteemed friend. Thrown together by accident, we performed the journey with much enjoyment on both sides.

I had left Rome on Monday in Passion Week, together with Pagolo and Ascanio.[3] At Monte Ruosi we joined the company which I have mentioned. Since I had expressed my intention of following the Cardinal, I did not anticipate that any of my enemies would be upon the watch to harm me. Yet I ran a narrow risk of coming to grief at Monte Ruosi; for a band of men had been sent forward, well armed, to do me mischief there. It was so ordained by God that, while we were at dinner, these fellows, on the news that I was not travelling in the Cardinal's suite, made preparation to attack me. Just at that moment the Cardinal's retinue arrived, and I was glad enough to travel with their escort safely to Viterbo. From that place onward I had no apprehension of danger, especially as I made a point of travelling a few miles in front, and the best men of the retinue kept a good watch over me.[4] I arrived by God's grace safe and sound at Viterbo, where my cousins and all the convent received me with the greatest kindness.

IV

After leaving Viterbo with the comrades I have mentioned, we pursued our journey on horseback, sometimes in front and sometimes behind the Cardinal's household. This brought us upon Maundy Thursday at twenty-two o'clock within one stage of Siena. At this place there happened to be some return-horses; and the people of the post were waiting for an opportunity to hire them at a small fee to any traveller who would take them back to the post-station in Siena. When I was aware of this, I dismounted from my horse

3 This was March 22, 1540.

4 *Tenevano molto conto di me.* This is perhaps equivalent to *held me in high esteem.* But Cellini uses the same phrase with the meaning I have given above, in Book I. chap. lxxxvi.

Tornon, saddled one of the beasts with my pad and stirrups, and gave a giulio to the groom in waiting.[1]

I left my horse under the care of my young men to bring after me, and rode on in front, wishing to arrive half-an-hour earlier in Siena, where I had some friends to visit and some business to transact. Although I went at a smart pace, I did not override the post-horse. When I reached Siena, I engaged good rooms at the inn for five persons, and told the groom of the house to take the horse back to the post, which was outside the Camollía gate; I forgot, however, to remove my stirrups and my pad.

That evening at Holy Thursday we passed together with much gaiety; and next morning, which was Good Friday, I remembered my stirrups and my pad. On my sending for them, the postmaster replied that he did not mean to give them up, because I had overridden his horse. We exchanged messages several times, and he kept saying that he meant to keep them, adding expressions of intolerable insult. The host where I was lodging told me: "You will get off well if he does nothing worse than to detain your gear; for you must know that he is the most brutal fellow that ever disgraced our city, and has two sons, soldiers of great courage, who are even more brutal than he is. I advise you then to purchase what you want, and to pursue your journey without moving farther in this matter."

I bought a new pair of stirrups, although I still hoped to regain my good pad by persuasion; and since I was very well mounted, and well armed with shirt and sleeves of mail, and carried an excellent arquebuse upon my saddle-bow, I was not afraid of the brutality and violence which that mad beast was said to be possessed of. I had also accustomed my young men to carry shirts of mail, and had great confidence in the Roman, who, while we were in Rome together, had never left it off, so far as I could see; Ascanio too, although he was but a stripling, was in the habit of wearing one. Besides, as it was Good Friday, I imagined that the madnesses of madmen might be giving themselves a holiday. When we came to the Camollía gate, I at once recognised the postmaster by the indications given me; for he was blind of the left eye. Riding up to him then, and leaving my young men and companions at a little distance, I courteously addressed him: "Master of the post, if I assure you that I did not override your horse, why are you unwilling to give me back

[1] The word I have translated by "pad" above is *cucino* in the original. It seems to have been a sort of cushion flung upon the saddle, and to which the stirrups were attached.

my pad and stirrups?" The reply he made was precisely as mad and brutal as had been foretold me. This roused me to exclaim: "How then! are you not a Christian? or do you want upon Good Friday to force us both into a scandal?" He answered that Good Friday or the Devil's Friday was all the same to him, and that if I did not take myself away, he would fell me to the ground with a spontoon which he had taken up—me and the arquebuse I had my hand on. Upon hearing these truculent words, an old gentleman of Siena joined us; he was dressed like a citizen, and was returning from the religious functions proper to that day. It seems that he had gathered the sense of my arguments before he came up to where we stood; and this impelled him to rebuke the postmaster with warmth, taking my side, and reprimanding the man's two sons for not doing their duty to passing strangers; so that their manners were an offence to God and a disgrace to the city of Siena. The two young fellows wagged their heads without saying a word, and withdrew inside the house. Their father, stung to fury by the scolding of that respectable gentleman, poured out a volley of abusive blasphemies, and levelled his spontoon, swearing he would murder me. When I saw him determined to do some act of bestial violence, I pointed the muzzle of my arquebuse, with the object only of keeping him at a distance. Doubly enraged by this, he flung himself upon me. Though I had prepared the arquebuse for my defence, I had not yet levelled it exactly at him; indeed it was pointed too high. It went off of itself; and the ball, striking the arch of the door and glancing backwards, wounded him in the throat, so that he fell dead to earth. Upon this the two young men came running out; one caught up a partisan from the rack which stood there, the other seized the spontoon of his father. Springing upon my followers, the one who had the spontoon smote Pagolo the Roman first above the left nipple. The other attacked a Milanese who was in our company, and had the ways and manners of a perfect fool. This man screamed out that he had nothing in the world to do with me, and parried the point of the partisan with a little stick he held; but this availed him naught: in spite of his words and fencing, he received a flesh wound in the mouth. Messer Cherubino wore the habit of a priest; for though he was a clockmaker by trade, he held benefices of some value from the Pope. Ascanio, who was well armed, stood his ground without trying to escape, as the Milanese had done; so these two came off unhurt. I had set spurs to my horse, and while he was galloping, had charged and got my arquebuse in readiness again; but now I turned back, burning with fury, and meaning to play my part this time in earnest. I thought that my young men had been killed, and was resolved to die with them. The horse had not gone many paces when I met them riding toward me, and asked if they were hurt. Ascanio answered that Pagolo was wounded to the death. Then I said: "O Pagolo, my son did the spontoon then pierce through your armour?" "No," he replied, "for I put my shirt of mail in the valise this morning." "So then, I suppose, one wears chain-mail in Rome to swagger before ladies, but where there is danger, and one wants it, one keeps it locked up in a portmanteau? You deserve what you have got, and you are now the cause of sending me back to die here too." While I was uttering these words, I kept riding briskly onward; but both the young men implored me for the love of God to save myself and them, and not to rush on certain death. Just then I met Messer Cherubino and the wounded Milanese. The former cried out that no one was badly wounded; the blow given to Pagolo had only grazed the skin;[2] but the old postmaster was stretched out dead; his sons with other folk were getting ready for attack, and we must almost certainly be cut to pieces: "Accordingly, Benvenuto, since fortune has saved us from this first tempest, do not tempt her again, for things may not go so favourably a second time." To this I replied: "If you are satisfied to have it thus, so also am I;" and turning to Pagolo and Ascanio, I said: "Strike spurs to your horses, and let us gallop to Staggia without stopping;[3] there we shall be in safety." The wounded Milanese groaned out: "A pox upon our peccadilloes! the sole cause of my misfortune was that I sinned by taking a little broth this morning, having nothing else to break my fast with." In spite of the great peril we were in, we could not help laughing a little at the donkey and his silly speeches. Then we set spurs to our horses, and left Messer Cherubino and the Milanese to follow at their leisure.

V

While we were making our escape, the sons of the dead man ran to the Duke of Melfi, and begged for some light horsemen to catch us up and take us prisoners.[1] The Duke upon being informed that

2 The Italian is peculiar: *il colpo di Pagolo era ito tanto ritto che non era isfondato.*
3 Staggia is the next post on the way to Florence.
1 The Duke of Melfi, or Amalfi, was at this time Alfonso Piccolomini, acting as captain-general of the Sienese in the interests of Charles V.

we were the Cardinal of Ferrara's men, refused to give them troops or leave to follow. We meanwhile arrived at Staggia, where we were in safety. There we sent for a doctor, the best who could be had in such a place; and on his examining Pagolo, we discovered that the wound was only skin-deep; so I felt sure[2] that he would escape without mischief. Then we ordered dinner; and at this juncture there arrived Messer Cherubino and that Milanese simpleton, who kept always muttering: "A plague upon your quarrels," and complaining that he was excommunicated because he had not been able to say a single Paternoster on that holy morning. He was very ugly, and his mouth, which nature had made large, had been expanded at least three inches by his wound; so that what with his ludicrous Milanese jargon and his silly way of talking, he gave us so much matter for mirth, that, instead of bemoaning our ill-luck, we could not hold from laughing at every word he uttered. When the doctor wanted to sew up his wound, and had already made three stitches with his needle, the fellow told him to hold hard a while, since he did not want him out of malice to sew his whole mouth up. Then he took up a spoon, and said he wished to have his mouth left open enough to take that spoon in, in order that he might return alive to his own folk. These things he said with such odd waggings of the head, that we never stopped from laughing, and so pursued our journey mirthfully to Florence.

We dismounted at the house of my poor sister, who, together with her husband, overwhelmed us with kind attentions. Messer Cherubino and the Milanese went about their business. In Florence we remained four days, during which Pagolo got well. It was lucky for us that whenever we talked about that Milanese donkey, we laughed as much as our misfortunes made us weep, so that we kept laughing and crying both at the same moment.

Pagolo recovered, as I have said, with ease; and then we travelled toward Ferrara, where we found our lord the Cardinal had not yet arrived. He had already heard of all our accidents, and said, when he expressed his concern for them: "I pray to God that I may be allowed to bring you alive to the King, according to my promise." In Ferrara he sent me to reside at a palace of his, a very handsome place called Belfiore, close under the city walls. There he provided me with all things necessary for my work. A little later, he arranged to leave for France without me; and observing that I was very ill

2 *Cognobbi.* The subject of this verb may be either Cellini or the doctor.

pleased with this, he said to me: "Benvenuto, I am acting for your welfare; before I take you out of Italy, I want you to know exactly what you will have to do when you come to France. Meanwhile, push on my basin and the jug with all the speed you can. I shall leave orders with my factor to give you everything that you may want."

He then departed, and I remained sorely dissatisfied, and more than once I was upon the point of taking myself off without license. The only thing which kept me back was that he had procured my freedom from Pope Paolo; for the rest, I was ill-contented and put to considerable losses. However, I clothed my mind with the gratitude due to that great benefit, and disposed myself to be patient and to await the termination of the business. So I set myself to work with my two men, and made great progress with the jug and basin. The air was unwholesome where we lodged, and toward summer we all of us suffered somewhat in our health. During our indisposition we went about inspecting the domain; it was very large, and left in a wild state for about a mile of open ground, haunted too by multitudes of peacocks, which bred and nested there like wildfowl. This put it into my head to charge my gun with a noiseless kind of powder; then I tracked some of the young birds, and every other day killed one, which furnished us with abundance of meat, of such excellent quality that we shook our sickness off. For several months following we went on working merrily, and got the jug and basin forward; but it was a task that required much time.

VI

At that period the Duke of Ferrara came to terms with Pope Paul about some old matters in dispute between them relating to Modena and certain other cities. The Church having a strong claim to them, the Duke was forced to purchase peace by paying down an enormous sum of money; I think that it exceeded three hundred thousand ducats of the Camera. There was an old treasurer in the service of the Duke, who had been brought up by his father, Duke Alfonso, and was called Messer Girolamo Giliolo. He could not endure to see so much money going to the Pope, and went about the streets crying: "Duke Alfonso, his father, would sooner have attacked and taken Rome with this money than have shown it to the Pope." Nothing would induce him to disburse it; at last, however, the Duke compelled him to make payments, which caused the old man such anguish that he sickened of a dangerous colic and was brought to death's door. During this man's illness the Duke sent for me, and bade me take his portrait; this I did upon a circular piece of black stone about the size of a little trencher. The duke took so much pleasure in my work and conversation, that he not unfrequently posed through four or five hours at a stretch for his own portrait, and sometimes invited me to supper. It took me eight days to complete his likeness; then he ordered me to design the reverse. On it I modelled Peace, giving her the form of a woman with a torch in her hand, setting fire to a trophy of arms; I protrayed her in an attitude of gladness, with very thin drapery, and below her feet lay Fury in despair, downcast and sad, and loaded with chains. I devoted much study and attention to this work, and it won me the greatest honour. The Duke was never tired of expressing his satisfaction, and gave me inscriptions for both sides of the medal. That on the reverse ran as follows: *Pretiosa in conspectu Domini;* it meant that his peace with the Pope had been dearly bought.

VII

While I was still engaged upon the reverse of this medal, the Cardinal sent me letters bidding me prepare for my journey, since the King had asked after me. His next communication would contain full details respecting all that he had promised. Accordingly, I had my jug and basin packed up, after showing them to the Duke. Now a Ferrarese gentleman named Alberto Bendedio was the Cardinal's agent, and he had been twelve years confined to his house, without once leaving it, by reason of some physical infirmity. One day he sent in a vast hurry for me, saying I must take the post at once, in order to present myself before the King of France, who had eagerly been asking for me, under the impression that I was in France. By way of apology, the Cardinal told him that I was staying, slightly indisposed, in his abbey at Lyons, but that he would have me brought immediately to his Majesty. Therefore I must lose no time, but travel with the post.

Now Messer Alberto was a man of sterling worth, but proud, and illness had made his haughty temper insupportable. As I have just said, he bade me to get ready on the spot and take the journey by the common post. I said that it was not the custom to pursue my profession in the post, and that if I had to go, it was my intention to make easy stages and to take with me the workmen Ascanio and Pagolo, whom I had brought from Rome. Moreover, I wanted a servant on horseback to be at my orders, and money sufficient for my costs upon the way. The infirm old man replied, upon a tone of mighty haughtiness, that the sons of dukes were wont to travel as I had described, and in no other fashion. I retorted that the sons of my art travelled in the way I had informed him, and that not being a duke's son, I knew nothing about the customs of such folk; if he treated me to language with which my ears were unfamiliar, I would not go at all; the Cardinal having broken faith with me, and such scurvy words having been spoken, I should make up my mind once for all to take no further trouble with the Ferrarese. Then I turned my back, and, he threatening, I grumbling took my leave.

I next went to the Duke with my medal, which was finished. He received me with the highest marks of honour and esteem. It seems that he had given orders to Messer Girolamo Giliolo to reward me for my labour with a diamond ring worth two hundred crowns, which was to be presented by Fiaschino, his chamberlain. Accordingly, this fellow, on the evening after I had brought the medal, at one hour past nightfall, handed me a ring with a diamond of showy appearance, and spoke as follows on the part of his master: "Take this diamond as a remembrance of his Excellency, to adorn the unique artist's hand which has produced a masterpiece of so singular merit." When day broke, I examined the ring, and found the stone to be a miserable thin diamond, worth about ten crowns. I felt sure that the Duke had not meant to accompany such magnificent compliments with so trifling a gift, but that he must have intended to reward me handsomely. Being then convinced that the trick proceeded from his rogue of a treasurer, I gave the ring to a friend of mine, begging him to return it to the chamberlain, Fiaschino, as he best could. The man I chose was Bernardo Saliti, who executed his commission admirably. Fiaschino came at once to see me, and declared, with vehement expostulations, that the Duke would take it very ill if I refused a present he had meant so kindly; perhaps I should have to repent of my waywardness. I answered that the ring his Excellency had given me was worth about ten crowns, and that the work I had done for him was worth more than two hundred. Wishing, however, to show his Excellency how highly I esteemed his courtesy, I should be happy if he bestowed on me only one of those rings for the cramp, which come from England and are worth tenpence.[1] I would treasure that so long as I lived in remembrance of his Excellency, together with the honourable message he had sent me; for I considered that the splendid favours of his Excellency had amply recompensed my pains, whereas that paltry stone insulted them. This speech annoyed the Duke so much that he sent for his treasurer, and scolded him more sharply than he had ever done before. At the same time he gave me orders, under pain of his displeasure, not to leave Ferrara without duly informing him; and commanded the treasurer to present me with a diamond up to three hundred crowns in value. The miserly official found a stone rising a trifle above sixty crowns, and let it be heard that it was worth upwards of two hundred.

VIII

Meanwhile Messer Alberto returned to reason, and provided me with all I had demanded. My mind was made up to quit Ferrara without fail that very day; but the Duke's attentive chamberlain arranged with Messer Alberto that I should get no horses then. I had loaded a mule with my baggage, including the case which held the Cardinal's jug and basin. Just then a Ferrarese nobleman named Messer Alfonso de' Trotti arrived.[1] He was far advanced in years, and a person of excessive affectation; a great dilettante of the arts, but one of those men who are very difficult to satisfy, and who, if they chance to stumble on something which suits their taste, exalt it so in their own fancy that they never expect to see the like of it again. Well, this Messer Alfonso arrived, and Messer Alberto said to him: "I am sorry that you are come so late; the jug and basin we are sending to the Cardinal in France have been already packed." He answered that it did not signify to him; and beckoning to his servant, sent him home to fetch a jug in white Faenzo clay, the workmanship of which was very exquisite. During the time the servant took to go and return, Messer Alfonso said to Messer Alberto: "I will tell you why I do not care any longer to look at vases; it is that I once beheld a piece of silver, antique, of such beauty and such finish that the human imagination cannot possibly conceive its rarity.

1 *Anello del granchio,* a metal ring of lead and copper, such as are now worn in Italy under the name of *anello di salute.*

1 This man was a member of a very noble Ferrarese family, and much esteemed for his official talents.

Therefore I would rather not inspect any objects of the kind, for fear of spoiling the unique impression I retain of that. I must tell you that a gentleman of great quality and accomplishments, who went to Rome upon matters of business, had this antique vase shown to him in secret. By adroitly using a large sum of money, he bribed the person in whose hands it was, and brought it with him to these parts; but he keeps it jealously from all eyes, in order that the Duke may not get wind of it, fearing he should in some way be deprived of his treasure." While spinning out this lengthy yarn, Messer Alfonso did not look at me, because we were not previously acquainted. But when that precious clay model appeared, he displayed it with such airs of ostentation, pomp, and mountebank ceremony, that, after inspecting it, I turned to Messer Alberto and said: "I am indeed lucky to have had the privilege to see it!"[2] Messer Alfonso, quite affronted, let some contemptuous words escape him, and exclaimed: "Who are you, then, you who do not know what you are saying?" I replied: "Listen for a moment, and afterwards judge which of us knows best what he is saying." Then turning to Messer Alberto, who was a man of great gravity and talent, I began: "This is a copy from a little silver goblet, of such and such a weight, which I made at such and such a time for that charlatan Maestro Jacopo, the surgeon from Carpi. He came to Rome and spent six months there, during which he bedaubed some scores of noblemen and unfortunate gentlefolk with his dirty salves, extracting many thousands of ducats from their pockets. At that time I made for him this vase and one of a different pattern. He paid me very badly; and at the present moment in Rome all the miserable people who used his ointment are crippled and in a deplorable state of health.[3] It is inded great glory for me that my works are held in such repute among you wealthy lords; but I can assure you that during these many years past I have been progressing in my art with all my might, and I think that the vase I am taking with me into France is far more worthy of cardinals and kings than that piece belonging to your little quack doctor."

After I had made this speech, Messer Alfonso seemed dying with desire to see the jug and basin, but I refused to open the box. We remained some while disputing the matter, when he said that he would go to the Duke and get an order from his Excellency to have it shown him. Then Messer Alberto Bendedio, in the high and

[2] *Pur beato che io l' ho veduto!* Leclanché translates thus: *"Par Dieu! il y a longtemps que je l'ai vu!"* I think Cellini probably meant to hint that he had seen it before.

[3] See above, book i., p. 47, for this story.

mighty manner which belonged to him, exclaimed: "Before you leave this room, Messer Alfonso, you shall see it, without employing the Duke's influence." On hearing these words I took my leave, and left Ascanio and Pagolo to show it. They told me afterwards that he had spoken enthusiastically in my praise. After this he wanted to become better acquainted with me; but I was wearying to leave Ferrara and get away from all its folk. The only advantages I had enjoyed there were the society of Cardinal Salviati and the Cardinal of Ravenna, and the friendship of some ingenious musicians;[4] no one else had been to me of any good; for the Ferrarese are a very avaricious people, greedy of their neighbours' money, however they may lay their hands on it; they are all the same in this respect.

At the hour of twenty-two Fiaschino arrived, and gave me the diamond of sixty crowns, of which I spoke above. He told me, with a hang-dog look and a few brief words, that I might wear it for his Excellency's sake. I replied: "I will do so." Then putting my foot in the stirrup in his presence, I set off upon my travels without further leave-taking. The man noted down my act and words, and reported them to the Duke, who was highly incensed, and showed a strong inclination to make me retrace my steps.

IX

That evening I rode more than ten miles, always at a trot; and when, upon the next day, I found myself outside the Ferrarese domain, I felt excessively relieved; indeed I had met with nothing to my liking there, except those peacocks which restored my health. We journeyed by the Monsanese, avoiding the city of Milan on account of the apprehension I have spoken of;[1] so that we arrived safe and sound at Lyons. Counting Pagolo and Ascanio and a servant, we were four men, with four very good horses. At Lyons we waited several days for the muleteer, who carried the silver cup and basin, as well as our other baggage; our lodging was in an abbey of the Cardinal's. When the muleteer arrived, we loaded all our goods upon a little cart, and then set off toward Paris. On the road we met with some annoyances, but not of any great moment.

[4] Cardinal Giovanni Salviati was Archbishop of Ferrara; Cardinal Benedetto Accolti, Archbishop of Ravenna, was then staying at Ferrara; the court was famous for its excellent orchestra and theatrical display of all kinds.

[1] The *Monsanese* is the *Mont Cenis*. Cellini forgets that he has not mentioned this apprehension which made him turn aside from Milan. It may have been the fear of plague, or perhaps of some enemy.

We found the Court of the King at Fontana Beliò;[2] there we presented ourselves to the Cardinal, who provided us at once with lodgings, and that evening we were comfortable. On the following day the cart turned up; so we unpacked our things, and when the Cardinal heard this he told the King, who expressed a wish to see me at once. I went to his Majesty with the cup and basin; then, upon entering his presence, I kissed his knee, and he received me very graciously. I thanked his Majesty for freeing me from prison, saying that all princes unique for generosity upon this earth, as was his Majesty, lay under special obligations to set free men of talent, and particularly those that were innocent, as I was; such benefits, I added, were inscribed upon the book of God before any other good actions. The King, while I was delivering this speech, continued listening till the end with the utmost courtesy, dropping a few words, such as only he could utter. Then he took the vase and basin, and exclaimed: "Of a truth I hardly think the ancients can have seen a piece so beautiful as this. I well remember to have inspected all the best works, and by the greatest masters of all Italy, but I never set my eyes on anything which stirred me to such admiration." These words the King addressed in French to the Cardinal of Ferrara, with many others of even warmer praise. Then he turned to me and said in Italian: "Benvenuto, amuse yourself for a few days, make good cheer, and spend your time in pleasure; in the meanwhile we will think of giving you the wherewithal to execute some fine works of art for us."

X

The Cardinal of Ferrara saw that the King had been vastly pleased by my arrival; he also judged that the trifles which I showed him of my handicraft had encouraged him to hope for the execution of some considerable things he had in mind. At this time, however, we were following the court with the weariest trouble and fatigue; the reason of this was that the train of the King drags itself along with never less than 12,000 horse behind it; this calculation is the very lowest; for when the court is complete in times of peace, there are some 18,000, which makes 12,000 less than the average. Consequently we had to journey after it through places where sometimes there were scarcely two houses to be found; and then we sat

[2] It is thus that Cellini always writes Fontainebleau.

up canvas tents like gipsies, and suffered at times very great discomfort. I therefore kept urging the Cardinal to put the King in mind of employing me in some locality where I could stop and work. The Cardinal answered that it was far better to wait until the King should think of it himself, and that I ought to show myself at times to his Majesty while he was at table. This I did then; and one morning, at his dinner, the King called me. He began to talk to me in Italian, saying that he had it in his mind to execute several great works, and he would soon give orders where I was to labour, and provide me with all necessaries. These communications he mingled with discourse on divers pleasant matters. The Cardinal of Ferrara was there, because he almost always ate in the morning at the King's table. He had heard our conversation, and when the King rose, he spoke in my favour to this purport, as I afterwards was informed: "Sacred Majesty, this man Benvenuto is very eager to get to work again; it seems almost a sin to let an artist of his abilities waste his time." The King replied that he had spoken well, and told him to arrange with me all things for my support according to my wishes.

Upon the evening of the day when he received this commission, the Cardinal sent for me after supper, and told me that his Majesty was resolved to let me begin working, but that he wanted me first to come to an understanding about my appointments. To this the Cardinal added: "It seems to me that if his Majesty allows you three hundred crowns a year, you will be able to keep yourself very well indeed; furthermore, I advise you to leave yourself in my hands, for every day offers the opportunity of doing some service in this great kingdom, and I shall exert myself with vigour in your interest." Then I began to speak as follows: "When your most reverend lordship left me in Ferrara, you gave me a promise, which I had never asked for, not to bring me out of Italy before I clearly understood the terms on which I should be placed here with his Majesty. Instead of sending to communicate these details, your most reverend lordship urgently ordered me to come by post, as if an art like mine was carried on post-haste. Had you written to tell me of three hundred crowns, as you have now spoken, I would not have stirred a foot for twice that sum. Nevertheless, I thank God and your most reverend lordship for all things, seeing God has employed you as the instrument for my great good in procuring my liberation from imprisonment. Therefore I assure your lordship that all the troubles you are now causing me fall a thousand times short of the great good which you have done me. With all my heart I thank you, and take good leave of you; wherever I may be, so long as I have life, I will pray God for you." The Cardinal was greatly irritated, and cried out in a rage: "Go where you choose; it is impossible to help people against their will." Some of his good-for-nothing courtiers who were present said: "That fellow sets great store on himself, for he is refusing three hundred ducats a year." Another, who was a man of talent, replied: "The King will never find his equal, and our Cardinal wants to cheapen him, as though he were a load of wood." This was Messer Luigi Alamanni who spoke to the above effect, as I was afterwards informed. All this happened on the last day of October, in Dauphiné, at a castle the name of which I do not remember.

XI

On leaving the Cardinal I repaired to my lodging, which was three miles distant, in company with a secretary of the Cardinal returning to the same quarters. On the road, this man never stopped asking me what I meant to do with myself, and what my own terms regarding the appointment would have been. I gave him only one word back for answer, which was that—I knew all. When we came to our quarters, I found Pagolo and Ascanio there; and seeing me much troubled, they implored me to tell them what was the matter. To the poor young men, who were all dismayed, I said for answer: "To-morrow I shall give you money amply sufficient for your journey home. I mean myself to go about a most important business without you, which for a long time I have had it in my mind to do." Our room adjoined that of the secretary; and I think it not improbable that he wrote to the Cardinal, and informed him of my purpose. However, I never knew anything for certain about this. The night passed without sleep, and I kept wearying for the day, in order to carry out my resolution.

No sooner did it dawn than I ordered out the horses, made my preparations in a moment, and gave the two young men everything which I had brought with me, and fifty ducats of gold in addition. I reserved the same sum for myself, together with the diamond the Duke had given me; I only kept two shirts and some well-worn riding-clothes which I had upon my back. I found it almost impossible to get free of the two young men, who insisted upon going with me, whatever happened. At last I was obliged to treat them with contempt, and use this language: "One of you has his first beard, and the other is just getting it; and both of you have learned as much from me as I could teach in my poor art, so that you are now the first craftsmen among the youths of Italy. Are you not ashamed to have no courage to quit this go-cart, but must always creep about in leading-strings? The thing is too disgraceful! Or if I were to send you away without money, what would you say then? Come, take yourselves out of my sight, and may God bless you a thousand times. Farewell!"

I turned my horse and left them weeping. Then I took my way along a very fair road through a forest, hoping to make at least forty miles that day, and reach the most out-of-the-way place I could. I had already ridden about two miles, and during that short time had resolved never to revisit any of those parts where I was known. I also determined to abandon my art so soon as I had made a Christ three cubits in height, reproducing, so far as I was able, that infinite beauty which He had Himself revealed to me. So then, being thoroughly resolved, I turned my face toward the Holy Sepulchre.[1] Just when I thought I had got so far that nobody could find me, I heard horses galloping after. They filled me with some uneasiness, because that district is infested with a race of brigands, who bear the name of Venturers, and are apt to murder men upon the road. Though numbers of them are hanged every day, it seems as though they did not care. However, when the riders approached, I found they were a messenger from the King and my lad Ascanio. The former came up to me and said: "From the King I order you to come immediately to his presence." I replied: "You have been sent by the Cardinal, and for this reason I will not come." The man said that since gentle usage would not bring me, he had authority to raise the folk, and they would take me bound hand and foot like a prisoner. Ascanio, for his part, did all he could to persuade me, reminding me that when the King sent a man to prison, he kept him there five years at least before he let him out again. This word about the prison, when I remembered what I had endured in Rome, struck such terror into me, that I wheeled my horse round briskly and followed the King's messenger. He kept perpetually chattering in French through all our journey, up to the very precincts of the court, at one time bullying,

[1] See above, p. 215, for Cellini's vow in the Castle of S. Angelo.

now saying one thing, then another, till I felt inclined to deny God and the world.

XII

On our way to the lodgings of the King we passed before those of the Cardinal of Ferrara. Standing at his door, he called to me and said: "Our most Christian monarch has of his own accord assigned you the same appointments which his Majesty allowed the painter Lionardo da Vinci, that is, a salary of seven hundred crowns; in addition, he will pay you for all the works you do for him; also for your journey hither he gives you five hundred golden crowns, which will be paid you before you quit this place." At the end of this announcement, I replied that those were offers worthy of the great King he was. The messenger, not knowing anything about me, and hearing what splendid offers had been made me by the King, begged my pardon over and over again. Pagolo and Ascanio exclaimed: "It is God who has helped us to get back into so honoured a go-cart!"

On the day following I went to thank the King, who ordered me to make the models of twelve silver statues, which were to stand as candelabra round his table. He wanted them to represent six gods and six goddesses, and to have exactly the same height as his Majesty, which was a trifle under four cubits. Having dictated this commission, he turned to his treasurer, and asked whether he had paid me the five hundred crowns. The official said that he had received no orders to that effect. The King took this very ill, for he had requested the Cardinal to speak to him about it. Furthermore, he told me to go to Paris and seek out a place to live in, fitted for the execution of such work; he would see that I obtained it.

I got the five hundred crowns of gold, and took up my quarters at Paris in a house of the Cardinal of Ferrara. There I began, in God's name, to work, and fashioned four little waxen models, about two-thirds of a cubit each in height. They were Jupiter, Juno, Apollo, and Vulcan. In this while the King returned to Paris; whereupon I went to him at once, taking my models with me, and my two prentices, Ascanio and Pagolo. On perceiving that the King was pleased with my work, and being commissioned to execute the Jupiter in silver of the height above described, I introduced the two young men, and said that I had brought them with me out of Italy to serve his Majesty; for inasmuch as they had been brought up by me, I could at the beginning get more help from them than from the Paris workmen. To this the King replied that I might name a salary which I thought sufficient for their maintenance. I said that a hundred crowns of gold apiece would be quite proper, and that I would make them earn their wages well. This agreement was concluded. Then I said that I had found a place which seemed to me exactly suited to my industry; it was his Majesty's own property, and called the Little Nello. The Provost of Paris was then in possession of it from his Majesty; but since the Provost made no use of the castle, his Majesty perhaps might grant it me to employ in his service.[1] He replied upon the instant: "That place is my own house, and I know well that the man I gave it to does not inhabit or use it. So you shall have it for the work you have to do." He then told his lieutenant to install me in the Nello. This officer made some resistance, pleading that he could not carry out the order. The King answered in anger that he meant to bestow his property on whom he pleased, and on a man who would serve him, seeing that he got nothing from the other; therefore he would hear no more about it. The lieutenant then submitted that some small force would have to be employed in order to effect an entrance. To which the King answered: "Go, then, and if a small force is not enough, use a great one."

The officer took me immediately to the castle, and there put me in possession, not, however, without violence; after that he warned me to take very good care that I was not murdered. I installed myself, enrolled serving-men, and bought a quantity of pikes and partisans; but I remained for several days exposed to grievous annoyances, for the Provost was a great nobleman of Paris, and all the other gentlefolk took part against me; they attacked me with such insults that I could hardly hold my own against them. I must not omit to mention that I entered the service of his Majesty in the year 1540, which was exactly the year in which I reached the age of forty.

XIII

The affronts and insults I received made me have recourse to the King, begging his Majesty to establish me in some other place. He answered: "Who are you, and what is your name?" I remained in great confusion, and could not comprehend what he meant. Holding

[1] This was the castle of Le Petit Nesle, on the site of which now stands the Palace of the Institute. The Provost of Paris was then Jean d'Estouteville, lord of Villebon.

my tongue thus, the King repeated the same words a second time angrily. Then I said my name was Benvenuto. "If, then, you are the Benvenuto of whom I have heard," replied the King, "act according to your wont, for you have my full leave to do so." I told his Majesty that all I wanted was to keep his favour; for the rest, I knew of nothing that could harm me. He gave a little laugh, and said: "Go your ways, then; you shall never want my favour." Upon this he told his first secretary, Monsignor di Villerois, to see me provided and accommodated with all I needed.[1]

This Villerois was an intimate friend of the Provost, to whom the castle had been given. It was built in a triangle, right up against the city walls, and was of some antiquity, but had no garrison. The building was of considerable size. Monsignor di Villerois counselled me to look about for something else, and by all means to leave this place alone, seeing that its owner was a man of vast power, who would most assuredly have me killed. I answered that I had come from Italy to France only in order to serve that illustrious King; and as for dying, I knew for certain that die I must; a little earlier or a little later was a matter of supreme indifference to me.

Now Villerois was a man of the highest talent, exceptionally distinguished in all points, and possessed of vast wealth. There was nothing he would not gladly have done to harm me, but he made no open demonstration of his mind. He was grave, and of a noble presence, and spoke slowly, at his ease. To another gentleman, Monsignor di Marmagna, the treasurer of Languedoc, he left the duty of molesting me.[2] The first thing which this man did was to look out the best apartments in the castle, and to have them fitted up for himself. I told him that the King had given me the place to serve him in, and that I did not choose it should be occupied by any but myself and my attendants. The fellow, who was haughty, bold, and spirited, replied that he meant to do just what he liked; that I should run my head against a wall if I presumed to oppose him, and that Villerois had given him authority to do what he was doing. I told him that, by the King's authority given to me, neither he nor Villerois could do it. When I said that he gave vent to offensive language in French, whereat I retorted in my own tongue that he lied. Stung with rage, he clapped his hand upon a little dagger which he had; then I set my hand also to a large dirk which I always wore for my defence,

[1] M. Nicholas de Neufville, lord of Villeroy.
[2] François l'Allemand, Seigneur de Marmagne.

and cried out: "If you dare to draw, I'll kill you on the spot." He had two servants to back him, and I had my two lads. For a moment or two Marmagna stood in doubt, not knowing exactly what to do, but rather inclined to mischief, and muttering: "I will never put up with such insults." Seeing then that the affair was taking a bad turn, I took a sudden resolution, and cried to Pagolo and Ascanio: "When you see me draw my dirk, throw yourselves upon those serving-men, and kill them if you can; I mean to kill this fellow at the first stroke, and then we will decamp together, with God's grace." Marmagna, when he understood my purpose, was glad enough to get alive out of the castle.

All these things, toning them down a trifle, I wrote to the Cardinal of Ferrara, who related them at once to the King. The King deeply irritated, committed me to the care of another officer of his bodyguard who was named Monsignor lo Iscontro d'Orbech.[8] By him I was accommodated with all that I required in the most gracious way imaginable.

XIV

After fitting up my own lodgings in the castle and the workshop with all conveniences for carrying on my business, and putting my household upon a most respectable footing, I began at once to construct three models exactly of the size which the silver statues were to be. These were Jupiter, Vulcan and Mars. I moulded them in clay, and set them well up on irons; then I went to the King, who disbursed three hundred pounds weight of silver, if I remember rightly, for the commencement of the undertaking. While I was getting these things ready, we brought the little vase and oval basin to completion, which had been several months in hand. Then I had them richly gilt, and they showed like the finest piece of plate which had been seen in France.

Afterwards I took them to the Cardinal, who thanked me greatly; and, without requesting my attendance, carried and presented them to the King. He was delighted with the gift, and praised me as no artist was ever praised before. In return, he bestowed upon the Cardinal an abbey worth seven thousand crowns a year, and expressed his intention of rewarding me too. The Cardinal, however, prevented him, telling his Majesty that he was going ahead too fast,

8 Le Vicomte d'Orbec. It seems that by *Iscontro* Cellini meant Viscount.

since I had as yet produced nothing for him. The King, who was exceedingly generous, replied: "For that very reason will I put heart and hope into him." The Cardinal, ashamed at his own meanness, said: "Sire, I beg you to leave that to me; I will allow him a pension of at least three hundred crowns when I have taken possession of the abbey." He never gave me anything; and it would be tedious to relate all the knavish tricks of this prelate. I prefer to dwell on matters of greater moment.

XV

When I returned to Paris, the great favour shown me by the King made me a mark for all men's admiration. I received the silver and began my statue of Jupiter. Many journeymen were now in my employ; and the work went onward briskly day and night; so that, by the time I had finished the clay models of Jupiter, Vulcan, and Mars, and had begun to get the silver statue forward, my workshop made already a grand show.

The King now came to Paris, and I went to pay him my respects. No sooner had his Majesty set eyes upon me than he called me cheerfully, and asked if I had something fine to exhibit at my lodging, for he would come to inspect it. I related all I had been doing; upon which he was seized with a strong desire to come. Accordingly, after his dinner, he set off with Madame de Tampes, the Cardinal of Lorraine, and some other of his greatest nobles, among whom were the King of Navarre, his cousin, and the Queen, his sister; the Dauphin and Dauphiness also attended him; so that upon that day the very flower of the French court came to visit me.[1] I had been some time at home, and was hard at work. When the King arrived at the door of the castle, and heard our hammers going, he bade his company keep silence. Everybody in my house was busily employed, so that the unexpected entrance of his Majesty took me by surprise. The first thing he saw on coming into the great hall was myself with a huge plate of silver in my hand, which I was beating for the body of my Jupiter; one of my men was finishing the head, another the legs; and it is easy to imagine what a din we made between us. It happened that a little French lad was working at my side, who had just been guilty of some

1 These personages were Madame d'Etampes, the King's mistress; John of Lorraine, son of Duke Renée II., who was made Cardinal in 1518; Henri d'Albret II. and Marguerite de Valois, his wife; the Dauphin, afterwards Henri II., and his wife, the celebrated Caterina de' Medici, daughter of Lorenzo, Duke of Urbino.

trifling blunder. I gave the lad a kick, and, as my good luck would have it, caught him with my foot exactly in the fork between his legs, and sent him spinning several yards, so that he came stumbling up against the King precisely at the moment when his Majesty arrived. The King was vastly amused, but I felt covered with confusion. He began to ask me what I was engaged upon, and told me to go on working; then he said that he would much rather have me not employ my strength on manual labour, but take as many men as I wanted, and make them do the rough work; he should like me to keep myself in health, in order that he might enjoy my services through many years to come. I replied to his Majesty that the moment I left off working I should fall ill; also that my art itself would suffer, and not attain the mark I aimed at for his Majesty. Thinking that I spoke thus only to brag, and not because it was the truth, he made the Cardinal of Lorraine repeat what he had said; but I explained my reasons so fully and clearly, that the Cardinal perceived my drift; he then advised the King to let me labour as much or little as I liked.

XVI

Being very well satisfied with what he had seen, the King returned to his palace, after bestowing on me too many marks of favour to be here recorded. On the following day he sent for me at his dinner-hour. The Cardinal of Ferrara was there at meat with him. When I arrived, the King had reached his second course; he began at once to speak to me, saying, with a pleasant cheer, that having now so fine a basin and jug of my workmanship, he wanted an equally handsome salt-cellar to match them; and begged me to make a design, and to lose no time about it. I replied: "Your Majesty shall see a model of the sort even sooner than you have commanded; for while I was making the basin, I thought there ought to be a salt-cellar to match it; therefore I have already designed one, and if it is your pleasure, I will at once exhibit my conception." The King turned with a lively movement of surprise and pleasure to the lords in his company—they were the King of Navarre, the Cardinal of Lorraine, and the Cardinal of Ferrara—exclaiming as he did so: "Upon my word, this is a man to be loved and cherished by every one who knows him." Then he told me that he would very gladly see my model.

I set off, and returned in a few minutes; for I had only to cross the river, that is, the Seine. I carried with me the wax model which I had made in Rome at the Cardinal of Ferrara's request. When I appeared again before the King and uncovered my piece, he cried out in astonishment: "This is a hundred times more divine a thing than I had ever dreamed of. What a miracle of a man! He ought never to stop working." Then he turned to me with a beaming countenance, and told me that he greatly liked the piece, and wished me to execute it in gold. The Cardinal of Ferrara looked me in the face, and let me understand that he recognised the model as the same which I had made for him in Rome. I replied that I had already told him I should carry it out for one who was worthy of it. The Cardinal, remembering my words, and nettled by the revenge he thought that I was taking on him, remarked to the King: "Sire, this is an enormous undertaking; I am only afraid that we shall never see it finished. These able artists who have great conceptions in their brain are ready enough to put the same in execution without duly considering when they are to be accomplished. I therefore, if I gave commission for things of such magnitude, should like to know when I was likely to get them." The King replied that if a man was so scrupulous about the termination of a work, he would never begin anything at all; these words he uttered with a certain look, which implied that such enterprises were not for folk of little spirit. I then began to say my say: "Princes who put heart and courage in their servants, as your Majesty does by deed and word, render undertakings of the greatest magnitude quite easy. Now that God has sent me so magnificent a patron, I hope to perform for him a multitude of great and splendid master-pieces." "I believe it," said the King, and rose from table. Then he called me into his chamber, and asked me how much gold was wanted for the salt-cellar. "A thousand crowns," I answered. He called his treasurer at once, who was the Viscount of Orbec, and ordered him that very day to disburse to me a thousand crowns of good weight and old gold.

When I left his Majesty, I went for the two notaries who had helped me in procuring silver for the Jupiter and many other things. Crossing the Seine, I then took a small hand-basket, which one of my cousins, a nun, had given me on my journey through Florence. It made for my good fortune that I took this basket and not a bag. So then, thinking I could do the business by daylight, for it was still early, and not caring to interrupt my workmen, and being indisposed to take a servant with me, I set off alone. When I reached the house of the treasurer, I found that he had the money laid out before him, and was selecting the best pieces as the King had ordered. It seemed to me, however, that that thief of a treasurer was doing all he could to postpone the payment of the money; nor were the pieces counted out until three hours after nightfall.

I meanwhile was not wanting in despatch, for I sent word to several of my journeymen that they should come and attend me, since the matter was one of serious importance. When I found that they did not arrive, I asked the messenger if he had done my errand. The rascal of a groom whom I had sent replied that he had done so, but that they had answered that they could not come; he, however, would gladly carry the money for me. I answered that I meant to carry the money myself. By this time the contract was drawn up and signed. On the money being counted, I put it all into my little basket, and then thrust my arm through the two handles. Since I did this with some difficulty, the gold was well shut in, and I carried it more conveniently than if the vehicle had been a bag. I was well armed with shirt and sleeves of mail, and having my sword and dagger at my side, made off along the street as quick as my two legs would carry me.

XVII

Just as I left the house, I observed some servants whispering among themselves, who also went off at a round pace in another direction from the one I took. Walking with all haste, I passed the bridge of the Exchange,[1] and went up along a wall beside the river which led to my lodging in the castle. I had just come to the Augustines—now this was a very perilous passage, and though it was only five hundred paces distant from my dwelling, yet the lodging in the castle being quite as far removed inside, no one could have heard my voice if I had shouted—when I saw four men with four swords in their hands advancing to attack me.[2] My resolution was taken in an instant. I covered the basket with my cape, drew my sword, and seeing that they were pushing hotly forward, cried aloud: "With soldiers there is only the cape and sword to gain; and these, before I give them up, I hope you'll get not much to your advantage." Then crossing my sword boldly with them, I more than once spread out my arms, in

1 The Pont du Change, replaced by the Pont Neuf.

2 The excitement of his recollection makes Cellini more than usually incoherent about this episode. The translator has to collect the whole sense of the passage.

order that, if the ruffians were put on by the servants who had seen me take my money, they might be led to judge I was not carrying it. The encounter was soon over; for they retired step by step, saying among themselves in their own language: "This is a brave Italian, and certainly not the man we are after; or if he be the man, he cannot be carrying anything." I spoke Italian, and kept harrying them with thrust and slash so hotly that I narrowly missed killing one or the other. My skill in using the sword made them think I was a soldier rather than a fellow of some other calling. They drew together and began to fall back, muttering all the while beneath their breath in their own tongue. I meanwhile continued always calling out, but not too loudly, that those who wanted my cape and blade would have to get them with some trouble. Then I quickened pace, while they still followed slowly at my heels; this augmented my fear, for I thought I might be falling into an ambuscade, which would have cut me off in front as well as rear. Accordingly, when I was at the distance of a hundred paces from my home, I ran with all my might, and shouted at the top of my voice: "To arms, to arms! out with you, out with you! I am being murdered." In a moment four of my young men came running, with four pikes in their hands. They wanted to pursue the ruffians, who could still be seen; but I stopped them, calling back so as to let the villains hear: "Those cowards yonder, four against one man alone, had not pluck enough to capture a thousand golden crowns in metal, which have almost broken this arm of mine. Let us haste inside and put the money away; then I will take my big two-handed sword, and go with you whithersoever you like." We went inside to secure the gold; and my lads, while expressing deep concern for the peril I had run, gently chided me, and said: "You risk yourself too much alone; the time will come when you will make us all bemoan your loss." A thousand words and exclamations were exchanged between us; my adversaries took to flight; and we all sat down and supped together with mirth and gladness, laughing over those great blows which fortune strikes, for good as well as evil, and which, what time they do not hit the mark, are just the same as though they had not happened.[8] It is very true that one says to oneself: "You will have had a lesson for next time." But that is not the case; for fortune always comes upon us in new ways, quite unforeseen by our imagination.

8 Cellini's philosophy is summed up in the proverb: "A miss is as good as a mile."

XVIII

On the morning which followed these events, I made the first step in my work upon the great salt-cellar, pressing this and my other pieces forward with incessant industry. My workpeople at this time, who were pretty numerous, included both sculptors and goldsmiths. They belonged to several nations, Italian, French, and German; for I took the best I could find, and changed them often, retaining only those who knew their business well. These select craftsmen I worked to the bone with perpetual labour. They wanted to rival me; but I had a better constitution. Consequently, in their inability to bear up against such a continuous strain, they took to eating and drinking copiously, some of the Germans in particular, who were more skilled than their comrades, and wanted to march apace with me, sank under these excesses, and perished.

While I was at work upon the Jupiter, I noticed that I had plenty of silver to spare. So I took in hand, without consulting the King, to make a great two-handled vase, about one cubit and a half in height. I also conceived the notion of casting the large model of my Jupiter in bronze. Having up to this date done nothing of the sort, I conferred with certain old men experienced in that art at Paris. and described to them the methods in use with us in Italy. They told me they had never gone that way about the business; but that if I gave them leave to act upon their own principles, they would bring the bronze out as clean and perfect as the clay. I chose to strike an agreement, throwing on them the responsibility, and promising several crowns above the price they bargained for. Thereupon they put the work in progress; but I soon saw that they were going the wrong way about it, and began on my own account a head of Julius Cæsar, bust and armour, much larger than the life, which I modelled from a reduced copy of a splendid antique portrait I had brought with me from Rome. I also undertook another head of the same size, studied from a very handsome girl, whom I kept for my own pleasures. I called this Fontainebleau, after the place selected by the King for his particular delight.

We constructed an admirable little furnace for the casting of the bronze, got all things ready, and baked our moulds; those French masters undertaking the Juoiter, while I looked after my two heads. Then I said: "I do not think you will succeed with your Jupiter, because you have not provided sufficient vents beneath for the air to circulate; therefore you are but losing your time and trouble." They replied that, if their work proved a failure, they would pay back the money I had given on account, and recoup me for current expenses; but they bade me give good heed to my own proceedings,[1] for the fine heads I meant to cast in my Italian fashion would never succeed.

At this dispute between us there were present the treasurers and other gentlefolk commissioned by the King to superintend my proceedings. Everything which passed by word or act was duly reported to his Majesty. The two old men who had undertaken to cast my Jupiter postponed the experiment, saying they would like to arrange the moulds of my two heads. They argued that, according to my method, no success could be expected, and it was a pity to waste such fine models. When the King was informed of this, he sent word that they should give their minds to learning, and not try to teach their master.

So then they put their own piece into the furnace with much laughter; while I, maintaining a firm carriage, showing neither mirth nor anger (though I felt it), placed my two heads, one on each side of the Jupiter. The metal came all right to melting, and we let it in with joy and gladness; it filled the mould of the Jupiter most admirably, and at the same time my two heads. This furnished them with matter for rejoicing and me with satisfaction; for I was not sorry to have predicted wrongly of their work, and they made as though they were delighted to have been mistaken about mine. Then, as the custom in France is, they asked to drink, in high good spirits. I was very willing, and ordered a handsome collation for their entertainment. When this was over, they requested me to pay the money due to them and the surplus I had promised. I replied: "You have been laughing over what, I fear, may make you weep. On reflection, it seems to me that too much metal flowed into your mould. Therefore I shall wait until to-morrow before I disburse more money." The poor fellows swallowed my words and chewed the cud of them; then they went home without further argument.

At daybreak they began, quite quietly, to break into the pit of the furnace. They could not uncover their large mould until they had extracted my two heads; these were in excellent condition, and they placed them where they could be well seen. When they came to Jupiter, and had dug but scarcely two cubits, they sent up such a yell, they and their four workmen, that it woke me up. Fancying it was

[1] *Ma che io guardassi bene, che, &c.* This is perhaps: *but they bade me note well that.*

a shout of triumph, I set off running, for my bedroom was at the distance of more than five hundred paces. On reaching the spot, I found them looking like the guardians of Christ's sepulchre in a picture, downcast and terrified. Casting a hasty glance upon my two heads, and seeing they were all right, I tempered my annoyance with the pleasure that sight gave me. Then they began to make excuses, crying: "Our bad luck!" I retorted: "Your luck has been most excellent, but what has been indeed bad is your deficiency of knowledge; had I only seen you put the soul [2] into your mould, I could have taught you with one word how to cast the figure without fault. This would have brought me great honour and you much profit. I shall be able to make good my reputation; but you will now lose both your honour and your profit. Let then this lesson teach you another time to work, and not to poke fun at your masters."

They prayed me to have pity on them, confessing I was right, but pleading that, unless I helped them, the costs they had to bear and the loss they had sustained would turn them and their families upon the street a-begging. I answered that if the King's treasurers obliged them to pay according to their contract, I would defray the cost out of my own purse, because I saw that they had honestly and heartily performed their task according to their knowledge. This way of mine in dealing with them raised the good-will of the King's treasurers and other officers toward me to a pitch which cannot be described. The whole affair was written to his Majesty, who being without a paragon for generosity, gave directions that all I ordered in this matter should be done.

XIX

About this time the illustrious soldier Piero Strozzi arrived in France, and reminded the King that he had promised him letters of naturalisation. These were accordingly made out; and at the same time the King said: "Let them be also given to Benvenuto, *mon ami,* and take them immediately to his house, and let him have them without the payment of any fees." Those of the great Strozzi [1] cost him several hundred ducats: mine were brought me by one of the King's

[2] I have here translated the Italian *anima* literally by the English word *soul.* It is a technical expression, signifying the block, somewhat smaller than the mould, which bronze-founders insert in order to obtain a hollow, and not a solid cast from the mould which gives form to their liquid metal.

[1] Piero was the son of Filippo Strozzi, and the general who lost the battle of Montemurlo, so disastrous to the Florentine exiles, in 1537.

chief secretaries, Messer Antonio Massone.[2] This gentleman presented them with many expressions of kindness from his Majesty, saying: "The King makes you a gift of these, in order that you may be encouraged to serve him; they are letters of naturalisation." Then he told me how they had been given to Piero Strozzi at his particular request, and only after a long time of waiting, as a special mark of favour; the King had sent mine of his own accord, and such an act of grace had never been heard of in that realm before. When I heard these words, I thanked his Majesty with heartiness; but I begged the secretary to have the kindness to tell me what letters of naturalisation meant. He was a man accomplished and polite, who spoke Italian excellently. At first my question made him laugh; then he recovered his gravity, and told me in my own language what the papers signified, adding that they conferred one of the highest dignities a foreigner could obtain: "indeed, it is a far greater honour than to be made a nobleman of Venice."

When he left me, he returned and told his Majesty, who laughed awhile, and then said: "Now I wish him to know my object in sending those letters of naturalisation. Go and install him lord of the castle of the Little Nello, where he lives, and which is a part of my demesne. He will know what that means better than he understood about the letters of naturalisation." A messenger brought me the patent, upon which I wanted to give him a gratuity. He refused to accept it, saying that his Majesty had so ordered. These letters of naturalisation, together with the patent for the castle, I brought with me when I returned to Italy; wherever I go and wherever I may end my days, I shall endeavour to preserve them.[3]

XX

I shall now proceed with the narration of my life. I had on hand the following works already mentioned, namely, the silver Jupiter, the golden salt-cellar, the great silver vase, and the two bronze heads. I also began to cast the pedestal for Jupiter, which I wrought very richly in bronze, covered with ornaments, among which was a bas-relief, representing the rape of Ganymede, and on the other side Leda and the Swan. On casting this piece it came out admirably. I

2 Antoine le Maçon secretary to Margaret of Navarre. He translated the *Decameron* at her instance into French.

3 The letter of naturalisation exists. See *Bianchi*, p. 583. For the grant of the castle, see *ibid.*, p. 585.

also made another pedestal of the same sort for the statue of Juno, intending to begin that too, if the King gave me silver for the purpose. By working briskly I had put together the silver Jupiter and the golden salt-cellar; the vase was far advanced; the two bronze heads were finished. I had also made several little things for the Cardinal of Ferrara, and a small silver vase of rich workmanship, which I meant to present to Madame d'Etampes. Several Italian noblemen, to wit, Signor Piero Strozzi, the Count of Anguillara, the Count of Pitigliano, the Count of Mirandola, and many others, gave me employment also.[1]

For my great King, as I have said, I had been working strenuously, and the third day after he returned to Paris, he came to my house, attended by a crowd of his chief nobles. He marvelled to find how many pieces I had advanced, and with what excellent results. His mistress, Madame d'Etampes, being with him, they began to talk of Fontainebleau. She told his Majesty he ought to commission me to execute something beautiful for the decoration of his favourite residence. He answered on the instant: "You say well, and here upon the spot I will make up my mind what I mean him to do." Then he turned to me, and asked me what I thought would be appropriate for that beautiful fountain.[2] I suggested several ideas, and his Majesty expressed his own opinion. Afterwards he said that he was going to spend fifteen or twenty days at San Germano del Aia,[3] a place twelve leagues distant from Paris; during his absence he wished me to make a model for that fair fountain of his in the richest style I could invent, seeing he delighted in that residence more than in anything else in his whole realm. Accordingly he commanded and besought me to do my utmost to produce something really beautiful; and I promised that I would do so.

When the King saw so many finished things before him, he exclaimed to Madame d'Etampes: "I never had an artist who pleased me more, nor one who deserved better to be well rewarded; we must contrive to keep him with us. He spends freely, is a boon companion, and works hard; we must therefore take good thought for him. Only think, madam, all the times that he has come to me or that I have

1 Anguillara and Pitigliano were fiefs of two separate branches of the Orsini family. The house of Pico lost their lordship of Mirandola in 1536, when Galeotto Pico took refuge with his sons in France. His descendants renewed their hold upon the fief, which was erected into a duchy in 1619.

2 *Per quella bella fonte.* Here, and below, Cellini mixes up Fontainebleau and the spring which gave its name to the place.

3 S. Germain-en-Laye is not so far from Paris as Cellini thought.

come to him, he has never once asked for anything; one can see that his heart is entirely devoted to his work. We ought to make a point of doing something for him quickly, else we run a risk of losing him." Madame d'Etampes answered: "I will be sure to remind you." Then they departed, and in addition to the things I had begun, I now took the model of the fountain in hand, at which I worked assiduously.

XXI

At the end of a month and a half the King returned to Paris; and I, who had been working day and night, went to present myself before him, taking my model, so well blocked out that my intention could be clearly understood. Just about that time, the devilries of war between the Emperor and King had been stirred up again, so that I found him much harassed by anxieties.[1] I spoke, however, with the Cardinal of Ferrara, saying I had brought some models which his Majesty had ordered, and begging him, if he found an opportunity, to put in a word whereby I might be able to exhibit them; the King, I thought, would take much pleasure in their sight. This the Cardinal did; and no sooner had he spoken of the models, than the King came to the place where I had set them up. The first of these was intended for the door of the palace at Fontainebleau. I had been obliged to make some alterations in the architecture of this door, which was wide and low, in their vicious French style. The opening was very nearly square, and above it was a hemicycle, flattened like the handle of a basket; here the King wanted a figure placed to represent the genius of Fontainebleau. I corrected the proportions of the doorway, and placed above it an exact half circle; at the sides I introduced projections, with socles and cornices properly corresponding: then, instead of the columns demanded by this disposition of parts, I fashioned two satyrs, one upon each side. The first of these was in somewhat more than half-relief, lifting one hand to support the cornice, and holding a thick club in the other; his face was fiery and menacing, instilling fear into the beholders. The other had the same posture of support; but I varied his features and some other details; in his hand, for instance, he held a lash with three balls attached to chains. Though I call them satyrs, they showed nothing of the satyr except little horns and a goatish head; all the rest of their form was human. In the lunette above I placed a female figure

1 Cellini refers to the renewal of hostilities in May 1542.

lying in an attitude of noble grace; she rested her left arm on a stag's neck, this animal being one of the King's emblems. On one side I worked little fawns in half relief, with some wild boars and other game in lower relief; on the other side were hounds and divers dogs of the chase of several species, such as may be seen in that fair forest where the fountain springs. The whole of this composition was enclosed in an oblong, each angle of which contained a Victory in bas-relief, holding torches after the manner of the ancients. Above the oblong was a salamander, the King's particular device, with many other ornaments appropriate to the Ionic architecture of the whole design.

XXII

When the King had seen this model, it restored him to cheerfulness, and distracted his mind from the fatiguing debates he had been holding during the past two hours. Seeing him cheerful as I wished, I uncovered the other model, which he was far from expecting, since he not unreasonably judged that the first had work in it enough. This one was a little higher than two cubits; it figured a fountain shaped in a perfect square, with handsome steps all round, intersecting each other in a way which was unknown in France, and is indeed very uncommon in Italy. In the middle of the fountain I set a pedestal, projecting somewhat above the margin of the basin, and upon this a nude male figure, of the right proportion to the whole design, and of a very graceful form. In his right hand he raised a broken lance on high; his left hand rested on a scimitar; he was poised upon the left foot, the right being supported by a helmet of the richest imaginable workmanship. At each of the four angles of the fountain a figure was sitting, raised above the level of the base, and accompanied by many beautiful and appropriate emblems.

The King began by asking me what I meant to represent by the fine fancy I had embodied in this design, saying that he had understood the door without explanation, but that he could not take the conception of my fountain, although it seemed to him most beautiful; at the same time, he knew well that I was not like those foolish folk who turn out something with a kind of grace, but put no intention into their performances. I then addressed myself to the task of exposition; for having succeeded in pleasing him with my work, I wanted him to be no less pleased with my discourse. "Let me inform your sacred Majesty," I thus began, "that the whole of this model is so exactly made to scale, that if it should come to being executed in the large, none of its grace and lightness will be sacrificed. The figure in the middle is meant to stand fifty-four feet above the level of the ground." At this announcement the King made a sign of surprise. "It is, moreover, intended to represent the god Mars. The other figures embody those arts and sciences in which your Majesty takes pleasure, and which you so generously patronise. This one, upon the right hand, is designed for Learning; you will observe that the accompanying emblems indicate Philosophy, and her attendant branches of knowledge. By the next I wished to personify the whole Art of Design, including Sculpture, Painting, and Architecture. The third is Music, which cannot be omitted from the sphere of intellectual culture. That other, with so gracious and benign a mien, stands for Generosity, lacking which the mental gifts bestowed on us by God will not be brought to view. I have attempted to portray your Majesty, your very self, in the great central statue; for you are truly a god Mars, the only brave upon this globe, and all your bravery you use with justice and with piety in the defence of your own glory." Scarcely had he allowed me to finish this oration, when he broke forth with a strong voice: "Verily I have found a man here after my own heart." Then he called the treasurers who were appointed for my supplies, and told them to disburse whatever I required, let the cost be what it might. Next, he laid his hand upon my shoulder, saying: *"Mon ami* (which is the same as *my friend*), I know not whether the pleasure be greater for the prince who finds a man after his own heart, or for the artist who finds a prince willing to furnish him with means for carrying out his great ideas." I answered that, if I was really the man his Majesty described, my good fortune was by far the greater. He answered laughingly: "Let us agree, then, that our luck is equal!" Then I departed in the highest spirits, and went back to my work.

XXIII

My ill-luck willed that I was not wide-awake enough to play the like comedy with Madame d'Etampes. That evening, when she heard the whole course of events from the King's own lips, it bred such poisonous fury in her breast that she exclaimed with anger: "If Benvenuto had shown me those fine things of his, he would have given me some reason to be mindful of him at the proper moment." The King sought to excuse me, but he made no impression on her temper. Being informed of what had passed, I waited fifteen days, during which they made a tour through Normandy, visiting Rouen and Dieppe; then, when they returned to S. Germain-en-Laye, I took the handsome little vase which I had made at the request of Madame d'Etampes, hoping, if I gave it her, to recover the favour I had lost. With this in my hand, then, I announced my presence to her nurse, and showed the gift which I had brought her mistress; the woman received me with demonstrations of good-will, and said that she would speak a word to Madame, who was still engaged upon her toilette; I should be admitted on the instant, when she had discharged her embassy. The nurse made her report in full to Madame, who retorted scornfully: "Tell him to wait." On hearing this, I clothed myself with patience, which of all things I find the most difficult. Nevertheless, I kept myself under control until the hour for dinner was past. Then, seeing that time dragged on, and being maddened by hunger, I could no longer hold out, but flung off, sending her most devoutly to the devil.

I next betook myself to the Cardinal of Lorraine, and made him a present of the vase, only petitioning his Eminence to maintain me in the King's good graces. He said there was no need for this; and if there were need he would gladly speak for me. Then he called his treasurer, and whispered a few words in his ear. The treasurer waited till I took my leave of the Cardinal; after which he said to me: "Benvenuto, come with me, and I will give you a glass of good wine to drink." I answered, not understanding what he meant: "For Heaven's sake, Mr. Treasurer, let me have but one glass of wine and a mouthful of bread; for I am really fainting for want of food. I have fasted since early this morning up to the present moment, at the door of Madame d'Etampes; I went to give her that fine piece of silver-gilt plate, and took pains that she would be informed of my intention; but she, with the mere petty will to vex me, bade me wait; now I am famished, and feel my forces failing; and, as God willed it, I have bestowed my gift and labour upon one who is far more worthy of them. I only crave of you something to drink; for being rather too bilious by nature, fast upsets me so that I run the risk now of falling from exhaustion to the earth." While I was pumping out these words with difficulty, they brought some admirable wine and other delicacies for a hearty meal. I refreshed myself, and having recovered my vital spirits, found that my exasperation had departed from me.

The good treasurer handed me a hundred crowns in gold. I sturdily refused to accept them. He reported this to the Cardinal, who swore at him, and told him to make me take the money by force, and not to show himself again till he had done so. The treasurer returned, much irritated, saying he had never been so scolded before by the Cardinal: but when he pressed the crowns upon me, I still offered some resistance. Then, quite angry, he said he would use force to make me take them. So I accepted the money. When I wanted to thank the Cardinal in person, he sent word by one of his secretaries that he would gladly do me a service whenever the occasion offered. I returned the same evening to Paris. The King heard the whole history, and Madame d'Etampes was well laughed at in their company. This increased her animosity against me, and led to an attack upon my life, of which I shall speak in the proper time and place.

XXIV

Far back in my autobiography I ought to have recorded the friendship which I won with the most cultivated, the most affectionate, and the most companionable man of worth I ever knew in this world. He was Messer Guido Guidi, an able physician and doctor of medicine, and a nobleman of Florence.[1] The infinite troubles brought upon me by my evil fortune caused me to omit the mention of him at an earlier date; and though my remembrance may be but a trifle, I deemed it sufficient to keep him always in my heart. Yet, finding that the drama of my life requires his presence, I shall introduce him here at the moment of my greatest trials, in order that, as he was then my comfort and support, I may now recall to memory the good he did me.[2]

Well, then, Messer Guido came to Paris; and not long after making his acquaintance, I took him to my castle, and there assigned him his own suite of apartments. We enjoyed our lives together in that place for several years. The Bishop of Pavia, that is to say, Mon-

1 Son of Giuliano Guidi and Costanza, a daughter of Domenico Ghirlandajo. François I. sent for him some time before 1542, appointed him his own physician, and professor of medicine in the Royal College. He returned to Florence in 1548.

2 *Qui mi faccia memoria di quel bene.* This is obscure. *Quel bene* may mean *the happiness of his friendship.*

signore de' Rossi, brother of the Count of San Secondo, also arrived.[3] This gentleman I removed from his hotel, and took him to my castle, assigning him in like manner his own suite of apartments, where he sojourned many months with serving-men and horses. On another occasion I lodged Messer Luigi Alamanni and his sons for some months. It was indeed God's grace to me that I should thus, in my poor station, be able to render services to men of great position and acquirements.

But to return to Messer Guido. We enjoyed our mutual friendship during all the years I stayed in Paris, and often did we exult together on being able to advance in art and knowledge at the cost of that so great and admirable prince, our patron, each in his own branch of industry. I can indeed, and with good conscience, affirm that all I am, whatever of good and beautiful I have produced, all this must be ascribed to that extraordinary monarch. So, then, I will resume the thread of my discourse concerning him and the great things I wrought for him.

XXV

I had a tennis-court in my castle, from which I drew considerable profit. The building also contained some little dwellings inhabited by different sorts of men, among whom was a printer of books of much excellence in his own trade. Nearly the whole of his premises lay inside the castle, and he was the man who printed Messer Guidos' first fine book on medicine.[1] Wanting to make use of his lodging, I turned him out, but not without some trouble. There was also a manufacturer of saltpetre; and when I wished to assign his apartments to some of my German workmen, the fellow refused to leave the place. I asked him over and over again in gentle terms to give me up my rooms, because I wanted to employ them for my workpeople in the service of the King. The more moderately I spoke, the more arrogantly did the brute reply; till at last I gave him three days' notice to quit. He laughed me in the face, and said that he would begin to think of it at the end of three years. I had not then learned that he was under the

[3] We have already met with him in the Castle of S. Angelo. His brother, the Count, was general in the French army. This brought the Bishop to Paris, whence he returned to Italy in 1545.

[1] *Chirurgia e Græco in Latinum Conversa, Vido Vidio Florentino interprete, &c. Excudebat Petrus Galterius Lutecia Parisiorum, prid. Cal. Mai.* 1544. So this printer was Pierre Sauthier.

protection of Madame d'Etampes; but had it not been that the terms on which I stood toward that lady made me a little more circumspect than I was wont to be, I should have ousted him at once; now, however, I thought it best to keep my temper for three days. When the term was over, I said nothing, but took Germans, Italians, and Frenchmen, bearing arms, and many hand-labourers whom I had in my employ, and in a short while gutted all his house and flung his property outside my castle. I resorted to these somewhat rigorous measures because he had told me that no Italian whom he knew of had the power or spirit to remove one ring of iron from its place in his house. Well, after the deed was done, he came to find me, and I said to him: "I am the least of all Italians in Italy, and yet I have done nothing to you in comparison with what I have the heart to do, and will do if you utter a single further word," adding other terms of menace and abuse. The man, dumbfounded and affrighted, got his furniture together as well as he was able; then he ran off to Madame d'Etampes, and painted a picture of me like the very fiend. She being my great enemy, painted my portrait still blacker to the King, with all her greater eloquence and all her greater weight of influence. As I was afterwards informed, his Majesty twice showed signs of irritation and was minded to use me roughly: but Henry the Dauphin, his son, now King of France, who had received some affronts from that imperious woman, together with the Queen of Navarre, sister to King Francis, espoused my cause so cleverly that he passed the matter over with a laugh. So with God's assistance I escaped from a great danger.

XXVI

I had to deal in like manner with another fellow, but I did not ruin his house; I only threw all his furniture out of doors. This time Madame d'Etampes had the insolence to tell the King: "I believe that devil will sack Paris one of these days." The King answered with some anger that I was only quite right to defend myself from the low rabble who put obstacles in the way of my serving him.

The rage of this vindictive woman kept continually on the increase. She sent for a painter who was established at Fontainebleau, where the King resided nearly all his time. The painter was an Italian and a Bolognese, known then as Il Bologna; his right name, however, was Francesco Primaticcio.[1] Madame d'Etampes advised him to beg that commission for the fountain which his Majesty had given me, adding that she would support him with all her ability; and upon this they agreed. Bologna was in an ecstasy of happiness, and thought himself sure of the affair, although such things were not in his line of art. He was, however, an excellent master of design, and had collected round him a troop of work-people formed in the school of Rosso, our Florentine painter, who was undoubtedly an artist of extraordinary merit; his own best qualities indeed were derived from the admirable manner of Rosso, who by this time had died.

These ingenious arguments, and the weighty influence of Madame d'Etampes, prevailed with the King; for they kept hammering at him night and day, Madame at one time, and Bologna at another. What worked most upon his mind was that both of them combined to speak as follows: "How is it possible, sacred Majesty, that Benvenuto should accomplish the twelve silver statues which you want? He has not finished one of them yet. If you employ him on so great an undertaking, you will, of necessity, deprive yourself of those other things on which your heart is set. A hundred of the ablest craftsmen could not complete so many great works as this one able man has taken in hand to do. One can see clearly that he has a passion for labour; but this ardent temper will be the cause of your Majesty's losing both him and his masterpieces at the same moment." By insinuating these and other suggestions of the same sort at a favourable opportunity, the King consented to their petition; and yet Bologna had at this time produced neither designs nor models for the fountain.

XXVII

It happened that just at this period an action was brought against me in Paris by the second lodger I had ousted from my castle, who pretended that on that occasion I had stolen a large quantity of his effects. This lawsuit tormented me beyond measure, and took up so much of my time that I often thought of decamping in despair from the country. Now the French are in the habit of making much capital out of any action they commence against a foreigner, or against such persons as they notice to be indolent in litigation. No sooner do

1 Primaticcio, together with Rosso, introduced Italian painting into France. Vassari says he came to Paris in 1541. He died in 1570. He was, like many other Lombard artists, an excellent master of stucco.

they observe that they are getting some advantage in the suit, than they find the means to sell it; some have even been known to give a lawsuit in dowry with their daughters to men who make a business out of such transactions. They have another ugly custom, which is that the Normans, nearly all of them, traffic in false evidence; so that the men who buy up lawsuits, engage at once the services of four or six of these false witnesses, according to their need; their adversary, if he neglect to produce as many on the other side, being perhaps unacquainted with the custom, is certain to have the verdict given against him.

All this happened in my case, and thinking it a most disgraceful breach of justice, I made my appearance in the great hall of Paris, to defend my right. There I saw a judge, lieutenant for the King in civil causes, enthroned upon a high tribunal. He was tall, stout, and fat, and of an extremely severe countenance. All round him on each side stood a crowd of solicitors and advocates, ranged upon the right hand and the left. Others were coming, one by one, to explain their several causes to the judge. From time to time, too, I noticed that the attorneys at the side of the tribunal talked all at once: and much admiration was roused in me by that extraordinary man, the very image of Pluto, who listened with marked attention first to one and then to the other, answering each with learning and sagacity. I have always delighted in watching and experiencing every kind of skill; so I would not have lost this spectacle for much. It happened that the hall being very large, and filled with a multitude of folk, they were strict in excluding every one who had no business there, and kept the door shut with a guard to hold it. Sometimes the guardian, in his effort to prevent the entrance of some improper person, interrupted the judge by the great noise he made, and the judge in anger turned to chide him. This happened frequently, so that my attention was directed to the fact. On one occasion, when two gentlemen were pushing their way in as spectators, and the porter was opposing them with violence, the judge raised his voice, and spoke the following words precisely as I heard them: "Keep peace, Satan, begone, and hold your tongue." These words in the French tongue sound as follows: *Phe phe, Satan, Phe Phe, alé, phe!*[1] Now I had learned the French

[1] *Paix, paix, Satan, allez, paix.* The line in Dante to which Cellini alludes is the first of the seventh canto of the *Inferno.* His suggestion is both curious and ingenious; but we have no reason to think that French judges used the same imprecations, when interrupted, in the thirteenth as they did in the sixteenth century, or that what Cellini heard on this occasion was more than an accidental similarity of sounds, striking his quick ear and awakening his lively memory.

tongue well; and on hearing this sentence, the meaning of that phrase used by Dante came into my memory, when he and his master Virgil entered the doors of Hell. Dante and the painter Giotto were together in France, and particularly in the city of Paris, where, owing to the circumstances I have just described, the hall of justice may be truly called a hell. Dante then, who also understood French well, made use of the phrase in question, and it has struck me as singular that this interpretation has never yet been put upon the passage; indeed, it confirms my opinion that the commentators make him say things which never came into his head.

XXVIII

Well, then, to return to my affairs. When certain decisions of the court were sent me by those lawyers, and I perceived that my cause had been unjustly lost, I had recourse for my defence to a great dagger which I carried; for I have always taken pleasure in keeping fine weapons. The first man I attacked was the plaintiff who had sued me; and one evening I wounded him in the legs and arms so severely, taking care, however, not to kill him, that I deprived him of the use of both his legs. Then I sought out the other fellow who had brought the suit, and used him also in such wise that he dropped it.

Returning thanks to God for this and every other dispensation, and hoping to be left awhile without worries, I bade the young men of my household, especially the Italians, for God's sake to attend each diligently to the work I set him, and to help me till such time as I could finish the things I had in hand. I thought they might soon be completed, and then I meant to return to Italy, being no longer able to put up with the rogueries of those Frenchmen; the good King too, if he once grew angry, might bring me into mischief for many of my acts of self-defence. I will describe who these Italians were; the first, and the one I liked best, was Ascanio, from Tagliacozzo in the kingdom of Naples; the second was Pagolo, a Roman of such humble origin that he did not know his own father. These were the two men who had been with me in Rome, and whom I had taken with me on the journey. Another Roman had also come on purpose to enter my service; he too bore the name of Pagolo, and was the son of a poor nobleman of the family of the Macaroni; he had small acquirements in our art, but was an excellent and courageous swordsman. I had another from Ferrara called Bartolommeo Chioccia. There was also another from Florence named Pagolo Micceri; his brother, nicknamed "Il Gatta," was a clever clerk, but had spent too much money in managing the property of Tommaso Guadagni, a very wealthy merchant. This Gatta put in order for me the books in which I wrote the accounts of his most Christian Majesty and my other employers. Now Pagolo Micceri, having learned how to keep them from his brother, went on doing this work for me in return for a liberal salary. He appeared, so far as I could judge, to be a very honest lad, for I noticed him to be devout, and when I heard him sometimes muttering psalms, and sometimes telling his beads, I reckoned much upon his feigned virtue.

Accordingly I called the fellow apart and said to him, "Pagolo, my dearest brother, you know what a good place you have with me, and how you formerly had nothing to depend on; besides, you are a Florentine. I have also greater confidence in you because I observe that you are pious and religious, which is a thing that pleases me. I beg you therefore to assist me, for I cannot put the same trust in any of your companions: so then I shall ask you to keep watch over two matters of the highest importance, which might prove a source of much annoyance to me. In the first place I want you to guard my property from being stolen, and not touch it yourself. In the next place, you know that poor young girl, Caterina; I keep her principally for my art's sake, since I cannot do without a model; but being a man also, I have used her for my pleasures, and it is possible that she may bear me a child. Now I do not want to maintain another man's bastards, nor will I sit down under such an insult. If any one in this house had the audacity to attempt anything of the sort, and I were to become aware of it, I verily believe that I should kill both her and him. Accordingly, dear brother, I entreat you to be my helper; should you notice anything, tell me at once; for I am sure to send her and her mother and her fellow to the gallows. Be you the first upon your watch against falling into this snare." The rascal made a sign of the cross from his head to his feet and cried out: "O blessed Jesus! God preserve me from ever thinking of such a thing! In the first place, I am not given to those evil ways; in the next place, do you imagine I am ignorant of your great benefits toward me?" When I heard these words, which he uttered with all appearance of simplicity and affection for me, I believed that matters stood precisely as he asserted.

XXIX

Two days after this conversation, M. Matti del Nazaro took the occasion of some feast-day to invite me and my workpeople to an entertainment in the garden.[1] He was an Italian in the King's service, and practiced the same art as we did with remarkable ability. I got myself in readiness, and told Pagolo that he might go abroad too and amuse himself with us; the annoyances arising from that lawsuit being, as I judged, now settled down. The young man replied in these words: "Upon my word, it would be a great mistake to leave the house so unprotected. Only look how much of gold, silver, and jewels you have here. Living as we do in a city of thieves, we ought to be upon our guard by day and night. I will spend the time in religious exercises, while I keep watch over the premises. Go then with mind at rest to take your pleasure and divert your spirits. Some other day another man will take my place as guardian here."

Thinking that I could go off with a quiet mind, I took Pagolo, Ascanio, and Chioccia to the garden, where we spent a large portion of the day agreeably. Toward the middle of the afternoon, however, when it began to draw toward sundown, a suspicion came into my head, and I recollected the words which that traitor had spoken with his feigned simplicity. So I mounted my horse, and with two servants to attend me, returned to the castle, where I all but caught Pagolo and that little wretch Caterina *in flagrante*. No sooner had I reached the place, than that French bawd, her mother, screamed out: "Pagolo! Caterina! here is the master!" When I saw the pair advancing, overcome with fright, their clothes in disorder, not knowing what they said, nor, like people in a trance, where they were going, it was only too easy to guess what they had been about. The sight drowned reason in rage, and I drew my sword, resolved to kill them both. The man took to his heels; the girl flung herself upon her knees and shrieked to Heaven for mercy. In my first fury I wanted to strike at the male; but before I had time to catch him up, second thoughts arose which made me think it would be best for me to drive them both away together. I had so many acts of violence upon my hands, that if I killed him I could hardly hope to save my life. I said then to Pagolo: "Had I seen with my own eyes, scoundrel, what your behavior and appearance force me to believe, I should

1 Matteo del Nassaro, a native of Verona, was employed in France as engraver, die-caster, and musician.

have run you with this sword here ten times through the guts. Get out of my sight; and if you say a Paternoster, let it be San Giuliano's."[2] Then I drove the whole lot forth, mother and daughter, lamming into them with fist and foot. They made their minds up to have the law of me, and consulted a Norman advocate, who advised them to declare that I had used the girl after the Italian fashion; what this meant I need hardly explain.[3] The man argued: "At the very least, when this Italian hears what you are after, he will pay down several hundred ducats, knowing how great the danger is, and how heavily that offence is punished in France." Upon this they were agreed. The accusation was brought against me, and I received a summons from the court.

XXX

The more I sought for rest, the more I was annoyed with all sorts of embarrassments. Being thus daily exposed to divers persecutions, I pondered which of two courses I ought to take; whether to decamp and leave France to the devil, or else to fight this battle through as I had done the rest, and to see to what end God had made me. For a long while I kept anxiously revolving the matter. At last I resolved to make off, dreading to tempt my evil fortune, lest this should bring me to the gallows. My dispositions were all fixed; I had made arrangements for putting away the property I could not carry, and for charging the lighter articles, to the best of my ability, upon myself and servants; yet it was with great and heavy reluctance that I looked forward to such a departure.

I had shut myself up alone in a little study. My young men were advising me to fly; but I told them that it would be well for me to meditate this step in solitude, although I very much inclined to their opinion. Indeed, I reasoned that if I could escape imprisonment and let the storm pass over, I should be able to explain matters to the King by letter, setting forth the trap which had been laid to ruin me by the malice of my enemies. And as I have said above, my mind was made up to this point; when, just as I rose to act on the decision, some power took me by the shoulder and turned me round, and I heard a voice which cried with vehemence: "Benvenuto, do as thou art wont, and fear not!" Then, on the instant, I changed the whole

2 See Boccaccio, *Decam.*, Gior. ii. Nov. ii.
3 *Qual modo s'intendeva contro natura, cioè in soddomia.*

course of my plans, and said to my Italians: "Take your good arms and come with me; obey me to the letter; have no other thought, for I am now determined to put in my appearance. If I were to leave Paris, you would vanish the next day in smoke; so do as I command, and follow me." They all began together with one heart and voice to say: "Since we are here, and draw our livelihood from him, it is our duty to go with him and bear him out so long as we have life to execute what he proposes. He has hit the mark better than we did in this matter; for on the instant when he leaves the place, his enemies will send us to the devil. Let us keep well in mind what great works we have begun here, and what vast importance they possess; we should not know how to finish them without him, and his enemies would say that he had taken flight because he shrank before such undertakings." Many other things bearing weightily upon the subject were said among them. But it was the young Roman, Macaroni, who first put heart into the company; and he also raised recruits from the Germans and the Frenchmen, who felt well disposed toward me.

We were ten men, all counted. I set out, firmly resolved not to let myself be taken and imprisoned alive. When we appeared before the judges for criminal affairs, I found Caterina and her mother waiting; and on the moment of my arrival, the two women were laughing with their advocate. I pushed my way in, and called boldly for the judge, who was seated, blown out big and fat, upon a tribunal high above the rest. On catching sight of me, he threatened with his head, and spoke in a subdued voice: "Although your name is Benvenuto, this time you are an ill-comer." I understood his speech, and called out the second time: "Despatch my business quickly. Tell me what I have come to do here." Then the judge turned to Caterina, and said: "Caterina, relate all that happened between you and Benvenuto." She answered that I had used her after the Italian fashion. The judge turned to me and said: "You hear what Caterina deposes, Benvenuto." I replied: "If I have consorted with her after the Italian fashion, I have only done the same as you folk of other nations do." He demurred: "She means that you improperly abused her." I retorted that, so far from being the Italian fashion, it must be some French habit, seeing she knew all about it, while I was ignorant; and I commanded her to explain precisely how I had consorted with her. Then the impudent baggage entered into plain and circumstantial details regarding all the filth she lyingly accused me of. I made her repeat her deposition three times in succession. When she had finished, I cried out with a loud voice: "Lord judge, lieutenant of the Most Christian King, I call on you for justice. Well I know that by the laws of his Most Christian Majesty both agent and patient in this kind of crime are punished with the stake. The woman confesses her guilt; I admit nothing whatsoever of the sort with regard to her; her go-between of a mother is here, who deserves to be burned for either one or the other offence. Therefore I appeal to you for justice." These words I repeated over and over again at the top of my voice, continually calling out: "To the stake with her and her mother!" I also threatened the judge that, if he did not send her to prison there before me, I would go to the King at once, and tell him how his lieutenant in criminal affairs of justice had wronged me. When they heard what a tumult I was making, my adversaries lowered their voices, but I lifted mine the more. The little hussy and her mother fell to weeping, while I shouted to the judge: "Fire, fire! to the stake with them!" The coward on the bench, finding that the matter was not going as he intended, began to use soft words and excuse the weakness of the female sex. Thereupon I felt that I had won the victory in a nasty encounter; and, muttering threats between my teeth, I took myself off, not without great inward satisfaction. Indeed, I would gladly have paid five hundred crowns down to have avoided that appearance in court. However, after escaping from the tempest, I thanked God with all my heart, and returned in gladness with my young men to the castle.

XXXI

When adverse fortune, or, if we prefer to call it, our malignant planet, undertakes to persecute a man, it never lacks new ways of injuring him. So now, when I thought I had emerged from this tempestuous sea of troubles, and hoped my evil star would leave me quiet for a moment, it began to set two schemes in motion against me before I had recovered my breath from that great struggle. Within three days two things happened, each of which brought my life into extreme hazard. One of these occurred in this way: I went to Fontainebleau to consult with the King; for he had written me a letter saying he wanted me to stamp the coins of his whole realm, and enclosing some little drawings to explain his wishes in the matter; at the same time he left me free to execute them as I liked; upon which

I made new designs according to my own conception, and according to the ideal of art. When I reached Fontainebleau, one of the treasurers commissioned by the King to defray my expenses (he was called Monsignor della Fa[1]) addressed me in these words: "Benvenuto, the painter Bologna has obtained commission from the King to execute your great Colossus, and all the orders previously given as on your behalf have been transferred to him.[2] We are all indignant; and it seems to us that that countryman of yours has acted towards you in a most unwarrantable manner. The work was assigned you on the strength of your models and studies. He is robbing you of it, only through the favour of Madame d'Etampes; and though several months have passed since he received the order, he has not yet made any sign of commencing it." I answered in surprise: "How is it possible that I should have heard nothing at all about this?" He then informed me that the man had kept it very dark, and had obtained the King's commission with great difficulty, since his Majesty at first would not concede it; only the importunity of Madame d'Etampes secured this favour for him.

When I felt how greatly and how wrongfully I had been betrayed, and saw a work which I had gained with my great toil thus stolen from me, I made my mind up for a serious stroke of business, and marched off with my good sword at my side to find Bologna.[3] He was in his room, engaged in studies; after telling the servant to introduce me, he greeted me with some of his Lombard compliments, and asked what good business had brought me hither. I replied: "A most excellent business, and one of great importance." He then sent for wine, and said: "Before we begin to talk, we must drink together, for such is the French custom." I answered: "Messer Francesco, you must know that the conversation we have to engage in does not call for drinking at the commencement; after it is over, perhaps we shall be glad to take a glass." Then I opened the matter in this way: "All men who wish to pass for persons of worth allow it to be seen that they are so by their actions; if they do the contrary, they lose the name of honest men. I am aware that you knew the King had commissioned me with that great Colossus; it had been talked of these eighteen months past; yet neither you nor anybody else came forward to speak a word about it. By my great labours I made myself known

1 His name in full was Jacques de la Fa. He and his son Pierre after him held the office of *tresorier de l'épargne*. See Plon, p. 63.

2 By *Colossus*, Cellini means the fountain with the great statue of Mars.

3 *i. e.* Primaticcio.

to his Majesty, who approved of my models and gave the work into my hands. During many months I have heard nothing to the contrary; only this morning I was informed that you have got hold of it, and have filched it from me. I earned it by the talents I displayed, and you are robbing me of it merely by your idle talking."

XXXII

To this speech Bologna answered: "O Benvenuto! all men try to push their affairs in every way they can. If this is the King's will, what have you to say against it? You would only throw away your time, because I have it now, and it is mine. Now tell me what you choose, and I will listen to you." I replied: "I should like you to know, Messer Francesco, that I could say much which would prove irrefragably, and make you admit, that such ways of acting as you have described and used are not in vogue among rational animals. I will, however, come quickly to the point at issue; give close attention to my meaning, because the affair is serious." He made as though he would rise from the chair on which he was sitting, since he saw my colour heightened and my features greatly discomposed. I told him that the time had not yet come for moving; he had better sit and listen to me. Then I recommenced: "Messer Francesco, you know that I first received the work, and that the time has long gone by during which my right could be reasonably disputed by any one. Now I tell you that I shall be satisfied if you will make a model, while I make another in addition to the one I have already shown. Then we will take them without any clamour to our great King; and whosoever in this way shall have gained the credit of the best design will justly have deserved the commission. If it falls to you, I will dismiss from my mind the memory of the great injury you have done me, and will bless your hands, as being worthier than mine of so glorious a performance. Let us abide by this agreement, and we shall be friends; otherwise we must be enemies; and God, who always helps the right, and I, who know how to assert it, will show you to what extent you have done wrong." Messer Francesco answered: "The work is mine, and since it has been given me, I do not choose to put what is my own to hazard." To this I retorted: "Messer Francesco, if you will not take the right course which is just and reasonable, I will show you another which shall be like your own, that is to say, ugly and disagreeable. I tell you plainly that if I ever hear that you have spoken one single word about this work of mine, I will kill you like a dog. We are neither in Rome, nor in Bologna, nor in Florence; here one lives in quite a different fashion; if then it comes to my ears that you talk about this to the King or anybody else, I vow that I will kill you. Reflect upon the way you mean to take, whether that for good which I formerly described, or this latter bad one I have just now set before you."

The man did not know what to say or do, and I was inclined to cut the matter short upon the spot rather than to postpone action. Bologna found no other words than these to utter: "If I act like a man of honesty, I shall stand in no fear." I replied: "You have spoken well, but if you act otherwise, you will have to fear, because the affair is serious." Upon this I left him, and betook myself to the King. With his Majesty I disputed some time about the fashion of his coinage, a point upon which we were not of the same opinion; his council, who were present, kept persuading him that the monies ought to be struck in the French style, as they had hitherto always been done. I urged in reply that his Majesty had sent for me from Italy in order that I might execute good work; if he now wanted me to do the contrary, I could not bring myself to submit. So the matter was postponed till another occasion, and I set off again at once for Paris.

XXXIII

I had but just dismounted from my horse, when one of those excellent people who rejoice in mischief-making came to tell me that Pagolo Micceri had taken a house for the little hussy Caterina and her mother, and that he was always going there, and whenever he mentioned me, used words of scorn to this effect: "Benvenuto set the fox to watch the grapes,[1] and thought I would not eat them! Now he is satisfied with going about and talking big, and thinks I am afraid of him. But I have girt this sword and dagger to my side in order to show him that my steel can cut as well as his, and that I too am a Florentine, of the Micceri, a far better family than his Cellini." The scoundrel who reported this poisonous gossip spoke it with such good effect that I felt a fever in the instant swoop upon me; and when I say fever, I mean fever, and no mere metaphor. The insane passion which took possession of me might have been my

[1] *Aveva dato a guardia la lattuga ai paperi.*

death, had I not resolved to give it vent as the occasion offered. I ordered the Ferrarese workman, Chioccia, to come with me, and made a servant follow with my horse. When we reached the house where that worthless villain was, I found the door ajar, and entered. I noticed that he carried sword and dagger, and was sitting on a big chest with his arm round Caterina's neck; at the moment of my arrival, I could hear that he and her mother were talking about me. Pushing the door open, I drew my sword, and set the point of it at his throat, not giving him time to think whether he too carried steel. At the same instant I cried out: "Vile coward! recommend your soul to God, for you are a dead man." Without budging from his seat he called three times: "Mother, mother, help me!" Though I had come there fully determined to take his life, half my fury ebbed away when I heard this idiotic exclamation. I ought to add that I had told Chioccia not to let the girl or her mother leave the house, since I meant to deal with those trollops after I had disposed of their bully. So I went on holding my sword at his throat, and now and then just pricked him with the point, pouring out a torrent of terrific threats at the same time. But when I found he did not stir a finger in his own defence, I began to wonder what I should do next; my menacing attitude could not be kept up for ever; so at last it came into my head to make them marry, and complete my vengeance at a later period. Accordingly, I formed my resolution, and began: "Take that ring, coward, from your finger, and marry her, that I may get satisfaction from you afterwards according to your deserts." He replied at once: "If only you do not kill me, I will do whatever you command." "Then," said I, "put that ring upon her hand." When the sword's point was withdrawn a few inches from his throat, he wedded her with the ring. But I added: "This is not enough. I shall send for two notaries, in order that the marriage may be ratified by contract." Bidding Chioccia go for the lawyers, I turned to the girl and her mother, and, using the French language, spoke as follows: "Notaries and witnesses are coming; the first of you who blabs about this affair will be killed upon the spot; nay, I will murder you all three. So beware, and keep a quiet tongue in your heads." To him I said in Italian: "If you offer any resistance to what I shall propose, upon the slightest word you utter I will stab you till your guts run out upon this floor." He answered: "Only promise not to kill me, and I will do whatever you command." The notaries and witnesses arrived; a contract, valid and in due form, was drawn up; then my heat and fever left me. I paid the lawyers and took my departure.

On the following day Bologna came to Paris on purpose, and sent for me through Mattio del Nasaro. I went to see him; and he met me with a glad face, entreating me to regard him as a brother, and saying that he would never speak about that work again, since he recognised quite well that I was right.

XXXIV

If I did not confess that in some of these episodes I acted wrongly, the world might think I was not telling the truth about those in which I say I acted rightly. Therefore I admit that it was a mistake to inflict so singular a vengeance upon Pagolo Micceri. In truth, had I believed him to be so utterly feeble, I should not have conceived the notion of branding him with such infamy as I am going to relate.

Not satisfied with having made him take a vicious drab to wife, I completed my revenge by inviting her to sit to me as a model, and dealing with her thus. I gave her thirty sous a day, paid in advance, and a good meal, and obliged her to pose before me naked. Then I made her serve my pleasure, out of spite against her husband, jeering at them both the while. Furthermore, I kept her for hours together in position, greatly to her discomfort. This gave her as much annoyance as it gave me pleasure; for she was beautifully made, and brought me much credit as a model. At last, noticing that I did not treat her with the same consideration as before her marriage, she began to grumble and talk big in her French way about her husband, who was now serving the Prior of Capua, a brother of Piero Strozzi.[1] On the first occasion when she did this, the mere mention of the fellow aroused me to intolerable fury; still I bore it, greatly against the grain, as well as I was able, reflecting that I could hardly find so suitable a subject for my art as she was. So I reasoned thus in my own mind: "I am now taking two different kinds of revenge. In the first place, she is married; and what I am doing to her husband is something far more serious than what he did to me, when she was only a girl of loose life. If then I wreak my spite so fully upon him, while upon her I inflict the discomfort of posing in

1 Leone, son of Filippo Strozzi, Knight of Jerusalem and Prior of Capua, was, like his brother Piero, a distinguished French general.

such strange attitudes for such a length of time—which, besides the pleasure I derive, brings me both profit and credit through my art—what more can I desire?" While I was turning over these calculations, the wretch redoubled her insulting speeches, always prating big about her husband, till she goaded me beyond the bounds of reason. Yielding myself up to blind rage, I seized her by the hair, and dragged her up and down my room, beating and kicking her till I was tired. There was no one who could come to her assistance. When I had well pounded her she swore that she would never visit me again. Then for the first time I perceived that I had acted very wrongly; for I was losing a grand model, who brought me honour through my art. Moreover, when I saw her body all torn and bruised and swollen, I reflected that, even if I persuaded her to return, I should have to put her under medical treatment for at least a fortnight before I could make use of her.

XXXV

Well, to return to Caterina. I sent my old serving-woman, named Ruberta, who had a most kindly disposition, to help her dress. She brought food and drink to the miserable baggage; and after rubbing a little bacon fat into her worst wounds, they ate what was left of the meat together. When she had finished dressing, she went off blaspheming and cursing all Italians in the King's service, and so returned with tears and murmurs to her home.

Assuredly, upon that first occasion, I felt I had done very wrong, and Ruberta rebuked me after this fashion: "You are a cruel monster to maltreat such a handsome girl so brutally." When I excused my conduct by narrating all the tricks which she and her mother had played off upon me under my own roof, Ruberta scoldingly replied that *that* was nothing—that was only French manners, and she was sure there was not a husband in France without his horns. When I heard this argument, I laughed aloud, and then told Ruberta to go and see how Caterina was, since I should like to employ her again while finishing the work I had on hand. The old woman took me sharply up, saying that I had no *savoir vivre:* "Only wait till daybreak, and she will come of herself; whereas, if you send to ask after her or visit her, she will give herself airs and keep away."

On the following morning Caterina came to our door, and knocked so violently, that, being below, I ran to see whether it was a madman or some member of the household. When I opened, the creature laughed and fell upon my neck, embracing and kissing me, and asked me if I was still angry with her. I said, "No!" Then she added: "Let me have something good to break my fast on." So I supplied her well with food, and partook of it at the same table in sign of reconciliation. Afterwards I began to model from her, during which occurred some amorous diversions; and at last, just at the same hour as on the previous day, she irritated me to such a pitch that I gave her the same drubbing. So we went on several days, repeating the old round like clockwork. There was little or no variation in the incidents.

Meanwhile, I completed my work in a style which did me the greatest credit. Next I set about to cast it in bronze. This entailed some difficulties, to relate which would be interesting from the point of view of art; but since the whole history would occupy too much space, I must omit it. Suffice it to say, that the figure came out splendidly, and was as fine a specimen of foundry as had ever been seen.[1]

XXXVI

While this work was going forward, I set aside certain hours of the day for the salt-cellar, and certain others for the Jupiter. There were more men engaged upon the former than I had at my disposal for the latter, so the salt-cellar was by this time completely finished. The King had now returned to Paris; and when I paid him my respects, I took the piece with me. As I have already related, it was oval in form, standing about two-thirds of a cubit, wrought of solid gold, and worked entirely with the chisel. While speaking of the model, I said before how I had represented Sea and Earth, seated, with their legs interlaced, as we observe in the case of firths and promontories; this attitude was therefore metaphorically appropriate. The Sea carried a trident in his right hand, and in his left I put a ship of delicate workmanship to hold the salt. Below him were his four sea-horses, fashioned like our horses from the head to the front hoofs; all the rest of their body, from the middle backwards, resembled a fish, and the tails of these creatures were agreeably interwoven. Above this group the Sea sat throned in an attitude of pride and dignity; around him were many kinds of fishes and other crea-

1 This figure was undoubtedly the Nymph of Fontainebleau.

tures of the ocean. The water was represented with its waves, and enamelled in the appropriate colour. I had portrayed earth under the form of a very handsome woman, holding her horn of plenty, entirely nude like the male figure; in her left hand I placed a little temple of Ionic architecture, most delicately wrought, which was meant to contain the pepper. Beneath her were the handsomest living creatures which the earth produces; and the rocks were partly enamelled, partly left in gold. The whole piece reposed upon a base of ebony, properly proportioned, but with a projecting cornice, upon which I introduced four golden figures in rather more than half-relief. They represented Night, Day, Twilight, and Dawn. I put, moreover, into the same frieze four other figures, similar in size, and intended for the four chief winds; these were executed, and in part enamelled, with the most exquisite refinement.[1]

When I exhibited this piece to his Majesty, he uttered a loud outcry of astonishment, and could not satiate his eyes with gazing at it. Then he bade me take it back to my house, saying he would tell me at the proper time what I should have to do with it. So I carried it home, and sent at once to invite several of my best friends; we dined gaily together, placing the salt-cellar in the middle of the table, and thus we were the first to use it. After this, I went on working at my Jupiter in silver, and also at the great vase I have already described, which was richly decorated with a variety of ornaments and figures.

XXXVII

At that time Bologna, the painter, suggested to the King that it would be well if his Majesty sent him to Rome, with letters of recommendation, to the end that he might cast the foremost masterpieces of antiquity, namely, the Laocoon, the Cleopatra, the Venus, the Commodus, the Zingara, and the Apollo.[1] These, of a truth, are by far the finest things in Rome. He told the King that when his Majesty had once set eyes upon those marvellous works, he would then, and not till then, be able to criticise the arts of design, since everything which he had seen by us moderns was far removed from

1 This salt-cellar is now at Vienna. It is beautifully represented by two photogravures in Plon's great book on Cellini.

1 The Cleopatra is that recumbent statue of a sleeping Ariadne or Bacchante now in the Vatican. The Venus (neither the Medicean nor the Capitoline) represents the goddess issuing from the bath; it is now in the Museo Pio Clementino of the Vatican. The Commodus is a statue of Hercules, with the lion's skin and an infant in his arms, also in the Vatican. The Zingara may be a statue of Diana forming part of the Borghese collection. The Apollo is the famous Belvedere Apollo of the Vatican.

the perfection of the ancients. The King accepted his proposal, and gave him the introductions he required. Accordingly that beast went off, and took his bad luck with him. Not having the force and courage to contend with his own hands against me, he adopted the truly Lombard device of depreciating my performances by becoming a copyist of antiques. In its own proper place I shall relate how, though he had these statues excellently cast, he obtained a result quite contrary to his imagination.

I had now done for ever with that disreputable Caterina, and the unfortunate young man, her husband, had decamped from Paris. Wanting then to finish off my Fontainebleau, which was already cast in bronze, as well as to execute the two Victories which were going to fill the angles above the lunette of the door, I engaged a poor girl of the age of about fifteen. She was beautifully made and of a brunette complexion. Being somewhat savage in her ways and spare of speech, quick in movement, with a look of sullenness about her eyes, I nicknamed her Scorzone;[2] her real name was Jeanne. With her for model, I gave perfect finish to the bronze Fontainebleau, and also to the two Victories.

Now this girl was a clean maid, and I got her with child. She gave birth to a daughter on the 7th of June, at thirteen hours of the day, in 1544, when I had exactly reached the age of forty-four. I named the infant Costanza; and M. Guido Guidi, the King's physician, and my most intimate friend, as I have previously related, held her at the font. He was the only godfather; for it is customary in France to have but one godfather and two godmothers. One of the latter was Madame Maddalena, wife of M. Luigi Alamanni, a gentleman of Florence and an accomplished poet. The other was the wife of M. Ricciardo del Bene, our Florentine burgher, and a great merchant in Paris; she was herself a French lady of distinguished family. This was the first child I ever had, so far as I remember. I settled money enough upon the girl for dowry to satisfy an aunt of hers, under whose tutelage I placed her, and from that time forwards I had nothing more to do with her.

XXXVIII

By labouring incessantly I had now got my various works well forward; the Jupiter was nearly finished, and the vase also; the door

[2] That is, in Italian, "the rough rind," a name given to rustics. *Scorzone* is also the name for a little black venomous serpent.

began to reveal its beauties. At that time the King came to Paris; and though I gave the right date of the year 1544 for my daughter's birth, we were still in 1543; but an opportunity of mentioning my daughter having arisen, I availed myself of it, so as not to interrupt the narrative of more important things. Well, the King, as I have said, came to Paris, and paid me a visit soon after his arrival. The magnificent show of works brought well-nigh to completion was enough to satisfy anybody's eye; and indeed it gave that glorious monarch no less contentment than the artist who had worked so hard upon them desired. While inspecting these things, it came into his head that the Cardinal of Ferrara had fulfilled none of his promises to me, either as regarded a pension or anything else. Whispering with his Admiral, he said that the Cardinal of Ferrara had behaved very badly in the matter; and that he intended to make it up to me himself, because he saw I was a man of few words, who in the twinkling of an eye might decamp without complaining or asking leave.

On returning home, his Majesty, after dinner, told the Cardinal to give orders to his treasurer of the Exchequer that he should pay me at an early date seven thousand crowns of gold, in three or four instalments, according to his own convenience, provided only that he executed the commission faithfully. At the same time he repeated words to this effect: "I gave Benvenuto into your charge, and you have forgotten all about him." The Cardinal said that he would punctually perform his Majesty's commands; but his own bad nature made him wait till the King's fit of generosity was over. Meanwhile wars and rumours of wars were on the increase; it was the moment when the Emperor with a huge army was marching upon Paris. Seeing the realm of France to be in great need of money, the Cardinal one day began to talk of me, and said: "Sacred Majesty, acting for the best, I have not had that money given to Benvenuto. First, it is sorely wanted now for public uses. Secondly, so great a donation would have exposed you to the risk of losing Benvenuto altogether; for if he found himself a rich man, he might have invested his money in Italy, and the moment some caprice took hold of him, he would have decamped without hesitation. I therefore consider that your Majesty's best course will be to present him with something in your kingdom, if you want to keep him in your service for any length of time."

1 In 1544 Charles V. advanced toward Champagne and threatened Paris, while the English were besieging Boulogne.

The King, being really in want of money, approved of these arguments; nevertheless, like the noble soul he was, and truly worthy of his royal station, he judged rightly that the Cardinal had acted thus in order to curry favour rather than from any clear prevision of distressed finances in so vast a realm.

XXXIX

As I have just said, his Majesty affected to concur with the Cardinal, but his own private mind was otherwise made up. Accordingly, upon the day after his arrival, without solicitation upon my part, he came of his own accord to my house. I went to meet him, and conducted him through several rooms where divers works of art were on view. Beginning with the less important, I pointed out a quality of things in bronze; and it was long since he had seen so many at once. Then I took him to see the Jupiter in silver, now nearly completed, with all its spendid decorations. It so happened that a grievous disappointment which he had suffered a few years earlier, made him think this piece more admirable than it might perhaps have appeared to any other man. The occasion to which I refer was this: After the capture of Tunis, the Emperor passed through Paris with the consent of his brother-in-law, King Francis,[1] who wanted to present him with something worthy of so great a potentate. Having this in view, he ordered a Hercules to be executed in silver, exactly of the same size as my Jupiter. The King declared this Hercules to be the ugliest work of art that he had ever seen, and spoke his opinion plainly to the craftsmen of Paris. They vaunted themselves to be the ablest craftsmen in the world for works of this kind, and informed the King that nothing more perfect could possibly have been produced in silver, insisting at the same time upon being paid two thousand ducats for their filthy piece of work. This made the King, when he beheld mine, affirm that the finish of its workmanship exceeded his highest expectations. Accordingly he made an equitable judgment, and had my statue valued also at two thousand ducats, saying: "I gave those other men no salary; Cellini, who gets about a thousand crowns a year from me, can surely let me have this masterpiece for two thousand crowns of gold, since he had his salary into the bargain." Then I exhibited other things in gold and silver, and a variety of

1 In the year 1539 Charles V. obtained leave to traverse France with his army on the way to Flanders.

models for new undertakings. At the last, just when he was taking leave, I pointed out upon the lawn of the castle that great giant, which roused him to higher astonishment than any of the other things he had inspected. Turning to his Admiral, who was called Monsignor Aniballe,[2] he said: "Since the Cardinal has made him no provision, we must do so, and all the more because the man himself is so slow at asking favours—to cut it short, I mean to have him well provided for; yes, these men who ask for nothing feel that their masterpieces call aloud for recompense; therefore see that he gets the first abbey that falls vacant worth two thousand crowns a year. If this cannot be had in one benefice, let him have two or three to that amount, for in his case it will come to the same thing." As I was standing by, I could hear what the King said, and thanked his Majesty at once for the donation, as though I were already in possession. I told him that as soon as his orders were carried into effect, I would work for his Majesty without other salary or recompense of any kind until old age deprived me of the power to labour, when I hoped to rest my tired body in peace, maintaining myself with honour on that income, and always bearing in mind that I had served so great a monarch as his Majesty. At the end of this speech the King turned toward me with a lively gesture and a joyous countenance, saying, "So let it then be done." After that he departed, highly satisfied with what he had seen there.

XL

Madame d'Etampes, when she heard how well my affairs were going, redoubled her spite against me, saying in her own heart: "It is I who rule the world to-day, and a little fellow like that snaps his fingers at me!" She put every iron into the fire which she could think of, in order to stir up mischief against me. Now a certain man fell in her way, who enjoyed great fame as a distiller; he supplied her with perfumed waters, which were excellent for the complexion, and hitherto unknown in France. This fellow she introduced to the King, who was much delighted by the processes for distilling which he exhibited. While engaged in these experiments, the man begged his Majesty to give him a tennis-court I had in my castle, together with some little apartments which he said I did not use. The good King,

2 Claude d'Annebault; captured at Pavia with François; Marshal in 1538; Admiral of France in 1543.

guessing who was at the bottom of the business, made no answer; but Madame d'Etampes used those wiles with which women know so well to work on men, and very easily succeeded in her enterprise; for having taken the King at a moment of amorous weakness, to which he was much subject, she wheedled him into conceding what she wanted.

The distiller came, accompanied by Treasurer Grolier, a very great nobleman of France, who spoke Italian excellently, and when he entered my castle, began to jest with me in that language.[1] Watching his opportunity,[2] he said: "In the King's name I put this man here into possession of that tennis-court, together with the lodgings that pertain to it." To this I answered: "The sacred King is lord of all things here: so then you might have effected an entrance with more freedom: coming thus with notaries and people of the court looks more like a fraud than the mandate of a powerful monarch. I assure you that, before I carry my complaints before the King, I shall defend my right in the way his Majesty gave me orders two days since to do. I shall fling the man whom you have put upon me out of windows if I do not see a warrant under the King's own hand and seal." After this speech the treasurer went off threatening and grumbling, and I remained doing the same, without, however, beginning the attack at once. Then I went to the notaries who had put the fellow in possession. I was well acquainted with them; and they gave me to understand that this was a formal proceeding, done indeed at the King's orders, but which had not any great significance; if I had offered some trifling opposition the fellow would not have installed himself as he had done. The formalities were acts and customs of the court, which did not concern obedience to the King; consequently, if I succeeded in ousting him, I should have acted rightly, and should not incur any risk.

This hint was enough for me, and next morning I had recourse to arms; and though the job cost me some trouble, I enjoyed it. Each day that followed, I made an attack with stones, pikes and arquebuses, firing, however, without ball; nevertheless, I inspired such terror that no one dared to help my antagonist. Accordingly, when I noticed one day that his defence was feeble, I entered the house by force, and expelled the fellow, turning all his goods and chattels into the street. Then I betook me to the King, and told him that I had

1 Jean Grolier, the famous French Mæcenas, collector of books, antiquities, &c.
2 *Vedendo il bello.*

done precisely as his Majesty had ordered, by defending myself against every one who sought to hinder me in his service. The King laughed at the matter, and made me out new letters-patent to secure me from further molestation.[3]

XLI

In the meantime I brought my silver Jupiter to completion, together with its gilded pedestal, which I placed upon a wooden plinth that only showed a very little; upon the plinth I introduced four little round balls of hard wood, more than half hidden in their sockets, like the nut of a crossbow. They were so nicely arranged that a child could push the statue forward and backwards, or turn it round with ease. Having arranged it thus to my mind, I went with it to Fontainebleau, where the King was then residing.

At that time, Bologna, of whom I have already said so much, had brought from Rome his statues, and had cast them very carefully in bronze. I knew nothing about this, partly because he kept his doings very dark, and also because Fontainebleau is forty miles distant from Paris. On asking the King where he wanted me to set up my Jupiter, Madame d'Etampes, who happened to be present, told him there was no place more appropriate than his own handsome gallery. This was, as we should say in Tuscany, a loggia, or, more exactly, a large lobby; it ought indeed to be called a lobby, because what we mean by loggia is open at one side. The hall was considerably longer than 100 paces, decorated, and very rich with pictures from the hand of that admirable Rosso, our Florentine master. Among the pictures were arranged a great variety of sculptured works, partly in the round, and partly in bas-relief. The breadth was about twelve paces. Now Bologna had brought all his antiques into this gallery, wrought with great beauty in bronze, and had placed them in a handsome row upon their pedestals; and they were, as I have said, the choicest of the Roman antiquities. Into this same gallery I took my Jupiter; and when I saw that grand parade, so artfully planned, I said to myself: "This is like running the gauntlet;[1] now may God assist me." I placed the statue, and having arranged it as well as I was able, waited for the coming of the King. The Jupiter was raising his thunderbolt with the right hand in the act to hurl it; his left hand held the

[3] This document exists, and is dated July 15, 1544. See Bianchi, p. 585.
[1] *Questo si è come passare in fra le picche.*

globe of the world. Among the flames of the thunderbolt I had very cleverly introduced a torch of white wax. Now Madame d'Etampes detained the King till nightfall, wishing to do one of two mischiefs, either to prevent his coming, or else to spoil the effect of my work by its being shown off after dark; but as God has promised to those who trust in Him, it turned out exactly opposite to her calculations; for when night came, I set fire to the torch, which standing higher than the head of Jupiter, shed light from above and showed the statue far better than by daytime.

At length the King arrived; he was attended by his Madame d'Etampes, his son the Dauphin and the Dauphiness, together with the King of Navarre his brother-in-law, Madame Marguerite his daughter,[2] and several other great lords, who had been instructed by Madame d'Etampes to speak against me. When the King appeared, I made my prentice Ascalio push the Jupiter toward his Majesty. As it moved smoothly forwards, my cunning in its turn was amply rewarded, for this gentle motion made the figure seem alive; the antiques were left in the background, and my work was the first to take the eye with pleasure. The King exclaimed at once: "This is by far the finest thing that has ever been seen; and I, although I am an amateur and judge of art, could never have conceived the hundredth part of its beauty." The lords whose cue it was to speak against me, now seemed as though they could not praise my masterpiece enough. Madame d'Etampes said boldly: "One would think you had no eyes! Don't you see all those fine bronzes from the antique behind there? In those consists the real distinction of this art, and not in that modern trumpery." Then the King advanced, and the others with him. After casting a glance at the bronzes, which were not shown to advantage from the light being below them, he exclaimed: "Whoever wanted to injure this man has done him a great service; for the comparison of these admirable statues demonstrates the immeasurable superiority of his work in beauty and in art. Benvenuto deserves to be made much of, for his performances do not merely rival, but surpass the antique." In reply to this, Madame d'Etampes observed that my Jupiter would not make anything like so fine a show by daylight; besides, one had to consider that I had put a veil upon my statue to conceal its faults. I had indeed flung a gauze veil with elegance and delicacy over a portion of my statue, with the view of augmenting its majesty. This, when she had finished speaking, I lifted from beneath, uncovering

[2] Born 1523. Married Emmanuele Filiberto, Duke of Savoy, in 1559. Died 1574.

the handsome genital members of the god; then tore the veil to pieces with vexation. She imagined I had disclosed those parts of the statue to insult her. The King noticed how angry she was, while I was trying to force some words out in my fury; so he wisely spoke, in his own language, precisely as follows: "Benvenuto, I forbid you to speak; hold your tongue, and you shall have a thousand times more wealth than you desire." Not being allowed to speak, I writhed my body in a rage; this made her grumble with redoubled spite; and the King departed sooner than he would otherwise have done, calling aloud, however, to encourage me: "I have brought from Italy the greatest man who ever lived, endowed with all the talents."

XLII

I left the Jupiter there, meaning to depart the next morning. Before I took horse, one thousand crowns were paid me, partly for my salary, and partly on account of monies I had disbursed. Having received this sum, I returned with a light heart and satisfied to Paris. No sooner had I reached home and dined with merry cheer, than I called for all my wardrobe, which included a great many suits of silk, choice furs, and also very fine cloth stuffs. From these I selected presents for my workpeople, giving each something according to his desert, down to the servant-girls and stable-boys, in order to encourage them to aid me heartily.

Being then refreshed in strength and spirits, I attacked the great statue of Mars, which I had set up solidly upon a frame of well-connected woodwork.[1] Over this there lay a crust of plaster, about the eighth of a cubit in thickness, carefully modelled for the flesh of the Colossus. Lastly, I prepared a great number of moulds in separate pieces to compose the figure, intending to dovetail them together in accordance with the rules of art, and this task involved no difficulty.

I will not here omit to relate something which may serve to give a notion of the size of this great work, and is at the same time highly comic. It must first be mentioned that I had forbidden all the men who lived at my cost to bring light women into my house or anywhere within the castle precincts. Upon this point of discipline I was extremely strict. Now my lad Ascanio loved a very handsome girl,

1 This was what he called the Colossus above, p. 287. He meant it for the fountain of Fontainebleau. See p. 273.

who returned his passion. One day she gave her mother the slip, and came to see Ascanio at night. Finding that she would not take her leave, and being driven to his wits' ends to conceal her, like a person of resources, he hit at last upon the plan of installing her inside the statue. There, in the head itself, he made her up a place to sleep in; this lodging she occupied some time, and he used to bring her forth at whiles with secrecy by night. I meanwhile having brought this part of the Colossus almost to completion, left it alone, and indulged my vanity a bit by exposing it to sight; it could, indeed, be seen by more than half Paris. The neighbours, therefore, took to climbing their house-roofs, and crowds came on purpose to enjoy the spectacle. Now there was a legend in the city that my castle had from olden times been haunted by a spirit, though I never noticed anything to confirm this belief; and folk in Paris called it popularly by the name of Lemmonio Boreò.[2] The girl, while she sojourned in the statue's head, could not prevent some of her movements to and fro from being perceptible through its eye-holes; this made stupid people say that the ghost had got into the body of the figure, and was setting its eyes in motion, and its mouth, as though it were about to talk. Many of them went away in terror; others, more incredulous, came to observe the phenomenon, and when they were unable to deny the flashing of the statue's eyes, they too declared their credence in a spirit—not guessing that there was a spirit there, and sound young flesh to boot.

XLIII

All this while I was engaged in putting my door together, with its several appurtenances. As it is no part of my purpose to include in this autobiography such things an annalists record, I have omitted the coming of the Emperor with his great host, and the King's mustering of his whole army.[1] At the time when these events took place, his Majesty sought my advice with regard to the instantaneous fortification of Paris. He came on purpose to my house, and took me all round the city; and when he found that I was prepared to fortify the town with expedition on a sound plan, he gave express orders that all my suggestions should be carried out. His Admiral was directed to command the citizens to obey me under pain of his displeasure.

[2] Properly, *Le Moine Bourru*, the ghost of a monk dressed in drugget (*bure*). Le Petit Nesle had a bad reputation on account of the murders said to have been committed there in the fourteenth century by Queen Jeanne, wife of Philip V.

[1] Toward the end of August 1544, the Imperial army advanced as far as Epernay, within twenty leagues of Paris.

Now the Admiral had been appointed through Madame d'Etampes' influence rather than from any proof of his ability, for he was a man of little talent. He bore the name of M. d'Annebault, which in our tongue is Monsignor d'Aniballe; but the French pronounce it so that they usually made it sound like Monsignore Asino Bue.[2] This animal then referred to Madame d'Etampes for advice upon the matter, and she ordered him to summon Girolamo Bellarmato without loss of time.[3] He was an engineer from Siena, at that time in Dieppe, which is rather more than a day's journey distant from the capital. He came at once, and set the work of fortification going on a very tedious method, which made me throw the job up. If the Emperor had pushed forward at this time, he might easily have taken Paris. People indeed said that, when a treaty of peace was afterwards concluded, Madame d'Etampes, who took more part in it than anybody else, betrayed the King.[4] I shall pass this matter over without further words, since it has nothing to do with the plan of my *Memoirs*. Meanwhile, I worked diligently at the door, and finished the vase, together with two others of middling size, which I made of my own silver. At the end of those great troubles, the King came to take his ease awhile in Paris.

That accursed woman seemed born to be the ruin of the world. I ought therefore to think myself of some account, seeing she held me for her mortal enemy. Happening to speak one day with the good King about my matters, she abused me to such an extent that he swore, in order to appease her, he would take no more heed of me thenceforward than if he had never set eyes upon my face. These words were immediately brought me by a page of Cardinal Ferrara, called Il Villa, who said he had heard the King utter them. I was infuriated to such a pitch that I dashed my tools across the room and all the things I was at work on, made my arrangements to quit France, and went upon the spot to find the King. When he had dined, I was shown into a room where I found his Majesty in the company of a very few persons. After I had paid him the respects due to kings, he bowed his head with a gracious smile. This revived hope in me; so I drew nearer to his Majesty, for they were showing him some things in my own line of art; and after we had talked awhile about such

2 *i. e.,* ass-ox, *Ane-et-bo.*

3 Girolamo Bellarmati, a learned mathematician and military architect, banished from Siena for political reasons. He designed the harbour of Havre.

4 There is indeed good reason to believe that the King's mistress, in her jealousy of the Dauphin and Diane de Poitiers, played false, and enabled the Imperialists to advance beyond Epernay.

matters, he asked if I had anything worth seeing at my house, and next inquired when I should like him to come. I replied that I had some pieces ready to show his Majesty, if he pleased, at once. He told me to go home and he would come immediately.

XLIV

I went accordingly, and waited for the good King's visit, who, it seems, had gone meanwhile to take leave of Madame d'Etampes. She asked whither he was bound, adding that she would accompany him; but when he informed her, she told him that she would not go, and begged him as a special favour not to go himself that day. She had to return to the charge more than twice before she shook the King's determination; however, he did not come to visit me that day. Next morning I went to his Majesty at the same hour; and no sooner had he caught sight of me, than he swore it was his intention to come to me upon the spot. Going then, according to his wont, to take leave of his dear Madame d'Etampes, this lady saw that all her influence had not been able to divert him from his purpose; so she began with that biting tongue of hers to say the worst of me that could be insinuated against a deadly enemy of this most worthy crown of France. The good King appeased her by replying that the sole object of his visit was to administer such a scolding as should make me tremble in my shoes. This he swore to do upon his honour. Then he came to my house, and I conducted him through certain rooms upon the basement, where I had put the whole of my great door together. Upon beholding it, the King was struck with stupefaction, and quite lost his cue for reprimanding me, as he had promised Madame d'Etampes. Still he did not choose to go away without finding some opportunity for scolding; so he began in this wise: "There is one most important matter, Benvenuto, which men of your sort, though full of talent, ought always to bear in mind; it is that you cannot bring your great gifts to light by your own strength alone; you show your greatness only through the opportunities we give you. Now you ought to be a little more submissive, not so arrogant and headstrong. I remember that I gave you express orders to make me twelve silver statues; and this was all I wanted. You have chosen to execute a salt-cellar, and vases and busts and doors, and a heap of other things, which quite confound me, when I consider how you have neglected my wishes and worked for the fulfilment of your own.

If you mean to go on in this way, I shall presently let you understand what is my own method of procedure when I choose to have things done in my own way. I tell you, therefore, plainly: do your utmost to obey my commands; for if you stick to your own fancies, you will run your head against a wall." While he was uttering these words, his lords in waiting hung upon the King's lips, seeing him shake his head, frown, and gesticulate, now with one hand and now with the other. The whole company of attendants, therefore, quaked with fear for me; but I stood firm, and let no breath of fear pass over me.

XLV

When he had wound up this sermon, agreed upon beforehand with his darling Madame d'Etampes, I bent one leg upon the ground, and kissed his coat above the knee. Then I began my speech as follows: "Sacred Majesty, I admit that all that you have said is true. Only, in reply, I protest that my heart has ever been, by day and night, with all my vital forces, bent on serving you and executing your commands. If it appears to your Majesty that my actions contradict these words, let your Majesty be sure that Benvenuto was not at fault, but rather possibly my evil fate or adverse fortune, which has made me unworthy to serve the most admirable prince who ever blessed this earth. Therefore I crave your pardon. I was under the impression, however, that your Majesty had given me silver for one statue only; having no more at my disposal, I could not execute others; so, with the surplus which remained for use, I made this vase, to show your Majesty the grand style of the ancients. Perhaps you never had seen anything of the sort before. As for the salt-cellar, I thought, if my memory does not betray me, that your Majesty on one occasion ordered me to make it of your own accord. The conversation falling upon something of the kind which had been brought for your inspection, I showed you a model made by me in Italy; you, following the impulse of your own mind only, had a thousand golden ducats told out for me to execute the piece withal, thanking me in addition for my hint; and what is more, I seem to remember that you commended me highly when it was completed. As regards the door, it was my impression that, after we had chanced to speak about it at some time or other, your Majesty gave orders to your chief secretary, M. Villerois, from whom the order passed to M. de Marmagne and M. de la Fa, to this effect, that all these gentlemen should keep me going at the work, and see that I obtained the necessary funds. Without such commission I should certainly not have been able to advance so great an undertaking on my own resources. As for the bronze heads, the pedestal of Jupiter and other such-like things, I will begin by saying that I cast those heads upon my own account, in order to become acquainted with French clays, of which, as a foreigner, I had no previous knowledge whatsoever. Unless I had made the experiment, I could not have set about casting those large works. Now, touching the pedestals, I have to say that I made them because I judged them necessary to the statues. Consequently, in all that I have done, I meant to act for the best, and at no point to swerve from your Majesty's expressed wishes. It is indeed true that I set that huge Colossus up to satisfy my own desire, paying for it from my own purse, even to the point which it has reached, because I thought that, you being the great King you are, and I the trifling artist that I am, it was my duty to erect for your glory and my own a statue, the like of which the ancients never saw. Now, at the last, having been taught that God is not inclined to make me worthy of so glorious a service, I beseech your Majesty, instead of the noble recompense you had in mind to give me for my labours, bestow upon me only one small trifle of your favour, and therewith the leave to quit your kingdom. At this instant, if you condescend to my request, I shall return to Italy, always thanking God and your Majesty for the happy hours which I have passed in serving you."

XLVI

The King stretched forth his own hands and raised me very graciously. Then he told me that I ought to continue in his service, and that all that I had done was right and pleasing to him. Turning to the lords in his company, he spoke these words precisely: "I verily believe that a finer door could not be made for Paradise itself." When he had ceased speaking, although his speech had been entirely in my favour, I again thanked him respectfully, repeating, however, my request for leave to travel; for the heat of my indignation had not yet cooled down. His Majesty, feeling that I set too little store upon his unwonted and extraordinary condescension, commanded me with a great and terrible voice to hold my tongue, unless I wanted to incur his wrath; afterwards he added that he would drown me in gold, and that he gave me the leave I asked; and over and above the works he had commissioned,[1] he was very well satisfied with what I had done on my own account in the interval; I should never henceforth have any quarrels with him, because he knew my character; and for my part, I too ought to study the temper of his Majesty, as my duty required. I answered that I thanked God and his Majesty for everything; then I asked him to come and see how far I had advanced the Great Colossus. So he came to my house, and I had the statue uncovered; he admired it extremely, and gave orders to his secretary to pay me all the money I had spent upon it, be the sum what it might, provided I wrote the bill out in my own hand. Then he departed, saying: "Adieu, mon ami," which is a phrase not often used by kings.

XLVII

After returning to his palace, he called to mind the words I had spoken in our previous interview, some of which were so excessively humble, and others so proud and haughty, that they caused him no small irritation. He repeated a few of them in the presence of Madame d'Etampes and Monsignor di San Polo, a great baron of France.[1] This man had always professed much friendship for me in the past, and certainly, on that occasion, he showed his good-will, after the French fashion, with great cleverness. It happened thus: the King in the course of a long conversation complained that the Cardinal of Ferrara, to whose care he had entrusted me, never gave a thought to my affairs; so far as he was concerned, I might have decamped from the realm; therefore he must certainly arrange for committing me to someone who would appreciate me better, because he did not want to run a farther risk of losing me. At these words Monsieur de Saint Paul expressed his willingness to undertake the charge, saying that if the King appointed him my guardian, he would act so that I should never have the chance to leave the kingdom. The King replied that he was very well satisfied, if only Saint Paul would explain the way in which he meant to manage me. Madame sat by with an air of sullen irritation and Saint Paul stood on his dignity, declining to answer the King's question. When the King repeated it, he said, to curry favour with Madame d'Etampes: "I would hang that Ben-

1 The MSS. in this phrase vary, and the meaning is not quite clear. According to one reading, the sense would be: "Though the works he had commissioned were not yet begun." But this involves an awkward use of the word *dipoi.*

1 François de Bourbon, Comte de Saint Paul, one of the chief companions in arms and captains of François I.

venuto of yours by the neck, and thus you would keep him for ever in your kingdom." She broke into a fit of laughter, protesting that I richly deserved it. The King, to keep them company, began to laugh, and said he had no objection to Saint Paul hanging me, if he could first produce my equal in the arts; and although I had not earned such a fate, he gave him full liberty and license. In this way that day ended, and I came off safe and sound, for which may God be praised and thanked.

XLVIII

The King had now made peace with the Emperor, but not with the English, and these devils were keeping us in constant agitation.[1] His Majesty had therefore other things than pleasure to attend to. He ordered Piero Strozzi to go with ships of war into the English waters; but this was a very difficult undertaking, even for that great commander, without a paragon in his times in the art of war, and also without a paragon in his misfortunes. Several months passed without my receiving money or commissions; accordingly, I dismissed my workpeople with the exception of the two Italians, whom I set to making two big vases out of my own silver; for these men could not work in bronze. After they had finished these, I took them to a city which belonged to the Queen of Navarre; it is called Argentana, and is distant several days' journey from Paris.[2] On arriving at this place, I found that the King was indisposed; and the Cardinal of Ferrara told his Majesty that I was come. He made no answer, which obliged me to stay several days kicking my heels. Of a truth, I never was more uncomfortable in my life; but at last I presented myself one evening and offered the two vases for the King's inspection. He was excessively delighted, and when I saw him in good humour, I begged his Majesty to grant me the favour of permitting me to travel into Italy; I would leave the seven months of my salary which were due, and his Majesty might condescend to pay me when I required money for my return journey. I entreated him to grant this petition, seeing that the times were more for fighting than for making statues; moreover, his Majesty had allowed a similar license to Bologna the painter, wherefore I humbly begged him to concede the

1 The peace of Crépy was concluded September 18, 1544. The English had taken Boulogne four days earlier. Peace between France and England was not concluded till June 7, 1546.

2 Argentan, the city of the Duchy of Alençon. Margaret, it will be remembered, had been first married to the Duc d'Alençon, and after his death retained his fiefs.

same to me. While I was uttering these words the King kept gazing intently on the vases, and from time to time shot a terrible glance at me; nevertheless, I went on praying to the best of my ability that he would favour my petition. All of a sudden he rose angrily from his seat, and said to me in Italian: "Benvenuto, you are a great fool. Take these vases back to Paris, for I want to have them gilt." Without making any other answer he then departed.

I went up to the Cardinal of Ferrara, who was present, and besought him, since he had already conferred upon me the great benefit of freeing me from prison in Rome, with many others besides, to do me this one favour more of procuring for me leave to travel into Italy. He answered that he should be very glad to do his best to gratify me in this matter; I might leave it without farther thought to him, and even if I chose, might set off at once, because he would act for the best in my interest with the King. I told the Cardinal that since I was aware his Majesty had put me under the protection of his most reverend lordship, if he gave me leave, I felt ready to depart, and promised to return upon the smallest hint from his reverence. The Cardinal then bade me go back to Paris and wait there eight days, during which time he would procure the King's license for me; if his Majesty refused to let me go, he would without fail inform me; but if I received no letters, that would be a sign that I might set off with an easy mind.

XLIX

I obeyed the Cardinal, and returned to Paris, where I made excellent cases for my three silver vases. After the lapse of twenty days, I began my preparations, and packed the three vases upon a mule. This animal had been lent me for the journey to Lyons by the Bishop of Pavia, who was now once more installed in my castle.

Then I departed in my evil hour, together with Signor Ippolito Gonzaga, at that time in the pay of the King, and also in the service of Count Galeotto della Mirandola. Some other gentlemen of the said count went with us, as well as Lionardo Tedaldi, our fellow-citizen of Florence.

I made Ascanio and Pagolo guardians of my castle and all my property, including two little vases which were only just begun; those I left behind in order that the two young men might not be idle. I had lived very handsomely in Paris, and therefore there was a large amount of costly household furniture: the whole value of these effects exceeded 1500 crowns. I bade Ascanio remember what great benefits I had bestowed upon him, and that up to the present he had been a mere thoughtless lad; the time was now come for him to show the prudence of a man; therefore I thought fit to leave him in the custody of all my goods, as also of my honour. If he had the least thing to complain of from those brutes of Frenchmen, he was to let me hear at once, because I would take post and fly from any place in which I found myself, not only to discharge the great obligations under which I lay to that good King, but also to defend my honour. Ascanio replied with the tears of a thief and a hypocrite: "I have never known a father better than you are, and all things which a good son is bound to perform for a good father will I ever do for you." So then I took my departure, attended by a servant and a little French lad.

It was just past noon, when some of the King's treasurers, by no means friends of mine, made a visit to my castle. The rascally fellows began by saying that I had gone off with the King's silver, and told Messer Guido and the Bishop of Pavia to send at once off after his Majesty's vases; if not, they would themselves despatch a messenger to get them back, and do me some great mischief. The Bishop and Messer Guido were much more frightened than was necessary; so they sent that traitor Ascanio by the post off on the spot. He made his appearance before me about midnight. I had not been able to sleep, and kept revolving sad thoughts to the following effect: "In whose hands have I left my property, my castle? Oh, what a fate is this of mine, which forces me to take this journey! May God grant only that the Cardinal is not of one mind with Madame d'Etampes, who has nothing else so much at heart as to make me lose the grace of that good King."

L

While I was thus dismally debating with myself, I heard Ascanio calling me. On the instant I jumped out of bed, and asked if he brought good or evil tidings. The knave answered: "They are good news I bring; but you must only send back those three vases, for the rascally treasurers keep shouting, 'Stop, thief!' So the Bishop and Messer Guido say that you must absolutely send them back. For the rest you need have no anxiety, but may pursue your journey with a light heart." I handed over the vases immediately, two of them being my own property, together with the silver and much else besides.[1] I had meant to take them to the Cardinal of Ferrara's abbey at Lyons; for though people accused me of wanting to carry them into Italy, everybody knows quite well that it is impossible to export money, gold, or silver from France without special license. Consider, therefore, whether I could have crossed the frontier with those three great vases, which, together with their cases, were a whole mule's burden! It is certainly true that, since these articles were of great value and the highest beauty, I felt uneasiness in case the King should die, and I had lately left him in a very bad state of health; therefore I said to myself: "If such an accident should happen, having these things in the keeping of the Cardinal, I shall not lose them."

Well, to cut the story short, I sent back the mule with the vases, and other things of importance; then, upon the following morning, I travelled forward with the company I have already mentioned, nor could I, through the whole journey, refrain from sighing and weeping. Sometimes, however, I consoled myself with God by saying: "Lord God, before whose eyes the truth lies open! Thou knowest that my object in this journey is only to carry alms to six poor miserable virgins and their mother, my own sister. They have indeed their father, but he is very old, and gains nothing by his trade; I fear, therefore, lest they might too easily take to a bad course of life. Since, then, I am performing a true act of piety, I look to Thy Majesty for aid and counsel." This was all the recreation I enjoyed upon my forward journey.

We were one day distant from Lyons, and it was close upon the hour of twenty-two, when the heavens began to thunder with sharp rattling claps, although the sky was quite clear at the time.[2] I was riding a cross-bow shot before my comrades. After the thunder the heavens made a noise so great and horrible that I thought the last day had come; so I reined in for a moment, while a shower of hail began to fall without a drop of water. At first the hail was somewhat larger than pellets from a popgun, and when these struck me, they hurt considerably. Little by little it increased in size, until the stones might be compared to balls from a crossbow. My horse became restive with fright; so I wheeled round, and returned at a gallop to where I found

1 *Con l'argento e ogni cosa.* These words refer perhaps to the vases: *the silver and everything pertaining to them.*
2 *E l'aria era bianchissima.* Perhaps this ought to be: *and the air blazed with lightnings.* Goethe takes it as I do above.

my comrades taking refuge in a fir-wood. The hail now grew to the size of big lemons. I began to sing a Miserere; and while I was devoutly uttering this psalm to God, there fell a stone so huge that it smashed the thick branches of the pine under which I had retired for safety. Another of the hailstones hit my horse upon the head, and almost stunned him; one struck me also, but not directly, else it would have killed me. In like manner, poor old Lionardo Tedaldi, who like me was kneeling on the ground, received so shrewd a blow that he fell grovelling upon all fours. When I saw that the fir bough offered no protection, and that I ought to act as well as to intone my Misereres, I began at once to wrap my mantle round my head. At the same time I cried to Lionardo, who was shrieking for succour, "Jesus! Jesus!" that Jesus would help him if he helped himself. I had more trouble in looking after this man's safety than my own. The storm raged for some while, but at last it stopped; and we, who were pounded black and blue, scrambled as well as we could upon our horses. Pursuing the way to our lodging for the night, we showed our scratches and bruises to each other; but about a mile farther on we came upon a scene of devastation which surpassed what we had suffered, and defies description. All the trees were stripped of their leaves and shattered; the beasts in the field lay dead; many of the herdsmen had also been killed; we observed large quantities of hailstones which could not have been grasped with two hands. Feeling then that we had come well out of a great peril, we acknowledged that our prayers to God and Misereres had helped us more than we could have helped ourselves. Returning thanks to God, therefore, we entered Lyons in the course of the next day, and tarried there eight days. At the end of this time, being refreshed in strength and spirits, we resumed our journey, and passed the mountains without mishap. On the other side I bought a little pony, because the baggage which I carried had somewhat overtired my horses.

LI

After we had been one day in Italy, the Count Galeotto della Mirandola joined us. He was travelling by post; and stopping where we were, he told me that I had done wrong to leave France; I ought not to journey forwards, for, if I returned at once, my affairs would be more prosperous than ever. On the other hand, if I persisted in my course, I was giving the game up to my enemies, and furnishing them with opportunities to do me mischief. By returning I might put a stop to their intrigues; and those in whom I placed the most confidence were just the men who played most traitorously. He would not say more than that he knew very well all about it; and, indeed, the Cardinal of Ferrara had now conspired with the two rogues I left in charge of all my business. Having repeated over and over again that I ought absolutely to turn back, he went onward with the post, while I, being influenced by my companions, could not make up my mind to return. My heart was sorely torn asunder, at one moment by the desire to reach Florence as quickly as I could, and at another by the conviction that I ought to regain France. At last, in order to end the fever of this irresolution, I determined to take the post for Florence. I could not make arrangements with the first postmaster, but persisted in my purpose to press forward and endure an anxious life at Florence.[1]

I parted company with Signor Ippolito Gonzaga, who took the route for Mirandola, while I diverged upon the road to Parma and Piacenza. In the latter city I met Duke Pier Luigi upon the street, who stared me in the face, and recognised me.[2] Since I knew him to have been the sole cause of my imprisonment in the castle of St. Angelo, the sight of him made my blood boil. Yet being unable to escape from the man, I decided to pay him my respects, and arrived just after he had risen from table in the company of the Landi, who afterwards murdered him. On my appearance he received me with unbounded marks of esteem and affection, among which he took occasion to remark to the gentlemen present that I was the first artist of the world in my own line, and that I had been for a long while in prison at Rome. Then he turned to me and said: "My Benvenuto, I was deeply grieved for your misfortune, and knew well that you were innocent, but could not do anything to help you. In short, it was my father, who chose to gratify some enemies of yours, from whom, moreover, he heard that you had spoken ill of him. I am convinced this was not true, and indeed I was heartily sorry for your troubles." These words he kept piling up and repeating until he seemed to be

1 The text here is obscure. The words *venir a tribulare* might mean "to get, by any means, however inconvenient, to Florence." I have chosen another interpetation in the text, as more consonant with the Italian idiom. For Cellini's use of *tribulare* or *tribolare*, see lib. i. 112, *andando a tribolare la vita tua.*

2 Pier Luigi Farnese was not formally invested with the Duchy of Parma and Piacenza until September 1545. Cellini, therefore, gives him this title as Duke of Castro. He was assassinated on September 10, 1547. The Landi, among other noblemen of the duchy, took part in a conspiracy which had its ground in Pier Luigi's political errors no less than in his intolerable misgovernment and infamous private life.

begging my pardon. Afterwards he inquired about the work I had been doing for his Most Christian Majesty; and on my furnishing him with details, he listened as attentively and graciously as possible. Then he asked if I had a mind to serve him. To this I replied that my honour would not allow me to do so; but that if I had completed those extensive works begun for the King, I should be disposed to quit any great prince merely to enter his Excellency's service.

Hereby it may be seen how the power and goodness of God never leave unpunished any sort or quality of men who act unjustly toward the innocent. This man did what was equivalent to begging my pardon in the presence of those very persons who subsequently took revenge on him for me and many others whom he had massacred. Let then no prince, however great he be, laugh at God's justice, in the way that many whom I know are doing, and who have cruelly maltreated me, as I shall relate at the proper time. I do not write these things in any worldly spirit of boasting, but only to return thanks to God, my deliverer in so many trials. In those too which daily assail me, I always carry my complaint to Him, and call on Him to be my defender. On all occasions, after I have done my best to aid myself, if I lose courage and my feeble forces fail, then is the great might of God manifested, which descends unexpectedly on those who wrongfully injure their neighbours, or neglect the grave and honourable charge they have received from Him.

LII

When I returned to my inn, I found that the Duke had sent me abundance to eat and drink of very excellent quality. I made a hearty meal, then mounted and rode toward Florence. There I found my sister with six daughters, the eldest of whom was marriageable and the youngest still at nurse. Her husband, by reason of divers circumstances in the city, had lost employment from his trade. I had sent gems and French jewellery, more than a year earlier, to the amount of about two thousand ducats, and now brought with me the same wares to the value of about one thousand crowns. I discovered that, whereas I made them an allowance of four golden crowns a month, they always drew considerable sums from the current sale of these articles. My brother-in-law was such an honest fellow, that, fearing to give me cause for anger, he had pawned nearly everything he possessed, and was devoured by interest, in his anxiety to leave my monies untouched. It seems that my allowance, made by way of charity, did not suffice for the needs of the family. When then I found him so honest in his dealings, I felt inclined to raise his pension; and it was my intention, before leaving Florence, to make some arrangement for all of his daughters.[1]

LIII

The Duke of Florence at this time, which was the month of August 1545, had retired to Poggio a Cajano, ten miles distant from Florence. Thither then I went to pay him my respects, with the sole object of acting as duty required, first because I was a Florentine, and next because my forefathers had always been adherents of the Medicean party, and I yielded to none of them in affection for this Duke Cosimo. As I have said, then, I rode to Poggio with the sole object of paying my respects, and with no intention of accepting service under him, as God, who does all things well, did then appoint for me.

When I was introduced, the Duke received me very kindly; then he and the Duchess put questions concerning the works which I had executed for the King.[1] I answered willingly and in detail. After listening to my story, he answered that he had heard as much, and that I spoke the truth. Then he assumed a tone of sympathy, and added: "How small a recompense for such great and noble masterpieces! Friend Benvenuto, if you feel inclined to execute something for me too, I am ready to pay you far better than that King of yours has done, for whom your excellent nature prompts you to speak so gratefully." When I understood his drift, I described the deep obligations under which I lay to his Majesty, who first obtained my liberation from that iniquitous prison, and afterwards supplied me with the means of carrying out more admirable works than any artist of my quality had ever had the chance to do. While I was thus speaking, my lord the Duke writhed on his chair, and seemed as though he could not bear to hear me to the end. Then, when I had concluded, he rejoined: "If you are disposed to work for me, I will treat you in a way that will astonish you, provided the fruits of your labours give me satisfaction, of which I have no doubt." I, poor unhappy mortal,

[1] Though this paragraph is confused, the meaning seems to be that Cellini's brother-in-law did not use the money which accrued from the sale of jewellery, and got into debt, because his allowance was inadequate, and he was out of work.

[1] This Duchess was Eleonora di Toledo, well known to us through Bronzino's portrait.

burning with desire to show the noble school [2] of Florence that, after leaving her in youth, I had practised other branches of the art than she imagined, gave answer to the Duke that I would willingly erect for him in marble or in bronze a mighty statue on his fine piazza. He replied that, for a first essay, he should like me to produce a Perseus; he had long set his heart on having such a monument, and he begged me to begin a model for the same.[3] I very gladly set myself to the task, and in a few weeks I finished my model, which was about a cubit high, in yellow wax and very delicately finished in all its details. I had made it with the most thorough study and art.[4]

The Duke returned to Florence, but several days passed before I had an opportunity of showing my model. It seemed indeed as though he had never set eyes on me or spoken with me, and this caused me to augur ill of my future dealings with his Excellency. Later on, however, one day after dinner, I took it to his wardrobe, where he came to inspect it with the Duchess and a few gentlemen of the court. No sooner had he seen it than he expressed much pleasure, and extolled it to the skies; wherefrom I gathered some hope that he might really be a connoisseur of art. After having well considered it for some time, always with greater satisfaction, he began as follows: "If you could only execute this little model, Benvenuto, with the same perfection on a large scale, it would be the finest piece in the piazza." I replied: "Most excellent my lord, upon the piazza are now standing works by the great Donatello and the incomparable Michel Angelo, the two greatest men who have ever lived since the days of the ancients.[5] But since your Excellence encourages my model with such praise, I feel the heart to execute it at least thrice as well in bronze." [6] No slight dispute arose upon this declaration; the Duke protesting that he understood these matters perfectly, and was quite aware what could be done. I rejoined that my achievements would resolve his dubitations and debates; I was absolutely sure of being able to perform far more than I had promised for his Excellency, but that

2 This school was the Collegio dei Maestri di Belle Arti in Florence, who had hitherto known of Cellini mainly as a goldsmith.

3 Cosimo chose the subject of Perseus because it symbolised his own victory over the Gorgon of tyrannicide and Republican partisanship. Donatello's Judith, symbolising justifiable regicide, and Michel Angelo's David, symbolising the might of innocent right against an overbearing usurper, already decorated the Florentine piazza. Until lately, both of these masterpieces stood together there with the Perseus of Cellini.

4 This is probably the precious model now existing in the Bargello Palace at Florence, in many points more interesting than the completed bronze statue under the Loggia de' Lanzi.

5 Donatello's Judith and Holofernes; Michel Angelo's David.

6 It is difficult to give the exact sense of *pertanto* and *perchè* in the text, but I think the drift of the sentence is rendered above.

he must give me means for carrying my work out, else I could not fulfil my undertaking. In return for this his Excellency bade me formulate my demands in a petition, detailing all my requirements; he would see them liberally attended to.

It is certain that if I had been cunning enough to secure by contract all I wanted for my work, I should not have incurred the great troubles which came upon me through my own fault. But he showed the strongest desire to have the work done, and the most perfect willingness to arrange preliminaries. I therefore, not discerning that he was more a merchant than a duke, dealt very frankly with his Excellency, just as if I had to do with a prince, and not with a commercial man. I sent in my petition, to which he replied in large and ample terms. The memorandum ran as follows: "Most rare and excellent my patron, petitions of any validity and compacts between us of any value do not rest upon words or writings; the whole point is that I should succeed in my work according to my promise; and if I so succeed, I feel convinced that your most illustrious Excellency will very well remember what you have engaged to do for me." This language so charmed the Duke both with my ways of acting and of speaking that he and the Duchess began to treat me with extraordinary marks of favour.

LIV

Being now inflamed with a great desire to begin working, I told his Excellency that I had need of a house where I could install myself and erect furnaces, in order to commence operations in clay and bronze, and also, according to their separate requirements, in gold and silver. I knew that he was well aware how thoroughly I could serve him in those several branches, and I required some dwelling fitted for my business. In order that his Excellency might perceive how earnestly I wished to work for him, I had already chosen a convenient house, in a quarter much to my liking.[1] As I did not want to trench upon his Excellency for money or anything of that sort, I had brought with me from France two jewels with which I begged him to purchase me the house, and to keep them until I earned it with my labour. These jewels were excellently executed by my workmen, after my own designs. When he had inspected them with minute attention,

1 This house is in the Via del Rosaio, entered from Via della Pergola, No. 6527.

he uttered these spirited words, which clothed my soul with a false hope: "Take back your jewels, Benvenuto! I want you, and not them; you shall have your house free of charges." After this, he signed a rescript underneath the petition I had drawn up, and which I have always preserved among my papers. The rescript ran as follows: *"Let the house be seen to, and who is the vendor, and at what price; for we wish to comply with Benvenuto's request."* [2] I naturally thought that this would secure me in possession of the house; being over and above convinced that my performances must far exceed what I promised.

His Excellency committed the execution of these orders to his majordomo, who was named Ser Pier Francesco Riccio.[3] The man came from Prato, and had been the Duke's pedagogue. I talked, then, to this donkey, and described my requirements, for there was a garden adjoining the house, on which I wanted to erect a workshop. He handed the matter over to a paymaster, dry and meagre, who bore the name of Lattanzio Gorini. This flimsy little fellow, with his tiny spider's hands and small gnat's voice, moved about the business at a snail's pace; yet in an evil hour he sent me stones, sand, and lime enough to build perhaps a pigeon-house with careful management. When I saw how coldly things were going forward, I began to feel dismayed; however, I said to myself: "Little beginnings sometimes have great endings;" and I fostered hope in my heart by noticing how many thousand ducats had recently been squandered upon ugly pieces of bad sculpture turned out by that beast of a Buaccio Bandinelli.[4] So I rallied my spirits and kept prodding at Lattanzio Gorini, to make him go a little faster. It was like shouting to a pack of lame donkeys with a blind dwarf for their driver. Under these difficulties, and by the use of my own money, I had soon marked out the foundations of the workshop and cleared the ground of trees and vines, labouring on, according to my wont, with fire, and perhaps a trifle of impatience.

On the other side, I was in the hands of Tasso the carpenter, a great friend of mine, who had received my instructions for making a wooden framework to set up the Perseus. This Tasso was a most

2 The petition and the rescript are in existence, and confirm Cellini's veracity in this transaction. See Bianchi, p. 587.

3 Varchi, *St. Fior.*, lib. xv. 44, gives to this man the character of a presumptuous conceited simpleton.

4 Cellini calls this man, his bitter foe and rival, *Buaccio* or the *great ox, blockhead,* instead of Baccio, which is shortened for Bartolommeo.

excellent craftsman, the best, I believe, who ever lived in his own branch of art.[5] Personally, he was gay and merry by temperament; and whenever I went to see him, he met me laughing, with some little song in falsetto on his lips. Half in despair as I then was, news coming that my affairs in France were going wrong, and these in Florence promising but ill through the luke-warmness of my patron, I could never stop listening till half the song was finished; and so in the end I used to cheer up a little with my friend, and drove away, as well as I was able, some few of the gloomy thoughts which weighed upon me.

LV

I had got all the above-mentioned things in order, and was making vigorous preparations for my great undertaking—indeed a portion of the lime had been already used—when I received sudden notice to appear before the majordomo. I found him, after his Excellency's dinner, in the hall of the clock.[1] On entering, I paid him marked respect, and he received me with the greatest stiffness. Then he asked who had installed me in the house, and by whose authority I had begun to build there, saying he marvelled much that I had been so headstrong and foolhardy. I answered that I had been installed in the house by his Excellency, and that his lordship himself, in the name of his Excellency, had given the orders to Lattanzio Gorini. "Lattanzio brought stone, sand, and lime, and provided what I wanted, saying he did so at your lordship's orders." When I had thus spoken, the brute turned upon me with still greater tartness, vowing that neither I nor any of those whom I had mentioned spoke the truth. This stung me to the quick, and I exclaimed: "O majordomo, so long as your lordship[2] chooses to use language befitting the high office which you hold, I shall revere you, and speak to you as respectfully as I do to the Duke; if you take another line with me, I shall address you as but one Ser Pier Francesco Riccio." He flew into such a rage that I thought he meant to go mad upon the spot,

5 See p. 23. Vasari introduced him, together with Cosimo's other favoured artists, in a fresco of the Palazzo Vecchio at Florence. See Plon, p. 124.

1 One of the rooms in the Palazzo Vecchio, so called because the famous cosmographical timepiece, made about 1484 for Lorenzo de' Medici by Lorenzo della Volpaia, stood there.

2 It was the custom at that epoch to address princes by the title of *Signore* or *Vostra Signoria;* gentlemen (armigeri) had the title of *Messer;* simple *Ser* was given to plebeians with some civil or ecclesiastical dignity.

anticipating the time ordained by Heaven for him to do so.[8] Pouring forth a torrent of abuse, he roared out that he was surprised at himself for having let me speak at all to a man of his quality. Thereupon my blood was up, and I cried: "Mark my words, then, Ser Pier Francesco Riccio! I will tell you what sort of men are my equals, and who are yours—mere teachers of the alphabet to children!" His face contracted with a spasm, while he raised his voice and repeated the same words in a still more insulting tone. I, too, assumed an air of menace, and matching his own arrogance with something of the same sort, told him plainly that men of my kind were worthy to converse with popes and emperors, and great kings, and that perhaps there were not two such men alive upon this earth, while ten of his sort might be met at every doorway. On hearing these words he jumped upon a window-seat in the hall there, and defied me to repeat what I had said. I did so with still greater heat and spirit, adding I had no farther mind to serve the Duke, and that I should return to France, where I was always welcome. The brute remained there stupefied and pale as clay; I went off furious, resolved on leaving Florence; and would to God that I had done so!

The Duke cannot, I think, have been informed at once of this diabolical scene, for I waited several days without hearing from him. Giving up all thoughts of Florence, except what concerned the settlement of my sister's and nieces' affairs, I made preparations to provide for them as well as I could with the small amount of money I had brought, and then to return to France and never set my foot in Italy again. This being my firm purpose, I had no intention to ask leave of the Duke or anybody, but to decamp as quickly as I could; when one morning the majordomo, of his own accord, sent very humbly to entreat my presence, and opened a long pedantic oration, in which I could discover neither method, nor elegance, nor meaning, nor head, nor tail. I only gathered from it that he professed himself a good Christian, wished to bear no man malice, and asked me in the Duke's name what salary I should be willing to accept. Hearing this, I stood a while on guard, and made no answer, being firmly resolved not to engage myself. When he saw that I refused to reply, he had at least the cleverness to put in: "Benvenuto, dukes expect to be answered; and what I am saying to you, I am saying from his Excellency's lips." Then I rejoined that if the message came

[8] Vasari, in his *Life of Montorsoli*, says in effect that this Riccio died about 1559, after having been insane several years.

from his Excellency, I would gladly reply, and told him to report to the Duke that I could not accept a position inferior to that of any one employed by him as artist. The majordomo answered: "Bandinelli receives two hundred crowns a year; if then you are contented with that, your salary is settled." I agreed upon these terms, adding that what I might earn in addition by the merit of my performances, could be given after they were seen; that point I left entirely to the good judgment of his Excellency. Thus, then, against my will, I pieced the broken thread again, and set to work; the Duke continually treating me with the highest imaginable marks of favour.

LVI

I received frequent letters from France, written by my most faithful friend Messer Guido Guidi. As yet they told nothing but good news; and Ascanio also bade me enjoy myself without uneasiness, since, if anything happened, he would let me know at once.

Now the King was informed that I had commenced working for the Duke of Florence, and being the best man in the world, he often asked: "Why does not Benvenuto come back to us?" He put searching questions on the subject to my two workmen, both of whom replied that I kept writing I was well off where I was, adding they thought I did not want to re-enter the service of his Majesty. Incensed by these presumptuous words, which were none of my saying, the King exclaimed: "Since he left us without any cause, I shall not recall him; let him e'en stay where he is." Thus the thievish brigands brought matters exactly to the pass they desired; for if I had returned to France, they would have become mere workmen under me once more, whereas, while I remained away, they were their own masters and in my place; consequently, they did everything in their power to prevent my coming back.

LVII

While the workshop for executing my Perseus was in building, I used to work in a ground-floor room. Here I modelled the statue in plaster, giving it the same dimensions as the bronze was meant to have, and intending to cast it from this mould. But finding that it would take rather long to carry it out in this way, I resolved upon another expedient, especially as now a wretched little studio had been erected, brick on brick, so miserably built that the mere recollection of it gives me pain. So then I began the figure of Medusa, and constructed the skeleton in iron. Afterwards I put on the clay, and when that was modelled, baked it.

I had no assistants except some little shopboys, among whom was one of great beauty; he was the son of a prostitute called La Gambetta. I made use of the lad as a model, for the only books which teach this art are the natural human body. Meanwhile, as I could not do everything alone, I looked about for workmen in order to put the business quickly through; but I was unable to find any. There were indeed some in Florence who would willingly have come, but Bandinello prevented them, and after keeping me in want of aid awhile, told the Duke that I was trying to entice his workpeople because I was quite incapable of setting up so great a statue by myself. I complained to the Duke of the annoyance which the brute gave me, and begged him to allow me some of the labourers from the Opera.[1] My request inclined him to lend ear to Bandinello's calumnies; and when I noticed that, I set about to do my utmost by myself alone. The labour was enormous: I had to strain every muscle night and day; and just then the husband of my sister sickened, and died after a few days' illness. He left my sister, still young, with six girls of all ages, on my hands. This was the first great trial I endured in Florence, to be made the father and guardian of such a distressed family.

LVIII

In my anxiety that nothing should go wrong, I sent for two hand-labourers to clear my garden of rubbish. They came from Ponte Vecchio, the one an old man of sixty years, the other a young fellow of eighteen. After employing them about three days, the lad told me that the old man would not work, and that I had better send him away, since, besides being idle, he prevented his comrade from working. The little I had to do there could be done by himself, without throwing money away on other people. The youth was called Bernardino Mannellini, of Mugello. When I saw that he was so inclined to labour, I asked whether he would enter my service, and we agreed upon the spot. He groomed my horse, gardened, and

[1] That is, the Opera del Duomo, or permanent establishment for attending to the fabric of the Florentine Cathedral.

soon essayed to help me in the workshop, with such success that by degrees he learned the art quite nicely. I never had a better assistant than he proved. Having made up my mind to accomplish the whole affair with this man's aid, I now let the Duke know that Bandinello was lying, and that I could get on famously without his workpeople.

Just at this time I suffered slightly in the loins, and being unable to work hard, I was glad to pass my time in the Duke's wardrobe with a couple of young goldsmiths called Gianpagolo and Domenico Poggini,[1] who made a little golden cup under my direction. It was chased in bas-relief with figures and other pretty ornaments, and his Excellency meant it for the Duchess to drink water out of. He furthermore commissioned me to execute a golden belt, which I enriched with gems and delicate masks and other fancies. The Duke came frequently into the wardrobe, and took great pleasure in watching me at work and talking to me. When my health improved, I had clay brought, and took a portrait of his Excellency, considerably larger than life-size, which I modelled while he stayed with me for pastime. He was highly delighted with this piece, and conceived such a liking for me that he earnestly begged me to take up my working quarters in the palace, selecting rooms large enough for my purpose, and fitting them up with furnaces and all I wanted, for he greatly enjoyed watching the processes of art. I replied that this was impossible; I should not have finished my undertakings in a hundred years.

LIX

The Duchess also treated me with extraordinary graciousness, and would have been pleased if I had worked for her alone, forgetting Perseus and everything besides. I for my part, while these vain favours were being showered upon me knew only too well that my perverse and biting fortune could not long delay to send me some fresh calamity, because I kept ever before my eyes the great mistake I had committed while seeking to do a good action. I refer to my affairs in France. The King could not swallow the displeasure he felt at my departure; and yet he wanted me to return, if only this could be brought about without concessions on his part. I thought that I was entirely in the right, and would not bend submissively, because I judged that if I wrote in humble terms, those enemies of mine

1 These two brothers were specially eminent as die-casters. Gianpagolo went to Spain and served Philip II.

would say in their French fashion that I had confessed myself to blame, and that certain misdoings with which they wrongfully taxed me were proved true. Therefore I stood upon my honour, and wrote in terms of haughty coldness, which was precisely what those two traitors, my apprentices, most heartily desired. In my letters to them I boasted of the distinguished kindness shown me in my own birthplace by a prince and princess the absolute masters of Florence. Whenever they received one of these despatches, they went to the King, and beseiged his Majesty with entreaties for the castle upon the same terms as he had granted it to me. The King, who was a man of great goodness and perspicacity, would never consent to the presumptuous demands of those scoundrels, since he scented the malignity of their aims. Yet, wishing to keep them in expectation, and to give me the opportunity of coming back, he caused an angry letter to be written to me by his treasurer, Messer Giuliano Buonaccorsi, a burgher of Florence. The substance was as follows: If I wanted to preserve the reputation for honesty which I had hitherto enjoyed, it was my plain duty, after leaving France with no cause whatsoever, to render an account of all that I had done and dealt with for his Majesty.

The receipt of this letter gave me such pleasure that, if I had consulted my own palate, I could not have wished for either more or less. I sat down to write an answer, and filled nine pages of ordinary paper. In this document I described in detail all the works which I had executed, and all the adventures I had gone through while performing them, and all the sums which had been spent upon them. The payments had always been made through two notaries and one of his Majesty's treasurers; and I could show receipts from all the men into whose hands they passed, whether for goods supplied or labour rendered. I had not pocketed one penny of the money, nor had I received any reward for my completed works. I brought back with me into Italy nothing but some marks of favour and most royal promises, truly worthy of his Majesty. "Now, though I cannot vaunt myself of any recompense beyond the salaries appointed for my maintenance in France, seven hundred golden crowns of which are still due, inasmuch as I abstained from drawing them until I could employ them on my return-journey; yet knowing that malicious foes out of their envious hearts have played some knavish trick against me, I feel confident that truth will prevail. I take pride in his Most Christian Majesty and am not moved by avarice. I am indeed aware of having performed for him far more than I undertook; and albeit the promised reward has not been given me, my one anxiety is to remain in his Majesty's opinion that man of probity and honour which I have always been. If your Majesty entertains the least doubt upon this point, I will fly to render an account of my conduct, at the risk even of my life. But noticing in what slight esteem I am held I have had no mind to come back and make an offer of myself, knowing that I shall never lack for bread whithersoever I may go. If, however, I am called for, I will always answer." The letter contained many further particulars worthy of the King's attention, and proper to the preservation of my honour. Before despatching it, I took it to the Duke, who read it with interest; than I sent it into France, addressed to the Cardinal of Ferrara.

LX

About this time Bernardone Baldini,[1] broker in jewels to the Duke, brought a big diamond from Venice, which weighed more than thirty-five carats. Antonio, son of Vittorio Landi, was also interested in getting the Duke to purchase it.[2] The stone had been cut with a point; but since it did not yield the purity of lustre which one expects in such a diamond, its owners had cropped the point, and, in truth, it was not exactly fit for either point or table cutting.[3] Our Duke, who greatly delighted in gems, though he was not a sound judge of them, held out good hopes to the rogue Bernardaccio that he would buy this stone; and the fellow, wanting to secure for himself alone the honour of palming it off upon the Duke of Florence, abstained from taking his partner Antonio Landi into the secret. Now Landi had been my intimate friend from childhood, and when he saw that I enjoyed the Duke's confidence, he called me aside (it was just before noon at a corner of the Mercato Nuovo), and spoke as follows: "Benvenuto, I am convinced that the Duke will show you a diamond, which he seems disposed to buy; you will find it a big stone. Pray assist the purchase; I can give it for seventeen thousand crowns. I feel sure he will ask your advice; and if you see that he has a mind for it, we will contrive that he secures

1 Varchi and Ammirato both mention him as an excellent jeweller.

2 Antonio Landi was a Florentine gentleman, merchant, and author. A comedy of his called *Commodo* is extant.

3 Italians distinguished cut diamonds of three sorts: *in tavola*, *a faccette*, and *in punta*. The word I have translated *cropped* is *ischericato*, which was properly applied to an unfrocked or degraded ecclesiastic.

it." Antonio professed great confidence in being able to complete the bargain for the jewel at that price. In reply, I told him that if my advice was taken, I would speak according to my judgment, without prejudice to the diamond.

As I have above related, the Duke came daily into our goldsmith's workshop for several hours; and about a week after this conversation with Antonio Landi he showed me one day after dinner the diamond in question, which I immediately recognised by its description, both as to form and weight. I have already said that its water was not quite transparent, for which reason it had been cropped; so, when I found it of that kind and quality, I felt certainly disinclined to recommend its acquisition. However, I asked his Excellency what he wanted me to say; because it was one thing for jewellers to value a stone after a prince had bought it, and another thing to estimate it with a view to purchase. He replied that he had bought it, and that he only wanted my opinion. I did not choose to abstain from hinting what I really thought about the stone. Then he told me to observe the beauty of its great facets.[4] I answered that this feature of the diamond was not so great a beauty as his Excellency supposed, but came from the point having been cropped. At these words my prince, who perceived that I was speaking the truth, made a wry face, and bade me give good heed to valuing the stone, and saying what I thought it worth. I reckoned that, since Landi had offered it to me for 17,000 crowns, the Duke might have got it for 15,000 at the highest; so, noticing that he would take it ill if I spoke the truth, I made my mind up to uphold him in his false opinion, and handing back the diamond, said: "You will probably have paid 18,000 crowns." On hearing this the Duke uttered a loud "Oh" opening his mouth as wide as a well, and cried out: "Now am I convinced that you understand nothing about the matter." I retorted: "You are certainly in the wrong there, my lord. Do you attend to maintaining the credit of your diamond, while I attend to understanding my trade. But pray tell me at least how much you paid, in order that I may learn to understand it according to the way of your Excellency." The Duke rose, and, with a little sort of angry grin, replied: "Twenty-five thousand crowns and more, Benvenuto, did that stone cost me!"

Having thus spoken he departed. Giovanpagolo and Domenico Poggini, the goldsmiths, were present; and Bachiacca, the embroid-

4 *Filette*, the sharp lines which divide one facet from another.

erer, who was working in an adjacent room, ran up at the noise.[5] I told them that I should never have advised the Duke to purchase it; but if his heart was set on having it, Antonio Landi had offered me the stone eight days ago for 17,000 crowns. I think I could have got it for 15,000 or less. But the Duke apparently wished to maintain his gem in credit; for when Antonio Landi was willing to let it go at that price, how the devil can Bernardone have played off such a shameful trick upon his Excellency? Never imagining that the matter stood precisely as the Duke averred, we laughingly made light of his supposed credulity.

LXI

Meanwhile I was advancing with my great statue of Medusa. I had covered the iron skeleton with clay, which I modelled like an anatomical subject, and about half an inch thinner than the bronze would be. This I baked well, and then began to spread on the wax surface, in order to complete the figure to my liking.[1] The Duke, who often came to inspect it, was so anxious lest I should not succeed with the bronze, that he wanted me to call in some master to cast it for me.

He was continually talking in the highest terms of my acquirements and accomplishments. This made his majordomo no less continually eager to devise some trap for making me break my neck. Now his post at court gave him authority with the chief-constables and all the officers in the poor unhappy town of Florence. Only to think that a fellow from Prato, our hereditary foeman, the son of a cooper, and the most ignorant creature in existence, should have risen to such a station of influence, merely because he had been the rotten tutor of Cosimo de' Medici before he became Duke! Well, as I have said, he kept ever on the watch to serve me some ill turn; and finding that he could not catch me out on any side, he fell at last upon this plan, which meant mischief. He betook himself to Gambetta, the mother of my apprentice Cencio; and this precious pair together—that knave of a pedant and that rogue of a strumpet

5 Antonio Ubertini, called Il Bachiacca, a brother of Cellini's friend in Rome. See p. 52. He enjoyed a great reputation, and was praised by Varchi in a sonnet for his mastery of embroidery.

1 This is an important passage, which has not, I think, been properly understood by Cellini's translators. It describes the process he now employed in preparing a mould for bronze-casting. First, it seems, he made a solid clay model, somewhat smaller than the bronze was meant to be. This he overlaid with wax, and then took a hollow mould of the figure thus formed. Farther on we shall see how he withdrew the wax from the hollow mould, leaving the solid model inside, with space enough between them for the metal to flow in.

—invented a scheme for giving me such a fright as would make me leave Florence in hot haste. Gambetta, yielding to the instinct of her trade, went out, acting under the orders of that mad, knavish pedant, the majordomo—I must add that they had also gained over the Bargello, a Bolognese, whom the Duke afterwards dismissed for similar conspiracies. Well, one Saturday evening, after sunset, Gambetta came to my house with her son, and told me she had kept him several days indoors for my welfare. I answered that there was no reason to keep him shut up on my account; and laughing her whorish arts to scorn, I turned to the boy in her presence, and said these words: "You know, Cencio, whether I have sinned with you!" He began to shed tears, and answered, "No!" Upon this the mother, shaking her head, cried out at him: "Ah! you little scoundrel! Do you think I do not know how these things happen?" Then she turned to me, and begged me to keep the lad hidden in my house, because the Bargello was after him, and would seize him anywhere outside my house, but there they would not dare to touch him. I made answer that in my house lived my widowed sister and six girls of holy life, and that I wanted nobody else there. Upon that she related that the majordomo had given orders to the Bargello, and that I should certainly be taken up: only, if I would not harbour her son, I might square accounts by paying her a hundred crowns; the majordomo was her crony, and I might rest assured that she could work him to her liking, provided I paid down the hundred crowns. This cozenage goaded me into such a fury that I cried: "Out with you, shameful strumpet! Were it not for my good reputation, and for the innocence of this unhappy boy of yours here, I should long ago have cut your throat with the dagger at my side; and twice or thrice I have already clasped my fingers on the handle." With words to this effect, and many ugly blows to boot, I drove the woman and her son into the street.

LXII

When I reflected on the roguery and power of that evil-minded pedant, I judged it best to give a wide berth to his infernal machinations; so early next morning I mounted my horse and took the road for Venice, leaving in my sister's hands jewels and articles to the value of nearly two thousand crowns. I took with me my servant Bernardino of Mugello; and when I reached Ferrara, I wrote word to his Excellency the Duke, that though I had gone off without being sent, I should come back again without being called for.

On arriving at Venice, and pondering upon the divers ways my cruel fortune took to torment me, yet at the same time feeling myself none the less sound in health and hearty, I made up my mind to fence with her according to my wont. While thus engrossed in thoughts about my own affairs, I went abroad for pastime through that beautiful and sumptuous city, and paid visits to the admirable painter Titian, and to Jacopo del Sansovino, our able sculptor and architect from Florence. The latter enjoyed an excellent appointment under the Signoria of Venice; and we had been acquainted during our youth in Rome and Florence. These two men of genius received me with marked kindness. The day afterwards I met Messer Lorenzo de' Medici,[1] who took me by the hand at once, giving me the warmest welcome which could be imagined, because we had known each other in Florence when I was coining for Duke Allessandro, and afterwards in Paris while I was in the King's service. At that time he sojurned in the house of Messer Giuliano Buonaccorsi, and having nowhere else to go for pastime without the greatest peril of his life, he used to spend a large part of the day in my house, watching me working at the great pieces I produced there. As I was saying, our former acquaintance led him to take me by the hand and bring me to his dwelling, where I found the Prior degli Strozzi, brother of my lord Piero. While making good cheer together, they asked me how long I intended to remain in Venice, thinking that I was on my return journey into France. To these gentlemen I replied that I had left Florence on account of the events I have described above, and that I meant to go back after two or three days, in order to resume my service with the Duke. On hearing this, the Prior and Messer Lorenzo turned round on me with such sternness that I felt extremely uneasy; then they said to me: "You would do far better to return to France, where you are rich and well known; for if you go back to Florence, you will lose all that you have gained in France, and will earn nothing there but annoyances."

I made no answer to these words, and departed the next day as secretly as I was able, turning my face again toward Florence. In the meanwhile that infernal plot had come to a head and broken, for I had written to my great master, the Duke, giving him a full ac-

1 This is Lorenzino de' Medici, the murderer of Alessandro, who was himself assassinated by two Tuscan bravi in 1548. See *Renaissance in Italy*, vol. vi. chap. 6.

count of the causes of my escapade to Venice. I went to visit him without any ceremony, and was received with his usual reserve and austerity. Having maintained this attitude awhile, he turned toward me pleasantly, and asked where I had been. I answered that my heart had never moved one inch from his most illustrious Excellency, although some weighty reasons had forced me to go a roaming for a little while. Then softening still more in manner, he began to question me concerning Venice, and after this wise we conversed some space of time. At last he bade me apply myself to business, and complete his Perseus. So I returned home glad and light-hearted, and comforted my family, that is to say, my sister and her six daughters. Then I resumed my work, and pushed it forward as briskly as I could.

LXIII

The first piece I cast in bronze was that great bust, the portrait of his Excellency, which I had modelled in the goldsmith's workroom while suffering from those pains in my back.[1] It gave much pleasure when it was completed, though my sole object in making it was to obtain experience of clays suitable for bronze-casting. I was of course aware that the admirable sculptor Donatello had cast his bronzes with the clay of Florence; yet it seemed to me that he had met with enormous difficulties in their execution. As I thought that this was due to some fault in the earth, I wanted to make these first experiments before I undertook my Perseus. From them I learned that the clay was good enough, but had not been well understood by Donatello, inasmuch as I could see that his pieces had been cast with the very greatest trouble. Accordingly, as I have described above, I prepared the earth by artificial methods, and found it served me well, and with it I cast the bust; but since I had not yet constructed my own furnace, I employed that of Maestro Zanobi di Pagno, a bell-founder.

When I saw that this bust came out sharp and clean, I set at once to construct a little furnace in the workshop erected for me by the Duke, after my own plans and design, in the house which the Duke had given me. No sooner was the furnace ready than I went to work with all diligence upon the casting of Medusa, that is, the woman twisted in a heap beneath the feet of Perseus. It was an ex-

1 Now in the Museum of the Bargello Palace at Florence.

tremely difficult task, and I was anxious to observe all the niceties of art which I had learned, so as not to lapse into some error. The first cast I took in my furnace succeeded in the superlative degree, and was so clean that my friends thought I should not need to retouch it. It is true that certain Germans and Frenchmen, who vaunt the possession of marvellous secrets, pretend that they can cast bronzes without retouching them; but this is really nonsense, because the bronze, when it has first been cast, ought to be worked over and beaten in with hammers and chisels, according to the manner of the ancients and also to that of the moderns—I mean such moderns as have known how to work in bronze.

The result of this casting greatly pleased his Excellency, who often came to my house to inspect it, encouraging me by the interest he showed to do my best. The furious envy of Bandinello, however, who kept always whispering in the Duke's ears, had such effect that he made him believe my first successes with a single figure or two proved nothing; I should never be able to put the whole large piece together, since I was new to the craft, and his Excellency ought to take good heed he did not throw his money away. These insinuations operated so efficiently upon the Duke's illustrious ears, that part of my allowance for workpeople was withdrawn. I felt compelled to complain pretty sharply to his Excellency; and having gone to wait on him one morning in the Via de' Servi, I spoke as follows: "My lord, I do not now receive the monies necessary for my task, which makes me fear that your Excellency has lost confidence in me. Once more then I tell you that I feel quite able to execute this statue three times better than the model, as I have before engaged my word."

LXIV

I could see that this speech made no impression on the Duke, for he kept silence; then, seized with sudden anger and a vehement emotion, I began again to address him: "My lord, this city of a truth has ever been the school of the most noble talents. Yet when a man has come to know what he is worth, after gaining some acquirements, and wishing to augment the glory of his town and of his glorious prince, it is quite right that he should go and labour elsewhere. To prove the truth of these words, I need only remind your Excellency of Donatello and the great Lionardo da Vinci in the past, and of our incomparable Michel Angelo Buonarroti in the present;

they augment the glory of your Excellency by their genius. I in my turn feel the same desire and hope to play my part like them; therefore, my lord, give me the leave to go. But beware of letting Bandinello quit you; rather bestow upon him always more than he demands; for if he goes into foreign parts, his ignorance is so presumptuous that he is just the man to disgrace our most illustrious school. Now grant me my permission, prince! I ask no further reward for my labours up to this time than the gracious favour of your most illustrious Excellency." When he saw the firmness of my resolution, he turned with some irritation and exclaimed: "Benvenuto, if you want to finish the statue, you shall lack for nothing." Then I thanked him and said I had no greater desire than to show those envious folk that I had it in me to execute the promised work. When I left his Excellency, I received some slight assistance; but this not being sufficient, I had to put my hand into my own purse, in order to push the work forward at something better than a snail's pace.

It was my custom to pass the evening in the Duke's wardrobe, where Domenico Poggini and his brother Gianpagolo were at work upon that golden cup for the Duchess and the girdle I have already described. His Excellency had also commissioned me to make a little model for a pendent to set the great diamond which Bernardone and Antonio Landi made him buy. I tried to get out of doing it, but the Duke compelled me by all sorts of kindly pressure to work until four hours after nightfall. He kept indeed enticing me to push this job forward by daytime also; but I would not consent, although I felt sure I should incur his anger. Now one evening I happened to arrive rather later than usual, whereupon he said: "Ill come may you be!" [1] I answered: "My lord, that is not my name; my name is Welcome! But, as I suppose your Excellency is joking, I will add no more." He replied that, far from joking, he meant solemn earnest. I had better look to my conduct, for it had come to his ears that I relied upon his favour to take in first one man and then another. I begged his most illustrious Excellency to name a single person whom I had ever taken in. At this he flew into a rage, and said: "Go, and give back to Bernardone what you have of his. There! I have mentioned one." I said: "My lord, I thank you, and beg you to condescend so far as to listen to four words. It is true that he lent me a pair of old scales, two anvils, and three little hammers, which articles I begged

[1] A play on *Benvenuto* and *Malvenuto*.

his workman, Giorgio da Cortona, fifteen days ago, to fetch back. Giorgio came for them himself. If your Excellency can prove, on referring to those who have spoken these calumnies, or to others, that I have ever, from the day of my birth till now, got any single thing by fraud from anybody, be it in Rome or be it in France, then let your Excellency punish me as immoderately as you choose." When the Duke saw me in this mighty passion, he assumed the air of a prudent and benevolent lord, saying: "Those words are not meant for well-doers; therefore, if it is as you say, I shall always receive you with the same kindness as heretofore." To this I answered: "I should like your Excellency to know that the rascalities of Bernardone compel me to ask as a favour how much that big diamond with the cropped point cost you. I hope to prove on what account that scoundrel tries to bring me into disgrace." Then his Excellency replied: "I paid 25,000 ducats for it; why do you ask me?" "Because, my lord, on such a day, at such an hour, in a corner of Mercato Nuovo, Antonio Landi, the son of Vittorio, begged me to induce your Excellency to buy it, and at my first question he asked 16,000 ducats for the diamond;[2] now your Excellency knows what it has cost you. Domenico Poggini and Gianpagolo his brother, who are present, will confirm my words; for I spoke to them at once about it, and since that time have never once alluded to the matter, because your Excellency told me I did not understand these things, which made me think you wanted to keep up the credit of your stone. I should like you to know, my lord, that I do understand, and that, as regards my character, I consider myself no less honest than any man who ever lived upon this earth. I shall not try to rob you of eight or ten thousand ducats at one go, but shall rather seek to earn them by my industry. I entered the service of your Excellency as sculptor, goldsmith, and stamper of coin; but to blab about my neighbour's private matters,—never! What I am now telling you I say in self-defence; I do not want my fee for information.[3] If I speak out in the presence of so many worthy fellows as are here, it is because I do not wish your Excellency to believe what Bernardone tells you."

When he had heard this speech, the Duke rose up in anger, and sent for Bernardone, who was forced to take flight as far as Venice, he and Antonio Landi with him. The latter told me that he had

2 He forgets that he has said above that it was offered him by Landi for 17,000 ducats.

3 This fee was *il quarto,* or the fourth part of the criminal's fine, which came to the delator.

not meant that diamond, but was talking of another stone. So then they went and came again from Venice; whereupon I presented myself to the Duke and spoke as follows: "My lord, what I told you is the truth; and what Bernardone said about the tools he lent me is a lie. You had better put this to the proof, and I will go at once to the Bargello." The Duke made answer: "Benvenuto, do your best to be an honest man, as you have done until now; you have no cause for apprehension." So the whole matter passed off in smoke, and I heard not one more word about it. I applied myself to finishing his jewel; and when I took it to the Duchess, her Grace said that she esteemed my setting quite as highly as the diamond which Bernardaccio had made them buy. She then desired me to fasten it upon her breast, and handed me a large pin, with which I fixed it, and took my leave in her good favour.[4] Afterwards I was informed that they had the stone reset by a German or some other foreigner—whether truly or not I cannot vouch—upon Bernardone's suggestion that the diamond would show better in a less elaborate setting.

LXV

I believe I have already narrated how Domenico and Giovanpagolo Poggini, goldsmiths and brothers, were at work in the Duke's wardrobe upon some little golden vases, after my design, chased with figures in bas-relief, and other ornaments of great distinction. I oftentimes kept saying to his Excellency: "My lord, if you will undertake to pay some work-people, I am ready to strike coins for your mint and medals with your portrait. I am willing to enter into competition with the ancients, and feel able to surpass them; for since those early days in which I made the medals of Pope Clement, I have learned so much that I can now produce far better pieces of the kind. I think I can also outdo the coins I struck for Duke Alessandro, which are still held in high esteem; in like manner I could make for you large pieces of gold and silver plate, as I did so often for that noble monarch, King Francis of France, thanks to the great conveniences he allowed me, without ever losing time for the execution of colossal statues or other works of the sculptor's craft." To this suggestion the Duke replied: "Go forward; I will see;" but he never supplied me with conveniences or aid of any kind.

[4] It is worthy of notice that from this point onward the MS. is written by Cellini in his own hand.

One day his most illustrious Excellency handed me several pounds weight of silver, and said: "This is some of the silver from my mines;[1] take it, and make a fine vase." Now I did not choose to neglect my Perseus, and at the same time I wished to serve the Duke, so I entrusted the metal, together with my designs and models in wax, to a rascal called Piero di Martino, a goldsmith by trade. He set the work up badly, and moreover ceased to labour at it, so that I lost more time than if I had taken it in hand myself. After several months were wasted, and Piero would neither work nor put men to work upon the piece, I made him give it back. I moved heaven and earth to get back the body of the vase, which he had begun badly, as I have already said, together with the remainder of the silver. The Duke, hearing something of these disputes, sent for the vase and the models, and never told me why or wherefore. Suffice it to say, that he placed some of my designs in the hands of divers persons at Venice and elsewhere, and was very ill served by them.

The Duchess kept urging me to do goldsmith's work for her. I frequently replied that everybody, nay, all Italy, knew well I was an excellent goldsmith; but Italy had not yet seen what I could do in sculpture. Among artists, certain enraged sculptors laughed at me, and called me the new sculptor. "Now I hope to show them that I am an old sculptor, if God shall grant me the boon of finishing my Perseus for that noble piazza of his most illustrious Excellency." After this I shut myself up at home, working day and night, not even showing my face in the palace. I wished, however, to keep myself in favour with the Duchess; so I got some little cups made for her in silver, no larger than twopenny milk-pots, chased with exquisite masks in the rarest antique style. When I took them to her Excellency, she received me most graciously, and repaid the gold and silver I had spent upon them. Then I made my suit to her and prayed her tell the Duke that I was getting small assistance for so great a work; I begged her also to warn him not to lend so ready an ear to Bandinello's evil tongue, which hindered me from finishing my Perseus. In reply to these lamentable complaints the Duchess shrugged her shoulders and exclaimed: "Of a surety the Duke ought only too well to know that this Bandinello of his is worth nothing."

1 Cosimo's silver mines were at Campiglia and Pietrasantra. He worked them, however, rather at a loss than profit.

LXVI

I now stayed at home, and went rarely to the palace, labouring with great diligence to complete my statue. I had to pay the workmen out of my own pocket; for the Duke, after giving Lattanzio Gorini orders to discharge their wages, at the end of about eighteen months, grew tired, and withdrew this subsidy. I asked Lattanzio why he did not pay me as usual. The man replied, gesticulating with those spidery hands of his, in a shrill gnat's voice: "Why do not you finish your work? One thinks that you will never get it done." In a rage I up and answered: "May the plague catch you and all who dare to think I shall not finish it!"

So I went home with despair at heart to my unlucky Perseus, not without weeping, when I remembered the prosperity I had abandoned in Paris under the patronage of that marvellous King Francis, where I had the abundance of all kinds, and here had everything to want for. Many a time I had it in my soul to cast myself away for lost. One day on one of these occasions, I mounted a nice nag I had, put a hundred crowns in my purse, and went to Fiesole to visit a natural son of mine there, who was at nurse with my gossip, the wife of one of my workpeople. When I reached the house, I found the boy in good health, and kissed him, very sad at heart. On taking leave, he would not let me go, but held me with his little hands and a tempest of cries and tears. Considering that he was only two years old or thereabouts, the child's grief was something wonderful. Now I had resolved, in the heat of my despair, if I met Bandinello, who went every evening to a farm of his above San Domenico, that I would hurl him to destruction; so I disengaged myself from my baby, and left the boy there sobbing his heart out. Taking the road toward Florence, just when I entered the piazza of San Domenico, Bandinello was arriving from the other side. On the instant I decided upon bloodshed; but when I reached the man and raised my eyes, I saw him unarmed, riding a sorry mule or rather donkey, and he had with him a boy of ten years old. No sooner did he catch sight of me than he turned the colour of a corpse, and trembled from head to foot. Perceiving at once how base the business would be, I exclaimed: "Fear not, vile coward! I do not condescend to smite you." He looked at me submissively and said nothing. Thereupon I recovered command of my faculties, and thanked God that His goodness had withheld me from so great an act of violence.

Then, being delivered from that fiendish fury, my spirits rose, and I said to myself: "If God but grant me to execute my work, I hope by its means to annihilate all my scoundrelly enemies; and thus I shall perform far greater and more glorious revenges than if I had vented my rage upon one single foe." Having this excellent resolve in heart, I reached my home. At the end of three days news was brought me that my only son had been smothered by his nurse, my gossip, which gave me greater grief than I have ever had in my whole life. However, I knelt upon the ground, and, not without tears, returned thanks to God, as I was wont, exclaiming, "Lord, Thou gavest me the child, and Thou hast taken him; for all Thy dealings I thank Thee with my whole heart." This great sorrow went nigh to depriving me of reason; yet, according to my habit, I made a virtue of necessity, and adapted myself to circumstances as well as I was able.

LXVII

About this time a young fellow called Francesco, the son of a smith, Matteo, left Bandinello's employment, and inquired whether I would give him work. I agreed, and sent him to retouch my Medusa, which had been new cast in bronze. After a fortnight he mentioned that he had been speaking with his master, that is, Bandinello, who told him, if I cared to make a marble statue, he would give me a fine block of stone. I replied at once: "Tell him I accept his offer; perhaps this marble will prove a stumbling-block to him, for he keeps on provoking me, and does not bear in mind the great peril he ran upon the piazza of San Domenico. Tell him I will have the marble by all means. I never speak about him, and the beast is perpetually causing me annoyance. I verily believe you came to work here at his orders for the mere purpose of spying upon me. Go, then, and tell him I insist on having the marble, even against his will: see that you do not come back without it."

LXVIII

Many days had elapsed during which I had not shown my face in the palace, when the fancy took me to go there one morning just as the Duke was finishing his dinner. From what I heard, his Excellency had been talking of me that morning, commending me highly, and in particular praising my skill in setting jewels. Therefore, when the Duchess saw me, she called for me by Messer Sforza;[1] and on my presenting myself to her most illustrious Excellency, she asked me to set a little point-diamond in a ring, saying she wished always to wear it; at the same time she gave me the measure and the stone, which was worth about a hundred crowns, begging me to be quick about the work. Upon this the Duke began speaking to the Duchess, and said: "There is no doubt that Benvenuto was formerly without his peer in this art; but now that he has abandoned it, I believe it will be too much trouble for him to make a little ring of the sort you want. I pray you, therefore, not to importune him about this trifle, which would be no trifle to him owing to his want of practice." I thanked the Duke for his kind words, but begged him to let me render this trifling service to the Duchess. Then I took the ring in hand, and finished it within a few days. It was meant for the little finger; accordingly I fashioned four tiny children in the round and four masks, which figures composed the hoop. I also found room for some enamelled fruits and connecting links, so that the stone and setting went uncommonly well together. Then I took it to the Duchess, who told me graciously that I had produced a very fine piece, and that she would remember me. She afterwards sent the ring as a present to King Philip, and from that time forward kept charging me with commissions, so kindly, however, that I did my best to serve her, although I saw but very little of her money. God knows I had great need of that, for I was eager to finish my Perseus, and had engaged some journeymen, whom I paid out of my own purse. I now began to show myself more often than I had recently been doing.

LXIX

It happened on one feast-day that I went to the palace after dinner, and when I reached the clockroom, I saw the door of the wardrobe standing open. As I drew nigh it, the Duke called me, and after a friendly greeting said: "You are welcome! Look at that box which has been sent me by my lord Stefano of Palestrina.[1] Open it, and let us see what it contains." When I had opened the box, I

[1] Sforza Almeni, a Perugian gentleman, the Duke's chamberlain. Cosimo killed this man with his own hand in the year 1566.

[1] Stefano Colonna, of the princely house of Palestrina. He was a general of considerable repute in the Spanish, French, and Florentine services successively.

cried to the Duke: "My lord, this is a statue in Greek marble, and it is a miracle of beauty. I must say that I have never seen a boy's figure so excellently wrought and in so fine a style among all the antiques I have inspected. If your Excellency permits, I should like to restore it—head and arms and feet. I will add an eagle, in order that we may christen the lad Ganymede. It is certainly not my business to patch up statues, that being the trade of botchers, who do it in all conscience villainously ill; yet the art displayed by this great master of antiquity cries out to me to help him." The Duke was highly delighted to find the statue so beautiful, and put me a multitude of questions, saying: "Tell me, Benvenuto, minutely, in what consists the skill of this old master, which so excites your admiration." I then attempted, as well as I was able, to explain the beauty of workmanship, the consummate science, and the rare manner displayed by the fragment. I spoke long upon these topics, and with the greater pleasure because I saw that his Excellency was deeply interested.

LXX

While I was thus pleasantly engaged in entertaining the Duke, a page happened to leave the wardrobe, and at the same moment Bandinello entered. When the Duke saw him, his countenance contracted, and he asked him drily: "What are you about here?" Bandinello, without answering, cast a glance upon the box, where the statue lay uncovered. Then breaking into one of his malignant laughs and wagging his head, he turned to the Duke and said: "My lord, this exactly illustrates the truth of what I have so often told your Excellency. You must know that the ancients were wholly ignorant of anatomy, and therefore their works abound in mistakes." I kept silence, and paid no heed to what he was saying; nay, indeed, I had turned my back on him. But when the brute had brought his disagreeable babble to an end, the Duke exclaimed: "O Benvenuto, this is the exact opposite of what you were just now demonstrating with so many excellent arguments. Come and speak a word in defence of the statue." In reply to this appeal, so kindly made me by the Duke, I spoke as follows: "My lord, your most illustrious Excellency must please to know that Baccio Bandinello is made up of everything bad, and thus has he ever been; therefore, whatever he looks at, be the thing superlatively excellent, becomes in his ungracious eyes as bad as can be. I, who incline to the good only, discern the truth with purer senses. Consequently, what I told your Excellency about this lovely statue is mere simple truth; whereas what Bandinello said is but a portion of the evil out of which he is composed." The Duke listened with much amusement; but Bandinello writhed and made the most ugly faces—his face itself being by nature hideous beyond measure—which could be imagined by the mind of man.

The Duke at this point moved away, and proceeded through some ground-floor rooms, while Bandinello followed. The chamberlains twitched me by the mantle, and sent me after; so we all attended the Duke until he reached a certain chamber, where he seated himself, with Bandinello and me standing at his right hand and his left. I kept silence, and the gentlemen of his Excellency's suite looked hard at Bandinello, tittering among themselves about the speech I had made in the room above. So then Bandinello began again to chatter, and cried out: "Prince, when I uncovered my Hercules and Cacus, I verily believe a hundred sonnets were written on me, full of the worst abuse which could be invented by the ignorant rabble." [1] I rejoined: "Prince, when Michel Agnolo Buonarroti displayed his Sacristy to view, with so many fine statues in it, the men of talent in our admirable school of Florence, always appreciative of truth and goodness, published more than a hundred sonnets, each vying with his neighbour to extol these masterpieces to the skies.[2] So then, just as Bandinello's work deserved all the evil which, he tells us, was then said about it, Buonarroti's deserved the enthusiastic praise which was bestowed upon it." These words of mine made Bandinello burst with fury; he turned on me, and cried: "And you, what have you got to say against my work?" "I will tell you if you have the patience to hear me out." "Go along then," he replied. The Duke and his attendants prepared themselves to listen. I began and opened my oration thus: "You must know that it pains me to point out the faults of your statue; I shall not, however, utter my own sentiments, but shall recapitulate what our most virtuous school of Florence says about it." The brutal fellow kept making disagreeable remarks and gesticulating with his hands and feet, until he enraged me so that I began again, and spoke far more rudely than I should otherwise have

1 Vasari confirms this statement. The statue, which may still be seen upon the great piazza, is, in truth, a very poor performance. The Florentines were angry because Bandinello had filched the commission away from Michel Angelo. It was uncovered in 1534, and Duke Alessandro had to imprison its lampooners.

2 Cellini alludes of course to the Sacristy of S. Lorenzo, designed by Michel Angelo, with the portraits of the Medici and statues of Day, Night, Dawn, and Twilight.

done, if he had behaved with decency. "Well, then, this virtuous school says that if one were to shave the hair of your Hercules, there would not be skull enough left to hold his brain; it says that it is impossible to distinguish whether his features are those of a man or of something between a lion and an ox; the face too is turned away from the action of the figure, and is so badly set upon the neck, with such poverty of art and so ill a grace, that nothing worse was ever seen; his sprawling shoulders are like the two pommels of an ass's pack-saddle; his breasts and all the muscles of the body are not portrayed from a man, but from a big sack full of melons set upright against a wall. The loins seem to be modelled from a bag of lanky pumpkins; nobody can tell how his two legs are attached to that vile trunk; it is impossible to say on which leg he stands, or which he uses to exert his strength; nor does he seem to be resting upon both, as sculptors who know something of their art have occasionally set the figure. It is obvious that the body is leaning forward more than one-third of a cubit, which alone is the greatest and most insupportable fault committed by vulgar commonplace pretenders. Concerning the arms, they say that these are both stretched out without one touch of grace or one real spark of artistic talents, just as if you had never seen a naked model. Again, the right leg of Hercules and that of Cacus have got one mass of flesh between them, so that if they were to be separated, not only one of them, but both together, would be left without a calf at the point where they are touching. They say, too, that Hercules has one of his feet underground, while the other seems to be resting on hot coals."

LXXI

The fellow could not stand quiet to hear the damning errors of his Cacus in their turn enumerated. For one thing, I was telling the truth; for another, I was unmasking him to the Duke and all the people present, who showed by face and gesture first their surprise, and next their conviction that what I said was true. All at once he burst out: "Ah, you slanderous tongue! why don't you speak about my design?" I retorted: "A good draughtsman can never produce bad works; therefore I am inclined to believe that your drawing is no better than your statues." When he saw the amused expression on the Duke's face and the cutting gestures of the bystanders, he let his insolence get the better of him, and turned to me with that most hideous face of his, screaming aloud: "Oh, hold your tongue, you ugly . . ."[1] At these words the Duke frowned, and the others pursed their lips up and looked with knitted brows toward him. The horrible affront half maddened me with fury; but in a moment I recovered presence of mind enough to turn it off with a jest: "You madman! you exceed the bounds of decency. Yet would to God that I understood so noble an art as you allude to; they say that Jove used it with Ganymede in paradise, and here upon this earth it is practised by some of the greatest emperors and kings. I, however, am but a poor humble creature, who neither have the power nor the intelligence to perplex my wits with anything so admirable." When I had finished this speech, the Duke and his attendants could control themselves no longer, but broke into such shouts of laughter that one never heard the like. You must know, gentle readers, that though I put on this appearance of pleasantry, my heart was bursting in my body to think that a fellow, the foulest villain who ever breathed, should have dared in the presence of so great a prince to cast an insult of that atrocious nature in my teeth; but you must also know that he insulted the Duke, and not me; for had I not stood in that august presence, I should have felled him dead to earth. When the dirty stupid scoundrel observed that those gentlemen kept on laughing, he tried to change the subject, and divert them from deriding him; so he began as follows: "This fellow Benvenuto goes about boasting that I have promised him a piece of marble." I took him up at once. "What! did you not send to tell me by your journeyman, Francesco, that if I wished to work in marble you would give me a block? I accepted it, and mean to have it." He retorted: "Be very well assured that you will never get it." Still smarting as I was under the calumnious insults he had flung at me, I lost my self-control, forgot I was in the presence of the Duke, and called out in a storm of fury: "I swear to you that if you do not send the marble to my house, you had better look out for another world, for if you stay upon this earth I will most certainly rip the wind out of your carcass."[2] Then suddenly awakening to the fact that I was standing in the presence of so great a duke, I turned submissively to his Excellency and said: "My lord, one fool makes a hundred; the follies of this man have blinded me for a moment to the glory of your most illustrious Excellency and to myself. I humbly crave your pardon."

1 *Oh sta cheto, soddomitaccio.*
2 *In questo (mondo) ti sgonfierò a ogni modo.*

Then the Duke said to Bandinello: "Is it true that you promised him the marble?" He replied that it was true. Upon this the Duke addressed me: "Go to the Opera, and choose a piece according to your taste." I demurred that the man had promised to send it home to me. The words that passed between us were awful, and I refused to take the stone in any other way. Next morning a piece of marble was brought to my house. On asking who had sent it, they told me it was Bandinello, and that this was the very block which he had promised.[3]

LXXII

I had it brought at once into my studio, and began to chisel it. While I was rough-hewing the block, I made a model. But my eagerness to work in marble was so strong, that I had not patience to finish the model as correctly as this art demands. I soon noticed that the stone rang false beneath my strokes, which made me oftentimes repent commencing on it. Yet I got what I could out of the piece—that is, the Apollo and Hyacinth, which may still be seen unfinished in my workshop. While I was thus engaged, the Duke came to my house, and often said to me: "Leave your bronze awhile, and let me watch you working on the marble." Then I took chisel and mallet, and went at it blithely. He asked about the model I had made for my statue; to which I answered: "Duke, this marble is all cracked, but I shall carve something from it in spite of that; therefore I have not been able to settle the model, but shall go on doing the best I can."

His Excellency sent to Rome post-haste for a block of Greek marble, in order that I might restore his antique Ganymede, which was the cause of that dispute with Bandinello. When it arrived, I thought it a sin to cut it up for the head and arms and other bits wanting in the Ganymede; so I provided myself with another piece of stone, and reserved the Greek marble for a Narcissus which I modelled on a small scale in wax. I found that the block had two holes, penetrating to the depth of a quarter of a cubit, and two good inches wide. This led me to choose the attitude which may be noticed in my statue, avoiding the holes and keeping my figure free from

3 Vasari, in his *Life of Bandinello,* gives a curious confirmation of Cellini's veracity by reporting this quarrel, with some of the speeches which passed between the two rival artists. Yet he had not read Cellini's *Memoirs,* and was far from partial to the man. Comparing Vasari's with Cellini's account, we only notice that the latter has made Bandinello play a less witty part in the wordy strife than the former assigned him.

them. But rain had fallen scores of years upon the stone, filtering so deeply from the holes into its substance that the marble was decayed. Of this I had full proof at the time of a great inundation of the Arno, when the river rose to the height of more than a cubit and a half in my workshop.[1] Now the Narcissus stood upon a square of wood, and the water overturned it, causing the statue to break in two above the breasts. I had to join the pieces; and in order that the line of breakage might not be observed, I wreathed that garland of flowers round it which may still be seen upon the bosom. I went on working at the surface, employing some hours before sunrise, or now and then on feast-days, so as not to lose the time I needed for my Perseus.

It so happened on one of those mornings, while I was getting some little chisels into trim to work on the Narcissus, that a very fine splinter of steel flew into my right eye, and embedded itself so deeply in the pupil that it could not be extracted. I thought for certain I must lose the sight of that eye. After some days I sent for Maestro Raffaello dé Pilli, the surgeon, who obtained a couple of live pigeons, and placing me upon my back across a table, took the birds and opened a large vein they have beneath the wing, so that the blood gushed out into my eye. I felt immediately relieved, and in the space of two days the splinter came away, and I remained with eyesight greatly improved. Against the feast of S. Lucia,[2] which came round in three days, I made a golden eye out of a French crown, and had it presented at her shrine by one of my six nieces, daughters of my sister Liperata; the girl was ten years of age, and in her company I returned thanks to God and S. Lucia. For some while afterwards I did not work on the Narcissus, but pushed my Perseus forward under all the difficulties I have described. It was my purpose to finish it, and then to bid farewell to Florence.

LXXIII

Having succeeded so well with the cast of the Medusa, I had great hope of bringing my Perseus through; for I had laid the wax on, and felt confident that it would come out in bronze as perfectly as the Medusa. The waxen model produced so fine an effect, that when the Duke saw it and was struck with its beauty—whether some-

1 Cellini alludes to a celebrated inundation of the year 1547.

2 S. Lucy, I need hardly remark, is the patroness of the eyes. In Italian art she is generally represented holding her own eyes upon a plate.

body had persuaded him it could not be carried out with the same finish in metal, or whether he thought so for himself—he came to visit me more frequently than usual, and on one occasion said: "Benvenuto, this figure cannot succeed in bronze; the laws of art do not admit of it." These words of his Excellency stung me so sharply that I answered: "My lord, I know how very little confidence you have in me; and I believe the reason of this is that your most illustrious Excellency lends too ready an ear to my calumniators, or else indeed that you do not understand my art." He hardly let me close the sentence when he broke in: "I profess myself a connoisseur, and understand it very well indeed." I replied: "Yes, like a prince, not like an artist; for if your Excellency understood my trade as well as you imagine, you would trust me on the proofs I have already given. These are, first, the colossal bronze bust of your Excellency, which is now in Elba;[1] secondly, the restoration of the Ganymede in marble, which offered so many difficulties and cost me so much trouble, that I would rather have made the whole statue new from the beginning; thirdly, the Medusa, cast by me in bronze, here now before your Excellency's eyes, the execution of which was a greater triumph of strength and skill than any of my predecessors in this fiendish art have yet achieved. Look you, my lord! I constructed that furnace anew on principles quite different from those of other founders; in addition to many technical improvements and ingenious devices, I supplied it with two issues for the metal, because this difficult and twisted figure could not otherwise have come out perfect. It is only owing to my intelligent insight into means and appliances that the statue turned out as it did; a triumph judged impossible by all the practitioners of this art. I should like you furthermore to be aware, my lord, for certain, that the sole reason why I succeeded with all those great arduous works in France under his most admirable Majesty King Francis, was the high courage which that good monarch put into my heart by the liberal allowances he made me, and the multitude of workpeople he left at my disposal. I could have as many as I asked for, and employed at times above forty, all chosen by myself. These were the causes of my having there produced so many masterpieces in so short a space of time. Now then, my lord, put trust in me; supply me with the aid I need. I am confident of being able to complete a work which will delight your soul. But if your Excellency goes on disheartening me, and does not

1 At Portoferraio. It came afterwards to Florence.

advance me the assistance which is absolutely required, neither I nor any man alive upon this earth can hope to achieve the slightest thing of value."

LXXIV

It was as much as the Duke could do to stand by and listen to my pleadings. He kept turning first this way and then that; while I, in despair, poor wretched I, was calling up remembrance of the noble state I held in France, to the great sorrow of my soul. All at once he cried: "Come, tell me, Benvenuto, how is it possible that yonder splendid head of Medusa, so high up there in the grasp of Perseus, should ever come out perfect?" I replied upon the instant: "Look you now, my lord! If your Excellency possessed that knowledge of the craft which you affirm you have, you would not fear one moment for the splendid head you speak of. There is good reason, on the other hand, to feel uneasy about this right foot, so far below and at a distance from the rest." When he heard these words, the Duke turned, half in anger, to some gentlemen in waiting, and exclaimed: "I verily believe that this Benvenuto prides himself on contradicting everything one says." Then he faced round to me with a touch of mockery, upon which his attendants did the like, and began to speak as follows: "I will listen patiently to any argument you can possibly produce in explanation of your statement, which may convince me of its probability." I said in answer: "I will adduce so sound an argument that your Excellency shall perceive the full force of it." So I began: "You must know, my lord, that the nature of fire is to ascend, and therefore I promise you that Medusa's head will come out famously; but since it is not in the nature of fire to descend, and I must force it downwards six cubits by artificial means, I assure your Excellency upon this most convincing ground of proof that the foot cannot possibly come out. It will, however, be quite easy for me to restore it." "Why, then," said the Duke, "did you not devise it so that the foot should come out as well as you affirm the head will?" I answered: "I must have made a much larger furnace, with a conduit as thick as my leg; and so I might have forced the molten metal by its own weight to descend so far. Now, my pipe, which runs six cubits to the statue's foot, as I have said, is not thicker than two fingers. However, it was not worth the trouble and expense to make a larger; for I shall easily be able to mend what is lacking. But when my mould is more than half full, as I expect, from this middle point upwards, the fire ascending by its natural property, then the heads of Perseus and Medusa will come out admirably; you may be quite sure of it." After I had thus expounded these convincing arguments, together with many more of the same kind, which it would be tedious to set down here, the Duke shook his head and departed without further ceremony.

LXXV

Abandoned thus to my own resources, I took new courage, and banished the sad thoughts which kept recurring to my mind, making me often weep bitter tears of repentance for having left France; for though I did so only to revisit Florence, my sweet birthplace, in order that I might charitably succour my six nieces, this good action, as I well perceived, had been the beginning of my great misfortune. Nevertheless, I felt convinced that when my Perseus was accomplished, all these trials would be turned to high felicity and glorious well-being.

Accordingly I strengthened my heart, and with all the forces of my body and my purse, employing what little money still remained to me, I set to work. First I provided myself with several loads of pinewood from the forests of Serristori, in the neighbourhood of Montelupo. While these were on their way, I clothed my Perseus with the clay which I had prepared many months beforehand, in order that it might be duly seasoned. After making its clay tunic (for that is the term used in this art) and properly arming it and fencing it with iron girders, I began to draw the wax out by means of a slow fire. This melted and issued through numerous air-vents I had made; for the more there are of these, the better will the mould fill. When I had finished drawing off the wax, I constructed a funnel-shaped furnace all round the model of my Perseus.[1] It was built of bricks, so interlaced, the one above the other, that numerous apertures were left for the fire to exhale at. Then I began to lay on wood by degrees, and kept it burning two whole days and nights. At length, when all the wax was gone, and the mould was well baked, I set to work at digging the pit in which to sink it. This I performed with scrupulous regard to all the rules of art. When I

[1] This furnace, called *manica*, was like a grain-hopper, so that the mould could stand upright in it as in a cup. The word *manica* is the same as our *manuch*, an antique form of sleeve.

had finished that part of my work, I raised the mould by windlasses and stout ropes to a perpendicular position, and suspending it with the greatest care one cubit above the level of the furnace, so that it hung exactly above the middle of the pit, I next lowered it gently down into the very bottom of the furnace, and had it firmly placed with every possible precaution for its safety. When this delicate operation was accomplished, I began to bank it up with the earth I had excavated; and, ever as the earth grew higher, I introduced its proper air-vents, which were little tubes of earthenware, such as folk use for drains and such-like purposes.[2] At length, I felt sure that it was admirably fixed, and that the filling-in of the pit and the placing of the air-vents had been properly performed. I also could see that my workpeople understood my method, which differed very considerably from that of all the other masters in the trade. Feeling confident, then, that I could rely upon them, I next turned to my furnace, which I had filled with numerous pigs of copper and other bronze stuff. The pieces were piled according to the laws of art, that is to say, so resting one upon the other that the flames could play freely through them, in order that the metal might heat and liquefy the sooner. At last I called out heartily to set the furnace going. The logs of pine were heaped in, and, what with the unctuous resin of the wood and the good draught I had given, my furnace worked so well that I was obliged to rush from side to side to keep it going. The labour was more than I could stand; yet I forced myself to strain every nerve and muscle. To increase my anxieties, the workshop took fire, and we were afraid lest the roof should fall upon our heads; while, from the garden, such a storm of wind and rain kept blowing in, that it perceptibly cooled the furnace.

Battling thus with all these untoward circumstances for several hours, and exerting myself beyond even the measure of my powerful constitution, I could at last bear up no longer, and a sudden fever,[3] of the utmost possible intensity, attacked me. I felt absolutely obliged to go and fling myself upon my bed. Sorely against my will having to drag myself away from the spot, I turned to my assistants, about ten or more in all, what with master-founders, hand-workers, country-fellows, and my own special journeymen, among whom was

[2] These air-vents, or *sfiatatoi*, were introduced into the outer mould, which Cellini calls the *tonaca*, or clay tunic laid upon the original model of baked clay and wax. They served the double purpose of drawing off the wax, whereby a space was left for the molten bronze to enter, and also of facilitating the penetration of this molten metal by allowing a free escape of air and gas from the outer mould.

[3] *Una febbre efimera.* Lit., *a fever of one day's duration.*

Bernardino Mannellini of Mugello, my apprentice through several years. To him in particular I spoke: "Look, my dear Bernardino, that you observe the rules which I have taught you; do your best with all despatch, for the metal will soon be fused. You cannot go wrong; these honest men will get the channels ready; you will easily be able to drive back the two plugs with this pair of iron crooks; and I am sure that my mould will fill miraculously. I feel more ill than I ever did in all my life, and verily believe that it will kill me before a few hours are over."[4] Thus, with despair at heart, I left them, and betook myself to bed.

LXXVI

No sooner had I got to bed, than I ordered my serving-maids to carry food and wine for all the men into the workshop; at the same time I cried: "I shall not be alive tomorrow." They tried to encourage me, arguing that my illness would pass over, since it came from excessive fatigue. In this way I spent two hours battling with the fever, which steadily increased, and calling out continually: "I feel that I am dying." My housekeeper, who was named Mona Fiore da Castel del Rio, a very notable manager and no less warm-hearted, kept chiding me for my discouragement; but, on the other hand, she paid me every kind attention which was possible. However, the sight of my physical pain and moral dejection so affected her, that, in spite of that brave heart of hers, she could not refrain from shedding tears; and yet, so far as she was able, she took good care I should not see them. While I was thus terribly afflicted, I beheld the figure of a man enter my chamber, twisted in his body into the form of a capital S. He raised a lamentable, doleful voice, like one who announces their last hour to men condemned to die upon the scaffold, and spoke these words: "O Benvenuto! your statue is spoiled, and there is no hope whatever of saving it." No sooner had I heard the shriek of that wretch than I gave a howl which might

[4] Some technical terms require explanation in this sentence. The *canali* or channels were sluices for carrying the molten metal from the furnace into the mould. The *mandriani*, which I have translated by *iron crooks*, were poles fitted at the end with curved irons, by which the openings of the furnace, *plugs*, or in Italian *spine*, could be partially or wholly driven back, so as to let the molten metal flow through the channels into the mould. When the metal reached the mould, it entered in a red-hot stream between the *tonaca*, or outside mould, and the *anima*, or inner block, filling up exactly the space which had previously been occupied by the wax extracted by a method of slow burning alluded to above. I believe that the process is known as casting *á cire perdue*. The *forma*, or mould, consisted of two pieces; one hollow (*la tonaca*), which gave shape to the bronze; one solid and rounded (*la anima*), which stood at a short interval within the former, and regulated the influx of the metal. See above, pp. 328, note.

have been heard from the sphere of flame. Jumping from my bed, I seized my clothes and began to dress. The maids, and my lads, and every one who came around to help me, got kicks or blows of the fist, while I kept crying out in lamentation: "Ah! traitors! enviers! This is an act of treason, done by malice prepense! But I swear by God that I will sift it to the bottom, and before I die will leave such witness to the world of what I can do as shall make a score of mortals marvel."

When I had got my clothes on, I strode with soul bent on mischief toward the workshop; there I beheld the men, whom I had left erewhile in such high spirits, standing stupefied and downcast. I began at once and spoke: "Up with you! Attend to me! Since you have not been able or willing to obey the directions I gave you, obey me now that I am with you to conduct my work in person. Let no one contradict me, for in cases like this we need the aid of hand and hearing, not of advice." When I had uttered these words, a certain Maestro Alessandro Lastricati broke silence and said: "Look you, Benvenuto, you are going to attempt an enterprise which the laws of art do not sanction, and which cannot succeed." I turned upon him with such fury and so full of mischief, that he and all the rest of them exclaimed with one voice: "On then! Give orders! We will obey your least commands, so long as life is left in us." I believe they spoke thus feelingly because they thought I must fall shortly dead upon the ground. I went immediately to inspect the furnace, and found that the metal was all curdled; an accident which we express by "being caked."[1] I told two of the hands to cross the road and fetch from the house of the butcher Capretta a load of young oak-wood, which had lain dry for above a year; this wood had been previously offered me by Madame Ginevra, wife of the said Capretta. So soon as the first armfuls arrived, I began to fill the grate beneath the furnace.[2] Now oak-wood of that kind heats more powerfully than any other sort of tree; and for this reason, where a slow fire is wanted, as in the case of gun-foundry, alder or pine is preferred. Accordingly, when the logs took fire, oh! how the cake began to stir beneath that awful heat, to glow and sparkle in a blaze! At the same time I kept stirring up the channels, and sent men upon the roof to stop the conflagration, which had gathered force from the increased combustion in the furnace; also I caused boards, carpets,

[1] *Essersi fatto un migliaccio.*
[2] The Italian is *bracciaiuola*, a pit below the grating, which receives the ashes from the furnace.

and other hangings to be set up against the garden, in order to protect us from the violence of the rain.

LXXVII

When I had thus provided against these several disasters, I roared out first to one man and then to another: "Bring this thing here! Take that thing there!" At this crisis, when the whole gang saw the cake was on the point of melting, they did my bidding, each fellow working with the strength of three. I then ordered half a pig of pewter to be brought, which weighed about sixty pounds, and flung it into the middle of the cake inside the furnace. By this means, and by piling on wood and stirring now with pokers and now with iron rods, the curdled mass rapidly began to liquefy. Then, knowing I had brought the dead to life again, against the firm opinion of those ignoramuses, I felt such vigour fill my veins, that all those pains of fever, all those fears of death, were quite forgotten.

All of a sudden an explosion took place, attended by a tremendous flash of flame, as though a thunderbolt had formed and been discharged amongst us. Unwonted and appalling terror astonied every one, and me more even than the rest. When the din was over and the dazzling light extinguished, we began to look each other in the face. Then I discovered that the cap of the furnace had blown up, and the bronze was bubbling over from its source beneath. So I had the mouths of my mould immediately opened, and at the same time drove in the two plugs which kept back the molten metal. But I noticed that it did not flow as rapidly as usual, the reason being probably that the fierce heat of the fire we kindled had consumed its base alloy. Accordingly I sent for all my pewter platters, porringers, and dishes, to the number of some two hundred pieces, and had a portion of them cast, one by one, into the channels, the rest into the furnace. This expedient succeeded, and every one could now perceive that my bronze was in most perfect liquefaction, and my mould was filling; whereupon they all with heartiness and happy cheer assisted and obeyed my bidding, while I, now here, now there, gave orders, helped with my own hands, and cried aloud: "O God! Thou that by Thy immeasurable power didst rise from the dead, and in Thy glory didst ascend to heaven!" . . . even thus in a moment my mould was filled; and seeing my work finished, I fell upon my knees, and with all my heart gave thanks to God.

After all was over, I turned to a plate of salad on a bench there, and ate with hearty appetite, and drank together with the whole crew. Afterwards I retired to bed, healthy and happy, for it was now two hours before morning, and slept as sweetly as though I had never felt a touch of illness. My good housekeeper, without my giving any orders, had prepared a fat capon for my repast. So that, when I rose, about the hour for breaking fast, she presented herself with a smiling countenance, and said: "Oh! is that the man who felt that he was dying? Upon my word, I think the blows and kicks you dealt us last night, when you were so enraged, and had that demon in your body as it seemed, must have frightened away your mortal fever! The fever feared that it might catch it too, as we did!" All my poor household, relieved in like measure from anxiety and overwhelming labour, went at once to buy earthen vessels in order to replace the pewter I had cast away. Then we dined together joyfully; nay, I cannot remember a day in my whole life when I dined with greater gladness or a better appetite.

After our meal I received visits from the several men who had assisted me. They exchanged congratulations, and thanked God for our success, saying they had learned and seen things done which other masters judged impossible. I too grew somewhat glorious; and deeming I had shown myself a man of talent, indulged a boastful humour. So I thrust my hand into my purse, and paid them all to their full satisfaction.

That evil fellow, my mortal foe, Messer Pier Francesco Ricci, majordomo of the Duke, took great pains to find out how the affair had gone. In answer to his questions, the two men whom I suspected of having caked my metal for me, said I was no man, but of a certainty some powerful devil, since I had accomplished what no craft of the art could do; indeed they did not believe a mere ordinary fiend could work such miracles as I in other ways had shown. They exaggerated the whole affair so much, possibly in order to excuse their own part in it, that the majordomo wrote an account to the Duke, who was then in Pisa, far more marvellous and full of thrilling incidents than what they had narrated.

LXXVIII

After I had let my statue cool for two whole days, I began to uncover it by slow degrees. The first thing I found was that the head of Medusa had come out most admirably, thanks to the air-vents; for, as I had told the Duke, it is the nature of fire to ascend. Upon advancing farther, I discovered that the other head, that, namely, of Perseus, had succeeded no less admirably; and this astonished me far more, because it is at a considerably lower level than that of the Medusa. Now the mouths of the mould were placed above the head of Perseus and behind his shoulders; and I found that all the bronze my furnace contained had been exhausted in the head of this figure. It was a miracle to observe that not one fragment remained in the orifice of the channel, and that nothing was wanting to the statue. In my great astonishment I seemed to see in this the hand of God arranging and controlling all.

I went on uncovering the statue with success, and ascertained that everything had come out in perfect order, until I reached the foot of the right leg on which the statue rests. There the heel itself was formed, and going farther, I found the foot apparently complete. This gave me great joy on the one side, but was half unwelcome to me on the other, merely because I had told the Duke that it could not come out. However, when I reached the end, it appeared that the toes and a little piece above them were unfinished, so that about half the foot was wanting. Although I knew that this would add a trifle to my labour, I was very well pleased, because I could now prove to the Duke how well I understood my business. It is true that far more of the foot than I expected had been perfectly formed; the reason of this was that, from causes I have recently described, the bronze was hotter than our rules of art prescribe; also that I had been obliged to supplement the alloy with my pewter cups and platters, which no one else, I think, had ever done before.

Having now ascertained how successfully my work had been accomplished, I lost no time in hurrying to Pisa, where I found the Duke. He gave me a most gracious reception, as did also the Duchess; and although the majordomo had informed them of the whole proceedings, their Excellencies deemed my performance far more stupendous and astonishing when they heard the tale from my own mouth. When I arrived at the foot of Perseus, and said it had not come out perfect, just as I previously warned his Excellency, I saw an expression of wonder pass over his face, while he related to the Duchess how I had predicted this beforehand. Observing the princes to be so well disposed towards me, I begged leave from the Duke to go to Rome. He granted it in most obliging terms, and bade me return as soon as possible to complete his Perseus; giving me letters of recommendation meanwhile to his ambassador, Averardo Serristori. We were then in the first years of Pope Giulio de Monti.[1]

LXXIX

Before leaving home, I directed my workpeople to proceed according to the method I had taught them. The reason of my journey was as follows. I had made a life-sized bust in bronze of Bindo Altoviti,[1] the son of Antonio, and had sent it to him at Rome. He set it up in his study, which was very richly adorned with antiquities and other works of art; but the room was not designed for statues or for paintings, since the windows were too low, so that the light coming from beneath spoiled the effect they would have produced under more favourable conditions. It happened one day that Bindo was standing at his door, when Michel Agnolo Buonarroti, the sculptor, passed by; so he begged him to come in and see his study. Michel Agnolo followed, and on entering the room and looking round, he exclaimed: "Who is the master who made that good portrait of you in so fine a manner? You must know that that bust pleases me as much, or even more, than those antiques; and yet there are many fine things to be seen among the latter. If those windows were above instead of beneath, the whole collection would show to greater advantage, and your portrait, placed among so many masterpieces would hold its own with credit." No sooner had Michel Agnolo left the house of Bindo than he wrote me a very kind letter, which ran as follows: "My dear Benvenuto, I have known you for many years as the greatest goldsmith of whom we have any information; and henceforward I shall know you for a sculptor of like quality. I must tell you that Master Bindo Altoviti took me to see his bust in bronze, and informed me that you had made it. I was greatly pleased with the work; but it annoyed me to notice that it was placed in a bad light; for if it were suitably illuminated, it would show itself to be the fine performance that it is." This letter abounded with the most affectionate and complimentary expressions towards myself; and before I left for Rome, I showed it to the Duke, who read it with much kindly interest, and said to me: "Benvenuto, if

1 Gio Maria del Monte Sansovino was elected Pope, with the title of Julius III., in February 1550.

1 This man was a member of a very noble Florentine family. Born in 1491, he was at this epoch Tuscan Consul in Rome. Cellini's bust of him still exists in the Palazzo Altoviti at Rome.

you write to him, and can persuade him to return to Florence, I will make him a member of the Forty-eight."[2] Accordingly I wrote a letter full of warmth, and offered in the Duke's name a hundred times more than my commission carried; but not wanting to make any mistake, I showed this to the Duke before I sealed it, saying to his most illustrious Excellency: "Prince, perhaps I have made him too many promises." He replied: "Michel Agnolo deserves more than you have promised, and I will bestow on him still greater favours." To this letter he sent no answer, and I could see that the Duke was much offended with him.

LXXX

When I reached Rome, I went to lodge in Bindo Altoviti's house. He told me at once how he had shown his bronze bust to Michel Agnolo, and how the latter had praised it. So we spoke for some length upon this topic. I ought to narrate the reasons why I had taken this portrait. Bindo had in his hands 1200 golden crowns of mine, which formed part of 5000 he had lent the Duke; 4000 were his own, and mine stood in his name, while I received that portion of the interest which accrued to me.[1] This led to my taking his portrait; and when he saw the wax model for the bust, he sent me fifty golden scudi by a notary in his employ, named Ser Giuliano Paccalli. I did not want to take the money, so I sent it back to him by the same hand, saying at a later time to Bindo: "I shall be satisfied if you keep that sum of mine for me at interest, so that I may gain a little on it." When we came to square accounts on this occasion, I observed that he was ill disposed towards me, since, instead of treating me affectionately, according to his previous wont, he put on a stiff air; and although I was staying in his house, he was never good-humoured, but always surly. However, we settled our business in a few words. I sacrificed my pay for his portrait, together with the bronze, and we arranged that he should keep my money at 15 per cent. during my natural life.

LXXXI

One of the first things I did was to go and kiss the Pope's feet; and while I was speaking with his Holiness, Messer Averardo Serristori,

2 This was one of the three Councils created by Clement VII. in 1532, when he changed the Florentine constitution. It corresponded to a Senate.
1 To make the sum correct, 5200 ought to have been lent the Duke.

our Duke's Envoy, arrived.[1] I had made some proposals to the Pope, which I think he would have agreed upon, and I should have been very glad to return to Rome on account of the great difficulties which I had at Florence. But I soon perceived that the ambassador had countermined me.

Then I went to visit Michel Agnolo Buonarroti, and repeated what I had written from Florence to him in the Duke's name. He replied that he was engaged upon the fabric of S. Peter's, and that this would prevent him from leaving Rome. I rejoined that, as he had decided on the model of that building, he could leave its execution to his man Urbino, who would carry out his orders to the letter. I added much about future favours, in the form of a message from the Duke. Upon this he looked me hard in the face, and said with a sarcastic smile: "And you! to what extent are you satisfied with him?" Although I replied that I was extremely contented and was very well treated by his Excellency, he showed that he was acquainted with the greater part of my annoyances, and gave as his final answer that it would be difficult for him to leave Rome. To this I added that he could not do better than to return to his own land, which was governed by a prince renowned for justice, and the greatest lover of the arts and sciences who ever saw the light of this world. As I have remarked above, he had with him a servant of his who came from Urbino, and had lived many years in his employment, rather as valet and housekeeper than anything else; this indeed was obvious, because he had acquired no skill in the arts.[2] Consequently, while I was pressing Michel Agnolo with arguments he could not answer, he turned round sharply to Urbino, as though to ask him his opinion. The fellow began to bawl out in his rustic way: "I will never leave my master Michel Agnolo's side till I shall have flayed him or he shall have flayed me." These stupid words forced me to laugh, and without saying farewell, I lowered my shoulders and retired.

LXXXII

The miserable bargain I had made with Bindo Altoviti, losing my bust and leaving him my capital for life, taught me what the faith

1 His despatches form a valuable series of historical documents. *Firenze*, Le Monnier, 1853.

2 Upon the death of this Urbino, Michel Angelo wrote a touching sonnet and a very feeling letter to Vasari.

of merchants is; so I returned in bad spirits to Florence. I went at once to the palace to pay my respects to the Duke, whom I found to be at Castello beyond Ponte a Rifredi. In the palace I met Messer Pier Francesco Ricci, the majordomo, and when I drew nigh to pay him the usual compliments, he exclaimed with measureless astonishment: "Oh, are you come back?" and with the same air of surprise, clapping his hands together, he cried: "The Duke is at Castello!" then turned his back and left me. I could not form the least idea why the beast behaved in such an extraordinary manner to me.

Proceeding at once to Castello, and entering the garden where the Duke was, I caught sight of him at a distance; but no sooner had he seen me than he showed signs of surprise, and intimated that I might go about my business. I had been reckoning that his Excellency would treat me with the same kindness, or even greater, as before I left for Rome; so now, when he received me with such rudeness, I went back, much hurt, to Florence. While resuming my work and pushing my statue forward, I racked my brains to think what could have brought about this sudden change in the Duke's manner. The curious way in which Messer Sforza and some other gentlemen close to his Excellency's person eyed me, prompted me to ask the former what the matter was. He only replied with a sort of smile: "Benvenuto, do your best to be an honest man, and have no concern for anything else." A few days afterwards I obtained an audience of the Duke, who received me with a kind of grudging grace, and asked me what I had been doing at Rome. To the best of my ability I maintained the conversation, and told him the whole story about Bindo Altoviti's bust. It was evident that he listened with attention; so I went on talking about Michel Agnolo Buonarroti. At this he showed displeasure; but Urbino's stupid speech about the flaying made him laugh aloud. Then he said: "Well, it is he who suffers!" and I took my leave.

There can be no doubt that Ser Pier Francesco, the majordomo, must have served me some ill turn with the Duke, which did not, however, succeed; for God, who loves the truth, protected me, as He hath ever saved me, from a sea of dreadful dangers, and I hope will save me till the end of this my life, however full of trials it may be. I march forward, therefore, with a good heart, sustained alone by His divine power; nor let myself be terrified by any furious assault of fortune or my adverse stars. May only God maintain me in His grace!

LXXXIII

I must beg your attention now, most gracious reader, for a very terrible event which happened.

I used the utmost diligence and industry to complete my statue, and went to spend my evenings in the Duke's wardrobe, assisting there the goldsmiths who were working for his Excellency. Indeed, they laboured mainly on designs which I had given them. Noticing that the Duke took pleasure in seeing me at work and talking with me. I took it into my head to go there sometimes also by day. It happened upon one of those days that his Excellency came as usual to the room where I was occupied, and more particularly because he heard of my arrival. His Excellency entered at once into conversation, raising several interesting topics, upon which I gave my views so much to his entertainment that he showed more cheerfulness than I had ever seen in him before. All of a sudden, one of his secretaries appeared, and whispered something of importance in his ear; whereupon the Duke rose, and retired with the official into another chamber. Now the Duchess had sent to see what his Excellency was doing, and her page brought back this answer: "The Duke is talking and laughing with Benvenuto, and is in excellent good-humour." When the Duchess heard this, she came immediately to the wardrobe, and not finding the Duke there, took a seat beside us. After watching us at work a while, she turned to me with the utmost graciousness, and showed me a necklace of large and really very fine pearls. On being asked by her what I thought of them, I said it was in truth a very handsome ornament. Then she spoke as follows: "I should like the Duke to buy them for me; so I beg you, my dear Benvenuto, to praise them to him as highly as you can." At these words I disclosed my mind to the Duchess with all the respect I could, and answered: "My lady, I thought this necklace of pearls belonged already to your most illustrious Excellency. Now that I am aware you have not yet acquired them, it is right, nay, more, it is my duty to utter what I might otherwise have refrained from saying, namely, that my mature professional experience enables me to detect very grave faults in the pearls, and for this reason I could never advise your Excellency to purchase them." She replied: "The merchant offers them for six thousand crowns; and were it not for some of those trifling defects you speak of, the rope would be worth over twelve thousand." To this I replied, that "even were the necklace of quite flawless quality,

I could not advise any one to bid up to five thousand crowns for it; for pearls are not gems; pearls are but fishes' bones, which in the course of time must lose their freshness. Diamonds, rubies, emeralds, and sapphires, on the contrary, never grow old; these four are precious stones, and these it is quite right to purchase." When I had thus spoken, the Duchess showed some signs of irritation, and exclaimed: "I have a mind to possess these pearls; so prithee, take them to the Duke, and praise them up to the skies; even if you have to use some words beyond the bounds of truth, speak them to do me service; it will be well for you!"

I have always been the greatest friend of truth and foe to lies: yet, compelled by necessity, unwilling to lose the favour of so great a princess, I took those confounded pearls sorely against my inclination, and went with them over to the other room, whither the Duke had withdrawn. No sooner did he set eyes upon me than he cried: "O Benvenuto! what are you about here?" I uncovered the pearls and said: "My lord, I am come to show you a most splendid necklace of pearls, of the rarest quality, and truly worthy of your Excellency; I do not believe it would be possible to put together eighty pearls which could show better than these do in a necklace. My counsel therefore is, that you should buy them, for they are in good sooth miraculous." He responded on the instant: "I do not choose to buy them; they are not pearls of the quality and goodness you affirm; I have seen the necklace, and they do not please me." Then I added: "Pardon me, prince! These pearls exceed in rarity and beauty any which were ever brought together for a necklace." The Duchess had risen, and was standing behind a door listening to all I said. Well, when I had praised the pearls a thousandfold more warmly than I have described above, the Duke turned towards me with a kindly look, and said: "O my dear Benvenuto, I know that you have an excellent judgment in these matters. If the pearls are as rare as you certify, I should not hesitate about their purchase, partly to gratify the Duchess, and partly to possess them, seeing I have always need of such things, not so much for her Grace, as for the various uses of my sons and daughters." When I heard him speak thus, having once begun to tell fibs, I stuck to them with even greater boldness; I gave all the colour of truth I could to my lies, confiding in the promise of the Duchess to help me at the time of need. More than two hundred crowns were to be my commission on the bargain, and the Duchess had intimated that I should receive so much; but I was firmly resolved not to touch a farthing, in order to secure my credit, and convince the Duke I was not prompted by avarice. Once more his Excellency began to address me with the greatest courtesy: "I know that you are a consummate judge of these things; therefore, if you are the honest man I always thought you, tell me now the truth." Thereat I flushed up to my eyes, which at the same time filled with tears, and said to him: "My lord, if I tell your most illustrious Excellency the truth, I shall make a mortal foe of the Duchess; this will oblige me to depart from Florence, and my enemies will begin at once to pour contempt upon my Perseus, which I have announced as a masterpiece to the most noble school of your illustrious Excellency. Such being the case, I recommend myself to your most illustrious Excellency."

LXXXIV

The Duke was now aware that all my previous speeches had been, as it were, forced out of me. So he rejoined: "If you have confidence in me, you need not stand in fear of anything whatever." I recommenced: "Alas! my lord, what can prevent this coming to the ears of the Duchess?" The Duke lifted his hand in sign of troth-pledge,[1] and exclaimed: "Be assured that what you say will be buried in a diamond casket!" To this engagement upon honour I replied by telling the truth according to my judgment, namely, that the pearls were not worth above two thousand crowns. The Duchess, thinking we had stopped talking, for we now were speaking in as low a voice as possible, came forward, and began as follows: "My lord, do me the favour to purchase this necklace, because I have set my heart on them, and your Benvenuto here has said he never saw a finer row of pearls." The Duke replied: "I do not choose to buy them." "Why, my lord, will not your Excellency gratify me by buying them?" "Because I do not care to throw my money out of the window." The Duchess recommenced: "What do you mean by throwing your money away, when Benvenuto, in whom you place such well-merited confidence, has told me that they would be cheap at over three thousand crowns?" Then the Duke said: "My lady! my Benvenuto here has told me that, if I purchase this necklace, I shall be throwing my money away, inasmuch as the pearls are neither round nor well-matched, and some of them are quite faded. To

1 *Alzò la fede.*

prove that this is so, look here! look there! consider this one and then that. The necklace is not the sort of thing for me." At these words the Duchess cast a glance of bitter spite at me, and retired with a threatening nod of her head in my direction. I felt tempted to pack off at once and bid farewell to Italy. Yet my Perseus being all but finished, I did not like to leave without exposing it to public view. But I ask every one to consider in what a grievous plight I found myself!

The Duke had given orders to his porters in my presence, that if I appeared at the palace, they should always admit me through his apartments to the place where he might happen to be. The Duchess commanded the same men, whenever I showed my face at that palace, to drive me from its gates. Accordingly, no sooner did I present myself, than these fellows left their doors and bade me begone; at the same time they took good care lest the Duke should perceive what they were after; for if he caught sight of me before those wretches, he either called me, or beckoned to me to advance.

At this juncture the Duchess sent for Bernardone, the broker, of whom she had so often complained to me, abusing his good-for-nothingness and utter worthlessness. She now confided in him as she had previously done in me. He replied: "My princess, leave the matter in my hands." Then the rascal presented himself before the Duke with that necklace in his hands. No sooner did the Duke set eyes on him than he bade him begone. But the rogue lifted his big ugly voice, which sounded like the braying of an ass through his huge nose, and spoke to this effect: "Ah! my dear lord, for Heaven's sake buy this necklace for the poor Duchess, who is dying to have it, and cannot indeed live without it." The fellow poured forth so much of this stupid nonsensical stuff that the Duke's patience was exhausted, and he cried: "Oh, get away with you, or blow your chaps out till I smack them!" The knave knew very well what he was after; for if by blowing out his cheeks or singing *La Bella Franceschina*,[2] he could bring the Duke to make that purchase, then he gained the good grace of the Duchess, and to boot his own commission, which rose to some hundreds of crowns. Consequently he did blow out his chaps. The Duke smacked them with several hearty boxes, and, in order to get rid of him, struck rather harder than his wont was. The sound blows upon his cheeks not only reddened them above their natural purple, but also brought tears into his eyes. All the same, while smart-

2 A popular ballad of the time.

ing, he began to cry: "Lo! my lord, a faithful servant of his prince, who tries to act rightly, and is willing to put up with any sort of bad treatment, provided only that poor lady have her heart's desire!" The Duke, tired of the ribald fellow, either to recompense the cuffs which he had dealt him, or for the Duchess's sake, whom he was ever most inclined to gratify, cried out: "Get away with you, with God's curse on you! Go, make the bargain; I am willing to do what my lady Duchess wishes."

From this incident we may learn to know how evil Fortune exerts her rage against a poor right-minded man, and how the strumpet Luck can help a miserable rascal. I lost the good graces of the Duchess once and for ever, and thereby went close to having the Duke's protection taken from me. He acquired that thumping fee for his commission, and to boot their favour. Thus it will not serve us in this world to be merely men of honesty and talent.

LXXXV

About this time the war of Siena broke out,[1] and the Duke, wishing to fortify Florence, distributed the gates among his architects and sculptors. I received the Prato gate and the little one of Arno, which is on the way to the mills. The Cavaliere Bandinello got the gate of San Friano; Pasqualino d'Ancona, the gate at San Pier Gattolini; Giulian di Baccio d'Agnolo, the wood-carver, had the gate of San Giorgio; Particino, the wood-carver, had the gate of Santo Niccolo; Francesco da San Gallo, the sculptor, called Il Margolla, got the gate of Santa Croce; and Giovan Battista, surnamed Il Tasso, the gate Pinti.[2] Other bastions and gates were assigned to divers engineers, whose names I do not recollect, nor indeed am I concerned with them. The Duke, who certainly was at all times a man of great ability, went round the city himself upon a tour of inspection, and when he had made his mind up, he sent for Lattanzio Gorini, one of his paymasters. Now this man was to some extent an amateur of military architecture; so his Excellency commissioned him to make designs for the fortifications of the gates, and sent each of us his own gate drawn according to the plan. After examining the

1 In the year 1552, when Piero Strozzi acted as general for the French King, Henri II., against the Spaniards. The war ended in the capitulation of Siena in 1555. In 1557 it was ceded by Philip II. to Cosimo de' Medici.

2 These artists, with the exception of Pasqualino, are all known to us in the conditions described by Cellini. Francesco da San Gallo was the son of Giuliano, and nephew of Antonio da San Gallo.

plan for mine, and perceiving that it was very incorrect in many details, I took it and went immediately to the Duke. When I tried to point out these defects, the Duke interrupted me and exclaimed with fury: "Benvenuto, I will give way to you upon the point of statuary, but in this art of fortification I choose that you should cede to me. So carry out the design which I have given you." To these brave words I answered as gently as I could, and said: "My lord, your most illustrious Excellency has taught me something even in my own fine art of statuary, inasmuch as we have always exchanged ideas upon that subject; I beg you then to deign to listen to me upon this matter of your fortifications, which is far more important than making statues. If I am permitted to discuss it also with your Excellency, you will be better able to teach me how I have to serve you." This courteous speech of mine induced him to discuss the plans with me; and when I had clearly demonstrated that they were not conceived on a right method, he said: "Go, then, and make a design yourself, and I will see if it satisfies me." Accordingly, I made two designs according to the right principles for fortifying those two gates, and took them to him; and when he distinguished the true from the false system, he exclaimed good humouredly: "Go and do it in your own way, for I am content to have it so." I set to work then with the greatest diligence.

LXXXVI

There was on guard at the gate of Prato a certain Lombard captain; he was a truculent and stalwart fellow, of incredibly coarse speech, whose presumption matched his utter ignorance. This man began at once to ask me what I was about there. I politely exhibited my drawings, and took infinite pains to make him understand my purpose. The rude brute kept rolling his head, and turning first to one side and then to the other, shifting himself upon his legs, and twirling his enormous moustachios; then he drew his cap down over his eyes and roared out: "Zounds! deuce take it! I can make nothing of this rigmarole." At last the animal became so tiresome that I said: "Leave it then to me, who do understand it," and turned my shoulders to go about my business. At this he began to threaten me with his head, and, setting his left hand on the pommel of his sword, tilted the point up, and exclaimed: "Hullo, my master! you want perhaps to make me cross blades with you?" I faced round in a great fury, for the man had stirred my blood, and cried out: "It would be less trouble to run you through the body than to build the bastion of this gate." In an instant we both set hands to our swords, without quite drawing; for a number of honest folk, citizens of Florence, and others of them courtiers, came running up. The greater part of them rated the captain, telling him that he was in the wrong, that I was a man to give him as good as I got, and that if this came to the Duke's ears, it would be the worse for him. Accordingly he went off on his own business, and I began with my bastion.

After setting things in order there, I proceeded to the other little gate of Arno, where I found a captain from Cesena, the most polite, well-mannered man I ever knew in that profession. He had the air of a gentle young lady, but at need he could prove himself one of the boldest and bloodiest fighters in the world. This agreeable gentleman observed me so attentively that he made me bashful and self-conscious; and seeing that he wanted to understand what I was doing, I courteously explained my plans. Suffice it to say, that we vied with each other in civilities, which made me do far better with this bastion than with the other.

I had nearly finished the two bastions when an inroad of Piero Strozzi's people struck such terror into the countryfolk of Prati that they began to leave it in a body, and all their carts, laden with the household goods of each family, came crowding into the city. The number of them was so enormous, cart jostling with cart, and the confusion was so great, that I told the guards to look out lest the same misadventure should happen at this gate as had occurred at the gates of Turin; for if we had once cause to lower the portcullis, it would not be able to perform its functions, but must inevitably stick suspended upon one of the waggons. When the big brute of a captain heard these words, he replied with insults, and I retorted in the same tone. We were on the point of coming to a far worse quarrel than before. However, the folk kept us asunder; and when I had finished my bastions, I touched some score of crowns, which I had not expected, and which were uncommonly welcome. So I returned with a blithe heart to finish my Perseus.

LXXXVII

During those days some antiquities had been discovered in the country round Arezzo. Among them was the Chimæra, that bronze lion which is to be seen in the rooms adjacent to the great hall of the palace.[1] Together with the Chimæra a number of little statuettes, likewise in bronze, had been brought to light; they were covered with earth and rust, and each of them lacked either head or hands or feet. The Duke amused his leisure hours by cleaning up these statuettes himself with certain little chisels used by goldsmiths. It happened on one occasion that I had to speak on business to his Excellency; and while we were talking, he reached me a little hammer, with which I struck the chisels the Duke held, and so the figures were disengaged from their earth and rust. In this way we passed several evenings, and then the Duke commissioned me to restore the statuettes. He took so much pleasure in these trifles that he made me work by day also, and if I delayed coming, he used to send for me. I very often submitted to his Excellency that if I left my Perseus in the daytime, several bad consequences would ensue. The first of these, which caused me the greatest anxiety, was that, seeing me spend so long a time upon my statue, the Duke himself might get disgusted; which indeed did afterwards happen. The other was that I had several journeymen who in my absence were up to two kinds of mischief; first, they spoilt my piece, and then they did as little work as possible. These arguments made his Excellency consent that I should only go to the palace after twenty-four o'clock.

I had now conciliated the affection of his Excellency to such an extent, that every evening when I came to him he treated me with greater kindness. About this time the new apartments were built toward the lions;[2] the Duke then wishing to be able to retire into a less public part of the palace, fitted up for himself a little chamber in these new lodgings, and ordered me approach to it by a private passage. I had to pass through his wardrobe, then across the stage of the great hall, and afterwards through certain little dark galleries and cabinets. The Duchess, however, after a few days, deprived me of this means of access by having all the doors upon the path I had to traverse locked up. The consequence was that every evening when I arrived at the palace, I had to wait a long while, because the Duchess occupied the cabinets for her personal necessities.[3] Her habit of body was unhealthy, and so I never came without incommoding her. This and other causes made her hate the very sight of me. However, notwithstanding great discomforts and daily annoyances, I persevered in

1 Now in the Uffizzi.
2 Lions from a very early period had always been kept in part of the Palazzo Vecchio.
3 *Alle sue comodità.*

going. The Duke's orders, meanwhile, were so precise, that no sooner did I knock at those doors, than they were immediately opened, and I was allowed to pass freely where I chose. The consequence was that occasionally, while walking noiselessly and unexpectedly through the private rooms, I came upon the Duchess at a highly inconvenient moment. Bursting then into such a furious storm of rage that I was frightened, she cried out: "When will you ever finish mending up those statuettes? Upon my word, this perpetual going and coming of yours has grown to be too great a nuisance." I replied as gently as I could: "My lady and sole mistress, I have no other desire than to serve you loyally and with the strictest obedience. This work to which the Duke has put me will last several months; so tell me, most illustrious Excellency, whether you wish me not to come here any more. In that case I will not come, whoever calls me; nay, should the Duke himself send for me, I shall reply that I am ill, and by no means will I intrude again." To this speech she made answer: "I do not bid you not to come, nor do I bid you to disobey the Duke; but I repeat that your work seems to me as though it would never be finished."

Whether the Duke heard something of this encounter, or whatever the cause was, he began again as usual. Toward twenty-four o'clock he sent for me; and his messenger always spoke to this effect: "Take good care, and do not fail to come, for the Duke is waiting for you." In this way I continued, always with the same inconveniences, to put in an appearance on several successive evenings. Upon one occasion among others, arriving in my customary way, the Duke, who had probably been talking with the Duchess about private matters, turned upon me in a furious anger. I was terrified, and wanted to retire. But he called out: "Come in, friend Benvenuto; go to your affairs; I will rejoin you in a few moments." While I was passing onward, Don Garzia, then quite a little fellow, plucked me by the cape, and played with me as prettily as such a child could do. The Duke looked up delighted, and exclaimed: "What pleasant and friendly terms my boys are on with you!"

LXXXVIII

While I was working at these bagatelles, the Prince, and Don Giovanni, and Don Arnando, and Don Garzia kept always hovering around me, teasing me whenever the Duke's eyes were turned.[1] I

[1] The Prince was Don Francesco, then aged twelve; Don Giovanni was ten, Don Garzia was six, and Don Ferdinando four.

begged them for mercy's sake to hold their peace. They answered: "That we cannot do." I told them: "What one cannot is required of no one! So have your will! Along with you!" At this both Duke and Duchess burst out laughing.

Another evening, after I had finished the small bronze figures which are wrought into the pedestal of Perseus, that is to say, the Jupiter, Mercury, Minerva, and Danæ, with the little Perseus seated at his mother's feet, I had them carried into the room where I was wont to work, and arranged them in a row, raised somewhat above the line of vision, so that they produced a magnificent effect. The Duke heard of this, and made his entrance sooner than usual. It seems that the person who informed his Excellency praised them above their merit, using terms like "far superior to the ancients," and so forth; wherefore the Duke came talking pleasantly with the Duchess about my doings. I rose at once and went to meet them. With his fine and truly princely manner he received me, lifting his right hand, in which he held as superb a pear-graft as could possibly be seen. "Take it, my Benvenuto!" he exclaimed; "plant this pear in your garden." To these words I replied with a delighted gesture: "O my lord, does your most illustrious Excellency really mean that I should plant it in the garden of my house?" "Yes," he said, "in the garden of the house which belongs to you. Have you understood me?" I thanked his Excellency, and the Duchess in like manner, with the best politeness I could use.

After this they both took seats in front of the statues, and for more than two hours went on talking about nothing but the beauties of the work. The Duchess was wrought up to such an enthusiasm that she cried out: "I do not like to let those exquisite figures be wasted on the pedestal down there in the piazza, where they will run the risk of being injured. I would much rather have you fix them in one of my apartments, where they will be preserved with the respect due to their singular artistic qualities." I opposed this plan with many forcible arguments; but when I saw that she was determined I should not place them on the pedestal where they now stand, I waited till next day, and went to the palace about twenty-two o'clock. Ascertaining that the Duke and Duchess were out riding, and having already prepared the pedestal, I had the statues carried down, and soldered them with lead into their proper niches. Oh, when the Duchess knew of this, how angry she was! Had it not been for the Duke, who manfully defended me, I should have paid dearly for my daring. Her indignation about the pearls, and now again about this matter of the statues, made her so contrive that the Duke abandoned his amusements in our workshop. Consequently I went there no more, and was met again with the same obstructions as formerly whenever I wanted to gain access to the palace.

LXXXIX

I returned to the Loggia,[1] whither my Perseus had already been brought, and went on putting the last touches to my work, under the old difficulties always; that is to say, lack of money, and a hundred untoward accidents, the half of which would have cowed a man armed with adamant.

However, I pursued my course as usual; and one morning, after I had heard mass at San Piero Scheraggio, that brute Bernardone, broker, worthless goldsmith, and by the Duke's grace purveyor to the mint, passed by me. No sooner had he got outside the church than the dirty pig let fly four cracks which might have been heard from San Miniato. I cried: "Yah! pig, poltroon, donkey! is that the noise your filthy talents make?" and ran off for a cudgel. He took refuge on the instant in the mint; while I stationed myself inside my house-door, which I left ajar, setting a boy at watch upon the street to warn me when the pig should leave the mint. After waiting some time, I grew tired, and my heat cooled. Reflecting, then, that blows are not dealt by contract, and that some disaster might ensue, I resolved to wreak my vengeance by another method. The incident took place about the feast of our San Giovanni, one or two days before; so I composed four verses, and stuck them up in an angle of the church where people go to ease themselves. The verses ran as follows:—

"Here lieth Bernardone, ass and pig,
  Spy, broker, thief in whom Pandora planted
  All her worst evils, and from thence transplanted
Into that brute Buaccio's carcass big." [2]

Both the incident and the verses went the round of the palace, giving the Duke and Duchess much amusement. But, before the man himself

[1] That is, the Loggia de' Lanzi, on the great piazza of Florence, where Cellini's statue still stands.

[2] If I understand the obscure lines of the original, Cellini wanted to kill two birds with one stone by this epigram—both Bernardone and his son Baccio. But by Buaccio he generally means Baccio Bandinelli.

knew what I had been up to, crowds of people stopped to read the lines and laughed immoderately at them. Since they were looking towards the mine and fixing their eyes on Bernardone, his son, Maestro Baccio, taking notice of their gestures, tore the paper down with fury. The elder bit his thumb, shrieking threats out with that hideous voice of his, which comes forth through his nose; indeed he made a brave defiance.[3]

XC

When the Duke was informed that the whole of my work for the Perseus could be exhibited as finished, he came one day to look at it. His manner showed clearly that it gave him great satisfaction; but afterwards he turned to some gentlemen attending him and said: "Although this statue seems in our eyes a very fine piece, still it has yet to win the favour of the people. Therefore, my Benvenuto, before you put the very last touches on, I should like you, for my sake, to remove a part of the scaffolding on the side of the piazza, some day toward noon, in order that we may learn what folk think of it. There is no doubt that when it is thrown open to space and light, it will look very differently from what it does in this enclosure." I replied with all humility to his Excellency: "You must know, my lord, that it will make more than twice as good a show. Oh, how is it that your most illustrious Excellency has forgotten seeing it in the garden of my house? There, in that large extent of space, it showed so bravely that Bandinello, coming through the garden of the Innocents to look at it, was compelled, in spite of his evil and malignant nature, to praise it, he who never praised aught or any one in all his life! I perceive that your Excellency lends too ready an ear to that fellow." When I had done speaking, he smiled ironically and a little angrily; yet he replied with great kindness: "Do what I ask, my Benvenuto, just to please me."

When the Duke had left, I gave orders to have the screen removed. Yet some trifles of gold, varnish, and various other little finishings were still wanting; wherefore I began to murmur and complain indignantly, cursing the unhappy day which brought me to Florence. Too well I knew already the great and irreparable sacrifice I made when I left France; nor could I discover any reasonable ground for hope that I might prosper in the future with my prince and patron.

[3] To bite the thumb at any one was, as students of our old drama know, a sign of challenge or provocation.

From the commencement to the middle and the ending, everything that I had done had been performed to my great disadvantage. Therefore, it was with deep ill-humour that I disclosed my statue on the following day.

Now it pleased God that, on the instant of its exposure to view, a shout of boundless enthusiasm went up in commendation of my work, which consoled me not a little. The folk kept on attaching sonnets to the posts of the door, which was protected with a curtain while I gave the last touches to the statue. I believe that on the same day when I opened it a few hours to the public, more than twenty were nailed up, all of them overflowing with the highest panegyrics. Afterwards, when I once more shut it off from view, every day brought sonnets, with Latin and Greek verses; for the University of Pisa was then in vacation, and all the doctors and scholars kept vying with each other who could praise it best. But what gratified me most, and inspired me with most hope of the Duke's support, was that the artists, sculptors and painters alike, entered into the same generous competition. I set the highest value on the eulogies of that excellent painter Jacopo Pontormo, and still more on those of his able pupil Bronzino, who was not satisfied with merely publishing his verses, but sent them by his lad Sandrino's hand to my own house.[1] They spoke so generously of my performance, in that fine style of his which is most exquisite, that this alone repaid me somewhat for the pain of my long troubles. So then I closed the screen, and once more set myself to finishing my statue.

XCI

The great compliments which this short inspection of my Perseus had elicited from the noble school of Florence, though they were well known to the Duke, did not prevent him from saying: "I am delighted that Benvenuto has had this trifling satisfaction, which will spur him on to the desired conclusion with more speed and diligence. Do not, however, let him imagine that, when his Perseus shall be finally exposed to view from all sides, folk in general will be so lavish of their praises. On the contrary, I am afraid that all its defects will then be brought home to him, and more will be detected than the

1 Jacopo Carrucci da Pontormo was now an old man. He died in 1558, age sixty-five years. Angelo Allori, called Il Bronzino, one of the last fairly good Florentine painters, won considerable distinction as a writer of burlesque poems. He died in 15/1, aged sixty-nine years. We possess his sonnets on the Perseus.

statue really has. So let him arm himself with patience." These were precisely the words which Bandinello had whispered in the Duke's ears, citing the works of Andrea del Verrocchio, who made that fine bronze of Christ and S. Thomas on the front of Orsammichele; at the same time he referred to many other statues, and dared even to attack the marvellous David of divine Michel Agnolo Buonarroti, accusing it of only looking well if seen in front; finally, he touched upon the multitude of sarcastic sonnets which were called forth by his own Hercules and Cacus, and wound up with abusing the people of Florence. Now the Duke, who was too much inclined to credit his assertions, encouraged the fellow to speak thus, and thought in his own heart that things would go as he had prophesied, because that envious creature Bandinello never ceased insinuating malice. On one occasion it happened that the gallows bird Bernardone, the broker, was present at these conversations, and in support of Bandinello's calumnies, he said to the Duke: "You must remember, prince, that statues on a large scale are quite a different dish of soup from little figures. I do not refuse him the credit of being excellent at statuettes in miniature. But you will soon see that he cannot succeed in that other sphere of art." To these vile suggestions he added many others of all sorts, plying his spy's office, and piling up a mountain of lies to boot.

XCII

Now it pleased my glorious Lord and immortal God that at last I brought the whole work to completion: and on a certain Thursday morning I exposed it to the public gaze.[1] Immediately, before the sun was fully in the heavens, there assembled such a multitude of people that no words could describe them. All with one voice contended which should praise it most. The Duke was stationed at a window low upon the first floor of the palace, just above the entrance; there, half hidden, he heard everything the folk were saying of my statue. After listening through several hours, he rose so proud and happy in his heart that he turned to his attendant, Messer Sforza, and exclaimed: "Sforza, go and seek out Benvenuto; tell him from me that he has delighted me far more than I expected: say too that I shall reward him in a way which will astonish him; so bid him be of good courage."

[1] April 27, 1554.

In due course, Messer Sforzo discharged this glorious embassy, which consoled me greatly. I passed a happy day, partly because of the Duke's message, and also because the folk kept pointing me out as something marvellous and strange. Among the many who did so, were two gentlemen, deputed by the Viceroy of Sicily [2] to our Duke on public business. Now these two agreeable persons met me upon the piazza: I had been shown them in passing, and now they made monstrous haste to catch me up; then, with caps in hand, they uttered an oration so ceremonious, that it would have been excessive for a Pope. I bowed, with every protestation of humility. They meanwhile continued loading me with compliments, until at last I prayed them, for kindness' sake, to leave the piazza in my company, because the folk were stopping and staring at me more than at my Perseus. In the midst of all these ceremonies, they went so far as to propose that I should come to Sicily, and offered to make terms which should content me. They told me how Fra Giovan Agnolo de' Servi [3] had constructed a fountain for them, complete in all parts, and decorated with a multitude of figures; but it was not in the same good style they recognised in Perseus, and yet they had heaped riches on the man. I would not suffer them to finish all their speeches, but answered: "You give me much cause for wonder, seeking as you do to make me quit the service of a prince who is the greatest patron of the arts that ever lived; and I too here in my own birthplace, famous as the school of every art and science! Oh, if my soul's desire had been set on lucre, I could have stayed in France, with that great monarch Francis, who gave me a thousand golden crowns a year for board, and paid me in addition the price of all my labour. In his service I gained more than four thousand golden crowns the year."

With these and such like words I cut their ceremonies short, thanking them for the high praises they had bestowed upon me, which were indeed the best reward that artists could receive for their labours. I told them they had greatly stimulated my zeal, so that I hoped, after a few years were passed, to exhibit another masterpiece, which I dared believe would yield far truer satisfaction to our noble school of Florence. The two gentlemen were eager to resume the thread of their complimentary proposals, whereupon I, lifting my cap and making a profound bow, bade them a polite farewell.

2 Don Juan de Vega.
3 Giovanni Angelo Montorsoli entered the Order of the Servites in 1530. This did not prevent him from plying his profession of sculptor. The work above alluded to is the fountain at Messina.

XCIII

When two more days had passed, and the chorus of praise was ever on the increase, I resolved to go and present myself to the Duke, who said with great good-humour: "My Benvenuto, you have satisfied and delighted me; but I promise that I will reward you in such wise as will make you wonder; and I tell you that I do not mean to delay beyond to-morrow." On hearing this most welcome assurance, I turned all the forces of my soul and body to God, fervently offering up thanks to Him. At the same moment I approached the Duke, and almost weeping for gladness, kissed his robe. Then I added: "O my glorious prince, true and most generous lover of the arts, and of those who exercise them! I entreat your most illustrious Excellency to allow me eight days first to go and return thanks to God; for I alone know what travail I have endured, and that my earnest faith has moved Him to assist me. In gratitude for this and all other marvellous mercies, I should like to travel eight days on pilgrimage, continually thanking my immortal God, who never fails to help those who call upon Him with sincerity." The Duke then asked me where I wished to go. I answered: "To-morrow I shall set out for Vallombrosa, thence to Camaldoli and the Ermo, afterwards I shall proceed to the Bagni di Santa Maria, and perhaps so far as Sestile, because I hear of fine antiquities to be seen there.[1] Then I shall retrace my steps to San Francesco della Vernia, and, still with thanks to God, return light-hearted to your service." The Duke replied at once with cheerful kindness: "Go and come back again, for of a truth you please me; but do not forget to send a couple of lines by way of memorandum, and leave the rest to me."

I wrote four lines that very day, in which I thanked his Excellency for expected favours, and gave these to Messer Sforza, who placed them in the Duke's hands. The latter took them, and then handed them to Messer Sforza, remarking: "See that you put these lines each day where I can see them; for if Benvenuto comes back and finds I have not despatched his business, I think that he will murder me." Thus laughing, his Excellency asked to be reminded. Messer Sforza reported these precise words to me on the same evening, laughing too and expressing wonder at the great favour shown me by the Duke. He pleasantly added: "Go, Benvenuto, and come again quickly, for indeed I am jealous of you."

[1] The Ermo is more correctly Eremo, and Vernia is Alvernia.

XCIV

In God's name then I left Florence, continually singing psalms and prayers in His honour upon all that journey. I enjoyed it extremely; for the season was fine, in early summer, and the country through which I travelled, and which I had never seen before, struck me as marvellously beautiful. Now I had taken with me to serve as guide a young workman in my employ, who came from Bagno, and was called Cesare. Thanks to him, then, I received the kindest hospitality from his father and all his family, among whom was an old man of more than seventy, extremely pleasant in his conversation. He was Cesare's uncle, a surgeon by profession, and a dabbler in alchemy. This excellent person made me observe that the Bagni contained mines of gold and silver, and showed me many interesting objects in the neighbourhood; so that I enjoyed myself as much as I have ever done.

One day, when we had become intimate and he could trust me, he spoke as follows: "I must not omit to tell you a thought of mine, to which his Excellency might with advantage pay attention. It is, that not far from Camaldoli there lies a mountain pass so ill defended, that Piero Strozzi could not only cross it without risk, but might also seize on Poppi [1] unmolested." Not satisfied with this description, he also took a sheet of paper from his pouch, upon which the good old man had drawn the whole country, so that the seriousness of the danger could be manifest upon inspection of the map. I took the design and left Bagno at once, travelling homeward as fast as I could by Prato Magno and San Francesco della Vernia. On reaching Florence, I only stopped to draw off my riding-boots, and hurried to the palace. Just opposite the Badia I met the Duke, who was coming by the palace of the Podesta. When he saw me he gave me a very gracious reception, and showing some surprise, exclaimed: "Why have you come back so quickly; I did not expect you for eight days at least." I answered: "The service of your most illustrious Excellency brings me back, else I should very willingly have stayed some few days longer on my journey through that lovely country." "Well, and what good news have you?" said he. I answered: "Prince, I must talk to you about things of the greatest importance which I have to disclose." So I followed him to the palace, and when we were there, he took me privately into a chamber where we stayed a while alone

1 A village in the Castenino. Piero Strozzi was at this time in Valdichiana.

together. I then unfolded the whole matter and showed him the little map, with which he seemed to be much gratified. When I told his Excellency that one ought to take measures at once, he reflected for a little while and then said: "I may inform you that we have agreed with the Duke of Urbino that he should guard the pass; but do not speak about it." Then he dismissed me with great demonstrations of good-will, and I went home.

XCV

Next day I presented myself, and, after a few words of conversation, the Duke addressed me cheerfully: "Tomorrow, without fail, I mean to despatch your business; set your mind at rest, then." I, who felt sure that he meant what he said, waited with great impatience for the morrow. When the longed-for day arrived, I betook me to the palace; and as it always happens that evil tidings travel faster than good news, Messer Giacopo Guidi,[1] secretary to his Excellency, called me with his wry mouth and haughty voice; drawing himself up as stiff as a poker, he began to speak to this effect: "The Duke says he wants you to tell him how much you ask for your Perseus." I remained dumbfounded and astonished; yet I quickly replied that it was not my custom to put prices on my work, and that this was not what his Excellency had promised me two days ago. The man raised his voice, and ordered me expressly in the Duke's name, under the penalty of his severe displeasure, to say how much I wanted. Now I had hoped not only to gain some handsome reward, trusting to the mighty signs of kindness shown me by the Duke, but I had still more expected to secure the entire good graces of his Excellency, seeing I never asked for anything, but only for his favour. Accordingly, this wholly unexpected way of dealing with me put me in a fury, and I was especially enraged by the manner which that venomous toad assumed in discharging his commission. I exclaimed that if the Duke gave me ten thousand crowns I should not be paid enough, and that if I had ever thought things would come to this haggling, I should not have settled in his service. Thereupon the surly fellow began to abuse me, and I gave it him back again.

Upon the following day, when I paid my respects to the Duke, he beckoned to me. I approached, and he exclaimed in anger: "Cities

[1] It appears from a letter written by Guidi to Bandinelli that he hated Cellini, whom he called *pessimo mostro di natura.* Guidi was made Bishop of Penna in 1561, and attended the Council of Trent.

and great palaces are built with ten thousands of ducats." I rejoined: "Your Excellency can find multitudes of men who are able to build you cities and palaces, but you will not, perhaps, find one man in the world who could make a second Perseus." Then I took my leave without saying or doing anything farther. A few days afterwards the Duchess sent for me, and advised me to put my difference with the Duke into her hands, since she thought she could conduct the business to my satisfaction. On hearing these kindly words I replied that I had never asked any other recompense for my labours than the good graces of the Duke, and that his most illustrious Excellency had assured me of this; it was not needful that I should place in their Excellencies' hands what I had always frankly left to them from the first days when I undertook their service. I farther added that if his most illustrious Excellency gave me but a *crazia*,[2] which is worth five farthings, for my work, I should consider myself contented, providing only that his Excellency did not deprive me of his favour. At these words the Duchess smiled a little and said: "Benvenuto, you would do well to act as I advise you." Then she turned her back and left me. I thought it was my best policy to speak with the humility I have above described; yet it turned out that I had done the worst for myself, because, albeit she had harboured some angry feelings toward me, she had in her a certain way of dealing which was generous.

XCVI

About that time I was very intimate with Girolamo degli Albizzi,[1] commissary of the Duke's militia. One day this friend said to me: "O Benvenuto, it would not be a bad thing to put your little difference of opinion with the Duke to rights; and I assure you that if you repose confidence in me, I feel myself the man to settle matters. I know what I am saying. The Duke is getting really angry, and you will come badly out of the affair. Let this suffice; I am not at liberty to say all I know." Now, subsequently to that conversation with the Duchess, I had been told by some one, possibly a rogue, that he had heard how the Duke said upon some occasion which offered itself: "For less than two farthings I will throw Perseus to the dogs, and

2 A small Tuscan coin.

1 A warm partisan of the Medici. He was a cousin of Maria Salviati, Cosimo's mother. It was rumoured that he caused the historian Francesco Guicciardini's death by poison. We find him godfather to one of Cellini's children.

so our differences will be ended." This, then, made me anxious, and induced me to entrust Girolamo degli Albizzi with the negotiations, telling him anything would satisfy me provided I retained the good graces of the Duke. That honest fellow was excellent in all his dealings with soldiers, especially with the militia, who are for the most part rustics; but he had no taste for statuary, and therefore could not understand its conditions. Consequently, when he spoke to the Duke, he began thus: "Prince, Benvenuto has placed himself in my hands, and has begged me to recommend him to your Excellency." The Duke replied: "I too am willing to refer myself to you, and shall be satisfied with your decision." Thereupon Girolamo, composed a letter, with much skill and greatly in my honour, fixing the sum which the Duke would have to pay me at 3500 golden crowns in gold; and this should not be taken as my proper recompense for such a masterpiece, but only as a kind of gratuity; enough to say that I was satisfied; with many other phrases of like tenor, all of which implied the price which I have mentioned.

The Duke signed this agreement as gladly as I took it sadly. When the Duchess heard, she said: "It would have been better for that poor man if he had placed himself in my hands; I could have got him five thousand crowns in gold." One day, when I went to the palace, she repeated these same words to me in the presence of Messer Alamanno Salviati,[2] and laughed at me a little, saying that I deserved my bad luck.

The Duke gave orders that I should be paid a hundred golden crowns in gold per month, until the sum was discharged; and thus it ran for some months. Afterwards, Messer Antonio de' Nobili, who had to transact the business, began to give me fifty, and sometimes later on he gave me twenty-five, and sometimes nothing. Accordingly, when I saw that the settlement was being thus deferred, I spoke good-humouredly to Messer Antonio, and begged him to explain why he did not complete my payments. He answered in a like tone of politeness; yet it struck me that he exposed his own mind too much. Let the reader judge. He began by saying that the sole reason why he could not go forward regularly with these payments, was the scarcity of money at the palace; but he promised, when cash came in, to discharge arrears. Then he added: "Oh heavens! if I did not pay you, I should be an utter rogue." I was somewhat surprised to hear

[2] This Salviati and the De' Nobili mentioned afterwards occupied a distinguished place in Florentine annals as partisans of the Medici.

him speak in that way; yet I resolved to hope that he would pay me when he had the power to do so. But when I observed that things went quite the contrary way, and saw that I was being pillaged, I lost temper with the man, and recalled to his memory hotly and in anger what he had declared he would be if he did not pay me. However, he died; and five hundred crowns are still owing to me at the present date, which is nigh upon the end of 1566.[3] There was also a balance due upon my salary which I thought would be forgotten, since three years had elapsed without payment. But it so happened that the Duke fell ill of a serious malady, remaining forty-eight hours without passing water. Finding that remedies of his physicians availed nothing, it is probable that he betook himself to God, and therefore decreed the discharge of all debts to his servants. I too was paid on this occasion, yet I never obtained what still stood out upon my Perseus.

XCVII

I had almost determined to say nothing more about that unlucky Perseus; but a most remarkable incident, which I do not like to omit, obliges me to do so; wherefore I must now turn back a bit, to gather up the thread of my narration. I thought I was acting for the best when I told the Duchess that I could not compromise affairs which were no longer in my hands, seeing I had informed the Duke that I should gladly accept whatever he chose to give me. I said this in the hope of gaining favour; and with this manifestation of submissiveness I employed every likely means of pacifying his resentment; for I ought to add that a few days before he came to terms with Albizzi, the Duke had shown he was excessively displeased with me. The reason was as follows: I complained of some abominable acts of injustice done to me by Messer Alfonso Quistelli, Messer Jacopo Polverino of the Exchequer, and more than all by Ser Giovanbattista Brandini of Volterra. When, therefore, I set forth my cause with some vehemence, the Duke flew into the greatest rage conceivable. Being thus in anger, he exclaimed: "This is just the same as with your Perseus, when you asked those ten thousand crowns. You let yourself be blinded by mere cupidity. Therefore I shall have the statue valued, and shall give you what the experts think it worth." To these words I replied with too much daring and a touch of indignation, which is always out of place in dealing with great princes:

[3] Cellini began to write his *Memoirs* in 1558. Eight years had therefore now elapsed.

"How is it possible that my work should be valued at its proper worth when there is not a man in Florence capable of performing it?" That increased his irritation; he uttered many furious phrases, and among them said: "There is in Florence at this day a man well able to make such a statue, and who is therefore highly capable of judging it." He meant Bandinello, Cavaliere of S. Jacopo.[1] Then I rejoined: "My lord, your most illustrious Excellency gave me the means of producing an important and very difficult masterpiece in the midst of this the noblest school of the world; and my work has been received with warmer praises than any other heretofore exposed before the gaze of our incomparable masters. My chief pride is the commendation of those able men who both understand and practise the arts of design—as in particular Bronzino, the painter; this man set himself to work, and composed four sonnets couched in the choicest style, and full of honour to myself. Perhaps it was his example which moved the whole city to such a tumult of enthusiasm. I freely admit that if sculpture were his business instead of painting, then Bronzino might have been equal to a task like mine. Michel Agnolo Buonarroti, again, whom I am proud to call my master; he, I admit, could have achieved the same success when he was young, but not with less fatigue and trouble than I endured. But now that he is far advanced in years, he would most certainly be found unequal to the strain. Therefore I think I am justified in saying that no man known upon this earth could have produced my Perseus. For the rest, my work has received the greatest reward I could have wished for in this world; chiefly and especially because your most illustrious Excellency not only expressed yourself satisfied, but praised it far more highly than any one beside. What greater and more honourable prize could be desired by me? I affirm most emphatically that your Excellency could not pay me with more glorious coin, nor add from any treasury a wealth surpassing this. Therefore I hold myself overpaid already, and return thanks to your most illustrious Excellency with all my heart." The Duke made answer: "Probably you think I have not the money to pay you. For my part, I promise you that I shall pay you more for the statue than it is worth." Then I retorted: "I did not picture to my fancy any better recompense from your Excellency; yet I account myself amply remunerated by that first reward which the school of Florence gave me. With this to console me, I shall take my departure on the instant, without returning to the

[1] Bandinelli was a Knight of S. James of Compostella.

house you gave me, and shall never seek to set my foot in this town again." We were just at S. Felicità, and his Excellency was proceeding to the palace. When he heard these choleric words, he turned upon me in stern anger and exclaimed: "You shall not go; take heed you do not go!" Half terrified, I then followed him to the palace.

On arriving there, his Excellency sent for the Archbishop of Pisa, named De' Bartolini, and Messer Pandolfo della Stufa,[2] requesting them to order Baccio Bandinelli, in his name, to examine well my Perseus and value it, since he wished to pay its exact price. These excellent men went forthwith and performed their embassy. In reply Bandinello said that he had examined the statue minutely, and knew well enough what it was worth; but having been on bad terms otherwise with me for some time past, he did not care to be entangled anyhow in my affairs. Then they began to put a gentle pressure on him, saying: "The Duke ordered us to tell you, under pain of his displeasure, that you are to value the statue, and you may have two or three days to consider your estimate. When you have done so, tell us at what price it ought to be paid." He answered that his judgment was already formed, that he could not disobey the Duke, and that my work was rich and beautiful and excellent in execution; therefore he thought sixteen thousand crowns or more would not be an excessive price for it. Those good and courteous gentlemen reported this to the Duke, who was mightily enraged; they also told the same to me. I replied that nothing in the world would induce me to take praise from Bandinello, "seeing that this bad man speaks ills of everybody." My words were carried to the Duke; and that was the reason why the Duchess wanted me to place the matter in her hands. All that I have written is the pure truth. I will only add that I ought to have trusted to her intervention, for then I should have been quickly paid, and should have received so much more into the bargain.

XCVIII

The Duke sent me word by Messer Lelio Torello,[1] his Master of the Rolls,[2] that he wanted me to execute some bas-reliefs in bronze

2 Onofrio de' Bartolini was made Archbishop of Pisa in 1518, at the age of about seventeen. He was a devoted adherent of the Medici. He was shut up with Clement in S. Angelo, and sent as hostage to the Imperial army. Pandolfo della Stufa had been cupbearer to Caterina de' Medici while Dauphiness.

1 A native of Fano. Cosimo's Auditore, 1539; first Secretary or Grand Chancellor, 1546. He was a great jurist.

2 *Suo auditore.*

for the choir of S. Maria del Fiore. Now the choir was by Bandinello, and I did not choose to enrich his bad work with my labours. He had not indeed designed it, for he understood nothing whatever about architecture; the design was given by Giuliano, the son of that Baccio d'Agnolo, the wood-carver, who spoiled the cupola.[3] Suffice it to say that it shows no talent. For both reasons I was determined not to undertake the task, although I told the Duke politely that I would do whatever his most illustrious Excellency ordered. Accordingly, he put the matter into the hands of the Board of Works for S. Maria del Fiore,[4] telling them to come to an agreement with me; he would continue my allowance of two hundred crowns a year, while they were to supply the rest out of their funds.

In due course I came before the Board, and they told me what the Duke had arranged. Feeling that I could explain my views more frankly to these gentlemen, I began by demonstrating that so many histories in bronze would cost a vast amount of money, which would be totally thrown away, giving all my reasons, which they fully appreciated. In the first place, I said that the construction of the choir was altogether incorrect, without proportion, art, convenience, grace, or good design. In the next place, the bas-reliefs would have to stand too low, beneath the proper line of vision; they would become a place for dogs to piss at, and be always full of ordure. Consequently, I declined positively to execute them. However, since I did not wish to throw away the best years of my life, and was eager to serve his most illustrious Excellency, whom I had the sincerest desire to gratify and obey, I made the following proposal. Let the Duke, if he wants to employ my talents, give me the middle door of the cathedral to perform in bronze. This would be well seen, and would confer far more glory on his most illustrious Excellency. I would bind myself by contract to receive no remuneration unless I produced something better than the finest of the Baptistery doors.[5] But if I completed it according to my promise, then I was willing to have it valued, and to be paid one thousand crowns less than the estimate made by experts.

The members of the Board were well pleased with this suggestion, and went at once to report the matter to the Duke, among them being Piero Salviati. They expected him to be extremely gratified

3 It was Baccio d'Agnolo who altered Brunelleschi's plan for the cupola. Buonarroti used to say that he made it look like a cage for crickets. His work remained unfinished.

4 *Operai di S. Maria del Fiore.*

5 He means Ghiberti's second door, in all probability.

with their communication, but it turned out just the contrary. He replied that I was always wanting to do the exact opposite of what he bade me; and so Piero left him without coming to any conclusion. On hearing this, I went off to the Duke at once, who displayed some irritation when he saw me. However, I begged him to condescend to hear me, and he replied that he was willing. I then began from the beginning, and used such convincing arguments that he saw at last how the matter really stood, since I made it evident that he would only be throwing a large sum of money away. Then I softened his temper by suggesting that if his most illustrious Excellency did not care to have the door begun, two pulpits had anyhow to be made for the choir, and that these would both of them be considerable works, which would confer glory on his reign; for my part, I was ready to execute a great number of bronze bas-reliefs with appropriate decorations. In this way I brought him round, and he gave me orders to construct the models.

Accordingly I set at work on several models, and bestowed immense pains on them. Among these there was one with eight panels, carried out with far more science than the rest, and which seemed to me more fitted for the purpose. Having taken them several times to the place, his Excellency sent word by Messer Cesare, the keeper of his wardrobe, that I should leave them there. After the Duke had inspected them, I perceived that he had selected the least beautiful. One day he sent for me, and during our conversation about the models, I gave many reasons why the octagonal pulpit would be far more convenient for its destined uses, and would produce a much finer effect. He answered that he wished me to make it square, because he liked that form better; and thus he went on conversing for some time very pleasantly. I meanwhile lost no opportunity of saying everything I could in the interest of art. Now whether the Duke knew that I had spoken the truth, or whether he wanted to have his own way, a long time passed before I heard anything more about it.

XCIX

About this time the great block of marble arrived which was intended for the Neptune. It had been brought up the Arno, and then by the Grieve [1] to the road at Poggio a Caiano, in order to be carried to Florence by that level way; and there I went to see it. Now

[1] Instead of the Grieve, which is not a navigable stream, it appears that Cellini ought to have written the Ombrone.

I knew very well that the Duchess by her special influence had managed to have it given to Bandinello. No envy prompted me to dispute his claims, but rather pity for that poor unfortunate piece of marble. Observe, by the way, that everything, whatever it may be, which is subject to an evil destiny, although one tries to save it from some manifest evil, falls at once into far worse plight; as happened to this marble when it came into the hands of Bartolommeo Ammanato,[2] of whom I shall speak the truth in its proper place. After inspecting this most splendid block, I measured it in every direction, and on returning to Florence, made several little models suited to its proportions. Then I went to Poggio a Caiano, where the Duke and Duchess were staying, with their son the Prince. I found them all at table, the Duke and Duchess dining in a private apartment; so I entered into conversation with the Prince. We had been speaking for a long while, when the Duke, who was in a room adjacent, heard my voice, and condescended very graciously to send for me. When I presented myself before their Excellencies, the Duchess addressed me in a very pleasant tone; and having thus opened the conversation, I gradually introduced the subject of that noble block of marble I had seen. I then proceeded to remark that their ancestors had brought the magnificent school of Florence to such a pitch of excellence only by stimulating competition among artists in their several branches. It was thus that the wonderful cupola and the lovely doors of San Giovanni had been produced, together with those multitudes of handsome edifices and statues which made a crown of artistic glory for their city above anything the world had seen since the days of the ancients. Upon this the Duchess, with some anger, observed that she very well knew what I meant, and bade me never mention that block of marble in her presence, since she did not like it. I replied: "So, then, you do not like me to act as the attorney of your Excellencies, and to do my utmost to ensure your being better served? Reflect upon it, my lady; if your most illustrious Excellencies think fit to open the model for a Neptune to competition, although you are resolved to give it to Bandinello, this will urge Bandinello for his own credit to display greater art and science than if he knew he had no rivals. In this way, my princes, you will be far better served, and will not discourage our school of artists; you will be able to perceive which of us is eager to excel in the grand style of our noble calling,

2 This sculptor was born in 1511, and died in 1592. He worked under Bandinelli and Sansovino.

and will show yourselves princes who enjoy and understand the fine arts." The Duchess, in a great rage, told me that I tired her patience out; she wanted the marble for Bandinello, adding: "Ask the Duke; for his Excellency also means Bandinello to have it." When the Duchess had spoken, the Duke, who had kept silence up to this time, said: "Twenty years ago I had that fine block quarried especially for Bandinello, and so I mean that Bandinello shall have it to do what he likes with it." I turned to the Duke and spoke as follows: "My lord, I entreat your most illustrious Excellency to lend a patient hearing while I speak four words in your service." He told me to say all I wanted, and that he would listen. Then I began: "You will remember, my lord, that the marble which Bandinello used for his Hercules and Cacus was quarried for our incomparable Michel Agnolo Buonarroti. He had made the model for a Samson with four figures, which would have been the finest masterpiece in the whole world; but your Bandinello got out of it only two figures, both ill-executed and bungled in the worst manner; wherefore our school still exclaims against the great wrong which was done to that magnificent block. I believe that more than a thousand sonnets were put up in abuse of that detestable performance; and I know that your most illustrious Excellency remembers the fact very well. Therefore, my powerful prince, seeing how the men to whose care that work was entrusted, in their want of taste and wisdom, took Michel Agnolo's marble away from him, and gave it to Bandinello, who spoilt it in the way the whole world knows, oh! will you suffer this far more splendid block, although it belongs to Bandinello, to remain in the hands of that man who cannot help mangling it, instead of giving it to some artist of talent capable of doing it full justice? Arrange, my lord, that every one who likes shall make a model; have them all exhibited to the school; you then will hear what the school thinks; your own good judgment will enable you to select the best; in this way, finally, you will not throw away your money, nor discourage a band of artists the like of whom is not to be found at present in the world, and who form the glory of your most illustrious Excellency."

The Duke listened with the utmost graciousness; then he rose from table, and turning to me, said: "Go, my Benvenuto, made a model, and earn that fine marble for yourself; for what you say is the truth, and I acknowledge it." The Duchess tossed her head defiantly, and muttered I know not what angry sentences.

I made them a respectful bow and returned to Florence, burning with eagerness to set hands upon my model.

C

When the Duke came to Florence, he sought me at my house without giving me previous notice. I showed him two little models of different design. Though he praised them both, he said that one of them pleased him better than the other; I was to finish the one he liked with care; and this would be to my advantage. Now his Excellency had already seen Bandinello's designs, and those of other sculptors; but, as I was informed by many of his courtiers who had heard him, he commended mine far above the rest. Among other matters worthy of record and of great weight upon this point, I will mention the following. The Cardinal of Santa Fiore was on a visit to Florence, and the Duke took him to Poggio a Caiano. Upon the road, noticing the marble as he passed, the Cardinal praised it highly, inquiring of his Excellency for what sculptor he intended it. The Duke replied at once: "For my good friend Benvenuto, who has made a splendid model with a view to it." This was reported to me by men whom I could trust.

Hearing what the Duke had said, I went to the Duchess, and took her some small bits of goldsmith's work, which greatly pleased her Excellency. Then she asked what I was doing, and I replied: "My lady, I have taken in hand for my pleasure one of the most laborious pieces which have ever been produced. It is a Christ of the whitest marble set upon a cross of the blackest, exactly of the same size as a tall man. She immediately inquired what I meant to do with it. I answered: "You must know my lady, that I would not sell it for two thousand golden ducats; it is of such difficult execution that I think no man ever attempted the like before; nor would I have undertaken it at the commission of any prince whatever, for fear I might prove inadequate to the task. I bought the marbles with my own money, and have kept a young man some two years as my assistant in the work. What with the stone, the iron frame to hold it up, and the wages, it has cost me above three hundred crowns. Consequently, I would not sell it for two thousand. But if your Excellency deigns to grant me a favour which is wholly blameless, I shall be delighted to make you a present of it. All I ask is that your Excellency will not use your influence either against or for the models which the Duke has ordered to be made of the Neptune for that great block of marble." She replied with mighty indignation: "So then you value neither my help nor my opposition?" "On the contrary, I value them highly, princess; or why am I offering to give you what I value at two thousand ducats? But I have such confidence in my laborious and well-trained studies, that I hope to win the palm, even against the great Michel Agnolo Buonarroti, from whom and from no one else I have learned all that I know. Indeed, I should be much better pleased to enter into competition with him who knows so much than with those others who know but little of their art. Contending with my sublime master, I could gain laurels in plenty, whereas there are but few to be reaped in a contest with these men." After I had spoken, she rose in a half-angry mood, and I returned to work with all the strength I had upon my model.

When it was finished, the Duke came to see it, bringing with him two ambassadors, one from the Duke of Ferrara, the other from the Signory of Lucca. They were delighted, and the Duke said to those two gentlemen: "Upon my word, Benvenuto deserves to have the marble." Then they both paid me the highest compliments, especially the envoy from Lucca, who was a person of accomplishments and learning.[1] I had retired to some distance in order that they might exchange opinions freely; but when I heard that I was being complimented, I came up, turned to the Duke, and said: "My lord, your most illustrious Excellency ought now to employ another admirable device: decree that every one who likes shall make a model in clay, exactly of the same size as the marble has to be. In this way you will be able to judge far better who deserves the commission; and I may observe that if your Excellency does not give it to the sculptor who deserves it, this will not wrong the man so much, but will reflect great discredit upon yourself, since the loss and shame will fall on you. On the other hand, if you award it to the one who has deserved it, you will acquire great glory in the first place, and will employ your treasure well, while artists will believe that you appreciate and understand their business." No sooner had I finished speaking than the Duke shrugged his shoulders, and began to move away. While they were taking leave the ambassador of Lucca said to the Duke: "Prince, this Benvenuto of yours is a terrible man!" The Duke responded: "He is much more terrible than you imagine, and well were it for him if he were a little less terrible; then he would

1 Probably Girolamo Lucchesini.

possess at the present moment many things which he has not got." These precise words were reported to me by the envoy, by way of chiding and advising me to change my conduct. I told him that I had the greatest wish to oblige my lord as his affectionate and faithful servant, but that I did not understand the arts of flattery. Several months after this date, Bandinello died; and it was thought that, in addition to his intemperate habits of life, the mortification of having probably to lose the marble contributed to his decline.

CI

Bandinello had received information of the crucifix which, as I have said above, I was now engaged upon. Accordingly he laid his hands at once upon a block of marble, and produced the Pietà which may be seen in the church of the Annunziata. Now I had offered my crucifix to S. Maria Novella, and had already fixed up the iron clamps whereby I meant to fasten it against the wall. I only asked permission to construct a little sarcophagus upon the ground beneath the feet of Christ, into which I might creep when I was dead. The friars told me that they could not grant this without the consent of their building committee.[1] I replied: "Good brethren, why did not you consult your committee before you allowed me to place my crucifix? Without their leave you suffered me to fix my clamps and other necessary fittings."

On this account I refused to give those fruits of my enormous labours to the church of S. Maria Novella, even though the overseers of the fabric came and begged me for the crucifix. I turned at once to the church of the Annunziata, and when I explained the terms on which I had sought to make a present of it to S. Maria Novella, those virtuous friars of the Nunziata unanimously told me to place it in their church, and let me make my grave according to my will and pleasure. When Bandinello became aware of this, he set to work with great diligence at the completion of his Pietà, and prayed the Duchess to get for him the chapel of the Pazzi for his monument. This he obtained with some difficulty; and on receiving the permission, he erected his Pietà with great haste. It was not altogether completed when he died.

The Duchess then said that, even as she had protected him in life, so would she protect him in the grave, and that albeit he was

[1] *I loro Operai.*

dead, I need never try to get that block of marble. Apropos of which, the broken Bernardone, meeting me one day in the country, said that the Duchess had assigned the marble. I replied: "Unhappy piece of stone! In the hands of Bandinello it would certainly have come to grief; but in those of Ammanato its fate is a hundred times worse." Now I had received orders from the Duke to make a clay model, of the same size as the marble would allow; he also provided me with wood and clay, set up a sort of screen in the Loggia where my Perseus stands, and paid me one workman. I went about my business with all diligence, and constructed the wooden framework according to my excellent system. Then I brought the model successfully to a conclusion, without caring whether I should have to execute it in marble, since I knew the Duchess was resolved I should not get the commission. Consequently I paid no heed to that. Only I felt very glad to undergo this labour, hoping to make the Duchess, who was after all a person of intelligence, as indeed I had the means of observing at a later period, repent of having done so great a wrong both to the marble and herself. Giovanni the Fleming also made a model in the cloister of S. Croce; Vinzenzio Danti of Perugia another in the house of Messer Ottaviano de' Medici; the son of Moschino began a third at Pisa, and Bartolommeo Ammanato a fourth in the Loggia, which we divided between us.[2]

When I had blocked the whole of mine out well, and wanted to begin upon the details of the head, which I had already just sketched out in outline, the Duke came down from the palace, and Giorgetto, the painter,[3] took him into Ammanato's workshed. This man had been engaged there with his own hands several days, in company with Ammanato and all his workpeople. While, then, the Duke was inspecting Ammanato's model, I received intelligence that he seemed but little pleased with it. In spite of Giorgetto's trying to dose him with his fluent nonsense, the Duke shook his head, and turning to Messer Gianstefano,[4] exclaimed: "Go and ask Benvenuto if his colossal statue is far enough forward for him to gratify us with a

[2] Gian Bologna, or Jean Boullogne, was born at Douai about 1530. He went, while a very young man, to Rome, and then settled at Florence. There he first gained reputation by a Venus which the Prince Francesco bought. The Neptune on the piazza at Bologna, which is his work, may probably have been executed from the model he made in competition upon this occasion. Vincenzo Danti was born at Perugia in 1530. He produced the bronze statue of Pope Julius III., which may still be seen in his native city. Simone Cioli, called Il Mosca, was a very fair sculptor who died in 1554, leaving a son, Francesco, called Il Moschino, who was also a sculptor, and had reached the age of thirty at this epoch. It is therefore to this Moschino probably that Cellini refers above.

[3] Giorgio Vasari.

[4] Probably Gianstefano Lalli.

glance at it." Messer Gianstefano discharged his embassy with great tact, and in the most courteous terms. He added that if I did not think my work quite ready to be seen yet, I might say so frankly, since the Duke knew well that I had enjoyed but little assistance for so large an undertaking. I replied that I entreated him to do me the favour of coming; for though my model was not far advanced, yet the intelligence of his Excellency would enable him to comprehend perfectly how it was likely to look when finished. This kindly gentleman took back my message to the Duke, who came with pleasure. No sooner had he entered the enclosure and cast his eyes upon my work, than he gave signs of being greatly satisfied. Then he walked all round it, stopping at each of the four points of view, exactly as the ripest expert would have done. Afterwards he showed by nods and gestures of approval that it pleased him; but he said no more than this: "Benvenuto, you have only to give a little surface to your statue." Then he turned to his attendants, praising my performance, and saying: "The small model which I saw in his house pleased me greatly, but this has far exceeded it in merit."

CII

It pleased God, who rules all things for our good—I mean, for those who acknowledge and believe in Him; such men never fail to gain His protection—that about this time a certain rascal from Vecchio called Piermaria d'Anterigoli, and surnamed Lo Sbietta, introduced himself to me. He is a sheep-grazier; and being closely related to Messer Guido Guidi, the physician, who is now provost of Pescia, I lent ear to his proposals. The man offered to sell me a farm of his for the term of my natural life. I did not care to go and see it, since I wanted to complete the model of my colossal Neptune. There was also no reason why I should visit the property, because Sbietta only sold it to me for the income.[1] This he had noted down at so many bushels of grain, so much of wine, oil, standing corn, chestnuts, and other produce. I reckoned that, as the market then ran, these together were worth something considerably over a hundred golden crowns in gold; and I paid him 650 crowns, which included duties to the state. Consequently, when he left a

1 What Cellini means is that Sbietta was to work the farm, paying Cellini its annual value. It appears from some particulars which follow that the *entrate* were to be paid in kind.

memorandum written in his own hand, to the effect that he would always keep up these products of the farm in the same values during my lifetime, I did not think it necessary to inspect it. Only I made inquiries, to the best of my ability, as to whether Sbietta and his brother Ser Filippo were well off enough to give me good security. Many persons, of divers sorts, who knew them, assured me that my security was excellent. We agreed to call in Ser Pierfrancesco Bertoldi, notary at the Mercantanzia; and at the very first I handed him Sbietta's memorandum, expecting that this would be recited in the deed. But the notary who drew it up was so occupied with detailing twenty-two boundaries described by Sbietta,[2] that, so far as I can judge, he neglected to include in the contract what the vendor had proposed to furnish. While he was writing, I went on working; and since it took him several hours, I finished a good piece of my Neptune's head.

After the contract was signed and sealed, Sbietta began to pay me the most marked attentions, which I returned in like measure. He made me presents of kids, cheese, capons, fresh curds, and many sorts of fruits, until I began to be almost ashamed of so much kindness. In exchange for these courtesies I always took him from the inn to lodge with me when he came into Florence, often inviting a relative or two who happened to attend him. On one of these occasions he told me with a touch of pleasantry that it was really shameful for me to have bought a farm, and, after the lapse of so many weeks, not yet to have left my business for three days in the hands of my workpeople, so as to have come to look at it. His wheedling words and ways induced me to set off, in a bad hour for my welfare, on a visit to him. Sbietta received me in his own house with such attentions and such honours as a duke might covet. His wife caressed me even more than he did; and these excellent relations continued between us until the plans which he and his brother Ser Filippo had in mind were fully matured.

CIII

Meanwhile I did not suspend my labours on the Neptune, which was now quite blocked out upon an excellent system, undiscovered and unknown before I used it. Consequently, although I knew I

2 The word *confini*, which I have translated *boundaries*, may mean *limiting conditions*.

should not get the marble for the reasons above narrated, I hoped to have it soon completed, and to display it on the piazza simply for my satisfaction.

It was a warm and pleasant season; and this, together with the attentions of those two rascals, disposed me to set out one Wednesday, which happened to be a double holiday, for my country-house at Trespiano.[1] Having spent some time over an excellent lunch, it was past twenty o'clock when I reached Vicchio. There, at the town-gate, I met Ser Filippo, who appeared to know already whither I was bound. He loaded me with attentions, and took me to Sbietta's house, where I found that fellow's strumpet of a wife, who also overwhelmed me with caresses. I gave the woman a straw hat of the very finest texture, the like of which she told me she had never seen. Still, up to this time, Sbietta had not put in his appearance.

Toward the end of the afternoon we all sat down to supper in excellent spirits. Later on, they gave me a well appointed bedroom, where I went to rest in a bed of the most perfect cleanliness. Both of my servants, according to their rank, were equally well treated. On the morrow, when I rose, the same attentions were paid me. I went to see my farm, which pleased me much; and then I had some quantities of grain and other produce handed over. But when I returned to Vicchio, the priest Ser Filippo said to me: "Benvenuto, do not be uneasy; although you have not found here quite everything you had the right to look for, yet put your mind to rest; it will be amply made up in the future, for you have to deal with honest folk. You ought, by the way, to know that we have sent that labourer away, because he was a scoundrel." The labourer in question bore the name of Mariano Rosegli; and this man now kept frequently repeating in my ear: "Look well after yourself; in the end you will discover which of us here is the greatest villain." The country-fellow, when he spoke those words, smiled with an evil kind of sneer, and jerked his head as though to say: "Only go up there, and you will find out for yourself."

I was to some extent unfavourably influenced by these hints, yet far from forming a conception of what actually happened to me. So, when I returned from the farm, which is two miles distant from Vicchio, toward the Alpi,[2] I met the priest, who was waiting for me with his customary politeness. We then sat down together to break-

1 From Cellini's *Ricordi* it appears that he bought a farm at this village, north-east of Florence, on October 26, 1548. In 1556 he also purchased land there.
2 The Alpi are high mountain pastures in the Apennines.

fast; it was not so much a dinner as an excellent collation. Afterwards I took a walk through Vicchio—the market had just opened—and noticed how all the inhabitants fixed their eyes upon me, as on something strange. This struck me particularly in the case of a worthy old man, who has been living for many years at Vicchio, and whose wife bakes bread for sale. He owns some good property at the distance of about a mile; however, he prefers this mode of life, and occupies a house which belongs to me in the town of Vicchio. This had been consigned to me together with the farm above mentioned, which bears the name of Della Fonte. The worthy old man spoke as follows: "I am living in your house, and when it falls due I shall pay you your rent; but if you want it earlier, I will act according to your wishes. You may reckon on never having any disputes with me." While we were thus talking I noticed that he looked me hard in the face, which compelled me to address him thus: "Prithee, tell me, friend Giovanni, why you have more than once stared at me in that way?" He replied: "I am quite willing to tell you, if, being the man of worth I take you for, you will promise not to say that I have told you." I gave the promise and he proceeded: "You must know then that that worthless priest, Ser Filippo, not many days since, went about boasting of his brother Sbietta's cleverness, and telling how he had sold his farm to an old man for his lifetime, and that the purchaser could hardly live the year out. You have got mixed up with a set of rogues; therefore take heed to living as long as you are able, and keep your eyes open, for you have need of it. I do not choose to say more."

CIV

During my promenade through the market, I met Giovan Battista Santini, and he and I were taken back to supper by the priest. As I have related above, we supped at the early hour of twenty, because I made it known that I meant to return to Trespiano. Accordingly they made all ready; the wife of Sbietta went bustling about in the company of one Cecchino Buti, their knave of all work. After the salads had been mixed and we were preparing to sit down to table, that evil priest, with a certain nasty sort of grin, exclaimed: "I must beg you to excuse me, for I cannot sup with you; the reason is that some business of importance has occurred which I must transact for my brother Sbietta. In his absence I am obliged to act for him." We all begged him to stay, but could not alter his determination; so he departed and we began our supper. After we had eaten the salads on some common platters, and they were preparing to serve the boiled meat, each guest received a porringer for himself. Santini, who was seated opposite me at table exclaimed: "Do you notice that the crockery they give you is different from the rest? Did you ever see anything handsomer?" I answered that I had not noticed it. He also prayed me to invite Sbietta's wife to sit down with us; for she and that Cecchino Buti kept running hither and thither in the most extraordinary fuss and hurry. At last I induced the woman to join us; when she began to remonstrate: "You do not like my victuals, since you eat so little." I answered by praising the supper over and over again, and saying that I had never eaten better or with heartier appetite. Finally, I told her that I had eaten quite enough. I could not imagine why she urged me so persistently to eat. After supper was over, and it was past the hour of twenty-one, I became anxious to return to Trespiano, in order that I might recommence my work next morning in the Loggia. Accordingly I bade farewell to all the company, and having thanked our hostess, took my leave.

I had not gone three miles before I felt as though my stomach was on fire, and suffered such pain that it seemed a thousand years till I arrived at Trespiano. However, it pleased God that I reached it after nightfall with great toil, and immediately proceeded to my farm, where I went to bed. During the night I got no sleep, and was constantly disturbed by motions of my bowels. When day broke, feeling an intense heat in the rectum, I looked eagerly to see what this might mean, and found the cloth covered with blood. Then in a moment I conceived that I had eaten something poisonous, and racked my brains to think what it could possibly have been. It came back to my memory how Sbietta's wife had set before me plates, and porringers, and saucers different from the others, and how that evil priest, Sbietta's brother, after giving himself such pains to do me honour, had yet refused to sup with us. Furthermore, I remembered what the priest had said about Sbietta's doing such a fine stroke of business by the sale of his farm to an old man for life, who could not be expected to survive a year. Giovanni Sardella had reported these words to me. All things considered, I made my mind up that they must have administered a dose of sublimate in the sauce, which was very well made and pleasant to the taste, inasmuch as sublimate produces all the symptoms I was suffering from. Now it is my custom to take but little sauce or seasoning with my meat, excepting salt; and yet I had eaten two moderate mouthfuls of that sauce because it was so tasteful. On further thinking, I recollected how often that wife of Sbietta had teased me in a hundred ways to partake more freely of the sauce. On these accounts I felt absolutely certain that they had given me sublimate in that very dish.

CV

Albeit I was suffering so severely, I forced myself to work upon my Colossus in the Loggia; but after a few days I succumbed to the malady and took to my bed. No sooner did the Duchess hear that I was ill, than she caused the execution of that unlucky marble to be assigned to Bartolommeo Ammanato.[1] He sent word to me through Messer . . . living . . . Street, that I might now do what I liked with my model since he had won the marble. This Messer . . . was one of the lovers of Bartolommeo Ammanato's wife; and being the most favoured on account of his gentle manners and discretion, Ammanato made things easy for him. There would be much to say upon this topic; however, I do not care to imitate his master, Bandinello, who always wandered from the subject in his talk. Suffice it to say that I told Ammanato's messenger I had always imagined it would turn out thus; let the man strain himself to the utmost in proof of gratitude to Fortune for so great a favour so undeservedly conferred on him by her.

All this while I stayed with sorry cheer in bed, and was attended by that most excellent man and physician, Maestro Francesco da Montevarchi. Together with him Maestro Raffaello de' Pilli undertook the surgical part of my case, forasmuch as the sublimate had so corroded the intestines that I was unable to retain my motions. When Maestro Francesco saw that the poison had exerted all its strength, being indeed insufficient in quantity to overcome my vigorous constitution, he said one day: "Benvenuto, return thanks to God, for you have won the battle. Have no anxiety, since I mean to cure you in spite of the rogues who sought to work your ruin." Maestro Raffaello then put in: "This will be one of the finest and most difficult cures which was ever heard of; for I can tell you, Benvenuto, that you swallowed

[1] What follows has been so carefully erased, possibly by Cellini's own hand, in the autograph, that it is illegible. Laura Battiferra, Ammanato's wife, was a woman of irreproachable character, whom Cellini himself praised in a sonnet.

a good mouthful of sublimate." Thereupon Maestro Francesco took him up and said: "It may possibly have been some venomous caterpillar." I replied: "I know for certain what sort of poison it was, and who gave it to me;" upon which we all were silent. They attended me more than six full months, and I remained more than a whole year before I could enjoy my life and vigour.

CVI

At this time[1] the Duke went to make his triumphal entry into Siena, and Ammanato had gone there some months earlier to construct the arches. A bastard of his, who stayed behind in the Loggia, removed the cloths with which I kept my model of Neptune covered until it should be finished. As soon as I knew this, I complained to Signor Don Francesco, the Duke's son, who was kindly disposed toward me, and told him how they had disclosed my still imperfect statue; had it been finished, I should not have given the fact a thought. The Prince replied with a threatening toss of his head: "Benvenuto, do not mind your statue having been uncovered, because these men are only working against themselves; yet if you want me to have it covered up, I will do so at once." He added many other words in my honour before a crowd of gentlemen who were there. I then begged his Excellency to give me the necessary means for finishing it, saying that I meant to make a present of it together with the little model to his Highness. He replied that he gladly accepted both gifts, and that he would have all the conveniences I asked for put at my disposal. Thus, then, I fed upon this trifling mark of favour, which, in fact, proved the salvation of my life; for having been overwhelmed by so many evils and such great annoyances all at one fell swoop, I felt my forces failing; but this little gleam of encouragement inspired me with some hope of living.

CVII

A year had now passed since I bought the farm of Della Fonte from Sbietta. In addition to their attempt upon my life by poisoning and their numerous robberies, I noticed that the property yielded less than half what had been promised. Now, in addition to the deeds of contract, I had a declaration written by Sbietta's own hand, in which

1 October 28, 1560.

he bound himself before witnesses to pay me over the yearly income I have mentioned. Armed with these documents, I had recourse to the Lords Counsellors. At that time Messer Alfonso Quistello was still alive and Chancellor of the Exchequer; he sat upon the Board, which included Averardo Serristori and Federigo de' Ricci. I cannot remember the names of all of them, but I know that one of the Alessandri was a member. Suffice it to say, the counsellors of that session were men of weight and worth. When I had explained my cause to the magistracy, they all with one voice ruled that Sbietta should give me back my money, except Federigo de' Ricci, who was then employing the fellow himself; the others unanimously expressed sorrow to me that Federigo de' Ricci prevented them from despatching the affair. Averardo Serristori and Alessandri in particular made a tremendous stir about it, but Federigo managed to protect matters until the magistracy went out of office; whereupon Serristori, meeting me one morning after they had come out upon the Piazza dell' Annunziata, cried aloud, without the least regard to consequences: "Federigo de' Ricci has been so much stronger than all of us put together that you have been massacred against our will." I do not intend to say more upon this topic, since it would be too offensive to the supreme authorities of state; enough that I was cruelly wronged at the will of a rich citizen, only because he made use of that shepherd-fellow.

CVIII

The Duke was staying at Livorno, where I went to visit him in order merely to obtain release from his service. Now that I felt my vigour returning, and saw that I was used for nothing, it pained me to lose time which ought to have been spent upon my art. I made my mind up, therefore, went to Livorno, and found my prince, who received me with exceeding graciousness. Now I stayed there several days, and went out riding daily with his Excellency. Consequently I had excellent opportunities for saying all I wanted, since it was the Duke's custom to ride four miles out of Livorno along the sea-coast to the point where he was erecting a little fort. Not caring to be troubled with a crowd of people, he liked me to converse with him. So then, on one of these occasions, having observed him pay me some remarkable attentions, I entered into the affair of Sbietta and spoke as follows: "My lord, I should like to narrate to your most illustrious

Excellency a very singular incident, which will explain why I was prevented from finishing that clay model of Neptune on which I was working in the Loggia. Your Excellency must know that I bought a farm for my life from Sbietta—" To cut the matter short, I related the whole story in detail, without contaminating truth with falsehood. Now when I came to the poison, I remarked that if I had ever proved an acceptable servant in the sight of his most illustrious Excellency, he ought not to punish Sbietta or those who administered the poison, but rather to confer upon them some great benefit, inasmuch as the poison was not enough to kill me, but had exactly sufficed to cleanse me of a mortal viscosity from which I suffered in my stomach and intestines. "The poison," quoth I, "worked so well, that whereas, before I took it, I had perhaps but three or four years to live, I verily believe now that it has helped me to more than twenty years by bettering my constitution. For this mercy I return thanks to God with greater heartiness than ever; and this proves that a proverb I have sometimes heard spoken is true, which runs as follows:—

'God send us evil, that may work us good.'"

The Duke listened to my story through more than two miles of travel, keeping his attention fixed, and only uttering: "Oh, the villains!" I said, in conclusion, that I felt obliged to them, and opened other and more cheerful subjects of conversation.

I kept upon the look-out for a convenient day; and when I found him well disposed for what I wanted, I entreated his most illustrious Excellency to dismiss me in a friendly spirit, so that I might not have to waste the few years in which I should be fit to do anything. As for the balance due upon my Perseus, he might give this to me when he judged it opportune. Such was the pith of my discourse: but I expanded it with lengthy compliments, expressing my gratitude toward his most illustrious Excellency. To all this he made absolutely no answer, but rather seemed to have taken my communication ill. On the following day Messer Bartolommeo Concino,[1] one of the Duke's secretaries, and among the chiefest, came to me, and said with somewhat of a bullying air: "The Duke bids me tell you that if you want your dismissal, he will grant it; but if you choose work, he will give you plenty: God grant you may have the power to execute

[1] This man was the son of a peasant at Terranuova, in Valdarno. He acquired great wealth and honour at the court of Duke Cosimo, and was grandfather of the notorious Maréchal d'Ancre.

all he orders." I replied that I desired nothing more than work to do, and would rather take it from the Duke than from any man whatever in the world. Whether they were popes, emperors, or kings, I should prefer to serve his most illustrious Excellency for a halfpenny than any of the rest of them for a ducat. He then remarked: "If that is your mind, you and he have struck a bargain without the need of further speech. So, then, go back to Florence, and be unconcerned; rely on the Duke's goodwill towards you." Accordingly I made my way again to Florence.

CIX

Immediately after my arrival, there came to visit me a certain Raffaellone Scheggia, whose trade was that of a cloth-of-gold weaver. He began thus: "My Benvenuto, I should like to reconcile you with Piermaria Sbietta." I replied that nobody could settle the affairs between us except the Lords Counsellors; in the present court Sbietta would not have a Federigo de' Ricci to support him, a man willing, for the bribe of a couple of fatted kids, without respect of God or of his honour, to back so infamous a cause and do so vile a wrong to sacred justice. When I had uttered these words, and many others to the like effect, Raffaelo kept on blandly urging that it was far better to eat a thrush in peace than to bring a fat capon to one's table, even though one were quite sure to get it, after a hot fight. He further reminded me that lawsuits had a certain way of dragging on, and that I could employ the time far better upon some masterpiece of art, which would bring me not only greater honour, but greater profit to boot. I knew that he was speaking the mere truth, and began to lend ear to his arguments. Before long, therefore, we arranged the matter in this way: Sbietta was to rent the farm from me at seventy golden crowns in gold the year during the whole term of my natural life. But when we came to the contract, which was drawn up by Ser Giovanni, son of Ser Matteo da Falgano, Sbietta objected that the terms we had agreed on would involve our paying the largest duties to the revenue. He was not going to break his word; therefore we had better draw the lease for five years, to be renewed on the expiry of the term. He undertook to abide by his promise to renew, without raising further litigation. That rascal, the priest, his brother, entered into similar engagements; and so the lease was drawn for five years.

CX

Though I want to enter upon other topics, and to leave all this rascality alone awhile, I am forced to narrate what happened at the termination of this five years' contract. Instead of abiding by their promised word, those two rogues declared they meant to give me up my farm, and would not keep it any longer upon lease. I not unnaturally complained, but they retorted by ostentatiously unfolding the deed; and I found myself without any defence against their chicanery. When it came to this, I told them that the Duke and Prince of Florence would not suffer folk to be so infamously massacred in their cities. That menace worked so forcibly upon their minds that they once more despatched Raffaello Scheggia, the same man who negotiated the former arrangement. I must add that they professed their unwillingness to pay the same rent of seventy crowns as during the five years past, while I replied that I would not take a farthing less. So then Raffaello came to look me up, and spoke to this effect: "My Benvenuto, you know that I am acting in your interest. Now these men have placed themselves entirely in my hands;" and he showed me a writing to this effect signed by them. Not being aware that he was their close relative, I thought he would be an excellent arbitrator, and therefore placed myself also absolutely in his hands. This man of delicate honour then came one evening about a half hour after sunset, in the month of August, and induced me with the strongest pressure to draw up the contract then and there. He did so because he knew that if he waited till the morning, the deceit he wished to practise on me must have failed. Accordingly the deed was executed, to the effect that they were to pay me a rent of sixty-five crowns, in two half-yearly instalments, during the term of my natural life. Notwithstanding I rebelled against it, and refused to sit down quietly under the injustice, all was to no purpose, Raffaello exhibited my signature, and every one took part against me. At the same time he went on protesting that he acted altogether in my interest and as my supporter. Neither the notary nor any others who heard of the affair, knew that he was a relative of those two rogues; so they told me I was in the wrong. Accordingly, I was forced to yield with the best grace I could; and what I have now to do is to live as long as I can manage.

Close after these events, that is to say, in the December of 1566 following, I made another blunder. I bought half of the farm Del

Poggio from them, or rather from Sbietta, for two hundred crowns.[1] It marches with my property of La Fonte. Our terms were that the estate should revert at the term of three years,[2] and I gave them a lease of it. I did this for the best; but I should have to dilate too long upon the topic were I to enter into all the rascalities they practised on me. Therefore, I refer my cause entirely to God, knowing that He hath ever defended me from those who sought to do me mischief.

CXI

Having quite completed my crucifix, I thought that if I raised it to some feet above the ground, it would show better than it did upon a lower level. After I had done so, it produced a far finer effect than even it had made before, and I was greatly satisfied. So then I began to exhibit it to every one who had the mind to see it.

As God willed, the Duke and Duchess heard about it. On their arrival then from Pisa, both their Excellencies arrived one day quite unexpectedly, attended by all the nobles of their court, with the sole purpose of inspecting my crucifix. They were so much delighted, that each of these princes lavished endless praises on it, and all the lords and gentlefolk of their suites joined in chorus. Now, when I saw how greatly they were taken with the piece, I began to thank them with a touch of humour, saying that, if they had not refused me the marble for the Neptune, I should never have undertaken so arduous a task, the like whereof had not been attempted by any sculptor before me." "It is true," I added, "that this crucifix has cost me hours of unimaginable labour; yet they have been well expended, especially now when your most illustrious Excellencies have bestowed such praises on it. I cannot hope to find possessors of it worthier than you are; therefore I gladly present it to you as a gift."[1]

After speaking to this effect, I prayed them, before they took their leave, to deign to follow me into the ground-floor of my dwelling. They rose at once with genial assent, left the workshop, and on entering the house, beheld my little model of the Neptune and the fountain, which had not yet been seen by the Duchess. This struck

1 *Scudi di moneta*, not *d'oro*.

2 This seems to be the meaning of *comprare con riservo di tre anni*. Cellini elsewhere uses the equivalent term *patto resolutivo*. See Tassi, vol. ii. p. 583.

1 The Duchess would not take the crucifix as a gift. The Duke bought it for fifteen hundred golden crowns, and transferred it to the Pitti in 1565. It was given by the Grand Duke Francesco in 1576 to Philip II., who placed it in the Escorial, where it now is.

her with such force that she raised a cry of indescribable astonishment, and turning to the Duke, exclaimed: "Upon my life, I never dreamed it could be one-tenth part so beautiful!" The Duke replied by repeating more than once: "Did I not tell you so?" Thus they continued talking together for some while greatly in my honour. Afterwards the Duchess called me to her side; and when she had uttered many expressions of praise which sounded like excuses (they might indeed have been construed into asking for forgiveness), she told me that she should like me to quarry a block of marble to my taste, and then to execute the work. In reply to these gracious speeches I said that, if their most illustrious Excellencies would provide me with the necessary accommodations, I should gladly for their sakes put my hand to such an arduous undertaking. The Duke responded on the moment: "Benvenuto, you shall have all the accommodations you can ask for; and I will myself give you more besides, which shall surpass them far in value." With these agreeable words they left me, and I remained highly satisfied.

CXII

Many weeks passed, but of me nothing more was spoken. This neglect drove me half mad with despair. Now about that time the Queen of France sent Messer Baccio del Bene to our Duke for a loan of money, which the Duke very graciously supplied, as rumour went. Messer Baccio del Bene and I had been intimate friends in former times; so when we renewed our acquaintance in Florence, we came together with much mutual satisfaction. In course of conversation he related all the favours shown him by his most illustrious Excellency, and asked me what great works I had in hand. In reply, I narrated the whole story of the Neptune and the fountain, and the great wrong done me by the Duchess. He responded by telling me how her Majesty of France was most eager to complete the monument of her husband Henri II., and how Daniello da Volterra[1] had undertaken a great equestrian statue in bronze, but the time had already elapsed in which he promised to perform it, and that a multitude of the richest ornaments were required for the tomb. If, then, I liked to return to France and occupy my castle, she would supply me with all the conveniences I could ask for, provided only I cared to enter

[1] This painter is chiefly famous for his "Descent from the Cross" in the Church of the Trinità de' Monti at Rome. He died in 1566.

her service. These proposals he made on the part of the Queen. I told Messer Baccio to beg me from the Duke; if his most illustrious Excellency was satisfied, I should very willingly return to France. He answered cheerfully: "We will travel back together!" and considered the affair settled. Accordingly, next day, in course of conversation with the Duke, he alluded to myself, declaring that if his Excellency had no objection, the Queen would take me into her employ. The Duke replied without a moment's hesitation: "Benvenuto's ability in his profession is known to the whole world; but at the present time he does not care to go on working." Then they touched on other topics; and upon the day following I called on Messer Baccio, who reported what had passed between them. Then I lost all patience, and exclaimed: "Oh, me! His most illustrious Excellency gave me nothing to do, while I was bringing to perfection one of the most difficult master-pieces ever executed in this world; and it stands me in more than two hundred crowns, which I have paid out of my poverty! Oh, what could I not have done if his Excellency had but set me to work! I tell you in pure truth, that they have done me a great wrong!" The good-natured gentleman repeated to the Duke what I had answered. The Duke told him we were joking, and that he wanted me for his own service. The result was that in my irritation I more than once made up my mind to make off without asking leave. However, the Queen preferred to drop negotiations, in fear of displeasing the Duke and so I remained here, much to my regret.

CXIII

About that time the Duke went on a journey, attended by all his court and all his sons, except the prince, who was in Spain. They travelled through the Sienese Maremma, and by this route he reached Pisa. The poison from the bad air of those marshes first attacked the Cardinal, who was taken with a pestilential fever after a few days, and died at the end of a brief illness. He was the Duke's right eye, handsome and good, and his loss was most severely felt. I allowed several days to elapse, until I thought their tears were dried, and then I betook myself to Pisa.

Printed in the United States
85105LV00010B/3/A

9 781432 578060